IMMIGRATION AND THE POLITICS OF WELFARE EXCLUSION

Selective Solidarity in Western Democracies

Why do some governments try to limit immigrants' access to social benefits and entitlements while others do not? Through an in-depth study of Sweden, Canada, and the Netherlands, *Immigration and the Politics of Welfare Exclusion* maps the politics of immigrants' social rights in Western democracies. To achieve this goal, Edward Anthony Koning analyses policy documents, public opinion surveys, data on welfare use, parliamentary debates, and interviews with politicians and key players in the three countries.

Koning's findings are threefold. First, the politics of immigrant welfare exclusion have little to do with economic factors and are more about general opposition to immigration and multiculturalism. Second, proposals for exclusion are particularly likely to arise in a political climate that incentivizes politicians to appear "tough" on immigration. Finally, the success of anti-immigrant politicians in bringing about exclusionary reforms depends on the response of the political mainstream and the extent to which immigrants' rights are protected in national and international legal frameworks.

A timely investigation into an increasingly pressing subject, *Immigration and the Politics of Welfare Exclusion* will be essential reading for scholars and students of political science, comparative politics, and immigration studies.

(Studies in Comparative Political Economy and Public Policy)

EDWARD ANTHONY KONING is an associate professor in the Department of Political Science at the University of Guelph.

Studies in Comparative Political Economy and Public Policy

Editors: MICHAEL HOWLETT, DAVID LAYCOCK (Simon Fraser University), and STEPHEN MCBRIDE (McMaster University)

Studies in Comparative Political Economy and Public Policy is designed to showcase innovative approaches to political economy and public policy from a comparative perspective. While originating in Canada, the series will provide attractive offerings to a wide international audience, featuring studies with local, subnational, cross-national, and international empirical bases and theoretical frameworks.

Editorial Advisory Board

For a list of books published in the series, see page 305.

Immigration and the Politics of Welfare Exclusion

Selective Solidarity in Western Democracies

EDWARD ANTHONY KONING

UNIVERSITY OF TORONTO PRESS
Toronto Buffalo London

© University of Toronto Press 2019
Toronto Buffalo London
utorontopress.com
Printed and bound by CPI Group (UK) Ltd, Croydon, CR0 4YY

ISBN 978-1-4875-0466-3 (cloth)   ISBN 978-1-4875-2342-8 (paper)

♾ Printed on acid-free paper with vegetable-based inks.

Library and Archives Canada Cataloguing in Publication

Koning, Edward Anthony, 1982–, author
Immigration and the politics of welfare exclusion : selective solidarity in western
democracies

(Studies in comparative political economy and public policy ; 55)
Includes bibliographical references and index.
ISBN 978-1-4875-0466-3 (cloth). – ISBN 978-1-4875-2342-8 (paper)

1. Immigrants – Services for – Canada.   2. Immigrants – Services for – Sweden.
3. Immigrants – Services for – Netherlands.   4. Canada – Emigration and
immigration – Government policy.   5. Sweden – Emigration and immigration –
Government policy.   6. Netherlands – Emigration and immigration – Government
policy.   I. Title.   II. Series: Studies in comparative political economy and public
policy ; 55

JV6038.K66 2019   325'.1   C2018-905718-1

This book has been published with the help of a grant from the Federation for the
Humanities and Social Sciences, through the Awards to Scholarly Publications
Program, using funds provided by the Social Sciences and Humanities Research
Council of Canada.

University of Toronto Press acknowledges the financial assistance to its publishing
program of the Canada Council for the Arts and the Ontario Arts Council, an agency
of the Government of Ontario.

Canada Council   Conseil des Arts
for the Arts   du Canada

Funded by the   Financé par le
Government   gouvernement
of Canada   du Canada

ONTARIO ARTS COUNCIL
CONSEIL DES ARTS DE L'ONTARIO
an Ontario government agency
un organisme du gouvernement de l'Ontario

Contents

Acknowledgments

This book has benefited tremendously from the advice and support from a large number of individuals and institutions. This project started almost ten years ago, and I am deeply grateful to everyone who has encouraged and enabled me to continue and expand my research since then.

My first thanks are for Keith Banting. It was my interest in his work that made me decide to leave my native Netherlands and pursue graduate studies in Canada. He has not only been foundational to this project in particular, but has also made me a better academic in general. His guidance extended far beyond what any graduate student can reasonably expect. He consistently provided incisive, constructive, and challenging feedback, and went out of his way to assist me in advancing my publication record, expanding my professional network, and navigating the world of academia. Having worked with such a great mentor and role-model benefits me until this day.

Many thanks are due to my interviewees as well. I am grateful to parliamentarians Sietse Fritsma, Eddy van Hijum, Fatma Koşer Kaya, Cora van Nieuwenhuizen, Hans Spekman, and Paul Ulenbelt (the Netherlands), Don Davies, Rick Dykstra, and Kevin Lamoureux (Canada), and Erik Almqvist, Mikael Cederbratt, Fredrick Federley, Emma Henriksson, Christina Höj Larsen, Ulf Nilsson, and Magdalena Streijffert (Sweden), who all generously reserved time in their busy schedules to answer my questions. The 22 anonymous civil servants who agreed to participate in this research were also invaluable, especially those who were so kind to read early drafts of the country chapters and provide thoughtful and detailed feedback.

During my time at Queen's, I greatly enjoyed being surrounded by brilliant faculty and graduate students. For the constructive comments, the thought-provoking conversations, and the personal support, I want to thank in particular Randy Besco, Alan Bloomfield, Zsuzsa Csergo, Andrea Collins, Aaron Ettinger, Megan Gaucher, Will Kymlicka, Rémi Léger, Scott Matthews, Sara Pavan, Dan Pfeffer, Lucia Salazar, Beesan Sarrouh, and Erin Tolley.

Since my arrival at the University of Guelph, I have had the privilege of working in a department filled with impressive scholars, fantastic colleagues, and dear friends (and to be clear, these are not mutually exclusive categories). I thank in particular Janine Clarke, Jordi Diez, Kate Puddister, and Tamara Small for their help with this project, but I am grateful to everyone else as well for creating such a supportive, productive, and fun work environment.

Many more friends and peers contributed to this project – by providing useful feedback on presentations, assisting me in setting up interviews or accessing data, exchanging ideas related to my subject, and offering institutional support. I want to thank in particular Iris Alfredsson, Caroline Andrew, Anna Boucher, Jan Erk, Alain Gagnon, Alison Harell, Henk van der Kolk, Christel Koop, Monique Kremer, Jeff Moon, Irving Palm, Vincent Post, Tim Reeskens, Arthur Sweetman, Melanee Thomas, Luc Turgeon, and Steven Weldon.

My field research would not have been possible without the support from a number of institutions and academics. During my stay in the Netherlands, the European Research Center on Migration and Ethnic Relations at the University of Utrecht kindly provided me with an office and access to all university services. Thanks in particular to Louk Hagendoorn, David Ingleby, and Marcel Lubbers for their welcoming approach and helpful comments on my research. In Sweden, I was hosted at the renowned Stockholm University Linnaeus Center for Integration Studies. I want to thank Julia Boguslaw, Marieke Bos, Christer Gerdes, Bart Golsteyn, Markus Jäntti, Anders Stenberg, and Eskil Wadensjö for sharing constructive comments and for making my stay in Stockholm more enjoyable.

This research has been made possible by the financial assistance of a number of institutions. I would like to thank the Canadian Labour Market and Skills Researcher Network, Queen's University, and the Department of Political Studies at Queen's for the generous financial assistance. Many thanks as well to the Social Sciences and Humanities Research Council of Canada for helping to fund this book through the Awards to Scholarly Publications Program.

From the University of Toronto Press, I want to thank in particular Daniel Quinlan. His professionalism, availability, and insight have made the process of moving from a manuscript to a published book much more seamless than I had dared to hope. Thanks as well to Wayne Herrington and Matthew Kudelka for the helpful comments and suggestions at the stage of copy-editing and proofreading. I also want to express my gratitude to Riyad Al Abdullah, the gifted artist who generously agreed to the use of his gorgeous painting *Towards a better future* for the cover of this book.

On a more personal note, I want to thank my fantastic family in the Netherlands: Elly and Henk, Joëlle and Hugo, Naomi and Sander, and Vesper, Aris, Katelijn, Imme, and Bodile. They are a source of continuous encouragement and love.

My very last thanks are, of course, for my two favourite second-generation immigrants. Caroline has enthusiastically encouraged this project from the beginning, enduring far too many monologues on academic frustrations in the process. Much more importantly, I want to thank both her and Oscar for the unmeasurable contributions they make to my happiness.

Abbreviations

AIO	Aanvullende Inkomensvoorziening Ouderen (Dutch pension top up benefit)
AIP	Anti-immigrant party
BQ	Bloc Québécois (Canadian sub-state nationalist party)
C	Centerpartiet (Swedish social liberal party)
CA	Canadian Alliance (Canadian conservative party)
CBS	Centraal Bureau voor de Statistiek (Statistics Netherlands)
CD	Centrumdemocraten (Dutch anti-immigrant party)
CDA	Christen Democratisch Àppel (Dutch Christian democratic party)
CPC	Conservative Party of Canada
CU	ChristenUnie (Dutch leftish Christian party)
DPES	Dutch Parliamentary Election Study
D66	Democraten '66 (Dutch liberal party)
ECHR	European Convention on Human Rights
ECJ	European Court of Justice
EEA	European Economic Area
EU	European Union
FVD	Forum Voor Democratie (Dutch populist party)
GL	GroenLinks (Dutch environmentalist party)
ICESCR	International Covenant on Economic, Social and Cultural Rights
IEWR	Immigrant-excluding welfare reform
IFHP	Interim Federal Health Program (Canadian refugee health care benefit)
ILO	International Labour Organization
ISSP	International Social Survey Programme
KD	Kristdemokraterna (Swedish Christian democrats)

L	Liberalerna (former Folkpartiet Liberalerna; Swedish liberal party)
LIS	Luxembourg Income Study
LPC	Liberal Party of Canada
LPF	Lijst Pim Fortuyn (Dutch anti-immigrant party)
M	Moderata Samlingspartiet (Swedish conservative party)
MP	Member of Parliament
MP	Miljöpartiet (Swedish green party)
ND	Ny Demokrati (Swedish anti-immigrant party)
NDP	New Democratic Party (Canadian labour party)
OAS	Old Age Security (Canadian universal pension benefit)
OECD	Organization for Economic Cooperation and Development
OLP	Ontario Liberal Party
OPC	Ontario Progressive Conservatives
PCP	Progressive Conservative Party (Canadian conservative party)
PvdA	Partij van de Arbeid (Dutch labour party)
PVV	Partij voor de Vrijheid (Dutch anti-immigrant party)
RPC	Reform Party of Canada (Canadian populist right party)
S	Socialdemokratiska Arbetarepartiet (Swedish labour party)
SCB	Statistics Sweden (Statistiska Centralbyrån)
SCF	Survey of Consumer Finance
SD	Sverigedemokraterna (Swedish anti-immigrant party)
SFI	Svenska För Invandrare (Swedish immigrant language classes)
SLID	Survey of Labour and Income Dynamics
SNES	Swedish National Election Studies
SP	Socialistische Partij (Dutch socialist party)
UDHR	Universal Declaration of Human Rights
UN	United Nations
V	Vänsterpartiet (Swedish socialist party)
VVD	Volkspartij voor Vrijheid en Democratie (Dutch conservative party)
WVS	World Values Survey

IMMIGRATION AND THE POLITICS OF WELFARE EXCLUSION

Selective Solidarity in Western Democracies

Introduction

The Mediterranean refugee crisis brought immigration to the centre of political attention. More than 1.3 million people applied for asylum in Europe in 2015 alone, and almost four times as many have sought temporary accommodation in refugee centres in North Africa and West Asia. In Western Europe, where issues of immigration and integration have been politically volatile since the beginning of the century, the crisis reignited controversies about the admission of newcomers and the rights and responsibilities they should enjoy. One particularly common subject of discussion has been the kinds of benefits and services immigrants should be able to access. Government leaders in various countries have argued that the intake of refugees can only be managed if it is accompanied by a reduction of their social entitlements (Isitman 2015; *The Local* 2015).

This is by no means the first time that the social rights of immigrants have been contested. In 1994, for example, the state of California held a referendum on "Proposition 187," which proposed that undocumented immigrants be denied any access to health care and education and was supported by 59 per cent of the voting public. A federal court later overturned the initiative, but only two years later, a sweeping reform to welfare programs formalized dramatic cuts in immigrant eligibility. Since the mid-1990s, similar policy changes have been enacted on the other side of the Atlantic. The welfare systems of Austria, Denmark, Germany, the Netherlands, Norway, and the United Kingdom are now all less inclusive of immigrants than they were twenty years ago.

These changes are of clear social relevance. On the one hand, global migration continues to increase and the number of people who do not live in their country of birth is growing (UN 2016). On the other, in some countries this growing subset of the population is less protected by the institutions designed to guarantee a minimum standard of living and to reduce the inequalities that pure market capitalism would produce. The combination of increasing migration and increasing immigrant exclusion raises serious concerns about the future of equality in Western welfare states. Equally noteworthy is that these changes have mostly come as a surprise to social scientists. Until the early 1990s, welfare states were apparently becoming more and more accessible to immigrants. Social rights were increasingly detached from citizenship, and passports were becoming less relevant when it came to access to health care, education, and social benefits (Hammar 1990; Sassen 1996; Soysal 1994). As a result, academics predicted more inclusion to follow. In probably the best-known study in this tradition, Yasemin Soysal enthusiastically declared: "A new and more universal concept of citizenship has unfolded in the post-war era, one whose organizing and legitimating principles are based on universal personhood rather than national belonging" (1994, 1). Some twenty years later, these kinds of depictions no longer seem applicable.

This book investigates the politics of immigrant welfare exclusion. While this subject certainly has received academic attention (Boucher and Carney 2009; Fix 2009; Koning and Banting 2013; Sabates-Wheeler and Feldman 2011; Sainsbury 2012), few existing studies have investigated why these proposals have received so much currency over the last two decades and why they permeate political discussions so much more in some contexts than in others. To be clear, the goal of this book is not to provide an account of the politics of immigration in general terms: I do not seek to explain why opposition to immigration pervades some jurisdictions more than others or is more prevalent at certain times than at others. Instead, the key objective is to investigate the politics of immigrants' social rights in particular and to understand why we see such large differences across place and time both in how often attempts at welfare exclusion occur and in the extent to which those attempts are successful.

Considering the relative scarcity of systematic research on this question, my main purpose is to explore how much the politics of immigrants' social rights differ between one political setting and another and develop tentative explanations for that variation. Instead of attempting a comprehensive overview of this subject in all Western democracies, this investigation centres on an in-depth analysis of a small number of cases that are similar enough to allow for meaningful comparison yet very different in respects that are of likely theoretical relevance to the subject under investigation. This strategy admittedly raises possible concerns about the external validity of my conclusions, but it also has the considerable advantage of allowing for the kind of in-depth investigation that is most conducive to theory building.

A comparison of Sweden, Canada, and the Netherlands fits the purpose of this research well. Each of these countries has been a popular destination for migrants, and all three have experienced roughly similar economic fortunes over the last two decades.[1] At the same time, however, they differ dramatically from one another in ways that likely affect the politics of immigration and welfare (see the next chapter for more details on the theoretical relevance of these differences). The structure of the welfare state varies considerably between these countries, ranging from a very generous system based on principles of universalism in Sweden, to a system with more contributory and means-tested characteristics in the Netherlands, to an even more basic system in Canada. Popular conceptions of national identity are at least equally diverse: a history of immigration is crucial to the self-imagery of Canada, whereas Sweden's inclusive approach to immigration is more rooted in the national virtue of egalitarianism, and Dutch nationalism has become more exclusionary over the last few decades. Finally, the discursive climate on immigration is very different in the three cases under study: while the vast majority of politicians and public commentators discuss immigration in positive terms in Canada, there is a growing minority of immigration sceptics in Sweden, and anti-immigrant commentary has become a central feature of public debate in the Netherlands.

A comparison of these three cases should give us a comprehensive idea of how differently the politics of immigrants' social rights might play out in different political settings. For each of these countries I have interviewed civil servants and parliamentarians, and analysed public opinion surveys, data on immigrant use of welfare services, parliamentary debates, party manifestos, and policy documents. The analysis of parliamentary debates and policy documents relies on available data from 1990 to 2012; all other analyses draw on available data from 1990 to the summer of 2017. The interviews were conducted in 2011 and 2012.[2]

My main finding is that the politics of immigrant welfare exclusion are more about general opposition to immigration and multiculturalism than about concerns over the economic effects of immigration and the sustainability of the welfare state. More simply put, economic facts have little to do with calls for immigrant exclusion. This is not to say there are no conceivable arguments based on economic analysis in favour of restrictions on immigrants' benefit access. The point, rather, is that economic facts do not help us understand whether a political system moves in a restrictive direction, and that many times when we do hear economic arguments a closer investigation suggests they are more rooted in ideological objections. Several pieces of evidence support this conclusion. Calls for immigrant exclusion are not at their loudest where and when immigrants are most overrepresented among benefit recipients. Proposals for benefit exclusion are often strikingly vague about the costs they would save. In justifications for benefit exclusion, principled arguments are more common than economic ones. And when economic arguments do come up, they often exaggerate the supporting evidence or ignore countervailing evidence.

The belief that the welfare state should first and foremost protect native-born citizens, then, does not originate in concerns about the economic sustainability of the welfare state; it results instead from principled attitudes about the proper place of immigrants in a welfare system. More important than the actual costs of immigration is the attention these costs receive in a political system. In some countries, levels of immigrant welfare dependence not only feature prominently on the political agenda but also tend to be exaggerated and framed as evidence that immigrants are lazy welfare cheats. In other contexts, they are hardly discussed at all or are invoked to draw attention to the difficulties immigrants experience on the labour market. Which of these types of discourse is dominant is a key component of any plausible account of the origins of immigrant-excluding welfare reforms. Understanding the exclusion of immigrants from social programs and benefits therefore requires an understanding of what political scientists would call the political translation of immigrants' welfare dependence.

Deep-rooted historical features of a political system, in particular the structure of the welfare system and the nature of a country's national identity, shape the framework within which the politics of immigrants' social rights take place. Countries with universalist welfare traditions are unlikely to single out immigrants as undeserving recipients. In a similar vein, a community with an inclusive national identity is less likely to politicize immigrant entitlements. For a fuller understanding, however, we need to look at political factors. If the political climate is such that politicians feel pressured to "do something" about immigration, proposing to exclude immigrants from benefits can become an attractive electoral strategy. For that reason, the success of anti-immigrant politicians – especially when this involves an electoral breakthrough by an anti-immigrant party – can have a profound effect on the political attention to immigrants' use of welfare services. Since no anti-immigrant party can be realistically expected to win a majority of the seats in any Western parliament, however, the impact of such parties depends crucially on how more mainstream parties react to them. In some cases, anti-immigrant parties are met with a *cordon sanitaire* – a parliament-wide agreement to minimize the political clout of these newcomers. In other cases, however, anti-immigrant parties are more "contagious" (Norris 2005; Van Spanje 2010). Some of these parties have struck formal and informal agreements with coalition governments, and this has allowed them to table some of their exclusionary proposals. In addition, some mainstream parties have adopted a more restrictive position on immigration themselves as a strategic response to the sudden success of anti-immigrant politicians. In these latter cases, attempts at immigrant welfare exclusion are a much more likely occurrence.

This research aims to make at least three contributions. Perhaps most obviously, it seeks to contribute to the still rather small body of literature on immigrants' social rights. So far, the overwhelming majority of the literature on immigration and welfare has explored whether immigration and immigrant-induced diversity is having a negative effect on overall support for social programs and the overall generosity of welfare state structures. As such, more subtle effects have been largely overlooked. We know, for example, that immigration rarely leads people to withdraw their support for the welfare state altogether (Crepaz 2008; Mau and Burkhardt 2009), but only recently have scholars turned their attention to whether it might increase public calls for amendments in social policies aimed at excluding immigrants (Crepaz and Damron 2009; Reeskens and Van Oorschot 2012; Van der Waal et al. 2010). Even less has been written on whether those amendments have in fact materialized. Several studies have investigated how much effect immigration has had on overall welfare state generosity (Gerdes 2011; Soroka et al. 2013), but we know much less about the policy adjustments that disentitle immigrants specifically.

Second, my analysis suggests that there are important theoretical differences between immigrant-excluding welfare reforms and more general social policy change. Across-the-board retrenchment tends to invoke discussions about the appropriate role of the state in the market economy, while one of the main questions in the politics of immigrants' entitlements is whether the welfare state actually has a duty to take care of them. While it is true that general welfare reform often invokes considerations about which social groups are most deserving of protection as well, calls for immigrant exclusion can contest the very idea that recipients are part of the political community to begin with. The difference between this type of exclusion and more general cutbacks is at least equally striking when we investigate the institutional dynamics of policy implementation. While across-the-board cutbacks in social policy are almost invariably met with large and well-mobilized public opposition, the exclusion of immigrants has more often garnered public approval than social outrage. Legal prohibitions on differential treatment pose a much more important obstacle to this type of social policy change. In some cases, governments have withdrawn from international treaties before they could implement their desired restrictions. In other instances, the legal obstacles proved so formidable that policymakers abandoned their attempts altogether.

Third, my investigation reveals that immigration can become such a politically volatile issue that it can affect policy-making in areas that are at most indirectly related. In other words, attempts to appear "tough" on immigration can lead to suggestions that have little to do with the problems they aim to solve. The chapter on the Netherlands features an extreme but illustrative example: when asked, the spokesperson of the largest right-of-centre party justified a proposal to bar all newcomers from benefits during their first ten years in the country by referring to homophobia and sexism among some (second-generation) immigrant youth. Theoretically, this suggests that our understanding of policy change may remain limited if we confine our gaze to the policy areas that are directly affected. Politically, it means we should submit suggestions for exclusionary reform to empirical scrutiny. This is perhaps obvious when the relationship between the proposed solution and the identified problem is as tenuous as in this example. But also in other instances, my findings demonstrate the importance of investigating not only the validity of how politicians describe the problems they claim to address but also the extent to which their proposals are likely to tackle them.

This book is structured as follows. The first chapter develops a theoretical framework for understanding immigrant-excluding welfare reforms, drawing from the theoretical literature on new institutionalism, social policy change, and the comparative politics of immigration. This framework distinguishes between forces of continuity that shape the dominant understanding of immigrants' place in the welfare state on the one hand and forces of change that can make exclusionary reforms more likely to occur on the other.

The empirical investigation starts in chapter 2, which demonstrates that the economics of immigrants' integration are mostly unrelated to politicians' and citizens' views regarding the social rights of immigrants. It first illustrates in a quantitative analysis of twelve Western welfare states that there is no positive association between levels of immigrant welfare dependence and attitudes towards immigrants' benefit access. It then moves on to show the limited importance of economic motivations for the politics of immigrants' social rights in Sweden, Canada, and the Netherlands.

The bulk of this research consists of a more thorough investigation of these three cases. Chapter 3 discusses Sweden, where a universalist welfare regime and an egalitarian culture have resulted in a predominantly inclusive approach. Immigrant welfare dependence is certainly a frequent topic of discussion, but it is most commonly framed in terms of whether the Swedish welfare state is doing *enough* for its newcomer population. And while an anti-immigrant party is slowly but surely gaining ground in Swedish politics, it has (so far) suggested few immigrant-excluding welfare reforms, let alone convinced the political mainstream of their desirability.

Chapter 4 analyses recent policy developments in Canada, which has mostly escaped divisive politics for a different reason. Here we will see that the prominent place of immigration in popular conceptions of Canadian identity has provided a powerful bulwark against proposals for immigrant exclusion. Even when the costs of immigration are in the political spotlight, they tend to be discussed as the outgrowth of a defective admission policy, not as something newcomers themselves can be blamed for. And when politicians try to adopt a more accusatory tone, as happened with the Reform Party in the early 1990s and with Conservative leadership hopeful Kellie Leitch more recently, the reaction from the electorate and other politicians has been punitive rather than enthusiastic.

Chapter 5 moves to the Netherlands, which in recent years has seen a significant surge in support for immigrant exclusion and has introduced a wide variety of immigrant-excluding welfare reforms. With a comparatively generous welfare state and a national identity that describes tolerance and openness as primary Dutch virtues, the institutional conditions in the Netherlands initially seemed conducive to an inclusive treatment of immigrants. However, the increasing success of anti-immigrant politicians has slowly convinced large parts of the Dutch political elite that exclusionary welfare reforms are a reasonable and perhaps necessary strategy to preserve the welfare state in an era of immigration.

The final chapter discusses what we can learn from a focused comparison of the three case studies and reflects on the theoretical and political implications of the findings of this research.

Chapter One

Theorizing Immigrant-Excluding Welfare Reforms

The relationship between immigration and welfare state institutions has long been the focus of scholarly attention, but most contributions have analysed this relationship at the most aggregate level. In doing so, scholars have paid less attention to a set of policy changes that I will refer to as immigrant-excluding welfare reforms (IEWRs): adjustments that make it more difficult for immigrants to access benefits and services. Interestingly, the currency of these reforms differs dramatically from one political context to another. While some countries have attempted to restrict immigrants' access to social programs and benefits as much as possible, we have seen few such attempts elsewhere. This chapter develops a theoretical framework aimed at understanding these types of policy changes. This framework combines insights from institutionalist theory, the comparative literature on social policy change, and the literature on the comparative politics of immigration.

The chapter begins by reviewing the existing literature on the relationship between immigration and the welfare state. I then introduce the concept of IEWRs and offer analytical tools for making sense of the various ways that welfare states can differentiate between the native-born and immigrants on their territory. I then move to the core of this chapter and suggest a theoretical framework for understanding the emergence of IEWRs.

The Progressive's Dilemma: Immigration versus the Welfare State?

"You cannot simultaneously have free immigration and a welfare state." This quote, uttered by Milton Friedman during a libertarian conference in 1999, is perhaps the best-known expression of a consensus among public commentators and academics alike. Typically framed as the "Progressive's Dilemma," even the most careful analysts seem to agree that there is an inherent tension between liberal admission policies and generous social policies (Bommes and Geddes 2000; Entzinger and Van der Meer 2004).

To a certain extent, this tension is undeniable. Combining entirely open borders with generous social policies does risk significant increases in social expenditure. However, many paint the picture more darkly and suggest that a steady inflow of newcomers will inevitably lead to the demise of the welfare state as we know it. One of the most frequently mentioned pieces of evidence by proponents of this view is that the United States, with its long history of immigration, has developed a minimal social safety net, whereas the presumably more homogeneous and isolated populations of Western Europe have come to be covered by more expansive systems of social programs (Alesina and Glaeser 2004; Freeman 1986; Goodhart 2004). The explanation, so the argument goes, is that (immigration-induced) diversity makes it difficult to sustain the solidarity necessary to legitimize an extensive welfare system. This argument comes in at least five variations.

First, some defend a biological hypothesis, arguing that there is a strong and positive relationship between feelings of solidarity and similarity in genetic composition (Freeman 2009, 7). A second set of authors invoke social identity rather than biology and argue that native-born citizens will likely view newcomers with a different background as members of an "out-group" with whom they do not wish to share (Tajfel 1982). A third set of studies rely heavily on the assumptions of social identity theory but pay almost exclusive attention to the role of trust. According to this argument, diversity has a negative effect on trust, which in turn translates into lower levels of solidarity. In probably the best-known study in this tradition, Robert Putnam (2007) goes further, predicting that diversity even makes people less trusting of members of *their own* in-group. While Putnam does not in fact study the impact of diversity on support for social programs, it is often suggested he does, not only by public commentators (Caldwell 2009, 49; Goodhart 2004, 33) but by academics as well (Burgoon 2011, 2–3; Freeman 2009, 2–6).[1]

A fourth argument builds on the assumption that people are willing to contribute to a redistributive welfare state out of reciprocal altruism: in this account, the willingness to share does not have biological or socio-psychological origins, but is based on a rational calculation that all members of the community contribute when they can and receive support when they cannot (Fong 2007). From this perspective, there are at least three reasons why immigrants are likely to be seen as undeserving of state support and, therefore, why an increase in immigration could be hypothesized as leading to a decrease in solidarity. First, as newcomers to a community, immigrants have a shorter history of contributing to the system and therefore might seem less entitled to tax-financed benefits. Second, they tend to be overrepresented among recipients of exactly the types of benefits that a reciprocal altruist will dislike the most. And third, prejudicial stereotypes (such as beliefs that immigrants are lazy or prone to cheating the system) can reinforce the perception that immigrants are less deserving of entitlements than native-born citizens (Boeri 2009; Bommes and Geddes 2000; Burns and Gimpel 2000).

Finally, some authors describe diversity as a threat to the welfare state because they reason it reduces cohesion among the working class and therefore makes concerted efforts to achieve equality less likely. First proposed by Karl Marx (A.W. Schmidt and Spies 2014, 522), in contemporary political science this argument has most commonly been raised by power resource theorists, who express concern that an ethnically diverse workforce is harder to mobilize and therefore less likely to succeed in promoting redistributive policies (Castles and Kosack 1985; Korpi 1978, 314).

Despite the intuitive plausibility of many of these claims, the available empirical evidence for these arguments is mixed. The findings are more robust in some countries than in others, and there is more evidence for some observable implications of these arguments than for others.

One hypothesis that finds consistent support is that diversity has a negative effect on trust (Alesina and La Ferrara 2002; Lancee and Dronkers 2011; Leigh 2006; Letki 2008; Putnam 2007). However, the evidence is weaker that such a decrease in trust necessarily erodes support for redistribution and welfare programs. Almost all studies that directly measure this link find that the effect of diversity on support for redistribution is very small (Crepaz 2006; Mau and Burkhardt 2009), if not non-existent (Finseraas 2012; Soroka, Johnston, and Banting 2004) or even positive (Van Oorschot and Uunk 2007). The only two studies I am aware of that do find a strong negative effect are county-level analyses in Sweden (Dahlberg, Edmark, and Lundqvist 2012; Eger 2010).

The picture is similar when we look at studies that measure the effect of diversity on the size of the welfare state. There is some evidence for the claim that diverse communities have developed less generous welfare state structures (Alesina and Glaeser 2004, 141). It is more contested, however, whether this necessarily means that immigration-induced diversity will reduce the size of already existing welfare state structures (Crepaz 2008). A recent cross-national comparison does indeed find evidence for a negative effect (Soroka et al. 2013), but many other studies reach the opposite conclusion (Brooks and Manza 2007; Gerdes 2011, 90; Hainmueller and Hiscox 2010).

All in all, we can summarize the large body of empirical literature on the relationship between diversity and (support for) welfare state institutions with three observations: (1) there is some evidence of a negative relationship between diversity and solidarity, but very few studies conclude that the relationship is strong; (2) there are more indications that diversity erodes trust than that it reduces support for welfare programs; and (3) there is more evidence that historically diverse communities have developed weaker welfare states than that the recent inflows of migrants have decreased the generosity of already existing welfare state structures.

With the benefit of hindsight, these conclusions are not surprising. Most of the theoretical propositions reviewed above offer little reason to expect that diversity would induce people to stop supporting the principle of a welfare state they might benefit from themselves. All we can logically deduce from the arguments of biological animosity, social identity theory, and reciprocal altruism is that some parts of the native-born population will be unwilling to share the welfare state *with immigrants*.[2] That migration would lead to calls for across-the-board retrenchment seems even less likely when we consider that the strongest opposition to immigration tends to be found among blue-collar workers and the unemployed, exactly those groups of voters who can also be expected to support redistribution (Crepaz 2008; Scheve and Slaughter 2001; Svallfors 2006).

Of course, one might reply that these individuals can nevertheless be swayed in an electoral campaign by the most vocal critic of immigration and therefore forget about economic interests while casting a vote (Kitschelt and McGann 1995). This mechanism should not be overstated, however. For one thing, there is no evidence that support for redistribution declines when political parties politicize immigration-related problems (A.W. Schmidt and Spies 2014). More importantly, whereas anti-immigrant sentiment used to be voiced by parties with a right-wing economic agenda, modern anti-immigrant parties tend to defend a more centrist or even leftist position on issues of redistribution (J.G. Andersen and Bjørklund 2000; De Lange 2007; Hainsworth 2000, 10; Ignazi 2003; Ivarsflaten 2005; Mudde 2000, 174; Rydgren 2003, 56). Those voters who are most likely to be affected by a diversity-driven decrease in solidarity, therefore, now have the opportunity of acting on that sentiment in the voting booth without being afraid that their vote will dismantle the welfare state. In addition, the entrance of these parties on the political scene even makes it possible that unease about immigration will lead some people who otherwise would not vote for a pro-welfare party to do so.

Finally, there are strong institutional barriers to (support for) welfare retrenchment (Huber and Stephens 2001, 202–311; Pierson 1994, 1996). In virtually every capitalist society, the median voter benefits from redistribution, and furthermore, welfare state institutions enjoy much greater legitimacy than can be explained by economic self-interest alone (Brooks and Manza 2007). Therefore, any plans for widespread reductions in benefits will face an opposing majority. Conversely, as will be discussed in more detail below, suggestions to reduce immigrants' social rights will not be met by the type of large and well-mobilized opposition that general welfare retrenchment is likely to elicit. One group of people that will benefit most from a welfare system that is inclusive of immigrants is future newcomers, and they obviously have no role to play in the decision-making process. Conversely, among the people who *could* affect that process, few have anything to lose from these types of reforms.

In sum, then, it seems that worries about immigration's overall corrosive impact on the welfare state are exaggerated. The empirical evidence is mixed and ambiguous; and on closer inspection the theoretical grounds for this thesis are shaky at worst and in need of qualification at best. But just because immigration has not made native-born respondents dislike a redistributive welfare state does not mean they would not like to change any aspect of the welfare system. Indeed, a more likely outcome is support for excluding immigrants from access to benefits. I will refer to this sentiment as "selective solidarity." The key characteristic is that it does not entail opposition to welfare programs but rather a belief that native-born citizens are entitled to *more* or *more generous* programs than newcomers to the political community. In sum, I define selective solidarity as *general support for a redistributive welfare state, but also a desire to restrict its benefits to native-born citizens.*

Over the last few years a number of scholars have turned their attention to selective solidarity. This research has invariably found that large portions of the population believe that native-born citizens should be priviliged in systems of social policies and that a non-trivial minority even goes so far as to favour indefinite and categorical exclusion of everyone who was not born in the country (De Koster, Achterberg, and Van der Waal 2012; Ford 2015; Gorodzeisky and Semyonov 2009; Mewes and Mau 2013; Van der Waal et al. 2010). It is telling that Mau and Burkhardt (2009) find only a weak relationship between diversity and solidarity and no relationship at all between diversity and social expenditure, but observe a strong negative relationship between share of non-Western immigrants and citizens' willingness to grant equal rights to newcomers. Studies by Tim Reeskens and his colleagues (Reeskens and Van Oorschot 2012; M. Wright and Reeskens 2013) replicate this finding and conclude that increases in diversity tend to increase selective solidarity. Erzo Luttmer (2001), using a different way of capturing selective solidarity, finds that support for welfare decreases with an increase in the number of recipients in a local community, but that it increases with an increase in the number of recipients in the community with the same race as the respondent. Using yet another strategy, Ann-Helen Bay and Axel Pedersen (2006) survey support for universal welfare programs among the Norwegian electorate and find that this support drops when respondents are asked if they would still be in favour of such programs if they were to be extended to non-citizens.

In sum, the effects of immigration on the welfare state are more visible when we focus on selective rather than general solidarity. Unfortunately, the recent blossoming in studies of public opinion have so far not been accompanied by increased attention to policy changes in line with such a sentiment. This is all the more problematic because the link between public attitudes and policies tends to be tenuous when it comes to issues of immigration (see below). It is necessary, therefore, to move beyond studying sentiments of selective solidarity among the public and start investigating the institutionalization of such sentiment in public policy.

Immigrant-Excluding Welfare Reforms (and Their Alternatives)

As we have seen, there is only limited evidence that immigration-induced diversity has eroded overall welfare state generosity. However, to argue that immigration has not changed the configuration of

Western welfare states would be to deny the many IEWRs over the last two decades or so, which I will define as *reforms that restrict or qualify immigrants' access to social programs*. Scholars have noted the exclusion of immigrants from welfare state institutions in a multitude of countries, including Austria (Crepaz 2008, 75; Howard 2006, 445); Denmark (Østergaard-Nielsen 2003; Sainsbury 2012); Germany (Ireland 2004; Soysal 2012, p. 27); the Netherlands (Huisman 2009; Kremer 2013; Minderhoud 2004); the United Kingdom (Dwyer 2006; Mynott, Humphries, and Cohen 2002; M. Wilkinson and Craig 2012); and the United States (Demleitner 1998; Fragomen 1997; Graefe et al. 2008; Handler 2009; Hero and Preuhs 2007; Kretsedemas and Aparicio 2004; Sainsbury 2012).

While these policy changes have thus not been ignored, few observers have attempted to trace their origins and develop a systematic account of the conditions under which they are most likely to arise. There have been several contributions regarding the welfare–migration nexus discussing, for example, how welfare states have responded to cope with immigration, the consequences of Europeanization for migrants' social rights, and the extent to which existing social protection schemes are effective for the migrant population (Ireland 2004; Jurado and Brochmann 2013; Sabates-Wheeler and Feldman 2011; Schierup, Hansen, and Castles 2006), but these studies refer to IEWRs only in passing. An exception is a volume edited by Michael Fix (2009) that is specifically dedicated to the mid-1990s exclusion of migrants from benefits in the United States. However, this work mostly discusses the consequences this IEWR has had for the American immigrant population, not the reasons why it was implemented in the first place. So far, the most important work in understanding the origins of IEWRs has been done by Diane Sainsbury (2012) in her impressive comparison of immigrants' social rights in six countries. Even in this study, however, the emphasis is more on providing a comprehensive descriptive overview of cross-national differences in immigrants' access to social benefits than on developing a theoretical account of the nature and origins of those differences.[3]

In sum, we know little about why IEWRs have come about. But before I turn to that question, it is useful to start with a few conceptual observations about these policy changes. Immigrant-excluding welfare reforms come in different guises and entail different kinds of exclusion. For the sake of analytical clarity, it is useful to describe them in terms of three characteristics: the *grounds* for exclusion, the *severity* of exclusion, and the *formality* of exclusion.

To start with the first of these three characteristics, welfare states might differentiate between immigrants and native-born citizens for four reasons.[4] First, residence status matters. The immigrants with the weakest social position in this regard are undocumented immigrants, who are commonly barred from social services and insurance programs and who in many countries risk deportation if they apply for even the most residual benefit. Children without a legal permit tend to enjoy more rights, in particular when it comes to education and health care access. Better protected than undocumented migrants, but still in a clearly disadvantaged position, are migrants on a temporary permit. IEWRs in 1996 and 1999 in the United Kingdom, for example, excluded temporary migrants from non-contributory benefits and denied welfare to asylum seekers awaiting a decision on their application (Sales 2002). In most welfare states, immigrants with permanent residence status are well-protected and differ little in their social rights from citizens (Hammar 1990; Soysal 1994). However, this is not the case everywhere. The welfare reforms of the mid-1990s in the United States, for example, excluded *all* non-citizens from food stamps and Supplemental Security Income (Fragomen 1997).

A second type of reform differentiates between immigrants and native-born citizens by implementing or extending residence requirements for access to benefits. All welfare states require immigrants – regardless of their status – to have lived a minimum number of years in the country before being eligible for tax-funded pension programs. However, this minimum requirement can vary considerably from one country to another, and some governments have decided to place residence requirements on other benefits as well. Denmark, for example, has recently placed a residence requirement of seven years for access to a complete social assistance benefit (J. Andersen, Larsen, and Møller 2009).

Third, the location of residence matters. Some welfare states pay out benefits to people who do not reside within their borders on the basis of the entitlements those people built up in the past. But the possibilities for this type of benefit export differ considerably among different programs, different welfare states, and even different countries of residence. Fourth and finally, migrants' success in meeting integration requirements can affect benefit access. The German government, for instance, decided to cut the unemployment and social assistance benefits of immigrants who do not attend their integration courses (Soysal 2012). Table 1.1 summarizes the above discussion and lists the four *grounds* for exclusion that underpin most IEWRs.

Table 1.1. Grounds for social rights differentiation between immigrants and native-born citizens

Ground	Explanation
Residence status	Migrants with more robust status tend to have more rights
Duration of residence	Migrants who have been in the country for a longer period of time tend to have more rights
Location of residence	Individuals who reside in country of benefit extension tend to have more rights
Integration	Migrants who meet integration standards tend to have more rights

IEWRs differ from one another not only in the groups of immigrants they target but also in the type of exclusion they entail. In this context, it is useful to distinguish between the *severity* of exclusion and the *formality* of exclusion. To start with the former, some reforms make immigrants altogether ineligible (as with the UK's exclusion of temporary migrants from non-contributory benefits), while others make immigrants receive a lower benefit (such as Denmark's coupling of social assistance to duration of residence). Still other reforms do not exclude immigrants or lower their benefits but do make the requirements for access more onerous for newcomers than for native-born citizens (e.g., Germany's requirement to attend integration courses).

We can also make distinctions with regard to the formality of exclusion. Most straightforwardly, some reforms explicitly exclude a subset of the immigrant population. Other programs exclude immigrants more indirectly, for instance by rewarding life experiences that immigrants are unlikely to have (Sabates-Wheeler and Feldman 2011, 10). For instance, social insurance programs that determine benefits based on past employment, as well as special benefits for veterans, inevitably privilege those who have been in the country all their life over those who have arrived recently. In these examples the exclusion is most likely an unintended consequence, but some mechanisms of indirect exclusion are deliberate and intentional. For example, the Dutch government's proposal to cut social assistance benefits in cases where "the behaviour or clothing of someone factually reduces his [sic] chances on the labour market"[5] (Government of the Netherlands 2010b, 26) was clearly meant to target the (Muslim) immigrant population. Third and finally, even if immigrants are legally entitled to the same benefits, more subtle forms

Table 1.2. Severity and formality of immigrant exclusion from social programs

	No access	Lower benefits	More onerous requirements
Direct formal	Disentitlement of immigrant groups (e.g., no benefits for undocumented or recent immigrants)	Lower benefits for immigrants (e.g., pro-rated pension programs)	Conditionality requirements (e.g., integration course for unemployment benefits)
Indirect formal	Immigrants unlikely to be eligible (e.g., veteran benefits)	Benefits likely to be lower for immigrants (e.g., contributory sickness benefits)	Cultural/linguistic barriers
Informal	Discrimination	Discrimination	Cultural/linguistic barriers

of exclusion may still impede access to benefits. As feminist critiques of the welfare state have pointed out, formal equality does not necessarily guarantee social equality (O'Connor 1993; Orloff 1993). When it comes to immigrants, there is evidence that benefit access can be hindered by discrimination (Capps, Hagan, and Rodriguez 2004; Kahanec, Kim, and Zimmerman 2013; Sabates-Wheeler and Feldman 2011) and, more frequently, by cultural and linguistic barriers (Ma and Chi 2005; Simich et al. 2005). This is why the repeal of translation services and of other programs that increase immigrants' uptake should also be considered a type of IEWR.

By combining the dimensions of formality and severity, we can develop a 3-by-3 matrix that maps the variety of ways that social programs can differentiate between immigrants and the native-born (Table 1.2).

In investigating these forms of differentiation, it is important to distinguish reforms that intentionally restrict immigrants' access to benefits, on the one hand, from exclusions that are the collateral result of broader policy reforms, on the other. Unless we keep this distinction in mind, it is easy to misunderstand reforms that have little to do with the politics of selective solidarity. A case in point, as we will see in chapter 3, is the pension reform the Swedish government implemented as part of its preparation to join the European Union in 1995. In order to facilitate the free movement of people, Sweden was required to make its pension system more similar to that of other member-states. One consequence of this overhaul was that the residence requirement for a full, tax-funded *folkpension* increased from ten to forty years, with obvious consequences for the immigrant population. To describe this as an IEWR similar to the 1996 British exclusion of asylum seekers, however, would give a misleading impression of the motivations behind the reform. At any rate, the theoretical framework in this chapter is of limited use in understanding this type of policy change.

In sum, as a way to deal with the tension between open borders and generous welfare institutions, some policy-makers have resorted to various strategies to restrict or qualify immigrants' access to social programs. Yet it would be wrong to suggest that there is something inevitable or necessary about this response. Policy-makers who are eager to avoid a large immigrant welfare clientele can consider at least three alternatives: (1) making admission policies more selective so as to admit fewer and/or more highly skilled immigrants; (2) investing in integration policies and immigrant-targeted active labour market policies to enhance immigrants' chances on the labour market; and (3) implementing across-the-board welfare reforms to achieve an overall reduction in social spending.[6]

To start with the first strategy, many European countries have in recent years turned to the "Canadian" strategy of carefully selecting those migrants who are least likely to turn to the state for support (Menz 2013). Typically, this entails restrictive changes in the streams of family and refugee migration as well as the implementation of skill and language requirements in the labour migration stream. Rather than pushing immigrants in need off benefits, this approach aims to minimize the number of immigrants who end up claiming benefits in the first place.

Second, policy-makers can propose the exact opposite of IEWRs, namely, the introduction or expansion of programs and services aimed at ameliorating immigrants' position in the labour market. Well in line with recent moves in many welfare states towards a "social investment model" (Jenson and Saint-Martin 2003), some politicians contend that the most obvious strategy for alleviating immigrant welfare dependence is by implementing economic integration programs or immigrant-targeted labour market policies. Examples include state-funded language classes, internship programs, micro-credit initiatives for newcomers, efforts to recognize foreign credentials, tax breaks for employers who hire immigrants, and initiatives to counter discrimination in the labour market.

Finally, policy-makers can decide to tackle the tension between migration and welfare by implementing across-the-board changes in the structure of the welfare state. A number of social scientists have argued that the combination of extensive protections for employees and passive benefits for the unemployed will leave immigrants little choice but to depend on the system for their income (Ghorashi 2005; Kogan 2004; Miller and Neo 2003). The key to an immigration-proof welfare state, in this account, is not to target immigrants specifically but rather to make the labour market more flexible and to reduce the generosity of passive benefits for everyone.

It is interesting to reflect on which of the four options is most effective at reducing or avoiding large-scale immigrant welfare dependence. I will return to this question briefly in the conclusion. My main interest, however, is in exploring and understanding the large cross-national differences in the currency these four options enjoy. More specifically, I aim to investigate why in some settings politicians have opted for the strategy of disentitling immigrants while their counterparts elsewhere formulate different policy responses. As said, there have been few attempts in the literature to address this puzzle and to understand when and how IEWRs are most likely to come about. The next two sections aim to develop such an account.

The Political Translation of Economic Facts

In the general literature on social policy, a pervasive argument is that cutbacks in welfare generosity come about in response to economic pressures. Almost every student of social policy would agree that policy-makers today face strong incentives to pursue retrenchment. The recent slowdown in productivity growth and the massive increase in the size of the service sector (Huber and Stephens 2001; Pierson 2001), the aging of the population and the decline in fertility rates (Esping-Andersen 1996a; Myles 2002; Pierson 2001; Taylor-Gooby 2002), and economic globalization (Scharpf and Schmidt 2000) are all threatening the economic sustainability of the welfare state. In those accounts, welfare retrenchment is explained at least partially as a measure to cope with formidable economic pressures.

Similar economic considerations are common in discussions about the social rights of immigrants. Here, immigrants' relatively heavy reliance on transfer benefits is presented as the reason their entitlements should be scaled back. In essence, this line of reasoning insists that immigrants make so much use of benefits that full welfare inclusion for them would make a redistributive welfare state unsustainable. Politicians frequently reason along these lines, and this argumentation has traction among academics and public commentators as well (Engelen 2003; Goodhart 2004; Grubel and Grady 2011).

In almost every Western welfare state, there is indeed ample evidence that immigrants are more likely than native-born citizens to be poor, unemployed, and reliant on state support (Brochmann 1996; Clark and Schultz 1998). Nevertheless, as we will see in later chapters, there are large differences in this regard from one country to another and from one point in time to another. In some countries, immigrants are highly overrepresented among those who receive benefits targeting the poor and unemployed and are more likely to depend on those benefits as a major source of income and to stay on those programs for a long period of time (Barrett and McCarthy 2008; Chiswick and Hurst 1998; Clark and Schultz 1998; Voges, Frick, and Büchel 1998); in other countries, the degree of overrepresentation is much smaller (Adsera and Chiswick 2006; Van Tubergen 2006). Welfare dependency rates tend to be lower in classic countries of immigration, although these rates have gone up in recent years (DeVoretz 1995). Conversely, in many Western European countries the trajectory seems to be one of decreasing dependency, although levels are still comparatively high (Dagevos, Gijsberts, and Van Praag 2003; Hammarstedt 2009).

The existing literature typically points to two sets of institutional characteristics to explain these differences. First, admission policies are obviously relevant. While some countries employ a wide range of measures to minimize the likelihood that immigrants will end up depending on social programs – for instance, by employing skill and language criteria in their admission policies – other countries are much less demanding in that regard (Boeri, Hanson, and McCormick 2009; Borjas 1999). Moreover, the composition of the migrant population matters. While some countries specifically select the majority of incoming migrants based on human capital characteristics, other countries admit the bulk of newcomers for humanitarian reasons. In effect, admission policy functions as an institutional screen that lets through different levels and mixes of immigrants in different countries, with different implications for the welfare state.[7]

Second, many have pointed at welfare state institutions themselves to explain immigrants' overrepresentation among benefit recipients. A particularly common argument in public commentary is that immigrants are more likely to rely on social benefits when those benefits are higher. One version of this thesis posits that immigrants have a "welfare penchant" and are more likely than the native-born to draw benefits (Koopmans 2010; Mollenkopf 2000; Scheffer 2004). A second version maintains that a generous welfare state can function as a magnet for immigrants with a poor work ethic (Borjas 1999; Carens 1988; Freeman 1986; Heitmueller 2005). Neither of these arguments, however, has found confirmation in empirical research. Once one controls for eligibility, immigrants tend to be equally or, more often, *less* likely than the native-born to make use of social programs (Barrett and Maître 2013; Boeri 2009, 20; Castronova et al. 2001; Reitz 1995; Sainsbury 2012, 126; Tienda and Jensen 1986). Moreover, to the degree that immigrants are drawn by the economic characteristics of the destination country, standard of living, wage equality, and overall economic standing have been found to be much more important than the system of social benefits (Barrett and McCarthy 2008; Giulietti et al. 2013; Hooghe et al. 2008; Kaestner and Kaushal 2005; Kaushal 2005; Kvist 2004; Voss, Hammer, and Meier 2001; WRR 2001; Yang and Wallace 2007). Indeed, while some studies find evidence of a modest magnet effect (Borjas 1999; Kremer 2013, 23–4, 127), the literature as a whole tends to reject rather than confirm the hypothesis that the generosity of social benefits has an important effect on migration patterns.

This, however, does not mean that the structure of the welfare state is irrelevant. The extent to which immigrants have access to benefits differs considerably from one program to another. Obviously, immigrants are unlikely to be disproportionately receiving benefits for which they have difficulty qualifying. The more stringent the eligibility requirements for programs with generous benefits such as public pensions, unemployment benefits or sickness benefits, the more likely immigrants will, in times of need, be compressed into programs of last resort such as social assistance, where they are likely to stand out demographically in the caseload (Boeri 2009; Taylor-Gooby 2004, 23). A second crucial set of social policies are labour market regulations. As mentioned above, protective labour market institutions such as a high minimum wage, rigid dismissal laws, and tax increases for double employment make it hard for newcomers to the labour market such as immigrants to be vertically mobile and therefore increase the likelihood that they will need to rely on the state for income support (Engelen 2003; Esping-Andersen 1996b; Kogan 2004; Miller and Neo 2003; Nickel 1997).

In sum, immigrants indeed tend to make greater use of some transfer programs than the native-born population. Yet it would be premature to conclude that the desire to exclude migrants from welfare benefits therefore originates in the objective pressure immigrants exert on the welfare budget. On closer investigation, it seems unlikely that there is a straightforward one-to-one relationship between patterns of immigrant welfare dependence and IEWRs.

Social scientists have long recognized that objective facts are of limited relevance in the formation of public policy (Ader 1995; Kingdon and Thurber 1984; Pralle 2009). Different political communities have been found to respond very differently to similar developments, a process commonly referred to as *political translation*. There are two components to this process. The first concerns salience: the same social facts can receive no attention at all in one place but be at the top of the political agenda in another (Iyengar and Kinder 1987). For example, climate change is arguably of equal relevance to every country in the world, but policy-makers pay much more attention to it in Denmark than in the United States. The second component is often referred to as *framing* (Chong and Druckman 2007): even when two communities pay equal attention to the same social fact, they may still formulate very different policy responses if there is a difference in the dominant way that this fact is most commonly discussed and understood. For example, policy-makers who understand an increase in crime as the result of increased inequality are likely to propose different solutions than their counterparts who blame it on a specific social group.

These insights have often been applied to the study of social policy (Cox 2001; Heclo 1974; Kuipers 2006; V.A. Schmidt 2000). Indeed, while concerns about a declining workforce or rising structural unemployment rates might be the ultimate driver of cutbacks in social programs, few scholars would argue that the relationship between economic incentives for welfare retrenchment and actual cutbacks in social programs is straightforward.

When it comes to immigrants' use of welfare, we might expect the process of political translation to be even more important. In many European countries, immigrants' appropriate place in the welfare system did not appear on the political agenda as a particularly salient policy issue until the 1990s but has since become subject to vehement political contestation. There is no obvious basis in social facts for this increased salience considering that the economic integration of immigrants is improving in many countries. A more likely explanation is that more general concerns about immigration (e.g., its implications for national identity or security) have cast a stronger spotlight on immigrants' use of benefits. IEWRs, then, do not appear as a response to objective economic facts regarding immigrants' economic integration, but as "solutions" to problems they are unlikely to solve.[8]

Of particular relevance in this regard are what scholars of political translation call "focusing events": dramatic incidents that spur a sudden increase in issue salience (Birkland 1997; Kingdon and Thurber 1984). Much research suggests that the distortion of social facts is strongest when it comes to subjects that people are most worried about (Boin, 't Hart, and McConnell 2009; Kelleher and Wolak 2006; Soroka 2002). In recent years there has been no shortage of focusing events that have been linked to immigration, such as the terrorist attacks in Western Europe and the United States, the riots in Parisian *banlieues*, and the murders of Pim Fortuyn and Theo van Gogh (d'Appollonia and Reich 2008; Korteweg 2006; Leiken 2005). In many countries the public has become worried about the general effects of immigration, and such worries have led many individuals to distort and exaggerate facts about migration and ethnic diversity (Jedwab 2008; Nadeau, Niemi, and Levine 1993; Transatlantic Trends 2010; C.J. Wong 2007).

For many of the same reasons, we should expect similar patterns of immigrant welfare dependence to receive more attention in some jurisdictions than others and for there to be large differences in the way the issue is most commonly understood. As discussed above, policymakers who worry about this subject have different policy tools at their disposal. Even when the political elite are unanimous that immigrant welfare dependence requires attention, it is not obvious that IEWRs are to be preferred over alternatives, such as employing more selective admission policies or investing more heavily in integration policies. It matters, therefore, how immigrants' economic integration is framed. When high dependency rates are taken as evidence that immigrants are lazy or prone to abuse the system, exclusionary policy suggestions are more likely to be formulated than when those rates are framed as a result of discrimination in the labour market or a dysfunctional integration regime.

Of course, we see similar dynamics in more general discussions about social policy: support for retrenchment has consistently been linked to a belief that welfare dependence can mostly be blamed on a lack of effort (Appelbaum 2001; Bullock 1999). In discussions of immigrants' use of welfare, however, there is an added dimension: immigrants invoke considerations about who truly "belongs" in the political community. For that reason, whether immigrants contribute to the economy or not may matter little for whether they are perceived as deserving access to benefits – especially when such perceptions become racialized (Gilens 1999; Kretsedemas and Aparicio 2004; Neubeck and Cazenave 2001; G.C. Wright 1977). Indeed, survey research suggests that identity concerns tend to be more important than economic concerns in driving anti-immigrant sentiment in general (Sides and Citrin 2007) and support for welfare exclusion in particular (A.W. Schmidt and Spies 2014; Sniderman et al. 2000; Van der Waal et al. 2010).[9]

All in all, there are good reasons to reject the suggestion that IEWRs are a calculated response to patterns of immigrant welfare dependence. Characteristics of the political system influence not only whether the subject receives attention in the first place but also which policy response is most likely to be suggested as a way of tackling it. The next two sections discuss the characteristics that are most important in this regard.

Forces of Continuity: Institutionalizing Immigrants' Social Rights

Before considering under which conditions we are most likely to see IEWRs suggested and adopted, it is important to discuss long-standing structural–institutional factors that shape the context in which debates about immigrants' social rights take place.

To start, it is worth emphasizing that IEWRs are puzzling from the perspective of institutional "path dependency" (James Mahoney 2000; Pierson 2004). As a well-developed literature demonstrates, previously established institutional structures have a tendency to reproduce themselves, thereby limiting possible courses of action in the future. Such sources of reproduction clearly also exist in the context of the subject under study. The long-term historical trajectory in most Western democracies has been one of a gradual and self-perpetuating increase in the inclusion of minority groups and the recognition of human rights (Joppke 2001; Marshall 1950; Triadafilopolous 2012). On this basis, we should expect countries to expand rather than restrict immigrants' access to the welfare state, and that is indeed what we have seen until recently. Citizenship used to be the only route to social rights in most Western democracies, but since the mid-twentieth century, immigrants without citizenship status have gradually gained more and more access to social benefits (Hammar 1990; Soysal 1994).

Moreover, once immigrants gain access to social benefits any future attempt at restrictions faces legal obstacles. Most obviously, the constitution of every immigrant-receiving Western democracy prohibits discrimination based on national origin. In those jurisdictions in which the courts have the power of judicial review, they can overrule reforms that violate this principle. Moreover, not only national but also international law can constrain IEWRs. The Universal Declaration of Human Rights (UDHR), for example, includes the prohibition of discrimination on the basis of national origin (Article 2) as well as the right to social security (Article 22). Although the UDHR is not a legally binding document, it does constitute normative pressure. Besides, many of the UDHR's provisions are included in UN treaties that *do* have legal status in the countries that are party to them. Particularly important for our purposes here are the International Covenant on Economic, Social and Cultural Rights (which, like the UDHR, guarantees the non-discrimination principle and the right to social security), the Convention on the Rights of the Child (which stipulates that all children, regardless of status, should be treated equally and that all children have the right to benefit from social security), and the Convention relating to the Status of Refugees (which demands that all recognized refugees be extended the exact same rights to social benefits as native-born citizens).[10]

The importance of international law is even greater for member-states of the European Union (EU) (Geddes 2003; Stokke 2007). For one thing, a member-state can do little to exclude citizens of other member-states. Citizens of the EU have the right to move freely from one member-state to another, and this has important consequences for access to social benefits and programs. On the one hand, unemployed EU citizens cannot simply move to another member-state and claim means-tested benefits such as social assistance there. National governments have to right to deny such claims for at least the first three months that the migrant is in the country (directive 2004/38), and a recent ruling of the European Court of Justice (ECJ) confirmed that EU citizens are not entitled to social assistance if the sole reason they moved to another member-state was to receive such benefits (*Dano v. Jobcenter Leipzig*). On the other hand, however, ever since the early 1970s member-states have been obligated to open their social programs and benefits to all EU citizens who work on their territory (regulations 1408/71 and 574/72). The consequences for contributory programs are particularly large: EU citizens start building up eligibility from the moment they start working, and more controversially, they can also count the years they worked in other member-states when it comes to assessing eligibility and benefit level. Moreover, judgments from the ECJ have expanded the obligations that follow from this principle. For example, it ruled in 1986 that member-states are required to offer child benefits to migrant workers from within the EU even if their children still live in their country of origin (*Pinna* case, 41/84). Similarly, in the *Ten Holder* judgment the court ruled that a Dutch woman who had returned to the Netherlands after having lived and worked for a long period of time in Germany, and who started to experience serious back problems, was still covered by German social security law until she took up work in the Netherlands (*Ten Holder* case, 302/84).

Finally, all members of the Council of Europe[11] are signatory to the European Convention on Human Rights (ECHR), which has proven to be an obstacle for IEWRs. The best-known example is *Gaygusuz vs. Austria*, a case in which a Turkish man, lawfully resident in Austria for over ten years, was denied emergency assistance on the basis of his nationality. When his appeals to the Austrian authorities proved futile, he applied to the European Court of Human Rights. That court ruled unanimously in Mr Gaygusuz's favour, declaring that Austria's decision violated the prohibition of discrimination (Gortázar Rotaeche 1998).

In short, the institutional context matters because it can discourage the adoption of IEWRs. But it is also relevant to consider specific aspects of a political system because they create a framework within which discussions of immigrants' social rights take place. Two related characteristics are particularly relevant: the structure of the welfare system, and the nature of national identity.

Perhaps most obviously, the structure of the welfare state itself shapes discussions about what immigrants' place in the welfare state should be. A large body of research demonstrates that in countries with a universal welfare regime the public is most likely to consider recipients deserving of state support, to believe that individuals cannot be blamed for depending on welfare, and to think that unequal treatment between different social groups is unjustifiable (Esping-Andersen 1990; G. Evans 1996; Halvorsen 2007; Jaeger 2007; Korpi 1980; Matthews and Erickson 2008; Rothstein 1998). Particularly instructive for our current purposes is the work of Christian Larsen (2008), who reasons that the institutional structure of a welfare state frames the way government transfers are most commonly perceived and that this frame tends to be at its most positive in more generous welfare systems. He points out that universal welfare settings have framing effects that are likely to mute opposition to benefit recipients: they obviate discussions about whether recipients truly need the benefits they rely on and whether the recipients are to blame for their dependency; they are unlikely to create tensions between the employed and the unemployed; and they blur the boundary between those who contribute and those who benefit. Building on these insights, a number of authors have theorized that selective solidarity likely enjoys the least currency in universal settings (Banting 2000). Because such sentiments have been found to be tightly linked to perceptions of deservingness (Reeskens and Van Oorschot 2012), it indeed seems plausible that concerns about immigrants' use of benefits are least likely to arise in welfare regimes that discourage the drawing of boundaries between the deserving and the undeserving. And indeed, the recent literature on sentiments of welfare chauvinism among the public supports this expectation (Crepaz and Damron 2009; Mau and Burkhardt 2009; Mewes and Mau 2013; Reeskens and Van Oorschot 2012; Van der Waal, De Koster, and Van Oorschot 2013).

The welfare regime is not only important because it shapes public attitudes, however. In keeping with the above-mentioned theory of path dependency, policy reforms take place within pre-established boundaries. As Diane Sainsbury has repeatedly pointed out, the ways different countries have chosen to incorporate immigrants into the structure of social benefits is deeply influenced by the existing welfare regime (Sainsbury 2006, 2012). Some systems rely heavily on targeted and means-tested programs for the most "deserving" in the population – a designation unlikely to be extended to immigrants. Other systems tend to tie benefit levels to past contributions, which means that recent newcomers in particular are likely to enjoy less protection than the established population (Sciortino 2013). Still others follow principles of universality and are therefore most likely to adopt an inclusive approach to immigrants. Moreover, these last systems tend to make extensive use of active labour market policies to fight unemployment (Huber and Stephens 2001; Huo 2009), which makes it more likely for high levels of immigrant unemployment to be met by attempts to stimulate immigrants' labour market participation than by the adoption of IEWRs.

The second country characteristic that likely shapes discussions about immigrants' social rights is the nature of a country's national identity. Like the structure of the welfare state, dominant conceptions of the nation-state affect to what extent immigrants are framed as deserving of social benefits, although the precise mechanisms by which this occurs are somewhat different. Since the very sentiment of selective solidarity is predicated on the categorization of immigrants as an out-group (cf. Sniderman et al. 2000), we might expect more unease about immigrants' use of benefits where exclusionary nationalism enjoys more currency. Of course, concerns about national identity tend to feature prominently in the rhetoric of immigration critics of all nationalities, and more generally, there is much research suggesting that nationalism tends to be associated with anti-immigrant sentiment (Pettigrew and Meertens 1995; Shayo 2009; Sides and Citrin 2007; Skenderovic 2007; Sniderman and Hagendoorn 2007). Yet it would be wrong to suggest that an attachment to a nation-state necessarily leads to xenophobia. As the literature on comparative nationalism attests, there are significant differences between political communities in the criteria for "belonging" they formulate. While some require aspiring members to adhere to their political values and institutions, others stipulate more demanding membership requirements of ethnicity and ancestry (Greenfeld 1992; Koning 2011; Meinecke 1907/1970). These differences in national identity are likely to influence discussions about immigration in general and immigrants' social rights in particular. Cross-national research on public attitudes towards nationalism invariably finds that the meaning of nationalism differs considerably from one country to another and that this matters for attitudes towards immigrants (Ariely 2011; Escandell and Ceobanu 2010; Esses et al. 2006; E.G.T. Green et al. 2011; Kunovich 2009; Pehrson, Vignoles, and Brown 2009). While in some political communities there is a strong relationship between nationalism and anti-immigrant attitudes, in others that relationship appears to be much weaker or non-existent. In some countries, nationalism even appears to be associated with a positive stance towards immigration (Johnston et al. 2010).

In sum, we need to analyse long-standing characteristics of the political system before we can tackle the key question why IEWRs have been a more popular tool in some countries than in others. Not only does such an analysis highlight why the adoption of such policy changes is puzzling in the first place, but it also provides a country-specific framework by which we can understand processes of political translation that take place later on.

Forces of Change: Contesting Immigrants' Social Rights

So far, we have seen that attempts to restrict immigrants' benefit access are relatively recent, that we would expect stability or expansion based on forces of path dependency, and that objective patterns of immigrant

welfare dependence are of little help in unravelling this puzzle. Historical and economic factors, therefore, cannot explain where IEWRs come
from. We need to look at politics.

This section suggests that IEWRs will be enacted when politicians
propose them, convince others to support them, and are able to over-
come legal obstacles. In describing this process, I will pay particular
attention to anti-immigrant parties (AIPs), not because they are the only
parties that might host anti-immigrant politicians but simply because
they offer the most dramatic illustration. They are the most likely voices
of selective solidarity, not only because of their hostility towards the
immigrant population but also because most modern versions of this
type of party are in favour of a redistributive welfare state (J.G. Andersen and Bjørklund 2000, 203–5; Carter 2005, 32; Gibson 2002; Halvorsen
2007, 253).[12]

For IEWRs to come about, visible political actors first need to criticize immigration and its consequences and promote the adoption of
IEWRs as a viable solution. The most likely explanation for this cir-
cumstance is that political actors believe they can reap electoral benefits from taking such a position. Of course, one might ask where an
anti-immigrant backlash incentivizing politicians to suggest IEWRs
comes from in the first place. That question is largely beyond the
scope of this project but has been investigated extensively in existing research. Most of the literature points at two sets of explanations.
First, some scholars emphasize "demand-side" explanations, pointing
at developments such as globalization, the rise of structural unemployment, and the overlap between ethnicity and class in many new
immigration countries that have created a breeding ground for anti-
immigrant sentiment (Betz 2001; Guibernau 2010; Mudde 2010; Oesch
2008). Second, other scholars have suggested "supply-side" explanations and invoked the characteristics of political systems, such as
the electoral system, the predominance of class voting, and the party
system, to understand why such rhetoric has become more pervasive
in some places than in others (Carter 2002; De Lange 2007; O'Malley
2008; Spies 2013).

For our current investigation, of most importance are the *consequences*
of a political climate that makes appearing tough on immigration an
attractive electoral strategy. As was emphasized above, in such a context it does not matter whether a proposal for exclusionary reform
addresses any of the problems that gave rise to concerns about immigration.[13] What matters is that the reform is effectively framed as "doing

something" about immigration. And the more these kinds of discussions take place, the more they reinforce themselves.

For one thing, by repeatedly bringing up problems associated with immigration – in particular, the overrepresentation of immigrants on welfare rolls – anti-immigrant actors are able to increase the salience of the issue, bringing it to the front of everyone's mind. In such a discursive climate, immigration can be invoked as the cause of social ills or policy failures in virtually any policy area. Taken-for-granted norms and institutions, such as the freedom of religion and the responsibility to grant asylum to the persecuted, can then become objects of political contestation. In the context of this study, the suggestion that immigrants be excluded from benefits seems more viable once immigrants' overrepresentation among welfare dependents has become a prominent theme in political discourse (Faist 1996, 240).

Moreover, we can expect AIPs to make use of the discursive frames that are most conducive to sentiments of selective solidarity. The anti-immigrant frame, in addition to presenting immigration as the root of various evils and as a threat to national identity, security, and welfare state sustainability, typically has four components. First, it describes the anti-immigrant position as "common sense." Anti-immigrant politicians frequently argue that they are "saying out loud what people are thinking inside" (Rydgren 2003, 58). Second, and relatedly, it presents itself as the voice of democracy. Anti-immigrant politicians and commentators often complain that the public at large has never been asked if it favours open immigration policies, and refer to survey data (where available) that find a majority of the electorate in favour of restrictions (Huntington 2004, 82, 166–7). Another strategy is to publicly ask for more "openness" about immigration – for example, by requesting a parliamentary inquiry to calculate the net fiscal burden or contribution of immigration (J.G. Andersen and Bjørklund 2000, 205) – and to frame any opposition they might encounter to such requests as elitist and anti-democratic. Third, this self-portrayal as the true defenders of democracy allows for a powerful us-versus-them frame, in which "we, the ordinary citizens," are pitted against "they, the elite and its protégés": mainstream political parties, special interest groups, and, of course, newcomers to the political community (Betz and Johnson 2004, 316). The literature on framing suggests that these types of divisive frames are among the most effective rhetorical techniques because they mobilize social identity (Mols 2012, 332; Sniderman and Hagendoorn 2007, 120). The final component is exaggeration. Rather than saying that immigrants are overrepresented among welfare recipients, anti-immigrant actors prefer to speak of "foreigners who plunder our benefits." This technique is particularly fruitful because, as noted earlier, people tend to exaggerate the social developments they are most worried about – a process that is likely to be exacerbated if the political elite reinforces those exaggerations.

In sum, we can expect calls for IEWRs to arise in a political climate where concerns about immigration and multiculturalism are pervasive, regardless of whether immigrants' interactions with the welfare system are central to those concerns. The most likely political agents to coin these ideas are members of anti-immigrant parties, most of whom combine their anti-immigrant stance with a pro–welfare state position. And finally, we can expect that once calls go out for IEWRs, the political salience of the welfare costs of immigration will increase and the predominant way of discussing the issue will turn much more accusatory. Yet it would be premature to draw an immediate link to the adoption of IEWRs. After all, just because some politicians favour them does not mean they will materialize. It is crucial, then, to investigate how the political mainstream responds to these suggestions. I will discuss two mechanisms by which anti-immigrant politicians can make the mainstream adopt more restrictive policies in general and IEWRs in particular.

The first and most direct of these mechanisms is what I will refer to as *compromise*. The election of anti-immigrant politicians changes the distribution of power and brings a player to the bargaining table that will focus most of her legislative influence on bringing about restrictive immigration policies. In some cases (e.g., in Austria from 1999 to 2006 and since 2017, in the Netherlands from 2002 to 2003, and in Norway since 2013), AIPs have become part of a coalition government and as such acquired a major opportunity to introduce their desired restrictions. In other cases (e.g., in Denmark from 2001 to 2011, in the Netherlands from 2010 to 2012, and in Norway from 2001 to 2005), governing parties were wary of formally including AIPs in their coalition but nevertheless struck a deal with them: guaranteed support in parliament in return for policy concessions (in particular on the immigration file). Finally, even in opposition, AIPs can play an influential bargaining role. Especially when there is a minority government or a coalition government whose factions do not always see eye to eye, AIPs have the potential to occupy a pivotal position on some bills and hold leverage for compromise.

While there has been little systematic empirical investigation on this subject, centre-right parties seem the most likely candidates to engage in such compromise. At any rate, all the cabinets mentioned above were composed of conservative and/or Christian-democratic parties. Conservatives tend to be closest in their position on immigration to AIPs (Breunig and Luedtke 2008; Koning 2017b; Messina 2007), and may also reason that restrictions on immigrant entitlements fit well with an agenda to cut government spending.

Nevertheless, the extent to which AIPs are able to reach compromises is strikingly different from one country to another. In some contexts, mainstream parties of all political stripes respond to anti-immigrant politicians with a concerted effort to minimize their legislative influence. Perhaps the best-known example is the *cordon sanitaire* that parties in Belgium erected when the *Vlaams Blok* (Flemish Bloc, since renamed *Vlaams Belang* or Flemish Interest) won eleven seats in the 1991 elections (Erk 2005). While some scholars argue that these strategies are counterproductive and only enhance the popularity of anti-immigrant politicians in the long run (Damen 2001; Loxbo 2010), it seems clear that this response at any rate reduces their short-term legislative influence.

The second mechanism can be labelled *contagion*, following the work of Pippa Norris (2005): a sudden success for anti-immigrant politicians can lead other politicians to support IEWRs on their own initiative. This might be because politicians had never considered such ideas until others suggested them and consider them worthwhile. A more cynical reason to suspect contagion is electoral self-interest: mainstream politicians may conclude that a more restrictive line on immigration will improve their standing in upcoming elections. In this account, centrist parties propose exclusionary reforms not because they genuinely support them but because they fear that too generous a position on immigration could lead to even greater success for anti-immigrant politicians in the future.

Norris predicted right-of-centre parties to be most susceptible to contagion, reasoning that they are the most obvious competitors for the anti-immigrant vote. In subsequent research, however, Joost van Spanje (2010) and Tim Bale and his colleagues (2010) found evidence of this effect among some left-wing parties as well. The tendency of modern AIPs to combine a right-wing stance on immigration with a relatively left-wing position on redistribution is again of key importance here. Given that we typically find some of the most virulent critics of immigration among the traditional constituents of social democratic parties

(Derks 2008), it is not difficult to understand why social democrats fear politicians who advocate selective solidarity.

Again, it is important to stress that this mechanism is not inescapable. Indeed, Bale and his colleagues find considerable differences in the extent of contagion both between countries and between parties within a country (Bale et al. 2010). As we saw above, there is large cross-national divergence in the responses that anti-migrant politicians have provoked from the political mainstream. All else being equal, we should most expect compromise and contagion to take place after a strong electoral showing by an AIP. A sizeable surge in the number of seats for AIPs increases the sheer necessity to strike deals and also makes a *cordon sanitaire* seem like an elitist negation of the election result. Moreover, especially those parties the newcomer party managed to win seats from are likely to feel an incentive to change strategies. In line with such expectations, Van Spanje (2010) found a strong positive relationship between the number of seats won by AIPs and the extent to which opposition parties moved to the right on the immigration file.

In sum, it is essential to analyse the response that suggestions for immigrant exclusion trigger among the political mainstream. Where no compromise or contagion takes place, IEWRs are unlikely to come about. And even if support for IEWRs reaches the political mainstream, it is hardly certain that such reforms will take place, because some of them might prove impossible to implement within existing legal frameworks.

It is worth pointing out that in terms of institutional obstacles, there are large and theoretically relevant differences between IEWRs and more general welfare reforms. One of the main insights in the literature on welfare retrenchment is that politicians who want to reduce the overall generosity of the welfare state face formidable institutional obstacles. Many social programs are popular among the citizenry, which means that attempts to retrench them will be met by a well-mobilized opposition and that any party that suggests or implements such measures will be punished at the next election (Brooks and Manza 2007; Huber and Stephens 2001; Kitschelt 2001; Rehm 2001; Sachweh, Ullrich, and Christoph 2007). To get around this, politicians have been observed to make use of two strategies. First, they can engage in what Kent Weaver (2010) calls "blame avoidance." By obfuscating the severity of reforms, striking cross-party package deals that make it unclear to the electorate which party is primarily responsible, and compensating those who are most obviously hit, politicians can reform social policies without having to worry about the electoral repercussions. The second strategy is almost the exact opposite: instead of evading responsibility for them, politicians can get away with welfare reforms by successfully convincing the electorate that it was necessary to implement them (Cox 2001; Kuipers 2006, 147–78; V.A. Schmidt 2000).

In the case of IEWRs, both the institutional obstacles and the strategies politicians employ to navigate them are different. To begin with the former, while a large part of the electorate would object to general cutbacks, a much smaller portion would be affected by IEWRs. The targets of those policy changes – recent and future migrants – have limited access to the decision-making process and are therefore unlikely to pose an obstacle. And as discussed above, while left-wing parties may for ideological reasons be reluctant to propose restrictions on immigrants' social rights, even they may under certain circumstances feel compelled to support such policy changes. In other words, compared to more general welfare reforms, IEWRs are more likely to pass through the legislature because no party depends on the people affected by the reforms for its re-election.

This does not mean, however, that IEWRs face no institutional obstacles at all. As discussed in the previous section, national and international legal frameworks can thwart attempts at excluding migrants from benefits. Indeed, many scholars note that the most important source of the protection and advancement of immigrants' social rights are the courts and legal activists (Guiraudon 2000, 2002; Joppke 2001). Proposition 187 in California offers a forceful example. The bill garnered a handsome majority of the vote in the 1994 referendum, yet the result was overturned by a federal court shortly afterwards (Valenty and Sylvia 2004). Other examples of the judicial branch of government reversing attempts to exclude immigrants from welfare benefits abound (Geddes 2003, 157; Joppke 2001, 343–6; Minderhoud 1999, 146; Rosenhek 2000, 56; Sainsbury 2012, 185).

Since the obstacles to IEWRs are legal rather than democratic, politicians intent on implementing these changes are likely to resort to different strategies than their counterparts who are trying to bring about a more general cutback in welfare policies. First, they can try to work around the legal prohibitions. For example, attempts to exclude immigrant groups with weak legal status are less likely to be frustrated than attempts to curtail the benefits of citizens or permanent residents. In most Western welfare states, immigrants without permanent resident status have been excluded from a variety of social programs (Faist 1995;

Kvistad 1998; Soysal 1994), and their access has been further restricted in recent years (Kurthen 1998; Minderhoud 2004). Undocumented immigrants are most vulnerable in this regard. Except for emergency health care, and education for children, there is very little a state can be forced to offer people who are not legally entitled to stay within its borders. Temporary migrants are somewhat better protected, because denying them access to contributory programs they paid into is easily construed as discrimination, even though this has happened in the past on a fairly large scale (Ryner 2000, 60), still takes place in some instances (Nakache and Kinoshita 2010), and is actively promoted today by a large number of politicians. However, temporary migrants are much more vulnerable to exclusion from non-contributory programs such as social assistance. The justification here is that the very reason for their migration is employment and that temporary migrants who lose their job should therefore lose their residence permit rather than receive income support. And even though this justification does not apply to asylum seekers, their relatively weak legal status has made this group of migrants susceptible to welfare exclusion in recent years as well (Bloch and Schuster 2002; Minderhoud 1999; Mynott, Humphries, and Cohen 2002; Schuster 2000).

A related albeit more indirect strategy is what institutionalists call "patching up" or "policy layering" (Genschel 1997; Streeck and Thelen 2005): when institutions cannot be changed, policy-makers can instead add policies or amend existing ones so as to make them perform in new ways. In particular, when it is unfeasible to amend social policies, changing admission policies can bring about the same differentiation in access to benefits. For example, when the legal system prohibits residence requirements affecting permanent migrants, politicians who are intent on IEWRs can decide to implement a residence requirement to acquire permanent residency instead. Similarly, the more difficult a country makes it to acquire and maintain legal status, the easier it will be to exclude unwanted outsiders from benefits. These strategies avoid the legal roadblocks while still achieving the intended goal.

If such strategies are unavailable or unsuccessful, another option is to amend or abolish the legal obstacles. An example of the former took place in 2003, when the EU introduced the so-called Family Reunification Directive (directive 2003/86). This amendment to the unconditional right of a family life as enshrined in Article 8 ECHR allowed member-states to demand that people who want to bring family members over from outside the EU satisfy certain criteria (such as having stable financial resources and suitable accommodation) (Groenendijk 2006). Complete abolition of legal obstacles seems less likely. After all, many policy-makers would consider withdrawing from the EU or repealing constitutional rights too drastic a measure for both pragmatic and normative reasons. Nevertheless, this does not preclude that some politicians will advocate these strategies or even that such advocacy is successful, as the United Kingdom's expected departure from the EU illustrates forcefully.

In sum, IEWRs do not automatically follow when they enjoy support from a large parliamentary majority. National and international law constrains the extent to which governments can exclude immigrants from social benefits. Proponents of such reforms, therefore, have to find a way to abolish, amend, patch up, or work around obstinate legal protections. If none of these strategies prove successful or feasible, they have little choice but to abandon their proposals for exclusion.

By combining insights from the theoretical literature on new institutionalism, social policy change, and the politics of immigration, this chapter has developed a theoretical framework for understanding how and when we should expect IEWRs to come about. To reiterate, the main expectations of this framework are threefold. First, it is unlikely that IEWRs are a calculated response to the actual stresses that immigrants place on the welfare system. While proponents of IEWRs often invoke such objective pressures, we should not expect more calls for IEWRs where and when immigrants' reliance on the welfare system is largest. This is because of a process of political translation by which economic facts assume different levels of salience and different specific interpretations in different political systems. In short, calls to exclude immigrants from welfare benefits are more about general opposition to immigration than about economics or social policies.

Second, historical legacies tend to encourage welfare inclusion rather than exclusion, especially in universal welfare states that hold inclusionary conceptions of national identity. Considering the historical trajectory in Western democracies of gradual rights extension and the difficulty of institutionalizing differential treatment once legal protections against discrimination are in place, the spread of IEWRs is a puzzling phenomenon. This is even more so the case when they arise in welfare systems that are premised on the principle of universalism or in countries that have embraced diversity as a national virtue.

Third, political factors are an essential component of any investigation of IEWRs. In the context of widespread concern about immigration, some politicians will conclude that they will benefit electorally from promoting IEWRs. AIP politicians are the most likely to reach such conclusions, especially because their platforms tend to combine opposition to immigration with support for redistributive policies. Yet the mere presence of suggestions for IEWRs does not necessarily translate into actual policy change. The impact of anti-immigrant politicians only becomes consequential when mainstream politicians respond in accommodating ways. And even when they do, and a parliamentary majority emerges in support of immigrant exclusion, attempts at IEWRs can still fail if they are unable to navigate existing legal obstacles.

Taken together, these three expectations help us make sense of the politics of immigrants' social rights in different welfare states. More specifically, they offer an explanation why we see the adoption of IEWRs in some contexts but not in others. The following chapters will subject this theoretical framework to empirical investigation.

Chapter Two

The Limits of Economic Explanations

This chapter starts the empirical investigation by demonstrating the first major proposition about IEWRs from the previous chapter, namely, that economic explanations are of limited use in understanding these reforms. Of course, the observation that policy-making does not always follow careful economic analysis is hardly novel, and indeed, the main evidence in this chapter may come as little surprise to students of political science and public administration. Nevertheless, it seems worth demonstrating that economic facts are of little relevance to the politics of IEWRs for at least two reasons. First of all, the academic literature on the relationship between immigration and the welfare state continues to lend credence to the suggestion that support for welfare exclusion is mostly a response to immigrants' actual overrepresentation among benefit recipients (Hero and Preuhs 2007; O'Connell 2005). Second, and more importantly, the claim that IEWRs are a response to economic realities is prominent in political discussions. Anti-immigrant politicians often attempt to legitimize their exclusionary reforms by referring to "objective facts" concerning the use of social benefits by immigrants (Halvorsen 2007, 253; Menz 2006, 409). Indeed, over the last few years immigration sceptics in various countries have called for economic estimates of immigrants' "price tag" as a strategy for increasing public discomfort about (the costs of) immigration (Grubel and Grady 2011; House of Lords 2008; Van der Geest amd Dietvorst 2010).

This chapter will demonstrate the limited explanatory power of economic factors by dispelling several implications that would have to hold if it were truly the case that support for IEWRs is a response to the actual economic pressure that immigration places on the welfare system. More specifically, if this hypothesis were true, we would expect

(1) that public opinion is more supportive of IEWRs in countries where immigrants rely more heavily on welfare benefits; (2) that politicians propose more of these reforms when and where immigrants rely more heavily on welfare benefits; (3) that suggestions for IEWRs target the most costly policies; (4) that economic arguments are most common in justifications for these reforms; and (5) that economic justifications rely on accurate reflections of economic reality. As we will see, this chapter does not find support for any of these expectations.

Immigrants' Welfare Use and Public Opinion

We start our investigation by exploring whether sentiments of selective solidarity are most widespread in countries where immigrants rely most heavily on welfare state benefits. So far, the academic literature has not investigated this question systematically. While studies on the determinants of general unease about immigration are countless, only recently have scholars started to address selective solidarity in particular (Reeskens and Van Oorschot 2012; Van der Waal et al. 2013). Similarly, existing research has analysed the effect of all kinds of indicators on anti-immigrant attitudes, but rarely have scholars investigated the effect of immigrants' reliance on welfare programs. One study that comes close is an investigation by Gordon Hanson and his colleagues (2005), who include levels of immigrant welfare dependence in a multivariate analysis of admission preferences. This study (which finds inconsistent effects across survey waves and different sets of respondents) is limited to the United States, however, and therefore offers only a partial answer. Another relevant study investigates whether *perceptions* of immigrant welfare dependence have an effect on support for redistribution in Canada (Banting, Soroka, and Koning 2013) and finds that people who believe that immigrants rely heavily on welfare are less likely to support social assistance but more likely to support other redistributive measures of the welfare state.

To begin, let us briefly consider the main variables of interest: immigrants' overrepresentation in transfer benefits, and selective solidarity. Table 2.1 shows the level of immigrant overrepresentation among recipients of various transfer benefits according to data of the Luxembourg Income Study (LIS) of 2000 in twelve Western welfare states.[1] The table reports three different sets of government transfers: social assistance; social assistance and unemployment benefits combined; and social assistance, unemployment benefits, pensions, and family benefits

Table 2.1. Overrepresentation of immigrants in various transfer programs, 12 countries, 2000

Country	Social assistance	Social assistance and unemployment benefits	Social assistance, unemployment, pensions, and family benefits
Sweden	840.6	174.5	−2.8
Norway	731.0	279.0	−21.5
Denmark	448.0	182.2	12.3
UK	186.4	163.1	13.7
Belgium	158.5	96.0	17.1
Germany	142.3	62.8	−9.3
USA	104.5	82.5	−41.6
France	65.8	62.2	−3.4
Canada	30.8	10.2	34.7
Switzerland	24.0	58.1	−79.9
Austria	15.6	54.5	−4.2
Ireland	8.4	5.3	5.0

Source: LIS and authors' calculations[2]

combined. The cell numbers express how much more the average immigrant receives than the average native-born citizen. For example, the data for Switzerland show that in 2000 the average immigrant received 24 per cent more in social assistance than the average native-born citizen, but about 80 per cent *less* in the combined total of social assistance, unemployment, pensions, and family benefits.[3]

Looking at the table, it first seems worth noting that the degree of immigrants' overreliance on government transfers depends on the type of transfers. If we combine the four most typical transfer benefits, in more than half of the countries immigrants are receiving *less* than native-born citizens, and in none of the other countries is immigrants' overrepresentation particularly high. This is in large part because in most of the countries under study, immigrants are on average younger than the native-born population and therefore less likely to be receiving pension benefits. The picture becomes different when we focus on programs that target the poor and the unemployed. In all countries under study, immigrants receive more in combined social assistance and unemployment benefits than the non-immigrant population, and for ten of the twelve countries their overrepresentation becomes even higher when we look at social assistance alone. Even more striking than the differences between programs are the differences between countries, especially when we focus exclusively on social assistance. Immigrants' overrepresentation is massive in Sweden and Norway but modest to negligible in Canada, Switzerland, Austria, and Ireland.

Reliable longitudinal and cross-national data on the dependent variable are more challenging to acquire. Indeed, an important reason for the scarcity of cross-national studies of selective solidarity is the lack of useful survey data. There are some surveys that ask respondents specifically about the welfare use and welfare entitlements of immigrants, but none of these have been conducted on both sides of the Atlantic. Moreover, there are no cross-national surveys available that invite respondents specifically to compare the entitlements of immigrants and the native-born and judge whether immigrants should have the same social rights as the native-born. The next best thing is to use different questions from large cross-national surveys in order to offer a general impression of the degree to which respondents see the position of immigrants in the welfare system as a problem and are comfortable with differentiations between immigrants and the native-born. Figure 2.1 aims to do exactly that. It shows, for the same twelve countries

Figure 2.1. Average distance from mean score on selective solidarity, 12 countries

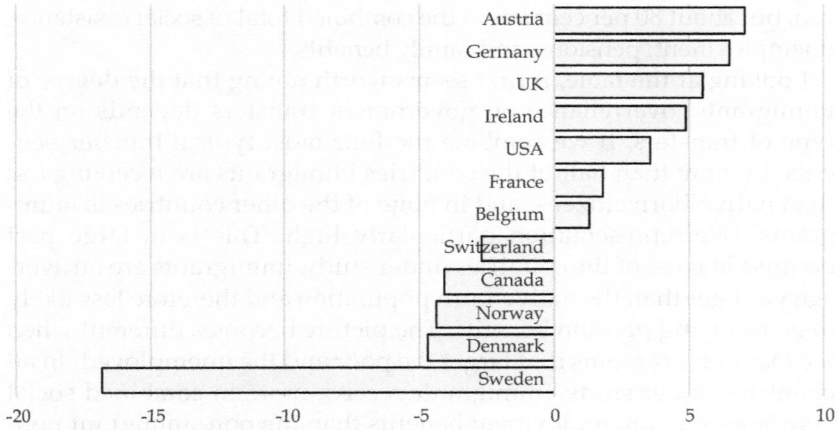

Source: WVS 2000 and 2005, ISSP 2003

Figure 2.2. Bivariate relationship between immigrant welfare dependence and selective solidarity among the public

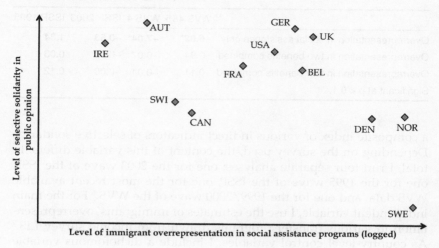

as in Table 2.1, the agreement with eight different indicators of selective solidarity drawn from the International Social Survey Program (ISSP) and the World Values Survey (WVS).[4] More specifically, it shows their average distance on these indicators from the mean for all countries. In doing so, it ranks these countries from those where selective solidarity seems to pervade public opinion the most (Austria) to where it seems to do so the least (Sweden).[5]

At this point it might already seem apparent that cross-national differences in immigrant welfare dependence are of limited help in understanding cross-national differences in public support for selective solidarity. If we plot a log of the level of overrepresentation of social assistance against the estimates of selective solidarity, as shown in Figure 2.2, we certainly do not observe a positive relationship. If anything, it suggests that the population shows most evidence of selective solidarity where immigrants are least overrepresented among welfare recipients ($r = -0.55$, two-tailed $p = 0.06$).

Of course, this is a rather crude analysis that ignores any other variables that might be relevant. We can therefore better estimate the relationship through multilevel modelling, a type of regression analysis also known as mixed modelling or hierarchical modelling (De Leeuw, Meijer, and Goldstein 2008). In this analysis, the main dependent variable is

Table 2.2. Effect of immigrants' overrepresentation in various transfer benefits on welfare chauvinism, multi-level model estimates (individual-level variables not shown)

	WVS 4&5	WVS 4	ISSP 2003	ISSP 1995
Overrepresentation in social assistance only	−5.02*	−7.04*	−0.53	1.34
Overrepresentation in two benefits combined	−0.94	−0.07	−0.06	0.03
Overrepresentation in four benefits combined	−0.11	−0.04	−0.00	0.12
Significant at p < 0.1.				

a composite index of various indirect indicators of selective solidarity. Depending on the survey used, the content of this variable differs. In total, I run four separate analyses: one for the 2003 wave of the ISSP, one for the 1995 wave of the ISSP, one for the most recent available WVS data, and one for the 1999/2000 wave of the WVS.[6] For the main independent variable, I use the estimates of immigrants' overrepresentation in various transfer programs drawn from income survey LIS.[7] As country-level control variables, I include a dichotomous variable for universal welfare states, an estimate of the inclusiveness of a country's national identity based on a combination of two scholarly indexes measuring the inclusiveness of naturalization policies (Koning 2011) and integration policies (Banting and Kymlicka 2011),[8] and the share of immigrants as percentage of the population in the survey year. On the individual level, I control where available for age, sex, education, employment status, occupation, income, religiosity, citizenship, and the citizenship of the respondents' parents at time of birth. In existing research, these generally appear to be the most important demographic predictors of attitudes towards immigrants in general (Hello, Scheepers, and Sleegers 2006; Masso 2009; Mau and Burkhardt 2009; Sides and Citrin 2007) and of selective solidarity in particular (Reeskens and Van Oorschot 2012; Van der Waal et al. 2010).

Table 2.2 summarizes the key findings from twelve separate regression models that estimate the relationship between immigrant welfare dependence and selective solidarity while controlling for individual-level variables. More specifically, it reports the coefficient of each of the three estimates of immigrant overrepresentation for each of the four sets of survey data in MLMs that include individual-level controls.

After controlling for demographic characteristics, we still observe no evidence that selective solidarity is a reaction to immigrants' actual reliance on transfer benefits. Only three of the twelve models suggest a

Table 2.3. Effect of immigrant overrepresentation in social assistance on selective solidarity, controlling for various country-level variables (individual-level variables not shown)

Model		WVS 4&5	WVS 4	ISSP 2003	ISSP 1995
I	Overrepresentation	−5.37*	−7.05*	−1.32	−1.61
	% Foreign-born	−0.47	−0.47*	−0.23	−1.14
II	Overrepresentation	−1.16*	−1.97*	3.27*	3.90
	Universality	−15.31	−10.68	−6.92	−11.11
III	Overrepresentation	−4.40*	−7.16*	−0.55	1.33
	Inclusive identity	−14.05*	1.45	−0.63	0.43
IV	Overrepresentation	−1.58*	−1.41*	2.55*	4.39*
	% Foreign-born	−0.43	−0.60	−0.27	−1.19
	Universality	−14.92	−11.90	−7.32	−12.05
V	Overrepresentation	−4.74*	−7.18*	−1.33	1.50
	% Foreign-born	−0.49*	−0.16	−0.23	−1.19
	Inclusive identity	−14.40	1.60	0.06	3.29
VI	Overrepresentation	−0.84*	−1.29*	3.74*	4.14
	Universality	−14.34*	−11.53	−7.90	−12.89
	Inclusive identity	−12.90	−3.23	−3.09	4.71
VII	Overrepresentation	−1.28*	−0.73*	2.98*	4.90*
	% Foreign-born	−0.46	−0.60	−0.24	−1.34
	Universality	−13.93*	−12.76	−8.04	−15.51
	Inclusive identity	−13.16	−3.26	−2.39	8.81

* Significant at $p < 0.1$.

positive effect, and the only coefficients that are statistically significant have a negative direction. Indeed, the WVS data suggest that when it comes to social assistance and unemployment benefits, selective solidarity is actually highest where immigrants' welfare reliance is lowest. This is all the more noteworthy because these are exactly the types of programs for which an "economic" hypothesis would predict immigrant overrepresentation to have the largest positive effect on selective solidarity.

Next, we consider the relationship while controlling for the three country-level variables (see Table 2.3). Because of the small number of cases on the country level, I introduce the control variables in a step-wise fashion: the first three models include only one of the control variables, the next three take in two of the variables, and the final model controls for all three variables at the same time. While this last model is perhaps the most interesting for theoretical reasons, the small number of cases troubles the interpretation of the coefficients. For that reason, it is useful to compare its results with those of less saturated models.

These results still do not offer any evidence that high levels of immigrant welfare dependence increase sentiments of selective solidarity, although they do qualify our earlier conclusions. Once we control for the type of welfare system, we no longer find a negative association between immigrants' overrepresentation on social assistance and selective solidarity. In other words, while on aggregate selective solidarity may be lower in countries where immigrants are most overrepresented among benefit recipients, upon closer inspection this result seems to be the product of the dual patterns that (1) immigrants' dependence on welfare benefits tends to be higher in universal welfare states, and (2) levels of selective solidarity tend to be lower in universal welfare states. The most important finding stands, however: there is no evidence that levels of immigrant welfare dependence increase sentiments of selective solidarity among the public.[9]

Immigrants' Welfare Use and Support for Welfare Exclusion in Three Countries

So far, the analysis has focused exclusively on public opinion and demonstrated that support for IEWRs among the public does not respond to actual patterns of immigrants' welfare uptake. This tells us little, however, about whether economic realities matter to the politicians who advocate such reforms. We therefore now turn our attention to politicians in three very different immigrant-receiving welfare states: Sweden, Canada, and the Netherlands. As we will see, this investigation suggests that the importance of economic reality for support for immigrant exclusion is as tenuous among politicians as it is among the public at large.

To begin, politicians are not making more calls for IEWRs where and when immigrants are most reliant on welfare benefits. As Figure 2.3 shows, immigrants' relative reliance on transfer benefits has in recent years been much stronger in the Netherlands and Sweden than in Canada. Yet when we turn our attention to parliamentary activity, the cross-national picture looks very different. Figure 2.4 shows the number of motions, petitions, and questions that parliamentarians have brought

Figure 2.3. Ratio of immigrant/native-born incidence of social assistance in Sweden, Canada, and the Netherlands, 1999–2010

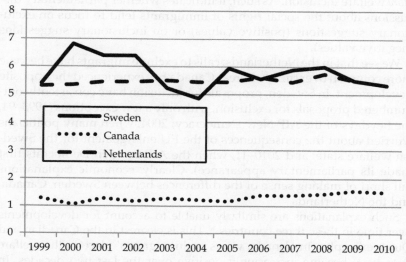

Source: CBS; SLID; SCB

Figure 2.4. Number of motions, interpellations, and petitions advocating immigrant welfare exclusion minus number advocating inclusion, Sweden, Canada, and the Netherlands, 1991–2012 (see legend in Figure 2.3)

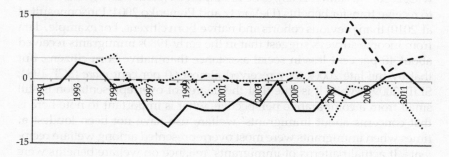

forward over the last twenty years advocating a reduction of immigrants' access to programs and benefits, minus the number proposing *more* welfare inclusion. As such, it indicates whether parliamentary discussions about the social rights of immigrants tend to focus on exclusionary suggestions (positive values) or on inclusionary suggestions (negative values).

We see that in the Netherlands, calls to exclude migrants have become more common over time, whereas Canada has experienced the opposite development. In Sweden, proposals for inclusion have consistently outnumbered proposals for exclusion, with only a few exceptions (1993–94, the heydays of the AIP New Democracy; 2004, when many politicians worried about the consequences of the EU enlargement for the Swedish welfare state; and 2010–11, when the AIP Sweden Democrats first made its parliamentary appearance). Clearly, economic explanations fall short of making sense of the differences between Sweden, Canada, and the Netherlands.

Such explanations are similarly unable to account for developments over time in these three countries.[10] This is clearest in the Canadian and Dutch examples. In Canada, views on immigrants' place in the welfare state have become increasingly positive over the last two decades. In that same period, however, the economic integration of immigrants has slowed down considerably. Until the mid-1990s, immigrants tended to outperform native-born citizens in economic terms and were actually *under*represented among benefit recipients (Akbari 1989; Baker and Benjamin 1995; Sweetman 2001). But this is no longer the case. Recent cohorts of immigrants are more likely to have a low income (D.A. Green and Worswick 2010; Waslander 2003), to be unemployed (Fleury 2007), and, indeed, to receive transfer benefits (DeVoretz and Pivnenko 2004; Pinsonneault et al. 2010) than previous cohorts and native-born citizens. For example, data from income surveys suggest that in the early 1980s immigrants received about 40 per cent less in social assistance than native-born citizens, but that by the late 2000s they received almost 60 per cent *more* (SCF 1984; SLID 2009). While it is true that the degree of overrepresentation is still small from a comparative perspective, what is important to note here is that concerns about immigrants' welfare use have not been loudest at times when immigrants were most overrepresented among welfare recipients. If actual patterns of immigrants' reliance on welfare benefits were truly the driving force behind selective solidarity, we would have seen an increase, not a decrease, in Canadian support for IEWRs.

The opposite trajectory is visible in the Netherlands. A series of reforms in the late 1980s and 1990s both made the labour market more flexible and made the system of benefits more active (Hartog 1999; Van der Veen and Trommel 1998). In February 2008 the fourth Balkenende cabinet loosened restrictions on asylum seekers' access to the labour market, allowing them to work twenty-four weeks per year. Moreover, a series of restrictions in admission policy in the late 1990s changed the composition of the immigration flow considerably. Whereas in the mid-1990s around 45 per cent of all incoming migrants came through the family stream, a decade later that share had been reduced to around 31 per cent. The decrease in the relative intake of refugees was even starker: from 33 per cent in 1995 to just over 3 (!) per cent in 2005 (CBS). As a result of these policy changes, the economic standing of the immigrant population as a whole has improved considerably. The unemployment rate for non-Western immigrants, for example, was as high as 34 per cent in the mid-1980s but had dropped to under 10 per cent by the late 2000s (before rising again somewhat in more recent years) (CBS).[11] A range of recent studies note similar improvements in migrants' labour market participation, employment, income, and education (Bijl et al. 2011; Dagevos et al. 2003; Entzinger 2006; Government of the Netherlands 2007; Kloosterman 2000; Lower House of Dutch Parliament 2003). In other words, while immigrants in the Netherlands are still worse off socio-economically than the native-born and are therefore still more likely to resort to the welfare state for support, it seems safe to assume that immigration is costing the Netherlands less today than it did a couple of decades ago. Yet as the costs of migration are declining, calls for IEWRs are becoming more pervasive. As we will see in chapter 5, welfare chauvinist rhetoric was rare in Dutch political debate before AIPs found a permanent place in the party system, and very few IEWRs were suggested, let alone implemented, before the late 1990s. If IEWRs are really a response to immigrants' reliance on welfare benefits, we should have seen a decline in their popularity over time, not an increase.

The next observation that casts doubt on the importance of economic facts to calls for welfare exclusion is that these calls often appear in reference to practices that involve very few costs, and relatedly, that they often suggest policy changes that would have very little economic effect. The examples are particularly pertinent in the Netherlands, which among the three cases under consideration has gone furthest in advocating and implementing IEWRs. When an internal report of a social security agency detailing cases of fraud in the export of child benefits to Turkey and Morocco leaked to the press, parliamentarians quickly demanded an emergency debate to urge the minister not only to increase efforts to combat fraud, but also to reduce the export of child benefits altogether. Yet the number of potential fraud cases that spurred the entire debate was estimated to be at most 371 – not even 2 per cent of the total caseload of exported child benefits. Similarly, suggestions that migrants from Central and Eastern European EU member-states be denied access to unemployment benefits have not been based on economic analysis either. In response to an article in the national newspaper *Algemeen Dagblad*, members of the anti-immigrant Freedom Party complained about the "massive" use of unemployment benefits among Polish migrants, argued that many Poles actually come to the Netherlands to exploit those benefits, and therefore proposed that all CEE migrants be refused access to the welfare state in the first ten years they are in the country (ah-tk1654, 2 May 2007). In reality, the use of unemployment benefits among Polish migrants was not "massive" at all: in the year that this debate took place, only 432 residents with a Polish background (barely 0.4 per cent of the estimated Polish population in the Netherlands) received unemployment benefits. Even after these data were communicated to Parliament, complaints about East Europeans' use of unemployment benefits persisted.

Besides criticizing inexpensive practices, Dutch proponents of IEWRs have frequently proposed exclusionary reforms that are likely to have little economic effect. In at least some of these cases, the proponents of the legislative reforms seem fully aware of this. Former MP Marcial Hernandez (2014) recounts in his memoirs of his time as a Freedom Party politician that his party often presented proposals they knew to be unfeasible or inconsequential. He reports the following interaction during a party program meeting between leader Geert Wilders and MP Wim Kortenoeven: "On the many questions Kortenoeven raised about the feasibility of the party program, he received a sneering comment from Wilders: he should stop with all the whining, because more than half of the program was not possible to carry out anyway. On the question if some points were actually responsible and legally possible, Wilders asked the faction cynically since when the Freedom Party is in the business of making legally feasible comments. Almost everyone laughed" (Hernandez 2014, 221).

It seems unlikely that *all* calls for IEWRs are guided by such opportunism. Nevertheless, on countless occasions politicians have proposed supposedly cost-saving measures they could anticipate to be ineffective. A good example is the suggestion (by the conservative VVD and the anti-immigrant PVV) that the residence requirement for access to social assistance be lengthened from five to ten years. Judges already often waive the current residence requirement, as several civil servants in the immigration and social affairs ministries explained to me (interviews NET12, NET13, NET15). Since municipalities already extend social assistance in cases of need after less than five years, extending the residence requirement to ten years is unlikely to have any significant economic impact. Much the same can be said about the 2010 proposal that eligibility for social assistance be linked to someone's "choice of clothing," clearly targeted at women who wear the burqa. Again, this policy is unlikely to have any economic impact worth mentioning. Even though exact numbers are unavailable, most estimate the number of burqa-wearing women in the Netherlands at between 150 and 200 (De Wijk 2008; Vermeulen et al. 2006). Moreover, it is not clear how the practical implications of this policy proposal are any different from the already existing requirement under social assistance law that applicants make a demonstrable effort to remove barriers to finding a job (Vermeulen et al. 2006, 6). Again, it seems clear that this proposal is not a response to demonstrable economic facts, but rather an attempt to appease public unease rooted more in cultural concerns than in economic considerations.

Indeed, it frequently happens that champions of IEWRs are unable to provide a rough estimate of how much money their proposals would save. For example, when the Dutch government was preparing to lengthen the period during which family migrants are ineligible for social benefits, the Christian Democrats submitted written questions to the minister asking how often it had happened that family migrants go on welfare immediately after they become eligible. In response, the government freely admitted that it did not collect the necessary information to provide answers to those questions (TK-32175–29, 13 April 2012). The same thing happened in discussions on the proposal to cut the welfare of migrants who do not speak Dutch (TK-43–9, 19 January 2012) and in a debate on reducing the export of child benefits (TK-95–11, 13 June 2012).

Perhaps the best evidence that economic realities are unimportant in the politics of immigrants' social rights is that even politicians who invoke economic facts admit themselves that other considerations are more important. A particularly illustrative example is the reaction of Saskatchewan premier Brad Wall to a recent decision in Canada to reduce refugees' health care benefits. In his response to the federal government's argument that the country was spending a disproportionate amount of money on refugee health care, he started by questioning the economics but quickly turned to a more principled point:

> We can't see a lot of evidence for that frankly. And you know what, even if that was the case, who cares? This country is rich beyond measure compared to the countries where these refugees are fleeing from and so it's our view that we should just be there to help. (Canadian Press 2012)

Similar examples can be found in recent Dutch and Swedish history. A particularly relevant episode in the Netherlands started on 17 July 2009, when Sietse Fritsma (Freedom Party) asked a wide range of departments how much money they spent on non-Western immigrants. The government provided only some of the calculations Fritsma asked for. This was partly because of limited data availability, but Eberhard van der Laan, the Labour immigration minister, indicated that there was also a "political" reason not to answer Fritsma's questions in full:

> Immigrants, both Western and non-Western, are members of our society. Their presence cannot be reduced to a simple cost–benefit analysis along the measuring rod of the euro. Just like that does not happen for the costs and benefits of native-born citizens, disabled people, pensioners, or whichever other category of people [sic]. We do not evaluate citizens, but we do evaluate policy. The answers to the questions are therefore aimed at the costs and benefits of [diversity] policies. (ah-tk-3692, 16 September 2009)

These kinds of comments are particularly common in Sweden. In almost exactly the same words as Van der Laan, Social Democratic minister Maj-Inger Klingvall commented as follows on a request for a comprehensive calculation of the costs of immigration:

> The question how much immigration costs pops up regularly in the debate about immigration and refugee policy. A pervasive theme is the hunt for a number which describes the total costs of immigration. The primary reason why the government has not actively worked to produce such a number either today or in the past is that there are other values and beliefs that underlie immigration and refugee policy. Sweden will continue to pursue a humane refugee policy, which means that people who flee from persecution or war will have a sanctuary here. No more than we measure the use of children and pensioners in crowns and ören should we treat immigrants as coldly calculated investments that we expect to deliver returns. (*Pr.* 1999/2000:99, *anf.* 24, 25 April 2000)[12]

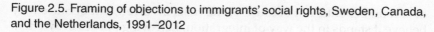

Figure 2.5. Framing of objections to immigrants' social rights, Sweden, Canada, and the Netherlands, 1991–2012

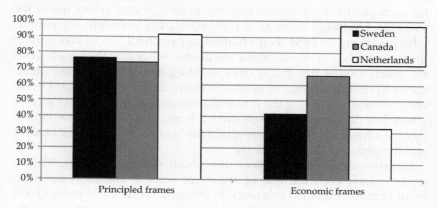

That economic considerations are often secondary among champions of inclusionary policies is perhaps not very surprising. But we see the same predominance of principled and ideological arguments in critiques of immigrants and their place in the welfare state. One way to illustrate this is by systematically analysing how politicians frame their objections. Figure 2.5 shows the results from such an analysis of all statements made in parliamentary debates in the three case studies from 1991 to 2012 that called for a reduction in immigrants' benefits and were accompanied by some sort of explanation.[13] For each of those statements, I recorded whether the explanation featured words like "abuse," "unlawful," and "fair," suggesting a "principled" objection or rather terms like "costs," "taxpayer," and "burden," suggesting an "economic" objection. While the terms "costs" and "taxpayer" indeed appear frequently in objections to immigrants' use of welfare, in all three cases politicians have been more likely to use principled than economic arguments. Equally noteworthy are the dual observations that principled arguments appear most frequently in the country under study that has introduced the most IEWRs (the Netherlands), and that the share of economic arguments is highest in the country with the lowest levels of immigrant welfare dependency (Canada).

Non-economic arguments usually come in three variations. First, in some cases politicians have expressed worries about immigrants' use of certain benefits, not because of the costs involved, but because they believe it stands in the way of integration. Left-wing parties in Sweden, for example, have repeatedly objected to immigrants' heavy use of the so-called Caretaker Allowance (*vårdnadsbidrag*), a benefit for parents who prefer not to send their children to preschool but to take care of them themselves. The reason for the unease is not that the benefit costs too much money, but that it risks isolating immigrant women (interviews SWE01, SWE06). For similar reasons, the Swedish Social Democrats advocate repealing the housing allowance asylum seekers receive when they find housing of their own. It is not that they are unwilling to pay the allowance, but they are afraid the benefit will lead to unhealthy and dangerous living conditions.

In other cases the objections are about system integrity. This is a particularly common line of argument when it comes to the treatment of undocumented migrants. In Sweden, centre-right parties have objected to the extension of health care benefits to newcomers without the appropriate documentation. However, interviewees from these parties explicitly denied there was any economic motivation behind their stance. Conservative Mikael Cederbratt said it makes for bad and counterproductive public policy to say "you are not allowed to be here, you are breaking the law, but we are giving you everything" (interview SWE02), while his colleague from the Centre Party, Fredrick Federley, argued that open access would lead to the curious situation that "an American [tourist] should pay for the operation him- or herself, but someone who is here not supported by the law should have it for free" (interview SWE04). This line of argument has been common in the occasional objections to immigrants' use of benefits in Canada. As we will see in chapter 4, many of these comments target those who receive benefits while they are technically not entitled to them – in particular, denied refugee claimants and recent family migrants who still fall under the conditions of their sponsorship agreement.

The third category of non-economic objections to immigrants' benefit use consists of comments that mostly reflect a generally hostile attitude towards diversity, a principled unwillingness to extend benefits to newcomers, and/or a desire to convince voters that "something" is being done about immigration.[14] Those who make such arguments tend to be the most ardent supporters of IEWRs. The Sweden Democrats, for example, commonly frame immigration as a threat to the welfare state, but economic considerations are far from central to their objections to immigration. It is worth quoting the party's immigration spokesperson, Erik Almqvist:

> The economic costs are actually more of a consequence of other problems that we can see with a multicultural system. I think the main problem is that the society gets split ... I am sure you know about Robert D. Putnam and his idea about social capital. I think you can see that social capital has decreased in Sweden where multicultural systems are growing. People don't trust each other as much when they don't relate to each other ... So I think it is a problem on a more basic level than just the economic costs. (interview SWE05)

When I asked him why his party then decided to use such a clear economic frame in a campaign video that featured burqa-clad women jumping the line at the welfare office, Almqvist said the video's main purpose was to "provoke the debate," not to "give a broader view on our basic ideology" (interview SWE05).

This line of argument came up frequently during my interviews in the Netherlands. When I asked the immigration spokesperson of the Freedom Party, Sietse Fritsma, why his party advocates scaling back the social rights of immigrants, he responded: "It is a matter of principle. I think that is the most important answer to your question. We can also expect migrants to make a contribution to Dutch society first" (interview NET03). Even when I explicitly inquired about the centrality of economic arguments, he emphasized that those are at best secondary: "We believe that we have to protect our identity, our core values. That is the primary, the most important consideration for us." His colleague of the VVD, Cora van Nieuwenhuizen, made a similar case:

> The basis is the principled point. The financial aspect is a consequence of that ... It starts with that there are simply problems in society. They are overrepresented in crime, large groups of people seclude themselves, also reject Dutch society ... You need to make it as unattractive as possible to take advantage of the system. Because that, in my mind, is the worst category: those who come here and do not want to integrate. People who detest Dutch society, who think that everything is too decadent here, object to the equality of men and women, object to our liberal position on homosexuals, constantly make a big fuss about those things, but at the same time do want to make use of our benefits and get a subsidy for

everything, et cetera et cetera. That is the group that we need to get rid of. (interview NET01)

Christian democrat Eddy van Hijum similarly denied the importance of economic factors ("I can't say that it has been based on a very rational cost–benefit analysis of the costs for the welfare state"), and emphasized general unease about immigration in explaining his party's restrictive line ("it is much more the societal debate that at a certain point was set in motion about the success of integration policy, or rather the lack thereof"; interview NET04). And also Paul Ulenbelt (SP) gave general cultural concerns precedence over economic arguments: "The biggest problem is not even financial in nature. The biggest problem has to do with that if you walk through certain neighbourhoods in large cities, you think you are on a holiday in a different country" (interview NET05). In sum, Labour MP Hans Spekman seemed right in his characterization of contemporary debates in the Netherlands about the exclusion of immigrants from welfare state benefits:

> [A concern for costs] might have something to do with it, but I rather feel that these arguments originate from the fact that in the Netherlands we do not have enough control over a couple of boys who botch up everything. And that creates so much irritation, fear, and anger, that everything that falls in this little box works. Among other things the costs. But rationally and emotionally as well, I think [that] once we get control over those boys who do not know how to behave themselves there is little ground left to still be talking about those costs. (interview NET02)

As a final piece of evidence against the suggestion that IEWRs respond to the actual economic realities of immigrants' integration, we might point out that even when champions of IEWRs use economic arguments, they often rely on the opportunistic selection, exaggeration, or even patent misrepresentation of economic facts. To start with the former, the use of facts in discussions about immigrants' place in the welfare state is often selective and opportunistic. A particularly blatant example in Canada is that some members of the Reform Party reported diametrically opposite "evidence" on immigrants' economic integration depending on the topic of discussion. In debates on immigration levels, the social rights of refugee claimants, or the enforcement of sponsorship agreements in family migration, Leon Benoit, Herbert Grubel, and Art Hanger repeatedly argued that restrictions were necessary because immigrants were placing a disproportionate burden on the welfare state. Yet when these same politicians commented on employment equity policies, they suddenly reported that immigrants were outperforming the native-born economically! [15]

Similar examples can be found in recent Dutch and Swedish history. A particularly telling episode in the Netherlands took place in 2011. Ever since the Eastern enlargement of the European Union in 2004, Dutch politicians have worried that Eastern European migrants will replace native-born workers, depress wages, and indeed, end up in massive numbers on social benefits. But when a parliamentary inquiry revealed that the use of social security among Eastern Europeans residing in the Netherlands was "generally small" and that there was hardly any evidence of replacement effects on the labour market (TK-32680–4, 29 September 2011), critics in Parliament did not revisit their arguments, but simply rejected the report's findings. Christian democrat Eddy van Hijum felt that the analysis lacked "detail," and conservative Cora van Nieuwenhuizen criticized the methodology of some of the studies the report relied on (TK-20–23–57, 8 November 2011). Sietse Fritsma of the Freedom Party did not even discuss the report's findings but instead continued warning for exactly the kinds of effects of which the inquiry did not find any evidence. While it is true that the parliamentary inquiry had its limitations (in particular, most of the studies it relied on included too few data points to warrant any conclusive statements regarding long-term developments), what is telling about this example is that economic objections to social rights for immigrants persisted even when there was no available evidence to support them.

A somewhat similar point can be made about one of the most vocal immigration critics among Swedish parliamentarians over the last two decades, conservative MP Sten Andersson. Three years in a row (from 1999 to 2002), he started the parliamentary year by submitting a motion asking for a comprehensive calculation of the costs of immigration (*Mo.* 1999/2000:*Sf*503, 24 September 1999; *Mo.* 2000/01:*Sf*603, 21 September 2000; *Mo.* 2001/02:*Sf*208, 21 September 2001). While he framed his requests as genuine attempts to acquire more evidence on the economic consequences of immigration, it is more likely that his main goal was merely to voice discontent. After all, at the time there were already numerous studies available that made exactly the calculations Andersson was supposedly interested in (Ekberg 1983, 1999; Gustafsson & Österberg 2001; Storesletten 2000; Wadensjö 1973). When another MP from Andersson's party, Gustaf von Essen, pointed this out to him, Andersson dismissed these studies without offering any real arguments: "there are people with a considerably higher education [than me] who question those numbers" (Pr. 1997/98; anf. 60–63, 25 March 1998). All in all, politicians may use economic data to advocate limitations on immigrants' access to social benefits, but they are just as comfortable criticizing those data when they do not support their case.

Similarly, economic facts regarding immigrants' benefit use are often exaggerated or misinterpreted. For one thing, it is important to emphasize that referring to levels of immigrant welfare dependence as a way to justify IEWRs on economic grounds rests on the assumption that immigrants are primarily to blame. If immigrants end up on welfare rolls against their will, there is little reason to expect that cutting their access will create additional incentives to become active on the labour market. Indeed, in that case it would make more sense to propose selective admission policies or investments in immigrants' human capital. In other words, a purely economic case for IEWRs has to depend on the assumption that immigrants are relying on the welfare state in disproportionate numbers by deliberate design. This assumption usually comes in one of two forms: the high levels of welfare dependence are taken as a sign that immigrants have a lousy work ethic, or they are interpreted as evidence that for many the very reason for migration is to take advantage of generous social benefits in the host country. While academic studies have found no evidence that immigrants are more likely to claim benefits than the native-born in similar situations (Barrett and Maître 2013; Boeri 2009, 20; Castronova et al. 2001; Reitz 1995; Sainsbury 2012, 126; Tienda and Jensen 1986), or that social benefits are an important consideration in migration decisions (Barrett and McCarthy 2008; Giulietti et al. 2013; Hooghe et al. 2008; Kaestner and Kaushal 2005; Kaushal 2005; Kvist 2004; Voss et al. 2001; WRR 2001; Yang and Wallace 2007), these arguments come up in almost every discussion of IEWRs. They have even been common in Canada, which, considering its comparatively residual welfare state, should receive very few migrants if the alleged magnet effect is actually at work. As early as the 1990s, members of the Reform Party were warning that many refugees "have come to exploit or drain our social services" (Jim Hart, House of Commons debate/19 September 1994), and this tune has changed little since then. In 2010, then immigration minister Jason Kenney (Conservative Party) complained that "the generosity of our welfare schemes ... creates incentives for dubious refugee claims" (Jill Mahoney 2010). In the Netherlands, one does not only encounter arguments about such magnet effects (see, e.g., TK-32500-XV-69, 9 March 2011; TK-33400-XV-13, 6 December 2012), but can also frequently hear the suggestion that immigrants are particularly prone to draw benefits (see, e.g., kst-32328–3, 4 March 2010; TK70–5527, 31 March 2009; 33000-XV-51, 14 December 2011).

Besides the use of these two specific unproven assumptions, exaggerations of economic facts are common in pleas for exclusion. I will give a few examples from each case under study. In Sweden, when Gustaf von Essen of the Moderates asserted that "most immigrants" were "permanently dependent on social assistance" (*Pr.* 1993/94:6, *anf.* 179, 13 October 1993), according to actual data only about 18 per cent of immigrants were receiving social assistance (SCB). Even more clearly unsubstantiated were Claus Zaar's suggestion that immigrants were responsible for the economic crisis in Sweden (*Pr.* 1992/93:91, *anf.* 81, 14 April 1993); Bert Karlsson's assertion that each year immigration costs 80 million crowns (about C$11 million) (*Pr.* 1993/94:6, *anf.* 188–192, 13 October 1993); Sten Andersson's theory that refugees tend to settle in those communities where social assistance levels are highest (*Pr.* 1994/95:16, *anf.* 34, 27 October 1994); Richard Jomshof's claim that all refugees were on "lifetime support financed by Swedish taxpayers" (*Pr.* 2010/11:120, *anf.* 100, 21 June 2011); and Erik Almqvist's comment that migration was leading to the complete destruction of the welfare state (*Pr.* 2011/12:100, 19 April 2012). The distortion of economic data was also clear in discussions about the 2004 EU expansion. Driven by fears of massive Eastern European welfare tourism, for some time the Social Democrats (and to a lesser degree, some of the centre-right parties) advocated transitional rules and temporary limits on rights in Sweden for citizens of the new member-states (Doyle, Hughes, and Wadensjö 2006; Eriksson 2006). In a public statement, Prime Minister Göran Persson explicitly worried that the welfare state could come under pressure as a result of the expansion (Eriksson 2006, 77). And when a documentary reported that Estonian women working as nurses for ten hours a week in Sweden would be allowed to bring their husbands and children over and then collectively live off state benefits, the Christian Democrats, Social Democrats, and Liberals all started to formulate objections to what became known as the "ten-hours rule." Many of these concerns were unfounded, especially with the benefit of hindsight. The documentary had made an unwarranted generalization based on an idiosyncratic case. As Jonas Eriksson puts it, "much energy was thus put into discussing a non-existent rule" (2006, 81). More importantly, Sweden ultimately did not implement any transitional rules, and economic analyses have found little evidence of the welfare tourism that Persson feared (Doyle et al. 2006; Gerdes and Wadensjö 2008; Ruist 2014).

In Canada, in the mid-1990s the Reform Party often drew attention to the use of welfare among refugees, arguing that refugees pose "an unacceptable drain on our already overburdened welfare system" (Jay Hill, House of Commons debate/31 January 1994) and that "social services ... are struggling with the flow of refugees" (Art Hanger, House of Commons debate/3 February 1994). But utilization data at the time hardly justified such strong language: around the time that these comments were being made, refugees constituted only 4 per cent of social assistance caseloads in the province of Ontario.[16] A particularly common exaggeration has been to argue that Canada has the most generous admission policy in the world and therefore cannot afford to be more generous. A good example is the following quote by Reform Party member Art Hanger:

> The minister's projected numbers continue the pattern of allowing numbers of family and refugee class immigrants that are virtually unheard of in the industrialized world today [...] Even today as a percentage of our population Canada is still accepting more immigrants than any other industrialized nation on earth. Why does this government want to up the number even more? (House of Commons debate/2 February 1994)

Such comments are patently false. In 1994 (when the comment above was made), there certainly were countries that admitted more immigrants than Canada, both in absolute and in relative terms.[17] Moreover, Canada has one of the most selective admission policies in the Western world and relies more on economic migration than almost all other immigrant-receiving nations. A comparison with the other two cases in this study is particularly instructive: during the five years before Hanger's comment, 12.6 per cent of all incoming migrants in Canada were refugees, whereas those percentages were as high as 37 for the Netherlands and even 50 for Sweden (OECD). The complaint that the level of refugee migration to Canada is "unheard of" thus has very little to do with actual facts. Interestingly, even after a series of restrictive policy changes to the refugee system this exaggeration still enjoys currency both in parliamentary debate (see, e.g., Jason Kenney, House of Commons debate/14 February 2011; Vic Toews, House of Commons debate/21 June 2011) and in public commentary (Simpson 2013; Stoffman 2002, 91).

In the Netherlands, the distortion of economic facts even became the explicit subject of a 2008 parliamentary debate on the welfare costs incurred by a general amnesty that took place that year. The centre-left government reasoned that these costs should be calculated by adding up the welfare costs paid out to all refugee claimants who would not have received legal status without the amnesty, but the Freedom Party argued that the calculation should also include those asylum seekers who would have acquired legal status in the absence of the amnesty.

On closer inspection, then, many of the ostensibly economic arguments that champions of IEWRs rely on are unconvincing. They tend to rely on the opportunistic use or exaggeration of economic facts. In addition, it is not clear that the solutions they offer would result in significant cost savings. Again, it is worth pointing out that these observations do not apply just to immigration critics. Indeed, we can say much the same about the arguments their opponents make. This is most clearly illustrated with examples from Sweden, where arguments for welfare inclusion have been most common.

Recent economic studies are unanimous that immigration poses a (small) net loss to the Swedish treasury (Ekberg 2009; Gerdes and Wadensjö 2012; Storesletten 2003), and comparative analyses suggest there are few countries where immigration costs more money than in Sweden (Boeri 2009). Yet politicians still claim, like Ulf Nilsson of the Liberals did when I asked him, that "it is more winning than losing with immigration in Sweden" (interview SWE03). With the exception of Sweden Democrat Erik Almqvist, none of my interviewees considered immigration an economic threat; instead, all argued the exact opposite – that Sweden would benefit economically from taking in more newcomers (interviews SWE01, SWE02, SWE03, SWE04, SWE06, SWE07). Such comments can be heard frequently in Parliament as well, especially from the mouths of Social Democrats (see, e.g., *Pr.* 2000/01:53, *anf.* 57, 19 January 2001; *Pr.* 2010/11:33, *anf.* 27, 13 December 2010; *Pr* 2010/11:37, *anf.* 42, 17 December 2010). Even when members of the Sweden Democrats explicitly cite credible studies showing the costs migration incurs (see, e.g., *Interp.* 2011/12:278, 5 March 2012; *Mo.* 2010/11: Fi11, 3 June 2011; and *Pr.* 2010/11:87, *anf.* 102, 13 April 2011), politicians from other parties typically respond by maintaining that migration poses an economic benefit but without offering any real evidence to support that claim (see, e.g., *Pr.* 2010/11: 79, *anf.* 20, 30 March 2011; *Pr.* 2011/12:56, *anf.* 84, 18 January 2012; and *Pr.* 2012/13:4, *anf.* 49, 20 September 2012).

One particularly common variant of this argument is that immigration is necessary to alleviate the straining effects of aging on the pension system. Again, the available evidence lends little credence to this theory. Most economic studies show that to make up for baby-boomers' mass retirement, much more immigration would be required than is either practically feasible or politically viable (Kleinman 2003; Venturini 2004).[18] In a study of the Swedish case, Jan Ekberg concludes that "even a modest increase in the employment rate among the population that already resides in the country will have a greater positive fiscal effect than large-scale migration" (Ekberg 2009, 21). Yet politicians continue to mention immigrants' supposedly benign impact in this regard when discussing the economics of immigration (see comments by Ulf Nilsson, *Pr.* 2010/11:16, *anf.* 8, 17 November 2010; Maria Ferm and Mikael Cederbratt, *Pr.* 2010/11:31, *anf.* 78, 85, 9 December 2010).

Other arguments that proponents of inclusion use to suggest that immigration has a positive effect on the economy have found more support in empirical research but seem poorly applicable to the Swedish case. For example, in a recent party document the conservative party maintains that immigration has a positive effect on employment levels, because it raises mobility, thereby expands the labour market, and in this way reduces frictional unemployment (Moderaterna 2010). Apart from the lack of convincing data,[19] it is difficult to see what this theory has to do with a country where only about 12 per cent of the foreign-born population came for reasons of work (SCB). Similarly, the argument that immigrants cost less money than the native-born because they tend to arrive after already having enjoyed a costly education – as made for example by Fredrik Lundh Sammeli (*Pr.* 2010/11:31, *anf.* 80, 9 December 2010) – seems unconvincing in Sweden, a country with some of the lowest immigrant self-sufficiency levels as well as one of the largest adult education systems (Nordlund, Stehlik, and Strandh 2013) in the world.

All in all, we have seen very little evidence that patterns of immigrant welfare dependence are important for the politics of immigrants' social rights. These patterns cannot explain cross-national or cross-temporal differences in selective solidarity among the public or among politicians. Parliamentary debates about immigrants' social rights rarely focus on proposals that could realistically result in cost savings. More often, they seem to be about principled rather than economic reasons to either include or exclude immigrants. And even when economic arguments do come up, it still seems difficult to believe that the policy suggestions are based on economic facts, considering how comfortable politicians seem to be about ignoring other facts, exaggerating or misrepresenting what the facts really mean, or even refusing to back up empirical claims with evidence. Again, on careful reflection these conclusions may not be very surprising. But they are highly relevant for both theoretical and societal reasons: apparently, politicians' views on immigrant inclusion have more to do with principled positions than with evidence-based reasoning. This implies not only that we should approach seemingly fact-based arguments with more scepticism, but also that if we want to understand where IEWRs come from we need to look at something other than economic facts.

Chapter Three

Sweden: Universalism, Even for Newcomers?

The Swedish welfare state has long drawn attention from admirers and critics alike. While some have pointed to its comparatively low levels of income inequality and poverty to argue that no other country has done a better job of offering its citizens a good life (Rothstein 1998), others have decried the lack of individual freedom in this system marked by a large public sector, high social spending, and heavy state intervention in most aspects of social life. An early critic even called Swedes the "new totalitarians," likening their welfare model to Aldous Huxley's dystopian *Brave New World* (Huntford 1971). Others reached a more nuanced conclusion: "To know Sweden is to be ambivalent about it" (Heclo and Madsen 1987, 4).

In recent years, this prototypical universal welfare state has become a country of immigration. Sweden still had a net emigration rate in 1973 but started soon after to welcome more and more immigrants. Especially in recent years the increase has been spectacular: annual intake levels have quadrupled since the mid-1990s. Today more than 17 per cent of the Swedish population consists of (first-generation) immigrants (in the early 1990s the figure was less than 10 per cent). These immigrants have been met by comparatively generous integration and naturalization policies. Moreover, as we will see in this chapter, today they face little formal exclusion in accessing the generous Swedish welfare state.

Yet it would be a grave mistake to assume that the integration of immigrants in Sweden has been seamless and unproblematic. Unemployment and welfare dependence rates are dizzyingly high, social interactions between immigrants and the native-born are few, organized political opposition to immigration is becoming more successful, and several times Sweden has been stirred by violent expressions of intergroup tension. Some academics describe the integration of immigrants as the "most important challenge" facing the Swedish welfare state (Hilson 2008, 114). Others have gone further and predicted that integration problems will result in a crumbling of social cohesion and as such, of the foundations of the welfare state for which Sweden is so well-known: "different groups will turn against one another, protecting their assets and interests in a future marked by drastic cuts in the welfare sector" (Westin 1996, 225). Yet another analysis predicts that Sweden will soon move in a decidedly xenophobic direction, both in political discourse and in public policy (Schierup and Ålund 2011).

Up until now, there has been little evidence to support such predictions. While immigrants are indeed heavily overrepresented among welfare recipients, few politicians have suggested disentitling newcomers from programs and benefits. Even in the wake of the Mediterranean refugee crisis, which led the left-of-centre government to install temporary restrictions in admission policy, immigrants' social rights seem protected from political attacks. In fact, recent social policy developments have been aimed at including immigrants *more*, not less. And this becomes even more relevant when we consider that the last two decades have seen considerable cutbacks in other areas of Swedish social policy. As we saw in the previous chapter, Sweden thus delivers a particularly damaging blow to the hypothesis that heavy overrepresentation of immigrants in the welfare system is associated with widespread support for IEWRs.

Much in line with the theoretical discussion in chapter 1, we will see that understanding the Swedish case requires an investigation of political translation. Instead of interpreting immigrants' welfare rates as evidence of laziness or of a penchant for welfare, policy-makers have taken them as a sign that the Swedish welfare state has not been successful *enough* at helping immigrants find employment and that it should therefore renew and expand its efforts to do so. This benign view can be traced back first and foremost to the structure of the Swedish welfare state, which has made egalitarianism a cornerstone of national identity and has institutionalized active labour market policies rather than disentitlement as the standard operating procedure for dealing with groups that face challenges in the labour market. And while the success of AIPs seems to be increasing, so far they have had limited success at convincing mainstream political parties to change their platforms on this issue. In this light, it is no surprise that Swedish governments have adopted almost no IEWRs over the last twenty years and have instead been more prone to amend the social policy apparatus to make it *more* inclusive of the immigrant population.

This chapter is structured as follows. The next section reviews recent policy developments in immigrants' access to social programs and benefits since 1991 and shows that by and large, the trend has been towards inclusion. I then illustrate that this trend reflects a particular political translation of immigrants' place in the welfare state, one that frames welfare dependents as people in a lamentable position who should be helped by the state to find their way in the labour market. The final section illustrates that anti-immigrant forces have so far had limited success in challenging this inclusionary approach and reflects on likely developments in the politics of immigrants' social rights in Sweden.

A Story of Gradual Inclusion

Over the last two decades the Swedish welfare state has become more inclusionary towards its immigrant population, even though there have been a few restrictive reforms as well. This section discusses the recent history of the social rights of different categories of immigrants and pays separate attention to the pension system, the export of benefits, and integration services.

As in all other welfare states, in Sweden immigrants without a legal permit to stay enjoy few social rights. In hardly any country, however, has the dividing line between inclusion and exclusion been as stark. Everyone who plans to stay in Sweden for more than three months is required to obtain a residence permit,[1] and anyone who is allowed to lawfully stay for at least a year will be registered in the national population register (*folkbokföringsregistret*). Migrants who do not go through this process or who overstay their permit become undocumented migrants. And while it is true that the number of undocumented migrants is small by comparative standards,[2] their exclusion is serious. While they are technically eligible to apply for social assistance, the municipality (which administers the welfare program) has the right to refuse if they suspect that applicants have the funds to finance travels to their country of origin. The municipality can also choose to arrange the travel itself (interview SWE14). Unsurprisingly, few undocumented migrants therefore attempt an application for social services in the first place: in a 2010 national survey, the vast majority of municipalities indicated they had not seen a single person without a legal residence permit at their welfare office (Socialstyrelsen 2010, 228).[3]

Undocumented migrants have also been excluded from other services. Until recently, children without at least a pending application for residence status had no access to public schools. The exclusion from health care has been similarly severe. While undocumented migrants below the age of eighteen were eligible for health care and dental care on the same terms as legally resident children, undocumented adults were barred from all health services except emergency care, and even for those services they were expected to foot the bill themselves. In addition, civil servants in the welfare, education, and health care sectors have a duty to report undocumented migrants to the migration board so that deportation can be arranged.

This policy regime made Sweden one of the most restrictive countries in the world in its treatment of undocumented migrants, and it has been criticized on that basis by a variety of organizations, including Doctors Without Borders (2005), the UN Human Rights Council (2007), and the Platform for International Cooperation on Undocumented Migrants (Socialstyrelsen 2010, 276). At the same time, it is worth noting that the treatment of undocumented migrants on the ground has not always been as strict as the formal regulations require. In practice, few municipal authorities observe the duty to report undocumented migrants (Socialstyrelsen 2010), and many health care providers follow their Hippocratic oath and offer health services to undocumented migrants anyway (Alexander 2010).[4] Moreover, a senior civil servant at the agency responsible for enforcing the eligibility requirements (the National Board of Health and Welfare, *Socialstyrelsen*) reported that the agency often looks sympathetically at these kinds of deviations from the regulations and that its enforcement role in those cases was "not clear" (SWE13).

As the number of people in Sweden without a legal residence permit grew, so did political opposition to the restrictive regime. Since the mid-1990s, especially parliamentarians from the Environment Party (*Miljöpartiet*, MP) have been vocal in their criticism, often joined by members of the socialist Left Party (*Vänsterpartiet*, V) and the Liberals (*Liberalerna*, L).[5] However, the Social Democratic Persson governments (in power from 1996 to 2006, see Table 3.1) were reluctant to heed these objections, and it took a right-wing coalition government to implement reforms in a more inclusionary direction. The first step, taken in 2008, was to make sure that undocumented migrants could no

Table 3.1. Cabinets of Sweden, 1986–2017

Administration	Political complexion	Takes office	Government part(y)(ies)	Majority/minority (initial seats of total 349)
Carlsson I	Left	1986/3/13	S	Minority (159)
Carlsson II	Left	1990/2/27	S	Minority (156)
Bildt	Centre-right	1991/10/4	M, L, C, KD	Minority (170)
Carlsson III	Left	1994//10/7	S	Minority (161)
Persson I	Left	1996/3/22	S	Minority (161)
Persson II	Left	1998/10/7	S	Minority (131)
Person III	Left	2002/10/21	S	Minority (144)
Reinfeldt I	Centre-right	2006/10/6	M, C, L, KD	Majority (178)
Reinfeldt II	Centre-right	2010/10/5	M, L, C, KD	Minority (173)
Löfven	Left	2014/10/3	S, MP	Minority (138)

longer be denied emergency care if they were unable to pay for it (*Pr.* 2008/2009:45, *anf.* 88–95, 9 December 2008). In March 2011 a majority of parliamentarians (the coalition partners in the Reinfeldt government, as well as the MP) agreed to a more encompassing inclusionary reform, making the children of undocumented migrants eligible for public education, and expanding the range of health care services that adults without a legal residence permit could make use of.

Nevertheless, the disparity between undocumented migrants and all other groups of newcomers is still pronounced. In sharp contrast to those without a permit, everyone who is registered in the *folkbokförings-register* has full access to health care, and migrants with a residence permit of more than one year can make use of all social provisions such as social assistance and child benefits.[6] In other words, all migrants (including, for example, temporary labour migrants and international students) who are expected to stay in Sweden for more than a year are fully included in the welfare state.

The regulations are somewhat different for refugee claimants. As in many European welfare states, asylum seekers can make use of designated accommodations (Hammar 1985; Westin 1996). On 30 March 1994 the centre-right Bildt government offered these migrants a modest housing allowance in case they preferred to find a place to stay for themselves (*SOU* 2003, 75, 163–96; Borevi 2012, 66). This policy, which has become known as the *EBO* Act,[7] has frequently been criticized. In December 2004 the Social Democratic minority government proposed to scrap the housing allowance, because it had the unintended consequences of overcrowding (many asylum seekers were claiming the housing allowance and then joined family members in already small apartments) and a concentration of refugee settlement in specific cities and neighbourhoods (*Pr.* 2004/05:46, *anf.* 163–207, 8 December 2004). The proposal did not receive majority support in Parliament because all parties except the conservative Moderates (*Moderata Samlingspartiet*, M) rejected it, but the critique of the *EBO* Act persisted. In 2009 the Social Democrats (*Socialdemokratiska Arbetarepartiet*, S) affirmed during their national congress that they would abolish the law as soon as they were in a position to do so (Lundgren 2009), and local branches of the party have recently repeated their objections to the policy (Barkman 2017). The AIP Sweden Democrats (*Sverigedemokraterna*, SD) have joined the Social Democrats in their opposition ever since it found representation in Parliament. In October 2011, for example, SD politician Carina Herrstedt introduced a (unsuccessful) motion proposing the abolishment of the *EBO* Act (*Mo.* 2011/12:Sf346, 5 October 2011).

Whether asylum seekers stay in an asylum centre or in a place of their own choosing, they can make use of a wide range of services and benefits. For one thing, they receive a cash benefit to cover daily expenses. Moreover, refugee claimants have access to some health care services, and the range of available services has become more encompassing over time. Since 1996, adult asylum seekers have been eligible for subsidized emergency health care (*Pr.* 1996/97:48, *anf.* 278–85). More recently they have also been granted access to subsidized health and dental care that cannot be deferred, as well as to contraceptive counselling, obstetric care, and abortion services (Socialstyrelsen 2010). While the overall direction of recent policy developments is thus inclusionary, there have been some exceptions. In 1992, for example, the centre-right government reduced the level of daily pocket money for asylum seekers as well as the expenditure on medical services (*Pr.* 1992/93:18, *anf.* 1–19, 6 November 1992; see also Sainsbury 2012, 223), and since 2000 some categories of refugee claimants have faced reductions in their health care access.[8]

The story for migrants with a permanent residence permit is largely similar: while there have been some exclusionary reforms, overall policy-makers have aimed at expanding rather than restricting their social rights. While access to some non-contributory benefits such as child allowance was initially tied to citizenship, this principle has been gradually replaced by a *ius domicili* that allows immediate and complete access to everyone with a legal residence permit (Sainsbury 2006, 237–9). From day one onwards, then, permanent migrants have full access to health care and social provisions such as social assistance.

The egalitarian thrust becomes even more apparent when we look at policy-making in times of economic austerity. Just as we will see in the Canadian and Dutch case studies, Sweden went through a deep recession in the mid-1990s. And as in the other two cases, this entailed a large increase in the number of welfare dependents, in particular among the immigrant population. But rather than restricting immigrants' access to benefits like the Dutch, or relying on a more selective admission policy like the Canadians, the Swedes opted for a cutback that affected native-born citizens and immigrants alike. The Persson government decided that *all* social assistance recipients who did not participate in labour market programs and other skill-enhancing activities they were offered would see their benefits cut (Socialstyrelsen 2005). As Diane Sainsbury puts it, "the Swedish economy was in serious trouble ... and policymakers responded by making *across the board cuts* in social benefits" (2012, 213; my emphasis). The example of regulations affecting family migrants is equally telling. As in many other immigration countries, some politicians have recently become concerned about the welfare use of family migrants. But the strategy for alleviating this concern has been very modest. While a few suggestions surfaced in the early 1990s to implement something like the sponsorship requirement we will see in the Canadian case,[9] those suggestions received very little support in Parliament and were quickly dismissed by the Social Democratic government. As the last country in the EU to do so (*SOU*, 2008:114, 11), in November 2009 Sweden ultimately did implement a mechanism aimed at reducing the welfare dependence of family migrants. Since the introduction of the so-called Support Requirement (*försörjningskrav*), before people can bring family members over, authorities first check whether the applicants make at least a minimum wage and have the housing space to accommodate the newcomers. According to the responsible minister, Tobias Billström (M), at least part of the rationale behind this requirement was that "it is not appropriate that Swedish taxpayers take the responsibility to arrange housing and support for those who have come to Sweden without an immediate need for protection" (*Pr.* 2009/10:85, *anf.* 34, 10 March 2010). Importantly, the Support Requirement only applies to about one quarter of all family migrants, because aspirant immigrants who are children, quota refugees, otherwise protected migrants, or citizens of Switzerland or any EEA country are all exempted from this policy (*SOU* 2008, 114).

In sum, every migrant who is expected to reside in Sweden for more than a year has full access to health care, social assistance, and residence-based insurance programs such as child care and a housing allowance. These rights have never been seriously challenged by any Swedish politician. Even the Sweden Democrats focus their efforts more on advocating an overall reduction in immigration levels than on attempting to curtail the social rights of those who are already legally in the country (see also below). And while it is true that the left-wing parties in Parliament have repeatedly criticized immigrants' use of a social benefit that compensates parents who prefer not to send their children to preschool (the so-called *vårdnadsbidrag*), these critiques should not be understood as sentiments of selective solidarity. In fact, these parties propose cutting the benefit primarily because they are afraid it will have a negative effect on (immigrant) women's participation in the labour market (see, e.g., *Pr.* 2010/11:53, *anf.* 1–7, 3 February 2011; *Mo.* 2012.13:A367).[10]

Work-related insurance programs such as unemployment insurance and sickness insurance, on the other hand, are a little different. To qualify for these benefits, immigrants need to work and pay premiums. This entails no direct exclusion, but it does privilege people with a long history in the Swedish labour market over newcomers. In practice, therefore, immigrants can rarely make use of these more generous entitlements during the first years they live in the country. Many studies have found that compared to their native-born counterparts, the immigrant unemployed are much more likely to rely on social assistance and much less likely to receive unemployment benefits (Hilson 2008; Lindquist 2007). For some migrants, this indirect exclusion disappeared when Sweden joined the EU in 1995. Since then, immigrants from EU member-states can apply the years they worked in their country of origin to the calculation of their access to work-related insurance programs. Migrants from other countries, however, still face the same difficulties in accessing contributory programs.

We see some of the same dynamics in the pension system. Since 1959, Sweden has had a residence-based pension paid out of general tax revenues as well as an employment-based pension program funded in large part by social premiums. The eligibility requirements of both tiers of the public pension system have changed considerably over time. It is the rules regarding the residence-based program that are of most concern to us here.[11]

First introduced in 1913, the *folkpension* was initially tied strictly to citizenship and residence in Sweden, thus excluding all foreigners in Sweden and all Swedish citizens abroad. While these rules were strict in one respect, they were generous in another. After all, they meant that immigrants could enjoy a full public pension as soon as they acquired Swedish citizenship (Johansson 2010). As mentioned above, Sweden has gradually abandoned the citizenship principle in its welfare system, and in 1978 it opened up the pension program to non-citizens. The reform made every elderly resident of Sweden, regardless of citizenship, eligible for the *folkpension* after a minimum residence of ten years (Försäkringskassan 2010) – which is very low by comparative standards (compare, for example, the residence requirement of fifty and forty years that the Netherlands and Canada, respectively, demand for a full public pension benefit).

This system was in need of overhaul, however, when Sweden decided to join the EU. To facilitate the free movement of people, the pension system needed to be aligned with that of other member-states. In 1993, therefore, the *folkpension* became a prorated benefit that required forty years' residence for complete access and that deducted 2.5 per cent for every year short of that number (Swedish Ministry of Health and Social Affairs 2003). As a result, many elderly immigrants had to turn to the municipal welfare office to receive a minimum income.

This consequence was quickly noted by politicians. In fact, when discussions about the pension reform were still in their earliest stages, Ragnhild Pohanka (MP) already made suggestions to counter the consequences the reform would have for the immigrant population: "I think it is important that we give immigrants a *folkpension*. Otherwise they are dependent to live only off social assistance" (1990/1991:96, *anf.* 90, 17 April 1991). Members from the Left Party quickly joined Pohanka in her pleas, but it was only in 1998 that a majority of the *Riksdag* agreed that policy changes were necessary. First, Parliament adopted a bill allowing UN-recognized refugees to count the years in their home country in satisfying the residence requirement. Coming into effect in January 1999, this meant that in practice this group of refugees had full access to a public pension when they reached retirement age, regardless of the number of years they had lived in Sweden (Försäkringskassan 2010). A second reform aided a much larger group of elderly immigrants. January 2003 saw the launch of the Income Support for Elderly (*äldreförsörjningsstöd*), a tax-free, income-tested benefit, at a slightly higher level than social assistance, specifically designed for seniors who did not qualify for a full public pension. These reforms did not quell all concerns, however, and the position of immigrants in the pension system has remained on the political agenda since 2003. The Reinfeldt government requested a public inquiry on the subject, which recommended increasing the level of the Income Support, raising the level of housing subsidies, and introducing additional pension benefits (Flood and Mitrut 2010).

When it comes to the possibility of taking benefits abroad, the distinction between residence-based and contributory programs is again crucial. Residence-based insurance programs can only be enjoyed abroad during temporary stays of up to six months, and most of these programs cannot be exported outside the EU (and, since June 2006, Switzerland; see Försäkringskassan 2010).[12] And while it is possible to receive the Swedish public pension benefit in Canada as well, this is only because of a bilateral agreement between the two countries. And even in this case there are additional requirements: only people who have resided in Sweden for a minimum of twenty years are eligible for this arrangement.

The export of contributory benefits is much less restricted. All emigrants remain entitled to the rights they accumulated by paying premiums, including rights to the contributory pension program. While awaiting a decision on their refugee claim, asylum seekers can choose to either opt into the insurance programs and bring all the premium rights with them in case their claim is denied, or opt out of the insurance programs and be exempted from paying insurance premiums (*Pr.* 2004/05:134, *anf.* 135–141, 7 June 2005).

Finally, the inclusionary character of the politics of immigrants' social rights in Sweden also becomes apparent when we look at integration programs and services. Over the last two decades, Swedish policy-makers have demonstrated a strong willingness to invest more in programs specifically designed to improve immigrants' position in the labour market and in society more generally. First, unlike in many other European countries, the integration budget has grown steadily in Sweden over the last ten years or so (*R.S.* 2009/10:233, 10 June 2010). Even in the period from 2009 to 2012, in the middle of the economic crisis, the Reinfeldt government increased the budget for integration services by 23 per cent (Collett 2011). Moreover, even though Sweden has offered a generous set of services ever since introducing a coherent immigration policy in 1975 (Hammar 1985), the range of available programs and services has become more encompassing over time (Olwig 2011). For example, in November 2002 the third Persson government announced extra investments in Swedish-language training, anti-discrimination campaigns, internship programs, and active labour market policies (Swedish Ministry of Finance 2007). And also the centre-right Reinfeldt government undertook a large number of new integration initiatives when it came to power in 2006 (*R.S.* 2009/2010:233, 10 June 2010). Moreover, after its re-election in 2010 it introduced a far-reaching overhaul of the integration system specifically aimed at enhancing the labour market opportunities of immigrants.[13]

Today, newcomers can avail themselves of a wide array of programs and services. Newly arrived migrants are welcome to discuss and plan an integration trajectory with local employment services. These "integration plans" are tailored to the skills and preferences of the individual migrant. Typically they entail language classes as well as lessons in civic orientation, but they can also include internship programs, mother-tongue education, additional schooling, integration coaches, and subsidized work offers. Separate from this integration trajectory, all immigrants are eligible to take state-funded classes in "Swedish For Immigrants" (*Svenska För Invandrare*, SFI).

It is worth emphasizing that two of the programs the Reinfeldt government introduced are specifically immigrant-targeted labour market programs.[14] First, immigrants in the first three years after their arrival (as well as Swedes who have been unemployed for more than twelve months) can take up "new start jobs" (*nystartjobb*): these jobs are partly subsidized by the state as a way to encourage employers to hire immigrants. Even more clearly targeting immigrants are "entry jobs" (*instegsjobb*): available for newly arrived immigrants only, these jobs require participants to take Swedish-language classes in addition to working for their new employer. To make it attractive for employers to make use of this program, the state subsidizes no less than 75 per cent of all wage costs (Government Offices of Sweden 2009).

Not only in expanding the available services does Sweden differ in its integration approach from countries that have moved in a more restrictive direction. Countries like the Netherlands use a "stick" to encourage participation in these programs, but Sweden has opted for the "carrot." For example, in 1992 the centre-right Bildt government introduced the Introduction Benefit (*introduktionsersättning*), a tax-free cash benefit at a higher level than social assistance, for all refugees, accepted asylum seekers as well as family members of refugees who participated in integration programs (Grönqvist, Johansson, and Niknami 2012; Westin 1996).[15] This benefit, which is available for up to two years, was welcomed by all politicians except those of the small AIP New Democracy (*Ny Demokrati*, ND), which described it as a form of positive discrimination.[16] A more recent example is the 2010 introduction of a financial reward for all immigrants who complete their introductory language class in one year (the so-called SFI bonus).

Certainly, there are political disagreements about the most appropriate integration strategy. For example, the Social Democrats have frequently questioned the effectiveness of a program assigning integration coaches to newcomers (see, e.g., *Pr.* 2010/11:95, *anf.* 23–35, 3 May 2011), left-wing parties in Parliament have criticized the SFI bonus for only helping those migrants who are already more likely to succeed in the first place (see, e.g., *Mo.* 2011/12:Fi241), and the Liberals have expressed worries that many immigrants stay in language classes for too long and thus do not become active on the labour market (see, e.g., *Pr.* 2010/11: 53, *anf.* 50–53, 3 February 2011). But except for the Sweden Democrats, no party in Parliament proposes reductions in integration spending or questions the merits of a broad set of policies aimed at ameliorating immigrants' chances on the labour market.

Overall, then, the Swedish welfare state has become *more* inclusionary towards its immigrant population over the last two decades. Compared to the reforms aimed at expanding immigrants' social rights that have taken place over the last few decades, the few reforms that entail some form of restriction are relatively marginal. The one case where immigrants' access did decrease significantly, namely the increase in the eligibility requirement for a public pension from ten to forty years, came about as a functional imperative of joining the EU, not as the result of the politics of selective solidarity. Moreover, even in that case we saw that politicians quickly made efforts to ameliorate the pension rights of immigrants. In the next section we will see that these inclusionary developments reflect a specific political translation of immigrants' position in the welfare state, one that frames immigrants' overrepresentation among welfare dependents largely as a failure by the state to integrate them properly.

Framing Welfare Dependence as *Utanförskap*

The comparatively inclusionary approach that successive Swedish governments have taken cannot be understood without an investigation of how the subject of immigrant welfare dependence is politically translated. This section will begin by describing this translation based on an analysis of recent Swedish political discourse. It will then discuss how this translation has contributed to a mostly inclusionary outlook among the public and, in particular, the political elite.

Contrary to what immigration critics have suggested (see, e.g., comments by AIP members Claus Zaar, *Pr.* 1992/93:18, *anf.* 5, 6 November 1992; and Erik Almqvist, *Pr.* 2010/11:31, *anf.* 79, 9 December 2010), Swedish politicians do not ignore the reality of immigrants' heavy dependence on welfare. The topic comes up in virtually every debate on immigration or welfare policy, and politicians of all stripes frequently quote statistics showing how dismal immigrants' position on the labour market is.[17] One could even argue that the fact that immigrants rely heavily on welfare benefits is such a common topic of discussion that the association between the two has become institutionalized (Eastmond 2011). In parliamentary debates it is not uncommon for politicians to use the words "welfare recipient" and "immigrant" interchangeably (see, e.g., *Pr.* 1996/97:112, *anf.* 77, 2 June 1997; *Pr.* 2001/02:114, *anf.* 47, 28 May 2002; *Pr.* 2010/11:42, 18 January 2011; *Pr.* 2011/12:61, 25 January 2012). Similarly, it would be wrong to suggest that there are politicians who positively evaluate the high levels of immigrant welfare dependence. See, for example, Ragnhild Pohanka's (MP) observation on this subject: "I completely agree that social assistance's goal is to offer a way out when nothing else is available. But it has now become a [permanent] source of support, and that is wrong" (*Pr.* 1996/97:65, *anf.* 2, 13 February 1997). Almost identical statements have been made by politicians from the Moderates (*Pr.* 1994/95:33, *anf.* 8, 1 December 1994), the Social Democrats (*Pr.* 1995/96:6, *anf.* 142, 11 October 1995), the Left Party (*Pr.* 1998/99:42, *anf.* 47, 20 January 1999), and the Liberals (*Pr.* 2000/01:53, *anf.* 58, January 2001).

The inclusive approach in Sweden, then, has nothing to do with a conspiracy of silence to cover up immigration-related challenges. Rather, what matters crucially is the way the subject is *framed*. Swedish politicians view being on welfare as a lamentable position, one that is associated with low income, few job prospects, and isolation – a situation most often captured by the term *utanförskap* (see, e.g., *Pr.* 1998/99:23, *anf.* 148, 26 November 1998; *Pr.* 1999/2000:51, *anf.* 69, 18 January 2000; and *Pr.* 2008/09:25, *anf.* 9, 11 November 2008). Fredrick Federley (C) described this concept, which can be translated loosely as social alienation, to me as follows:

> I don't know how many people I have seen, just sitting in their apartment and watching TV, saying: "I hate this life. It's like being in prison. I know nobody, I have no contacts, I don't learn Swedish, I'm not allowed to study, I'm not allowed to work, I can just sit here and watch Oprah all day." You know, it destroys people when you feel that you are not part of something, that you don't contribute, that you don't have any friends in your life, that you have no set times to hang your life onto: not getting up in the morning, not getting to bed in the evening in order to be fresh the next day, and so on. (interview SWE04)

In keeping with this understanding of what it is like to be a welfare recipient, few politicians argue that immigrants have deliberately chosen to be in this position. That is why immigrants are rarely blamed for their predicament or framed as lazy welfare cheats who should be pushed off their benefits (see also Borevi 2012, 83). Instead, the blame is laid elsewhere. Unsurprisingly, opposition parties are keen to blame the government (see, e.g., *Int.* 2010/11:277, 17 March 2011, or *Int.* 2011/12:78, 1 November 2011), while government parties tend to argue that the problems immigrants experience were caused mostly by past governments (see, e.g., *Pr.* 2010/11:78, *anf.* 102, 29 March 2011). But politicians do not simply blame their political opponents. In parliamentary debates we encounter a wide variety of explanations for integration difficulties: the rigid nature of the Swedish labour market (e.g., *Pr.* 2010/11:111, *anf.* 35, 8 June 2011; *Pr.* 2010/11:82, *anf.* 40, 5 April 2011), discrimination (see, e.g., 2011/12: 43, *anf.* 92, 7 December 2011; 2011/12: 48, *anf.* 121, 14 December 2011; 2011/12: 129, *anf.* 36, 13 June 2012), a lack of effort on behalf of public employment services (*Mo.* 2012/13:A272, October 3, 2012), or simply "the state" or "society" in general (e.g., *Pr.* 2011/12:36, *anf.* 93, 24 November 2011; *Pr.* 2011/12: 33, *anf.* 73, 18 November 2011).

Certainly, the anti-immigrant Sweden Democrats sometimes suggest that high levels of immigrant welfare dependence have something to do with laziness: they have argued, for example, that parental benefits reduce migrants' incentive to work (*Mo.* 2011/12:Sf347, 5 October 2011) and that immigrants tend to stay in language classes longer than necessary because of the benefits they are eligible for while taking them

(*Mo*. 2012/13:Ub323, 3 October 2012). But by and large, even these politicians tend to follow the dominant frame of blaming other factors than individual migrants themselves, and they typically identify integration policies or admission policies as the main culprit (see, e.g., *Pr*. 2010/11:61, *anf*. 86, 17 February 2011; *Pr*. 2010/11:71, *anf*. 7, 11 March 2011). A good example is a speech by David Lång, who began his contribution by describing immigration as an "economic and social burden" but quickly added: "It's not their fault that the rules are the way they are, that's the politicians' fault" (*Pr*. 2012/13:39, *anf*. 2, 7 December 2012).

In short, the dominant political translation of the high levels of immigrant welfare dependence is one that blames the state, not migrants themselves. Indeed, all the politicians I spoke to, except for the Sweden Democrats' Erik Almqvist, framed the integration challenges in this light. Magdalena Streijffert (S) said that "migration could be good, but then politicians need to change the policies" (interview SWE01); Mikael Cederbratt (M) declared that "we have to focus on getting them a job [and] if we do that, all the other questions are naturally resolved" (interview SWE02); Emma Henriksson (KD) said "the costs for the social benefit system" are merely the "minor problem," while the big problem is "that they don't get established in the labour market" (interview SWE07); and Ulf Nillsson (L), finally, said that while economic considerations might be important, "the biggest problem with if a person does not work but lives on benefits is that it is a risk of *utanförskap*" (interview SWE03).

This particular translation is well in line with both the nature of the welfare system and the Swedish national identity. For one thing, and in keeping with institutionalist theory, the structure of the Swedish welfare state has produced a climate in which recipients of government transfers are unlikely to be framed as undeserving. There is little reason for working citizens to look jealously at an immigrant on welfare, not only because almost everyone simultaneously pays to and draws benefits from the system, but also because in the event they become sick or unemployed they have access to more generous contributory insurance programs than newcomers do (Franzén 2004; Sjöberg 2005). Moreover, restricting immigrants' social rights is not an apparent option in a universalist context. Indeed, differentiation between immigrants and the native-born would go against the very foundations of the system of benefits (interview SWE12). Instead, ever since the 1950s a central characteristic of the Swedish welfare model has been the "work principle" (*arbetslinjen*), that is, a commitment to full employment based on the rationale that high employment levels are not only necessary to fund the expensive welfare system but also much more effective than any other instrument at lowering income inequality (Heclo and Madsen 1987, 196; Socialförsäkring 2005). Accordingly, the Swedish system has traditionally placed a much stronger emphasis on active labour market policies than on passive unemployment benefits (Bergmark and Palme 2003; Esping-Andersen 1992; Huo 2009), and this emphasis has become even more pronounced in recent years (Jenson 2012).

In the words of a government report, to be in favour of *arbetslinjen* is about as controversial in Swedish politics as being in favour of peace (Socialförsäkring 2005, 9). Unsurprisingly, then, politicians frequently express their commitment to this principle in discussions about the economic integration of immigrants (Borevi 2012, 44). Some of my interviewees did so even though I did not ask about the principle specifically (interviews SWE03, SWE04, SWE12), and the term often comes up in parliamentary discussions as well. Social affairs minister Lars Enqvist (S), for example, concluded a comment on high unemployment levels among immigrants by declaring that "the work principle is central in Swedish social policy ... Everything needs to be done to make it possible for people to support themselves with a job of their own" (*Pr.* 1999/2000:68, *anf.* 146, 17 February 2000). Ten years later, conservative finance minister Anders Borg (M) described the solution to integration difficulties in very similar terms: "We should build on the Nordic model we are so passionate about and believe in. It should be about multiple investments" (*Pr.* 2010/11:78, *anf.* 106, 29 March 2011). In other words, we can understand Swedish political parties responding to high immigrant welfare dependence with immigrant-targeted labour market programs as the institutionalized reaction to unemployment. Whenever a particular group of people are disproportionately unemployed, Swedish governments have responded with targeted programs (interview SWE11, Bergmark and Palme 2003, 112, 115; Heclo and Madsen 1987, 171). Some programs that target immigrants have been modelled explicitly on programs that were designed for other social groups. A job introduction program for immigrants (*arbetsplatsintroduktion för vissa invandrare*), for example, is based on an earlier program that targeted the unemployed with a disability (Swedish Ministry of Finance 2007, 127), and the "entry jobs" (*instegsjobb*) program has its roots in a program for young people who are struggling on the labour market.

For this reason, critiques of integration services and immigrant-targeted labour market programs that are often heard in other immigrant-receiving countries – in particular, that they are a form of positive discrimination or that they reward immigrants who do not try hard enough to integrate – have enjoyed little currency in Sweden. Certainly, Sten Andersson (M) (*Pr.* 1992/93:91, *anf.* 99, 14 April 1993), and members of the ND (*Pr.* 1992/93:16, *anf.* 103, 4 November 1992) and SD (*Pr.* 2010/11:30, *anf.* 48, 8 December 2010, SWE05), have made such arguments, but the mainstream majority views integration policies as an obvious part of the wide range of social programs the welfare state has to offer. Ulf Nilsson (L), for example, said that concerns about positive discrimination might be reasonable "if we hadn't something like that for Swedes, but we have" (interview SWE03). Fredrick Federley (C) said that the targeted programs are "just the same thing as we have for people who are born in Sweden" (interview SWE04), and Christina Höj Larsen (V) said that her party's support for targeted programs is "just the same as [our efforts] to get women into positions of power in society" (interview SWE06). This line of reasoning is frequently used in parliamentary debate as well. For example, when Sweden Democrat Sven-Olof Sällström advocated the abolition of the entry job program, Annika Qarlsson (C) brushed off the critique by arguing that the program is a normal and institutionalized feature of the Swedish welfare system: "I think it follows the same line we have in very many other measures and policies, in which we make sure to reduce the costs to hire those who are far from the labour market" (*Pr.* 2011/12:48, *anf.* 121, 14 December 2011).

A related factor shaping the discourse on immigrants' social rights is the Swedish national identity. The depiction of Sweden as one of the most progressive countries in the world is at the core of the national self-image. In the context of immigration, taking an open and tolerant approach to newcomers can therefore easily be framed as the Swedish thing to do. In a debate on migration requested by the Sweden Democrats, Fredrik Lundh Sammeli (S) invoked national hero Raoul Wallenberg, who saved between 20,000 and 100,000 Hungarian Jews during the Second World War, to explain his party's welcoming approach to newcomers:

> I am proud of Raoul Wallenberg and of what Sweden has done over the years. Just as he showed courage and civil bravery for those who once escaped the Nazis' persecution, we should both today and in the future

be able to offer a refuge for people who escape our time's totalitarian regimes. (*Pr.* 2010/11:79, *anf.* 4, 30 March 2011)

One could hear similar comments during a party leader debate in 2012, during which Åkesson (SD) criticized existing immigration and integration policies. Centre Party leader Annie Lööf, for example, countered Åkesson's criticisms with nationalist arguments: "I love Sweden. I love the diversity Sweden stands for. I love the tolerance that many with me show for the diversity and democracy that Sweden stands for" (*Pr.* 2011/12: 129, *anf.* 91, 13 June 2012). The response of Göran Hägglund, leader of the Christian Democrats, was similar (Ibid., *anf.* 99). Of course, these nationalist defences of open immigration policies often paint an overly rosy picture of Swedish history and understate the novelty of the current multicultural society (see, e.g., contributions by Social Democrat Jansson, *Pr.* 2011/12:94, *anf.* 30, 11 April 2012, and Liberal Ulf Nilsson, *Pr.* 2012/13:39, *anf.* 13, or the interactions between Sweden Democrat Johnny Skalin and his opponents, *Pr.* 2012/13:28, 21 November 2012). However, the accuracy of the picture of Sweden as a progressive, open, and tolerant country is only of limited relevance here – my point is merely that the image permeates political discourse and shapes the political translation of levels of immigrant welfare dependence.

A related characteristic of Swedish identity is the near-sanctity of egalitarianism. Foundational to Sweden's character is the history of its generous and encompassing welfare state. Per Albin Hansson, often credited as the founder of this system, famously argued that the state should offer a "people's home" (*folkhem*) where everyone is treated as equal brothers and sisters:

> In a good home there prevails equality, thoughtfulness, cooperation, help-fulness. As applied to the larger peoples' and citizens' home this implies a breaking down of all social and economic barriers which now divide citizens between the privileged and the forgotten, the rulers and the dependent, the rich and poor, the satiated and the utterly destitute, the plunderers and the plundered ... The foundation of the people's home is community and solidarity. The good home knows no privilege or neglect, no favourites and no stepchildren. (Quoted and translated by Heclo and Madsen 1987, 157)

This concept has found much popular resonance (Borevi 2012, 26–7). Many authors have noted that Swedes tend to pride themselves on the generous welfare state they live in and the comparatively low levels of inequality it has produced (Heclo and Madsen 1987, 154; Kvist et al. 2012; Sainsbury 2012, 222). In keeping with these findings, the Swedish "passion for equality" (Kvist et al. 2012, 6) has been of great importance in shaping immigration policies. Ever since the earliest attempts to formulate a coherent set of immigration policies in 1968, the political elite has been unanimous in emphasizing the importance of equality (*jämlikhet*), including equal access to social rights (Borevi 2012, 38–43). This institutionalization of egalitarianism has made proposals for differentiation in social rights difficult to defend. Indeed, politicians have often affirmed their commitment to egalitarianism in discussions about integration and immigrants' social rights. See for example, integration minister Mona Sahlin's (S) opening to a debate on the subject in 2002 (and note how she talks about more than the equality of all "Swedes" or "Swedish citizens"): "The goal is very clear ...: all human beings who live in our country should have the same rights, the same duties, but also the same possibilities. The changes we should discuss today are: how do we make that possible?" (*Pr.* 2002/03:25, *anf.* 1, 28 November 2002). Moreover, politicians frequently invoke the equality principle in objections to restrictive proposals. For example, when in the early 1990s a few Moderates suggested implementing sponsorship requirements in family migration, the Social Democratic government rejected the proposals on the grounds that "Swedish citizens were not required to support their elderly parents" either (Sainsbury 2006, 239; see also Borevi 2012, 74). Just as egalitarianism has offered a weapon against suggestions that immigrants' rights be restricted, so has it also been used as a tool to advocate further inclusion. For example, Gunilla Wahlén (V) argued that the children of asylum seekers should have more access to social services by saying that "an asylum-seeking child should have the same right to protection, support, and education as other children in Sweden" (*Pr.* 2003/04:115, *anf.* 143, 13 May 2004), and Ulf Nilsson (L) advocated increased health care access for undocumented migrants on the basis that "all human beings have the same human rights" (*Pr.* 2008/09, *anf.* 90, 9 December 2008).

In sum, us-versus-them frames go against both the structure of the welfare system and popular images of the Swedish nation. The public at large is thus discouraged from thinking of migrants as welfare leeches. And indeed, Swedish public opinion is largely sympathetic to the plight of immigrants and their position in the welfare system. An important qualification, however, is that there is a minority of (sometimes extremist) immigration critics. One of my interviewees at the Department of Health and Social Welfare told me that occasionally people call in to complain that immigrants are treated more generously than native-born Swedes (interview SWE12). In addition, public intellectuals such as Jonathan Friedman, taxpayer interest groups such as *skattebetalarna.se*, and explicit anti-immigrant networks such as Sweden Confidential frequently complain about the costs immigrants incur on the national budget. More generally, objections to immigration tend to be formulated by a vocal and at times aggressive minority (Eastmond 2011), and there have been several acts of xenophobic violence in Sweden (Geddes 2003; Johansson-Murie 2012; Ornbrant and Peura 1993; Rydgren 2006, 56)

Again, however, it is important to emphasize that critics of immigrants' rights are in the minority. We saw one indication of this in the previous chapter, where Sweden appeared as the country with the least welfare-chauvinist public of the twelve countries under study (see Figure 2.1). Longitudinal survey data, which allow us to trace the trajectory in sentiments of selective solidarity over time, suggest that the views of the average Swede have remained relatively stable over the last two decades. Figure 3.1 shows results from the Diversity Barometer (*Mångfaldsbarometern*), an annual mail survey that investigates public opinion on diversity issues, including immigrants' social rights (Ahmadi, Palm, and Ahmadi 2016). In each wave of the survey, the large majority of respondents agree with the statement that "all people of foreign background who come here should be given the same social rights as the rest of the population," and this majority seems to have grown gradually from 2005 (when the survey was first administered) to 2014. One more iteration of the survey took place in 2016, however, and it found much less support for that statement: only 55 per cent of respondents indicated agreement. (Because it is unclear at this point whether this unusual result is an anomaly or signals the beginning of a trend towards more selective solidarity in Sweden, it is omitted from Figure 3.1.)[18]

Unfortunately, questions asking directly about immigrants' social rights were not posed in longitudinal surveys before 2005. To probe Swedish views on this issue over a longer period, we therefore need to rely on indirect evidence. Figure 3.2 presents such evidence. First, it shows response patterns to a more general question about whether Sweden should admit fewer refugees, asked every year since 1990 by the Society, Opinion, and Media Survey (SOM). As the dotted line indicates, the proportion of people who believe that Sweden should admit

Figure 3.1. Support for giving immigrants the same social rights as native-born citizens, 2005–2014

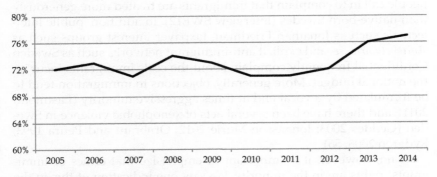

Source: Mångfaldsbarometern

Figure 3.2. Indirect evidence of selective solidarity, 1988–2015

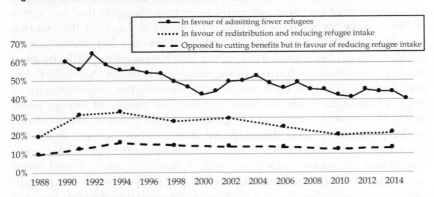

Source: SOM, SNES, and author's calculations

fewer refugees has declined considerably over time. In the absence of questions that directly measure feelings of selective solidarity, we can also look at the percentage of respondents who express support for redistribution and social benefits but simultaneously object to immigration. Figure 3.2 shows this information for each available wave of the Swedish National Election Study (SNES).[19] Overall, we see that the percentage of people who favour the welfare-chauvinist policy mix increased in the late 1980s but has been in decline since the mid-1990s.

In sum, then, there is scant evidence of selective solidarity among the Swedish population. Importantly, however, there is some evidence of tension between immigration and *general* solidarity. Some of the first academics to worry about the Progressive's Dilemma in fact singled out Sweden as an instructive example (see, e.g., Korpi 1978), and there is evidence to support those worries. For one thing, the increase in immigration in Sweden over the last twenty years did coincide with welfare retrenchment (Ginsburg, Lach and Rosenthal 2002; Kvist et al. 2012). And as we saw above, high levels of immigrant welfare dependence led policy-makers in the mid-1990s to make access to welfare more restrictive (see also Sainsbury 2006, 238; 2012, 213). More generally, the suggestion that the welfare state as a whole should be restructured because of the advent of immigration has commonly been made in Swedish political discourse (Borevi 2012, 57, 65; see also below). At the level of public opinion, there is evidence of this tension as well. For example, the percentage of people who give unconditional support for the welfare state has declined over the same time period that immigration has increased (Jaeger 2012). And as we saw in the first chapter, two recent studies conducted at the Swedish county level found a strong negative relationship between immigration inflows and support for social programs (Dahlberg, Edmark, and Lundqvist 2012; Eger 2010).

Thus it seems possible that immigration has had a negative effect on solidarity in Sweden. But it is worth repeating that there is no evidence that it has led to *selective* solidarity. In other words, diversity may have made Swedes less willing to share, but it has not make them supportive of differentiating in social rights between immigrants and the native-born.

We can characterize the views of the political elite in largely the same terms. In fact, politicians and policy-makers tend to maintain even *more* inclusionary views on immigration than the public at large. Carl Dahlström and Peter Esaiasson, for example, found that in survey questions about immigration, the views of Members of Parliament tend to be about 40 to 50 percentage points more favourable than those of general respondents (Dahlström and Esaiasson 2013). This does not mean that the costs of immigration have never led to controversy in the *Riksdag*. For one thing, the anti-immigrant parties ND and SD have made criticizing (the costs of) immigration a spearhead of their parliamentary activity. Parliamentarians of New Democracy (in Parliament from 1991 to 1994) frequently brought up the high welfare dependence of immigrants (*Pr.* 1993/94:6, *anf.* 169, 13 October 1993; *Pr.* 1993/94:21, *anf.* 72,

10 November 1993) and described immigration as a drain on the budget (*Pr.* 1992/93:6, *anf.* 61, 14 October 1992; *Pr.* 1992/93:18, *anf.* 5, 6 November 1993). In some of their contributions, they also accused newcomers of being welfare abusers. ND member Claus Zaar, for example, argued that many immigrants tend to use their welfare cheques to fund trips to their country of origin while covering their daily expenses with income from the black labour market (*Pr.* 1993/94:106, *anf.* 129, 18 May 1994. He even went so far as to suggest that immigrant families tend to be larger because they like to take as much advantage of child benefits as possible (*Pr.* 1992/93:91, *anf.* 81, 14 April 1993).

Unsurprisingly, the ND proposed a series of restrictions on immigrants' access to services and benefits: their long list of exclusionary proposals included ending funding for mother-tongue education, reducing financial assistance to refugees, halting the export of benefits, implementing more demanding requirements for accessing benefits for immigrants than for native-born Swedes, compelling asylum seekers to work in designated jobs while staying in asylum centres, and limiting refugee claimants' access to health and dental care (*Pr.* 1992/93:6, *anf.* 119, 14 October 1992; *Pr.* 1992/93:16, *anf.* 103, 4 November 1992; *Pr.* 1992/3:18, *anf.* 18, 6 November 1992; *Pr.* 1992/93:60, *anf.* 233, 11 February 1993). The party also proposed that the level of benefits be tied to the length of stay in Sweden, among other things by offering only 80 per cent of a full social assistance benefit to people who had lived in Sweden for two years or less (*Pr.* 1992/93:6, *anf.* 119, 14 October 1992).

The Sweden Democrats, the AIP that has been in Parliament since 2010, similarly brings up the costs of immigration on a regular basis (*Pr.* 2010/11:31, *anf.* 79, 9 December 2010; *Pr.* 2010/11:33, *anf.* 29, 13 December 2010). Even more strongly than the ND, the Sweden Democrats frame immigration as a direct threat to the redistributive welfare state. SD politician Johnny Skalin, for example, argued in Parliament that it is "unpleasant that much needed welfare investments have for so many years taken a backseat to an unmotivated and incomprehensible mass immigration policy" (*Pr.* 2010/11:30, *anf.* 3, 8 December 2010; also see *Pr.* 2010/11:36, *anf.* 61, 16 December 2010). Similarly, an SD motion proposing that family migrants be disentitled in the first five years after arrival explicitly states that "mass immigration constitutes a direct threat to Swedish welfare" (*Mo.* 2010/11:*Fi*231, 26 October 2010).

These kinds of comments are rarely heard, however, from mainstream party members. Until the early 2000s, Moderate politicians did occasionally express concern about immigrants' welfare dependence, sometimes accusing newcomers of drawing welfare while hiding assets in their country of origin or working in the underground economy.[20] Undoubtedly the loudest voice among immigration critics within the Moderate party was Sten Andersson's. Three years in a row, he started the parliamentary year by submitting a motion asking for a comprehensive calculation of the costs of immigration (*Mo.* 1999/2000:*Sf*503, 24 September 1999; *Mo.* 2000/01:*Sf*603, 21 September 2000; *Mo.* 2001/02:*Sf*208, 21 September 2001), and he repeatedly described immigrant integration in Sweden as a "total failure" (e.g., see *Pr.* 1994/95:84, *anf.* 36–42, 3 April 1995). As said, however, the Moderates have become an explicitly pro-immigration party since the early 2000s. In a telling illustration of this change, the party placed Sten Andersson at an unelectable position for the 2002 elections.[21] Since then, the party has maintained a decidedly inclusionary position on immigration, even though its recent overture to the Sweden Democrats has raised suspicions that this might change in the near future (Magnusson 2017).

Only in response to a few isolated events have the welfare costs of immigration led to widespread support for restrictive solutions. For example, the large intake of Bosnian refugees in the aftermath of the war in Yugoslavia led to fierce discussions in Parliament regarding the limits of Sweden's reception capacities (Eastmond 2011), the 2004 expansion of the EU made some parties (including Prime Minister Persson's Social Democrats) worry about possible "welfare tourism" from the new member-states (Doyle, Hughes, and Wadensjö 2006), and the large intake of Syrian refugees raised concern about its potential to strain social services in general and the immigration system in particular (Svensson 2015). But all in all, Swedish politicians have more often suggested inclusionary rather than restrictive measures to reduce immigrants' welfare dependence. Figure 3.3 shows all the motions and interpellations brought forward in Parliament from 1991 to 2012 that directly discussed the social rights of immigrants.[22] In some years, exclusionary suggestions could quite frequently be heard, in particular when New Democracy was still represented in the *Riksdag*. Overall, however, proposals to expand immigrants' social rights were much more numerous.

This becomes even more apparent when we look at how Swedish political parties assess the desirability of four different strategies for reducing immigrants' welfare dependence: (1) restricting immigrants' access to programs and benefits, (2) reducing the intake of immigrants, especially of those who are most likely to lay a claim on the state, (3) investing more

Figure 3.3. Motions and interpellations in Parliament advocating the expansion (black bars) and reduction (white bars) of immigrants' access to welfare state benefits in Sweden, 1991–2012

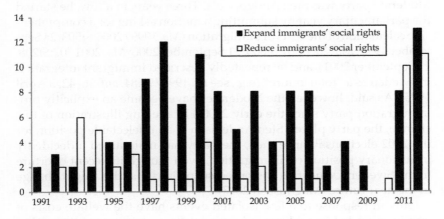

Table 3.2. Political parties' views on four possible strategies to avoid/reduce immigrant welfare dependence

Party	Ideology	% seats, (2014 elections)	Restrict access to benefits?	More selective intake?	More integration assistance?	General welfare reform?
S	Social-dem.	32	No	Some	Yes	No
M	Conservative	24	No	No	Some	Yes
SD	Anti-immigrant	14	Yes	Yes	No	No
MP	Green	7	No	No	Yes	No
C	Left-liberal	6	No	No	Yes	Yes
V	Socialist	6	No	No	Yes	No
L	Liberal	5	No	No	Yes	Yes
KD	Christian dem.	5	No	No	Yes	Yes

in integration assistance, and (4) reforming the welfare state in a more general manner.

Table 3.2 reports the position of seven parliamentary parties on this issue, based on an analysis of legislative behaviour, campaign manifestos, and interviews I conducted with the immigration spokesperson for each of these parties (Social Democrat Magdalena Streijffert, conservative Mikael Cederbratt, Liberal Ulf Nilsson, Centrist Fredrick Federley, Sweden Democrat Erik Almqvist, Socialist Christina Höj Larsen, and Christian Democrat Emma Henriksson).[23] The most important conclusion to draw is that neither of the restrictive options enjoys much support in the Swedish Parliament. In keeping with the dominant understanding of high levels of immigrant welfare dependence as a failure on the state's part to integrate immigrants properly, we see that Swedish politicians mostly advocate inclusionary strategies. In fact, parliamentary debates on immigration often take the form of a competition among politicians (in particular from L, C, MP, and V) vying to be the most immigrant-friendly.

To start with the first strategy, only the Sweden Democrats support curtailing access to social benefits. Its 2014 election manifesto suggests that non-refugee migrants be disentitled from social security during their first years in the country (Sverigedemokraterna 2014, 7), and both party documents and parliamentarians have made similar suggestions in the past (Sverigedemokraterna 2007, 4; Mo. 2010/11:Fi231, 26 October 2010; Mo. 2011/12:Sf346, 5 October 2011). Perhaps the most blatant support for this type of policy change came in the form of a campaign video the party ran in the 2010 elections, which showed a group of women in burqas jumping the queue at a welfare office and leaving an elderly white woman without a pension. Despite these clear examples of support for IEWRs, it is important to note that the party does not advocate restrictions on benefit access as ardently as anti-immigrant parties do elsewhere. It more commonly advocates reductions in intake levels rather than restrictions in the rights of those who have already arrived in the country. When I asked Erik Almqvist about residence requirements, conditionality requirements, and reduced rights for temporary migrants, he denied that the party ever supported any such restrictions:

> To be honest, we have almost never talked about immigrants in that way. [We do think] that immigration is too high ... But we very seldom talk about that too much subsidies, or too much pensions, are going to immigrants ... We think that everyone who has a permit to be here should of course have the same rights. (interview SWE05)

It is telling that Almqvist decided to claim that his party opposes reductions in immigrants' benefit access: just as we saw in their careful avoidance of blaming immigrants explicitly for their overrepresentation among benefit recipients, the Sweden Democrats apparently also try to avoid advocating differentiation in social rights too overtly.

Unsurprisingly, then, all the other politicians I spoke to also rejected this policy measure. Again, one could qualify these responses, pointing out, for example, that the Moderates and the Centre Party (C) object to an expansion of undocumented migrants' access to health care.[24] Overall, however, all mainstream parties have spent more time advocating further welfare inclusion than they have advocating exclusion, especially in recent years. To give just a few examples, the Moderates have repeatedly advocated expanding the export possibilities of pension benefits, the Social Democrats have suggested waiving the costs of naturalization for low-income immigrants, the Liberals have long been a champion of improving health care access for undocumented migrants, the Centre Party favours efforts to increase immigrants' uptake of social benefits and programs, the Environment Party advocates increasing financial assistance to asylum seekers, the Left Party wants to increase the Income Support for Elderly to the level of a full public pension benefit, and the Christian Democrats frequently promote more access to education for both immigrant adults and undocumented children.

The second restrictive strategy – making admission policies more selective – is almost as unpopular. Only the Sweden Democrats unequivocally embrace this option. As Almqvist explained to me, his party sees a reduction in family and asylum migration of 90 (!) per cent as the most effective strategy to alleviate difficulties in integration (interview SWE05). All other parties, by contrast, favour overall *increases* in immigration levels, although they differ in the type of migration they work hardest to attract. On the one hand, the Left Party proposes increasing the intake of refugee migrants (by expanding the definition of refugee) and of family migrants (by repealing the Support Requirement), but it is more hesitant about economic migration, fearing that too open a system might lead to the exploitation of migrant workers (interview SWE07; Vänsterpartiet 2014, 4). For that reason, it advocates reinstating the practice of setting annual labour migration targets that the Reinfeldt government ended in 2008. The Environment Party has defended similar policies, advocating in particular more relaxed admission criteria for family migrants and refugee migrants. The political right, on the other hand, targets its arrows precisely at attracting more labour migrants. The Moderates, Liberals, Center Party, and Christian Democrats all favour a further liberalization of Swedish economic admission policy, for example by making it easier for blue-collar workers to enter the labour migration stream and reducing the number of permits that tie immigrants to one specific field of employment. At the same time, it needs to be noted that these parties also look favourably on other migration streams. Other than the previously discussed Support Requirement, none of these parties formulate any restrictions on family migration. And even though the Moderate Party used to take a restrictive position on refugee migration, it no longer favours reductions in annual intake levels.[25] Indeed, when in September 2013 the Syrian refugee crisis prompted Swedish migration authorities to rule that all Syrian asylum seekers would be granted permanent residency, neither the Moderate Party nor any other mainstream party voiced opposition in Parliament.

The Social Democrats take the most ambiguous position. During the Carlsson and Persson governments, the party both curtailed refugee migration by narrowing the grounds for asylum (Borevi 2012; Geddes 2003, 119) and reduced the options for family migration outside the nuclear family (*Pr.* 1998/1999:95, *anf.* 36, 18 May 1999). Indeed, as Magdalena Streijffert admitted, for the Social Democrats a more selective intake for the purpose of reducing problems with immigrant integration "has been a strategy in the past" (interview SWE01). Today there are still Social Democrats who favour restrictions in admission policy,[26] but also many who favour liberalization. According to Streijffert, the party is now split into "two camps": "one that believes we have too restrictive policies in this area, and one that believe we ... have to have tougher policies" (interview SWE01). The coexistence of these two camps again became apparent in the aftermath of the refugee crisis. In November 2015, the Social Democratic Löfven government intensified border controls and sharpened requirements for family migration, but came under internal party criticism for doing so (Dagens Nyheter 2016).

In contrast to the limited support for restrictive options, almost all parties favour investing in integration policies and immigrant-targeted active labour market policies. Again, the Sweden Democrats are the exception, arguing that any service, program, or benefit that is exclusively available to immigrants is a form of positive discrimination (interview SWE05). All other parties, however, see integration policies as the most effective remedy for immigrant welfare dependence. This is clearest among the centre-right parties. As soon as the coalition government of Fredrik Reinfeldt took office, it introduced a sweeping reform of the integration regime, focusing on active labour market policies, internship programs, and skill enhancement initiatives. Moreover, even long before it took office politicians from the coalition parties argued in Parliament that the only way to reduce immigrant welfare dependence is to invest in integration initiatives.[27] The position of the left-wing parties is little different. Christina Höj Larsen (V) reluctantly agreed that the integration policies of the Reinfeldt government were "not too bad" (interview SWE06), and Streijffert even admitted that the plans her party proposed during the 2010 election campaign were very similar to the reforms the centre-right implemented in 2007: "we have the same solutions, but we call them by other names" (interview SWE01).

By far the most controversial question in Swedish immigration politics is whether general welfare and labour market reform would facilitate the economic integration of immigrants. Left-wing parties reason that since immigrants disproportionately rely on social programs and benefits, any type of retrenchment will hit immigrants harder than the native-born. Kalle Larsson (V), for example, repeatedly made this point, arguing that "being against the welfare state means being against immigrants" (Pr. 2000/2001:93, anf. 2, 6 April 2001). Equally telling is the Environment Party's Ywonne Ruwaida's response when Moderate Mikael Odenberg argued that labour market and welfare reform would improve the plight of immigrants:

> I listened very carefully to the Moderates today, and I am very concerned about the attitude. Indirectly the Moderates say, if I can be blunt: immigrants are welfare parasites. They don't talk about the discrimination there is against immigrants. (Pr. 2004/05:36, anf. 23, 24 November 2004)

In other words, the political left sees pleas to aid immigrants through welfare retrenchment as nothing more than a right-wing ploy to bring about a smaller and less generous welfare state. The Moderates, the Liberals, the Center Party, and the Christian Democrats, on the other hand, all see the structure of the Swedish welfare state as a partial culprit in creating current integration difficulties. For one thing, they view protective labour market institutions as an obstacle for immigrants' economic integration and therefore advocate more flexible dismissal laws, fewer regulations on small businesses, and more freedom in determining one's working hours.[28] When asked how the welfare state could best change to address immigrants' current economic problems, Emma Henriksson (KD) answered:

> Our labour market is a very fixed labour market. If you have a job, you don't quit. Because you know: "If I take a new job, I will be the last one to

be employed, and then if there is a crisis, I am the first one to go." [And for the] employer, because of the regulations we have, it is very difficult to get rid of someone if it is a bad match ... That's ... why it is difficult for young people and for immigrants to get into the labour market, because there is so little movement in the labour market. (interview SWE07)

Moreover, the centre-right parties believe that the difference between a wage income and a passive benefit has historically been too small to stimulate employment-seeking efforts, especially among newcomers on the labour market. For that reason, they favour lower benefits, lower taxes, and fewer possibilities to receive a benefit without having to do something in return (such as participating in a labour market program).[29] Indeed, Mikael Cederbratt (M) explained the policy changes his party implemented upon taking office in exactly this light (interview SWE02).

Finally, the Sweden Democrats oppose any reductions in welfare state generosity and can in this respect be understood as a largely left-of-centre party (interview SWE05). Indeed, political opponents agree with the characterization of the SD as a pro-welfare party,[30] and its MPs typically protest when they are labelled right-wing (see, e.g., the interaction between Jonas Sjöstedt from the Left Party and SD leader Jimmie Åkesson on 17 October 2012, *Pr.* 2012/13:11). This is noteworthy not only because this distinguishes the party from its anti-immigrant predecessor, New Democracy, but also because it makes it the first party in the Swedish Parliament to advocate selective solidarity.

Again, however, the Sweden Democrats are very much alone in this respect. As this section has shown, no mainstream political party today is in favour of reducing immigrants' access to welfare benefits. And by comparative standards, there is also little support for such policy changes among the public at large. As we have seen, much of this can be understood by the way the subject of immigrant welfare dependence is most commonly framed: as a lamentable situation for which the state rather than the immigrants themselves should largely be blamed. The next section discusses the possible future of the Swedish approach to immigration and welfare and reflects on the increasing pressure for restrictive reform –in particular, the rising popularity of the Sweden Democrats.

Anti-Migrant Politics in the Margins, but for How Long?

While the inclusionary approach towards immigrants' social rights seems pervasive today, there are of course no guarantees that it will persist in the indefinite future. As discussed in chapter 1, anti-immigrant politicians can potentially bring about a restrictive turn, in particular when they (1) are elected in large numbers, (2) manage to sway the mainstream in a more restrictive direction, and (3) are able to navigate institutional obstacles to IEWRs. This section discusses each of these three steps in turn. As we will see, anti-immigrant politicians in Sweden have had little success so far in challenging the dominant understanding of immigrants' place in the welfare state, but there are some signs that this could change in the near future. At any rate, the electoral success of the anti-immigrant Sweden Democrats is steadily increasing, and the political mainstream's dismissive approach to this party has started to show cracks. On the other hand, however, the party still faces more vociferous opposition than sympathy, and a parliamentary majority in favour of welfare exclusion remains highly unlikely.

Anti-immigrant politicians have long played a marginal role in Swedish politics. In 1991, New Democracy won 25 of the 349 seats in the *Riksdag*, but it disappeared again at the next election. It was not until 2010 that a new AIP managed to surpass the electoral threshold. The Sweden Democrats entered Parliament with a total of twenty seats, and since that first success they have gained in popularity. In May 2014 they managed to win two of the twenty seats Sweden occupies in the European Parliament, and a few months later they more than doubled their vote in the municipal and national elections that were taking place simultaneously. Today the party holds 49 seats in Parliament (out of a total of 349) and 1,324 seats in municipal councils across the country (up from 612 in the preceding election). Recent polls predict that it would win as many as seventy seats and become the second-largest party if there were elections today. Figure 3.4 shows results from the so-called "Voter Barometer" (TNS SIFO), a monthly poll conducted among an average of about 1,900 voters, ever since it first included the Sweden Democrats as an answer option. The increase in popularity, especially since 2010, has been spectacular.[31]

Other AIPs, such as the Skåne party, the Sjöbo Party, the Sweden Party, the National Democrats, Keep Sweden Swedish, and the Swedish Progress Party, have all tried their luck, but none of them have been able to win even 1 per cent of the vote in national elections (even though they have had some success in local elections). For most of recent history, therefore, parliamentary debates on immigration have not included any participants with an explicit anti-immigrant stance, with the exception of the above-mentioned Moderate rogue Sten Andersson.

Figure 3.4. Support for SD according to monthly poll, September 2006–June 2017 (dashed lines indicate 95% CI)

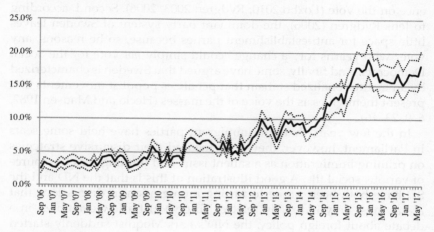

Source: TNS SIFO

While this is largely beyond the scope of this investigation, it is worthwhile to reflect on why AIPs have been so unsuccessful in Sweden. Important here are factors related to the parties themselves as well as the characteristics of the larger institutional structure. To start with the former, many Swedish AIPs were too closely associated with racism, fascism, and neo-Nazism to appeal to more than only the most xenophobic portions of the electorate. During the first election in which the Sweden Democrats participated (1998), it was still an extremist movement, and it won a meager 1,000 votes. Only after the party started to purge itself of all overtly extremist elements did it manage to broaden its appeal (Åkesson 2008; Rydgren 2006). The importance of party organization also becomes apparent when we look at the demise of New Democracy. The party was led by the team of aristocratic businessman Ian Wachtmeister and self-made record label director Bert Karlsson. The two became increasingly at odds, and when Karlsson started to criticize his fellow party leader in public, Wachtmeister resigned and the party quickly crumbled (J.G. Andersen and Bjørklund 2000; Rydgren 2006). As far as broader politico-institutional characteristics are concerned, most existing literature points to three explanations. One is the continued high salience of class voting in Sweden, which means that even if a sizeable portion of the Swedish electorate did harbour anti-immigrant feelings, it is unlikely that those sentiments would have a strong influence on the vote (Loxbo 2010; Rydgren 2003, 2006). Second, according to Jens Rydgren (2006), the dominant party system of Sweden leaves little space for anti-establishment parties because, so he reasons, any voter who yearns for "a change" could simply *not* vote for the Social Democrats. And finally, some have argued that Sweden is characterized by an institutionalized statism that penalizes populist movements that present themselves as the voice of the masses (Heclo and Madsen 1987, 6–9, 23–46).

In the few years that anti-immigrant parties have held some seats in Parliament, however, they have focused their discursive strategies on priming immigration as a salient issue and framing it as the source of various social ills. A good illustration of this is that the ND and the SD have both been prone to raising immigration in discussions that are at most only indirectly related. To give just a few examples, in a debate about foreign policy, the ND's Lars Moquist suddenly started to talk about illegal immigration (*Pr.* 1992/1993:67, *anf.* 12, 24 February 1993); his party colleague Leif Bergdahl started a discussion that was supposed to be about pension reform by arguing that immigrants are responsible for the strains on the pension system (*Pr.* 1993/94:120, *anf.* 1, 8 June 1994); SD politicians Johnny Skalin and Erik Almqvist argued in discussions about unemployment benefits that they could be much more generous if immigration levels were lowered (*Pr.* 2010/11:36, *anf.* 61, 16 December 2010; *Pr.* 2010/11:37, *anf.* 41, 17 December 2010); in a debate on the relatively poor performance of Sweden in an international study of skills and knowledge among fifteen-year-olds, Richard Jomshof (SD) dedicated most of his contribution to blaming immigrants (*Pr.* 2010/11:48, *anf.* 74, 26 January 2011); and in a discussion about a shortage on the housing market his party colleague Carina Herrstedt argued that there would be no shortage if only there were fewer immigrants (*Pr.* 2010/11:128, *anf.* 24, 8 September 2011).

Moreover, members of these AIPs (and in particular the SD) have often framed their arguments in a way that explicitly pits immigrants against native-born Swedes. Examples of this rhetoric abound, and I will limit myself here to a few:

I think it is painful not in the least for poor pensioners who despite an entire work life in Sweden live on or just over the social minimum. It is also painful for lone parents who do everything to get food on their children's plates. Why not give these people a bonus for their often heroic efforts instead of putting this money straight in the pocket of newly arrived people who apparently do not even want to be in our country? (Richard Jomshof, criticizing the financial bonus for immigrants who quickly finish their language classes 2010/11:120, anf. 100, 21 June 2011)

It is basically about which kind of society we want to have. It is about whether we want to continue to build a segregated Sweden ... or move away from the politics of segregation and instead focus on keeping Sweden together and using the money with which we are prioritizing mass migration and family migration today instead to protect and develop the welfare system, make it better for the elderly and sick, and make it possible to create security on the streets, squares, and so on. We cannot have it both ... Is it really the Swedish people who are responsible for that immigrants cannot find a job in this country? (Jimmie Åkesson, 2011/12: 15, anf. 101, 105; 12 October 2011)

They [the government] want to spend millions on illegal immigrants, criminals therefore, at the same time that they cut in other areas and increase the maximum rates for health care and medicine and so on. (Kent Ekeroth, 2011/12: 49, anf. 167, 15 December 2011)

I am convinced that many voters would prefer better welfare and tax cuts that are financed with a more responsible immigration policy instead of an increased immigration, like today, which is financed by worse welfare and higher taxes. (Erik Almqvist, 2011/12: 134, anf. 3, 20 June 2012)

It seems safe to predict that these kinds of parliamentary contributions will continue to be part of Swedish debate in the future, especially in light of the strides the Sweden Democrats have recently made. Besides these survey data, two other considerations are relevant here. First, the party does not seem to suffer from the defects that most often lead to the downfall of AIPs. The party leader, Jimmie Åkesson, is uncontested, and there is little sign of internal dissent within the party. Seven SD parliamentarians have been forced to leave the party, but these cases had little to do with disagreement over the direction of the party. Significantly, for five of these MPs the end of their political career seemed primarily the result of the SD's continued efforts to dissociate itself from the extremist image it had in the 1990s.[32] Lars Isovaara was forced to leave Parliament in November 2012 when he, after a night at the bar, accused two people of immigrant background of stealing his bag (which in reality he had forgotten in a restaurant) and subsequently on his way home subjected a foreign-born parliamentary guard to racist language (DN 2012). Somewhat similar was the case of Erik Almqvist, who left Parliament a month later, after a video started circulating that showed him harassing the immigrant comedian Soran Ismail on the street, kicking and pushing him while shouting racist insults (SvD Nyheter 2012). Thoralf Alfsson and Stellan Bojerud completed their parliamentary term, but were not placed on the SD list for the 2014 elections. While leader Jimmie Åkesson never explicitly explained this decision in public, it seems clear that the two were seen as too extremist: Alfsson was already under investigation for incitement to racial hatred because of comments he had made on his blog, while Bojerud became discredited when he expressed support for the extra-parliamentary neo-Nazi movement *Svenskarnas Parti* (Party of the Swedes) (Ekelund 2013; Expressen 2013). The final case occurred in October 2016, when the party leadership forced MP Anna Hagwall to leave when she suggested that Jews run Swedish media (Dagens Industri 2016).

Second, the party seems in a better position than New Democracy to spread unease about immigrants' place in the welfare state. The anti-immigrant message is much more central to the Sweden Democrats than it was to its predecessor (Ignazi 2003, 159; Rydgren 2006), and more importantly, it defends a more leftist position on issues of redistribution and social policy and is therefore better placed to capture the welfare chauvinist vote. New Democracy used to defend a squarely neoliberal economic agenda and tended to attract the vote of business owners and the middle class (Rydgren 2006, 10), but the Sweden Democrats have portrayed themselves as "middle-of-the-road" on economic issues (Åkesson 2008, 6) or even as adamant supporters of a generous welfare system (interview SWE13). As such, the party has been more popular among the unemployed and low-income workers than the ND (Eger 2010, 212).

It would be premature, however, to expect the increasing success of the Sweden Democrats to have a concomitant negative impact on immigrants' social rights. Even the most spectacular victory imaginable would not bring the party a parliamentary majority, and therefore we have to turn our attention to how other parties in Parliament have responded to the Sweden Democrats' success. Overall, anti-immigrant voices have received hostile and dismissive treatment for most of Swedish contemporary history. Nevertheless, there are reasons to suggest they have had some influence and might increase that influence in the near future.

For one thing, we can point to a few examples of a contagion effect. In particular, it does not seem coincidental that the Social Democrats and the centre-right Bildt government moved in a more restrictive direction on refugee policy at the time of New Democracy's ascendance (the former by formulating stricter criteria for admission, the latter by reducing the cash benefits of refugee claimants) (Eastmond 2011; Rydgren 2006). Maud Björnemalm (S) made a clear albeit implicit reference to New Democracy when justifying her party's stricter line on refugee issues: "We need to pursue a refugee policy with clear rules that are understandable for the Swedish people, because otherwise lies and myths will thrive, as well as xenophobia" (*Pr.* 1992/93:91, *anf.* 44, 14 April 1993). Social Democrat Magdalena Streijffert told me more explicitly that her party has occasionally defended restrictive policies precisely because they feared a nativist backlash that would result in success for AIPs:

> After the crisis in the beginning of the 1990s in Sweden, it was really sensitive. And the argument about this was: if we discuss those issues openly, the Sweden Democrats will come into the parliament ... [That is] also why we were quite restrictive when it comes to the health care system for undocumented migrants. (interview SWE01)

At the same time, however, the extent of this contagion has been limited. All political parties except the SD remain decidedly pro-immigrant. Politicians have repeatedly pointed to this consensus. In a discussion about the recognition of foreign credentials, for example, Ana Maria Narti (L) noted that "it is nice to take place in a debate where we don't immediately end up in party politics and controversy for controversy's sake" – a point that minister Leif Pagrotsky (S) was quick to agree with (*Pr.* 2004/05:50, *anf.* 47–48, 14 December 2004). Similarly, Göte Wahlström (S) started a more general debate about immigration policies by noting approvingly that "in large parts of the area of migration policy there is a large political consensus" (*Pr.* 2007/08:43, 13 December 2007).

This is not to say, however, that political stripe is irrelevant in the politics of immigrants' social rights. For one thing, a review of the interpellations and motions that were tabled from 1990 to 2012 on this issue suggests a clear difference between centre-left and centre-right parties. Of the 57 interpellations and motions that criticized immigrants' access to or use of social benefits and programs, 33 were submitted by New Democracy and the Sweden Democrats, 16 by the Moderates (seven of these by Sten Andersson), and another 5 by the Liberals. The Left Party and the Environment Party did not submit any such proposals (see appendix, Tables A1.1, A1.2). When it comes to suggestions for inclusion, we see similar left–right dynamics: of the 126 motions and interpellations advocating more inclusion, the Left Party and Environment Party are each responsible for 29 and the Social Democrats for another 26 (see appendix, Tables A1.3, A1.4). Moreover, even on the issues on which mainstream parties have reached agreement, there is still controversy. For example, although all parties except the SD now agree that undocumented migrants should have access to *some* health care services, disagreements are large regarding the exact scope of services they should be entitled to. And while every party agreed on the introduction of the Income Support for Elderly, there has been disagreement on how generous this benefit should be.

Again, however, it should be emphasized that political disagreements can best be understood as a matter of divergent views regarding the best ways to organize an immigrant society, not on whether Sweden should have a generous and open immigration system in the first place. Indeed, even the Christian Democrats, the Centre Party, the Liberals, and, since the turn of the century, the Moderates have more often advocated inclusionary rather than exclusionary reforms (see appendix, Tables A1.1–A1.4). In this light, it is unsurprising that mainstream parties have largely responded by refuting and dismissing the arguments and policy proposals of the ND and SD rather than adopting them (Dahlström and Esaiasson 2013; Rydgren 2003, 60). For one thing, all of the mainstream politicians I spoke to dismissed the strategy of taking a harsher line on immigration in order to reduce the SD's electoral niche as counterproductive. Ulf Nilsson (L) and Christina Höj Larsen (V), for example, referred to the example of Denmark, where the *Dansk Folkparti* only grew after mainstream parties moved in their direction (interview SWE03, SWE06). Fredrick Federley (C) referred to the situation in the Netherlands:

> I could see that clearly the VVD has been listening to other groups in parliament, and I think that's not taking the question seriously. That's just saying to people: what you have been told which is not actually the truth probably, that is what we will take into our concerns now. So we are confirming the scares in your beliefs, instead of saying how it actually is. (interview SWE04)

Similarly, Emma Henriksson (KD) argued that in other countries, adopting the views of AIPs had increased rather than decreased their success (interview SWE07). Magdalena Streijffert (S) and Mikael Cederbratt (M) even referred to a recent academic study that had reached that conclusion (Dahlström and Esaiasson 2013).[33]

Perhaps more importantly, these MPs also claimed that they would not change their position even if it promised greater electoral success. Voters' concerns about immigration are often "not true" (Cederbratt) and "miss the bigger picture" (Henriksson) – so my interviewees told me – and therefore an MP's role is to "explain" (Streijffert) and "inform" (Nilsson) rather than voice those concerns in Parliament.

This dismissive stance becomes even clearer when we look at parliamentary debates: virtually every politician who has advocated restrictions in immigration policies has met a hostile reaction (Borevi 2012). In some cases, that reaction has been respectful and nuanced (see, e.g., comments by Alf Svensson, KD, *Pr.* 1993/94:3, *anf.* 14, 6 October 1994). Often, however, the response has been more aggressive (Dahlström and Esaiasson 2013, 3). Anti-immigrant politicians have frequently been accused of discrimination and racism, and in some cases the critique has gone so far as to involve comparisons with Nazi Germany (see comments by the Left Party's Berith Eriksson, *Pr.* 1992/93:16, *anf.* 6, 6 November 1993; Christian Democrat Märtha Gårdestig, *Pr.* 1993/94:6, *anf.* 193, 13 October 1993; Social Democrat Juan Fonseca, *Pr.* 1996/97:106, *anf.* 5, 21 May 1997; and Left Party member Kalle Larsson, *Pr.* 2008/09:47, *anf.* 2, 11 December 2008).[34] A good example of this hostile treatment took place in April 1993, when Social Democrat Georg Andersson launched a personal attack against Claus Zaar (ND):

I feel disgust and repugnance for the cynicism and xenophobia that Claus Zaar just expressed. It is sickening that a member of the Swedish parliament in this way cultivates prejudice and creates the breeding ground for growing xenophobia and racism ... I have seldom met someone who admits he is xenophobic. But I have met some who are, and I include Claus Zaar as one of them. (*Pr.* 1992/93:91, *anf.* 87, 89, 6 October 1994)

Immediately afterwards, Berith Eriksson (V) stood up and proclaimed: "Mister Speaker! I first and foremost want to endorse Georg Andersson's last contribution. He spoke for many of us, I believe" (*Pr.* 1992/93:91, *anf.* 90, 6 October 1994).

The case of Sten Andersson offers another good illustration. After the elections of 1994 and the demise of New Democracy, the Moderate politician was left as the most outspoken critic of generous immigration policies in Parliament, and, as such, a welcome target for parliamentarians who wanted to paint the Moderate Party as a whole in a negative light (see, e.g., *Pr.* 1996/97:106, *anf.* 1–26, 21 May 1997). Andersson's contributions were typically met with dismissive reactions from politicians of all political stripes (see *Pr.* 1999/2000:76, *anf.* 76–93, 21 January 2000), and after 1998 even colleagues from his own party began to distance themselves from him (*Pr.* 1997/98:, *anf.* 60–63, 25 March 1998). In 2001 the Moderates placed Andersson on an unelectable position for the upcoming elections, and the Malmö politician quit the party. During the very first debate after his resignation, Moderate Anna Kinberg opened her speech by saying: "Let me first note that I am no longer a fellow party member of Sten Andersson. I am very proud of that" (*Pr.* 2001/02:35, *anf.* 14, 27 November 2001). In the remaining months until the elections, any comments and questions Andersson made in Parliament were ignored altogether (see *Pr.* 2001/02:35, *anf.* 9–11, 27 November 2001; *Pr.* 2001/02:76, *anf.* 9, 5 March 2002).

During their spell in Parliament, the Sweden Democrats have received a similar treatment. MPs of this party have been accused by their colleagues in Parliament of populism (*Pr.* 2012/13:11, *anf.* 98, 17 October 2012), racism (*Pr.* 2011/12:120, *anf.* 97, 30 May 2012; *Pr.* 2010/11:61, *anf.* 46, 17 February 2011), xenophobia (*Pr.* 2010/11:118, *anf.* 102, 17 June 2011), and heartlessness (*Pr.* 2010/11:73, *anf.* 20, 16 March 2011). In a debate on EU directives on integration policies, Patrick Björck (S) accused SD of spreading hate and racism, and when a Sweden Democrat objected to those labels, Björck replied: "Mister Speaker! Sven-Olof Sällström felt attacked when I was speaking of racism, right-wing extremism and xenophobia. That I can understand because Sven-Olof Sällström stands for racism, xenophobia and right-wing extremism" (*Pr.* 2011/12:86, *anf.* 144, 21 March 2012). Frederick Federley went even further in a debate on migration policy, comparing the SD to the Nazi Party:

> The blame you are laying on a particular group of Muslims is exactly the same thing that people have done for centuries with Roma and Jews. You have merely chosen to put the focus on a different group, but it is the same stale scent that spreads in the room where racism and xenophobia are expressed. (*Pr.* 2010/11:79, *anf.* 7, March 30, 2011)

Mainstream political parties have not only met anti-immigrant politicians with hostility, they have also long refused to cooperate with them in any way.[35] The Bildt government, for example, could have had a majority in Parliament if it had reached an agreement with New Democracy. It refused to do so, however, and thus had to rely on left-wing parties to pass their bills, as it did, for example, in a broad pension reform in the early 1990s (Gould 2001, 39–40; Lundberg 2005).

The initial consensus not to work with the Sweden Democrats was obvious even before the party achieved parliamentary representation. Two years before the 2010 election, Social Democrat Luciano Astudillo wanted to know whether the government would cooperate with the Sweden Democrats in the event that they won seats. Moderate party leader Reinfeldt declared that "me and the Moderates will forcefully work to make sure that the values that the Sweden Democrats stand for will not spread in Sweden," and seven politicians from various other parties (M, S, MP, L) affirmed (rather irrelevantly, one might add) that they would never work with the AIP either (Pr. 2008/09:25, anf. 1–21, 11 November 2008). True enough, even though the coalition parties (M, L, C, KD) lost their majority in 2010, they refused to negotiate with the Sweden Democrats. In order to pass a sweeping reform of immigration policies, for example, they reached an agreement with the Environment Party. At the presentation of that accord, Prime Minister Reinfeldt explicitly described it as "a way to close the door for xenophobic forces" (Magnussen and Larsson 2011). He repeated this statement in Parliament, adding the exhortation to his colleagues that "we have a common responsibility to guarantee that they [the Sweden Democrats] have no influence at all" (Pr. 2010/11:116, anf. 45, June 15, 2011).

The 2014 elections initially brought no change to this strategy. In its joint election manifesto, the right-wing coalition partners declared in a clear nod to the Sweden Democrats that they would "resist the forces that advocate protectionism and reduced openness" (Alliansen 2014, 13), and after the elections they struck a deal with left-wing parties to further isolate the anti-immigrant party. In what became known as the December Agreement, the centre-right and centre-left blocs agreed that whichever of the two blocs was smaller in Parliament would let the other govern, thereby effectively obviating the need to collaborate with the Sweden Democrats (Aylott 2015). This agreement, however, broke down in January 2017. The Moderates, presumably motivated by the growing numbers of their supporters that according to polling data were defecting to the Sweden Democrats, announced that they would consider cooperation with the anti-immigrant party in the future. Party leader Anna Kinberg declared that she "can no longer pretend that one of [the parties in Parliament] does not exist," because such a position "would not take voters seriously" (Sundberg 2017).

This surprising move certainly seems to have increased the future legislative influence of the Sweden Democrats. At least as far as the politics of immigrants' social rights is concerned, however, it is important not to overstate its significance. For one thing, Kinberg has (so far) continued to refuse collaboration with the Sweden Democrats on issues of refugee policy, foreign policy, and defence policy (Magnusson 2017). Moreover, the Moderates have been widely criticized for their change of heart, including by the other right-of-centre parties. Even if the Sweden Democrats were able to convince the Moderates of the merit of some IEWRs, therefore, such plans would only have a chance of success if the two parties reached a parliamentary majority together. That scenario seems unlikely, at least for now.

In sum, then, anti-immigrant politicians in Sweden still seem unable to change the dominant mode of discussing immigration and its inter-action with the welfare state. The Sweden Democrats continue to grow in popularity, but their legislative influence is still relatively weak. For that reason, the third component of our theoretical model – the legal-institutional hurdles that proposals for IEWRs are likely to encounter – is of only limited relevance to this case. This section briefly discusses how far IEWRs could realistically go if support somehow suddenly increased for such policy changes.

First, both domestic and international law is likely to thwart attempts to implement far-reaching cuts to immigrants' entitlements. The constitutionally enshrined principle of non-discrimination (Chapter 2, Article 12) makes it impossible to directly differentiate in social rights on the basis of national origin, and as an EU member-state and party to the ECHR, the UDHR, and the ICESCR, Sweden is bound by many of the international treaties that have obstructed IEWRs elsewhere (Migrationsverket 2010; Stokke 2007). In this light, it is unsurprising that the Sweden Democrats favour leaving the EU. As Erik Almqvist told me: "We are fully aware that the EU comes with more and more demands on immigration policy, and they want to form a common immigration policy for the entire EU ... But we don't want to be part of that" (interview SWE05).

Equally telling is that other parties have taken the opposite position and clung to international agreements in order to push their immigrant-inclusionary agendas. The Environment Party, for example, has argued since 2006 that Sweden should ratify the UN International Convention on the Protection of the Rights of All Migrant Workers and Members of Their Families as a way to further enshrine the (social) rights of immigrants (see, e.g., *Mo.* 2005/06:K22, 29 March 2006; *Mo.* 2012/13:Sf207, 10 September 2012). In a similar vein, some politicians have argued that inclusionary reforms are necessary in order to better live up to the international treaties Sweden is already party to. Before Sweden granted the children of undocumented migrants access to health care and education in 2011, politicians frequently argued that this policy regime violated the Convention of the Rights of the Child, in particular its directive to operate in the best interests of all children regardless of legal status. This argument was voiced as early as May 1994 by Brigitta Dahl (S) and Eva Zetterberg (V) (*Pr.* 1993/94:112, *anf* 2–3, 27 May 1994) and has since been repeated numerous times in motions and parliamentary commentary by politicians of the Liberals (*Pr.* 1998/99:63, *anf.* 78, 4 March 1999; *Mo.* 2004/05:So556, 30 September 2005), the Left Party (*Mo.* 1998/99:Sf612, 25 October 1998; *Mo.* 2003/04:So417, 10 October 2003; *Pr.* 2003/04:115, *anf.* 116, 13 May 2004), and the Environment Party (*Pr.* 2002/03:25, *anf.* 94, 28 November 2002).

In sum, in Sweden national and international legal obligations do more than shield against possible future attempts at IEWRs. They also serve as a tool for bringing about more inclusion. Yet the importance of these legal safeguards should not be overstated. While the Swedish judiciary technically has the right to strike down government bills on the grounds of unconstitutionality, it has never used that power (Nergelius 2011; Stjernquist 1990). Moreover, unlike their counterparts in other EU member-states, the national courts in Sweden have been disinclined to resort to supranational judicial review through the European Court of Justice (Wind 2010). And most importantly, as mentioned above, the best explanation for the absence of IEWRs in Sweden should be sought not in the legal context but rather in the mainstream consensus that such reforms are undesirable.

This brings us full circle. Sweden is an instructive case for understanding the politics of immigrants' social rights. There are few countries in the world where immigrants are as overrepresented in the welfare system, but this has not led to any IEWRs. Instead, when it comes to immigrant-targeted services, access to non-contributory programs, and the social rights of undocumented migrants, the Swedish welfare state has become *more* generous towards its immigrant population. The reason for this paradoxical outcome lies mainly in a political translation that frames high levels of immigrant welfare dependence as a sign that the state has not served immigrants *enough* and that it should undertake *more* efforts to improve immigrants' standing in the labour market. This frame can be traced back to long-standing institutional and cultural characteristics: IEWRs run counter not only to the structure of the welfare system but also to the value of egalitarianism that plays a central role in Swedish national identity. As a result, most citizens and almost all politicians reject differentiating between immigrants and native-born Swedes in the extension of social benefits. So far, anti-immigrant voices in Parliament have not been able to break down this inclusionary approach. Even though the popularity of the Sweden Democrats has been growing steadily in recent years, mainstream parties have responded to their success with hostility and unwillingness to cooperate. And while one party has started to entertain the possibility of co-legislating with them, it seems unlikely that attempts at IEWRs will become more frequent in the near future.

In sum, then, the Swedish case powerfully illustrates two of our key theoretical insights on the politics of immigrants' social rights. First, economic facts regarding immigrants' use of benefits are of limited importance. Politicians by no means ignore the reality of high levels of welfare dependence among immigrants, but they interpret these levels in ways that are conducive to inclusionary rather than exclusionary responses. Second, anti-immigrant voices can challenge immigrants' rights loudly, but their calls are ineffective as long as the political mainstream does not accommodate them. The Swedish Parliament is by no means empty of critics of immigration, but the influence of those critics has so far been limited. Indeed, other political parties have by and large maintained their inclusionary positions and refused any collaboration with anti-immigrant politicians. In sum, then, the reasons for the absence of IEWRs in contemporary Swedish politics lie both in the dominant way that immigrant welfare dependence is framed and in the dismissive response by the political mainstream to the increasingly popular anti-immigrant movement.

Chapter Four

Canada: Stability in a Country of Immigrants

Canada's history of immigration is a long one. Not only has immigration been of foundational importance, but it has also persisted as a source of demographic growth throughout the country's history (unlike in other settler societies such as the United States). During the twentieth century, Canada admitted more than 13 million immigrants. At times, as many as 2.5 million arrived within the span of ten years. As a result, foreign-born citizens make up a large part of the Canadian population, and the percentage continues to grow. In 1991, 15.5 per cent of Canadians were foreign-born, by 2016 that percentage had risen to 21.9 per cent, and the number is expected to rise to between 25 and 30 per cent by 2036 (Morency, Malenfant, and MacIsaac 2017).

The sheer amount of immigration is not the main reason for Canada's prominent place in the comparative immigration literature. Instead, it is the way that immigrants are accommodated and the outcome of that accommodation that has attracted many students of immigration to the Canadian case. The country has some of the most generous and inclusive naturalization and diversity policies in the Western world and has largely avoided the nativist backlash seen elsewhere. At least until recently, Canada also seemed to experience comparatively little trouble integrating its immigrant population into the labour market and society more generally. Indeed, in international comparisons the Canadian model of immigration and integration is often praised as a "success story" worthy of emulation (Aalandslid 2009; Hojem and Ådahl 2011).

There are some signs that things could change. The economic integration of immigrants has slowed down over the last decade and a half, and some members of the centre-right have started to cater to xenophobic and Islamophobic sentiments. In the last federal election (2015), the Conservative Party of Canada suggested the creation of a tip line for "barbaric cultural practices," and a subsequent leadership race in the party featured a candidate (Kellie Leitch) who indicated she was "excited" by Donald Trump and who suggested that all new arrivals should be screened for "Canadian values" (Minsky 2017a). The relevance of these developments should not be exaggerated, however. The Conservatives lost the 2015 election to a party that strongly advocated an inclusive stance on immigration and diversity, and Leitch ended up attracting the support of only 7 per cent of party members in the leadership race.

It is perhaps unsurprising, then, that Canada has largely steered clear of the politics of selective solidarity. Political discourse typically depicts immigration as a benefit to rather than a drain on the Canadian economy, and accordingly, it pays little attention to immigrants' reliance on transfer benefits. Calls for welfare exclusion have not been as uncommon as we saw in the Swedish case, however. When it comes to welfare use by undocumented migrants, refugee claimants, and recent family migrants, Canadian politicians have on occasion raised objections and suggested policy adjustments in an exclusionary direction. When the costs of immigration become the topic of parliamentary discussion, however, politicians more often advocate reducing those costs by amending admission policy rather than by disentitling immigrants from social benefits and programs. This follows a long-standing tradition in Canada of carefully selecting immigrants who are most likely to be self-sufficient, while treating those who ultimately pass the rigorous selection criteria in fundamentally the same way as native-born citizens. Broadly speaking, we can say that most immigrants are included in the Canadian welfare system as soon as they are admitted to the country and that this has changed little over the last two decades.

This chapter reviews the politics of immigrants' social rights in Canada over the last two decades. We will see that the policy stability in this area can be understood by analysing the political translation of immigrants' place in the welfare state and its effect on policy-making. While it is true that immigrants' reliance on transfer benefits is much lower than in other countries, the lack of a basis in economic facts is at best only a partial explanation for the relative absence of selective solidarity in Canada. More important is how immigrants' position in the welfare system tends to be discussed. The central place of immigration and immigrant diversity in popular conceptions of Canadian identity has left little space for divisive frames pitting "true Canadians" against immigrants. In fact, on those few occasions that politicians have advocated IEWRs, they have done so by framing the targets of their exclusionary reforms as "queue-jumpers" and therefore as enemies not only of native-born Canadians but also of law-abiding immigrants. The absence of successful anti-immigrant politicians further explains why the predominantly inclusive approach to immigrants' social rights has not been contested so far.

This chapter is structured as follows. The next section traces the relevant policy developments related to immigrants' access to social programs and benefits. Because a large portion of Canada's social programs are administered at the provincial level, I will refer in this section not only to federal politics but also to developments in Ontario, Canada's most immigrant-dense province.[1] I then examine the dominant political translation of immigrants' position in the welfare state and show that selective solidarity has limited traction among the public and the political elite. The final section discusses the fortunes of past and current anti-immigrant politicians and shows that they have been unable to challenge dominant conceptions of how best to integrate newcomers into the welfare state.

Continuation of the Canadian Model of Immigration and Welfare

This section reviews recent developments in the social rights of various immigrant groups. We will see that the entitlements of most immigrant groups have remained unchanged over the last twenty years. However, with regard to undocumented migrants, refugee claimants, and family migrants, politicians have occasionally expressed objections and formulated suggestions for exclusion.

As in any welfare state, undocumented migrants are in the most vulnerable position. They cannot access any transfer benefits, and politicians seem eager to keep it that way. Especially in the mid-1990s, provincial and federal politicians often brought up cases of "illegals on welfare" as a way to accuse the government of mismanagement. In 1989 a new right-wing party, the Reform Party of Canada (RPC), started to compete in federal elections, and by 1997 it had become the second-largest party in Parliament.[2] Reform's platform included a stricter line on immigration in general and on the entitlements of refugee claimants and undocumented migrants in particular. While Reform was certainly the most vocal party in raising these types of concerns,

Table 4.1. Governments of Canada, 1984–2017

Administration	Political party	Takes office	Majority/minority (initial House seats/total)
Mulroney I	PCP (conservative)	1984/09/17	Majority (211/282)
Mulroney II	PCP (conservative)	1988/12/12	Majority (169/295)
Campbell	PCP (conservative)	1993/06/25	Majority (167/295)
Chrétien I	LPC (liberal)	1993/11/04	Majority (177/295)
Chrétien II	LPC (liberal)	1997/09/22	Majority (155/301)
Chrétien III	LPC (liberal)	2001/01/29	Majority (172/301)
Martin I	LPC (liberal)	2003/12/12	Majority (172/301)
Martin II	LPC (liberal)	2004/10/04	Majority (172/308)
Harper I	CPC (conservative)	2006/02/06	Minority (124/308)
Harper II	CPC (conservative)	2008/11/18	Minority (143/308)
Harper III	CPC (conservative)	2011/06/02	Majority (166/308)
Trudeau	LPC (liberal)	2015/11/04	Majority (184/338)

similar arguments could be heard from centre-left politicians.[3] Partly in response to this political pressure, in 1994 the government led by Jean Chrétien of the Liberal Party of Canada (LPC) (see Table 4.1 for an overview of federal governments from 1984 to 2017) implemented Bill C-44, which increased identification controls and expanded the possibility of deportation with the specific aim of reducing the likelihood that undocumented migrants would end up in the refugee system and rely on welfare.

The exclusion of undocumented migrants is not limited to transfer benefits. The only service they have been able to make use of is temporary access to subsidized emergency health care. In 2009, an undocumented migrant who was denied treatment for her kidney problems because of her status appealed, arguing that the denial violated her right to life and security of the person (*Toussaint v. Canada*, 2009). In a unanimous verdict, the Federal Court of Appeal ruled in 2011 that undocumented migrants have no right to free medical services and cannot receive ongoing health care (Humphreys 2011). In sum, undocumented migrants are almost entirely excluded from the Canadian welfare state.

A second group of immigrants whose access to social benefits and services has often been the subject of discussion is refugee claimants. For as long as the federal government takes to administer their claims, these migrants are entitled to legal aid and social assistance, even though the precise eligibility requirements differ somewhat from one province to another. Since 1995 the federal government has also offered health care benefits to asylum seekers through the Interim Federal Health Program (IFHP). This program has frequently been criticized. Particularly contentious has been that the IFHP covers some supplemental services (in particular dental and ophthalmological care) that are not included in most provincial health care packages. The centre-right Harper government decided to remove those supplemental services as of June 2012, but the federal court reversed this policy change two years later on the grounds that it constituted a form of "cruel and unusual punishment" in violation of the Canadian constitution. The Harper government appealed that decision, but the following year a Liberal government came to power under Justin Tudeau and withdrew the appeal (Sheridan and Shankardass 2016). A proposal allowing provinces to impose residence requirements on social assistance benefits for this group of migrants met a similar fate: the Harper government fell before it was able to pass the bill through Parliament.

More generally, refugee claimants' use of financial support and medical care has repeatedly spurred objections in the federal and Ontario legislatures. The most common criticism has been that the costs would be much lower if only the federal government would process refugee claims more quickly.[4] But occasionally, some right-wing politicians have also directed their criticisms at the refugee claimants themselves.[5] It is important to note, however, that before the recent proposals to change the IFHP and to introduce residence requirements for accessing social assistance, the policy response to concerns about "bogus refugees" and the costs they were generating was to amend refugee admission policy, not refugee claimants' eligibility for social benefits. In 1987 the centre-right Mulroney government implemented the Refugee Deterrents and Detention Bill (C-84) as well as a subsequent 1992 reform (Bill C-86), which introduced "fingerprinting of refugee applicants to discourage welfare fraud, public hearings of refugee cases, harsher detention procedures, and deportations without hearings" (Knowles 2007, 239). During the Liberal governments that followed, three more bills on refugee policy passed: Bills C-44 (1994, mentioned earlier), C-84 (1997), and C-40 (1998) together facilitated the deportation of claimants with criminal records and further strengthened identification controls. The Harper government implemented additional changes. In 2010, Parliament passed the Balanced Refugee Reform Act (C-11), which among other things restricted the conditions under which refugee claimants could appeal a rejection of their claims. According to a senior civil servant at the immigration ministry, "one of the drivers ... in the reform was to reduce the overall cost of, mostly the negative, asylum seekers on the provincial welfare systems" (interview CAN11). Yet another piece of refugee legislation, Bill C-31, also known as the Protecting Canada's Immigration System Act passed in June 2012 and gave more individual leeway to the minister in deportation decisions. Again, the access to social benefits played a large role in public justifications for this change. Immigration minister Jason Kenney explained the need for the bill as follows:

> Canadians are also worried when they see a large number of false refugee claimants who do not need Canada's protection, but who file refugee claims because they see an opportunity in Canada's current refugee system to stay in Canada permanently and have access to social benefits [...] In too many cases the applicants do not show up for their hearings, but they do show up to collect Canadian social benefits. (House of Commons debate, 6 March 2012)

In sum, then, while concerns about the costs of refugee claimants are alive and well, they have led more to restrictions in admission policy than to cutbacks in refugee claimants' access to social benefits.

Other temporary migrants, most importantly temporary foreign workers and international students, are less protected than refugee claimants. Most of them are excluded from social assistance, they have no access to child benefits until they have spent eighteen months in the country, and they frequently experience practical problems in accessing health care services (Hennebry and Preibisch 2012; Koning and Banting 2013). This group of migrants is even excluded from some contribution-based programs. Temporary residents must pay monthly premiums for Employment Insurance, but many cannot access this program if they become unemployed (Basok 2003; Nakache and Kinoshita 2010).[6] Considering their limited eligibility, it is perhaps unsurprising that there has been little political outcry over these temporary migrants' reliance on the welfare system. When the social rights of temporary workers or international students are the topic of discussion, it is more often about expanding rather than restricting those rights. In particular, the federal left-wing New Democratic Party (NDP) has in recent years frequently advocated more inclusion. However, it has found little support for this from the Liberals and Conservatives.

In contrast to immigrants with a temporary residence permit, permanent residents are well protected. Canada places no residence requirement on a permanent residence permit. This means that from day one, recognized refugees and economic migrants have the exact same access to non-contributory transfer programs such as social assistance and child benefits as native-born citizens.[7] The health care system is only marginally less inclusive: the provincial health care programs of the three most popular destination provinces for migrants (British Columbia, Ontario, and Quebec) have a three-month waiting period for new arrivals, which means that in the interim, immigrants need to secure temporary private health insurance. (This does not apply to refugees, who can make use of the previously mentioned IFHP.) The equal treatment of permanent migrants and the native-born enjoys almost unanimous political support. It is true that in Ontario, the Ontario Progressive Conservative Party (OPC) has occasionally suggested exclusionary reforms. For example, MPP Cameron Jackson suggested cutting social assistance when immigrants are visiting their homeland (Legislative Assembly of Ontario debates/18 October 1993), and the 2011 OPC election platform proposed a one-year residence requirement for social assistance (Ontario Progressive Conservative Party 2011, 30). But such proposals have never been echoed by federal parties, let alone by non-conservative politicians.

The situation is different for one class of permanent migrants: family migrants can only enter the country on the condition that a relative will sponsor them – that is, the sponsor must sign a formal undertaking with the state to support them economically. For the duration of the sponsorship period (between three and ten years, depending on the nature of the relationship), these migrants are expected not to make use of social assistance or supplementary health care (and if they do, their sponsors are required to repay the costs to the province). These sponsorship agreements are not always observed for the full duration, however. Marriages or family relationships can collapse, or sponsors can get into economic difficulties themselves. In those cases, the individual sponsorship breaks down and the agreement is cancelled. In other cases, sponsorship agreements have not been enforced because officials have had difficulty monitoring them – the federal administration of immigration status is not linked to the provincial administration of social assistance, which raises the possibility of fraud.

Political parties have typically advocated the strict observance of sponsorship agreements.[8] Whenever stories emerge of sponsors who have reneged on their agreement, politicians have been quick to express their indignation. This has been especially the case for politicians in conservative parties, such as Reform's Ed Harper (House of Commons debate/14 April 1995) and Val Meredith (House of Commons debate/1 November 1995) and Ontario premier Mike Harris (OPC) (Blackwell 1999). However, similar criticisms have also been levelled by Liberal politicians (see, e.g., Paul Szabo's comment in the House of Commons on 1 February 1994). Federal and provincial governments have tried to reduce the number of sponsorship defaults by two strategies. The first has been to sharpen the requirements for sponsorship in admission policy. In May 2000, minister Eleanor Caplan (LPC) tabled Bill C-31, which among other things aimed to "tighten up sponsorship provisions to ensure that those who sponsor new immigrants are both able and willing to meet the financial obligations they undertake" (House of Commons debate/1 May 2000). The bill went through both houses of Parliament relatively quickly and received Royal Assent in November 2001.[9] The second strategy has been to exert greater effort to prevent sponsored immigrants from using social assistance. In 2004, when it was reported that 7,500 sponsored immigrants in Ontario (about 2 per cent of all sponsored immigrants) were on welfare, the province started to warn sponsors that social assistance benefits paid to the immigrants they were supposed to be sponsoring would be considered a debt to the Government of Ontario and that this debt could only be waived under extraordinary circumstances. By September 2009 the number of sponsored immigrants on social assistance had shrunk to 5,000. In a widely publicized court case that went all the way to the Supreme Court of Canada, eight sponsors who had been forced to repay a social assistance debt appealed to have their debt waived. The Supreme Court rejected the appeal unanimously (*Mavi v. Canada*, 2009).

The distinction between family migrants and other permanent residents is irrelevant for contributory programs such as Employment Insurance and the Canada Pension Plan. However, by their very nature these programs privilege those who have integrated themselves into the labour force over those who have had trouble doing so, and are therefore indirectly less generous to the immigrant population than to native-born citizens. Indeed, Michael Pal, Sujit Choudry, and Matthew Mendelsohn (2011) have found that, because of requirements placed on new entrants and the regional nature of the Employment Insurance system,[10] immigrants on average have to work for a longer period of time to qualify for benefits than the native-born do.[11] These differences are small, however, and by and large one can say that permanent migrants have almost the exact same access to premium-based programs as native-born Canadians.

The story is more complicated, however, for the Old Age Security (OAS) benefit, a pension program funded from general tax revenues. Immigrants must live in the country for ten years before they are eligible for OAS at all[12] and must be resident for forty years to receive the full benefit. For those residents in the country between ten and forty years, the benefit is proportional to the number of years spent in Canada. However, the effects of prorating are mitigated for low-income immigrant elderly: they can receive a top-up benefit, the Guaranteed Income Supplement (Baker, Benjamin, and Fan 2009). To make things even more confusing, since 1984 recent elderly immigrants to Canada can also apply for a partial OAS and the additional top-up if they have spent at least ten years in Canada *and* a country with which Canada has a bilateral social security agreement. The size of the OAS is still determined on the basis of the number of years spent in Canada, but the provision can lead to earlier access to the top-up benefit, which can provide a total benefit as high as the full OAS. However, this practice has come to be seen as abuse of the system, and when a 1996 reform denied this option to elderly immigrants under a sponsorship agreement,[13] the party-wide support was striking. Even critical opposition members such as Richard Bélisle (BQ) hailed the reform as "only fair to all taxpayers" (House of Common Debates/24 April 1996).

Further changes to this policy constellation seem unlikely in the near future. There have been no suggestions to lengthen the residence requirement or reduce the top-up benefit, and even centre-right politicians are generally supportive of immigrants' pension rights. In February 2012, for example, MP Joe Daniel (CPC) boasted in Parliament that the current government had increased the uptake of pension benefits among immigrant elderly (House of Commons debate/2 February 2012). And while it is true that a number of politicians from the NDP, the LPC, the BQ, and even the Conservatives have occasionally suggested shortening the residence requirement for accessing OAS,[14] all of those proposals have been made by individual MPs and have never become the official position of any Canadian party.

Finally, when mapping the position of immigrants in the Canadian welfare state it is important to discuss the various programs designed specifically to improve the economic fortunes of immigrants. Once immigrants are admitted as permanent residents, they can make use of a wide range of federal and provincial settlement programs, most importantly language training, employment assistance, and skills development (Biles 2008; W. Wong 2008). Moreover, even though 2012 saw a small cut in the funding of settlement services, over a longer period of time the budget for integration services has increased significantly. A senior civil servant in the integration department characterized recent developments as follows:

> Our budgets have been growing quite dramatically ... The most recent motions in the House have just been to spend more money. The exceptional thing about settlement and integration is that while in many files ... different parties take different approaches, there seems to be a party-wide consensus on settlement and integration. The Liberals, Conservatives, and NDP all have been keen on doing more, doing it better, and doing it faster. (interview CAN12)

One barrier to integration that has recently received much attention is that the credentials of high-skilled immigrants are often not recognized by Canadian employers. According to some observers, this is one of the most significant obstacles to their successful economic participation (Ferrer and Riddell 2008; Girard and Bauder 2007; Reitz 2001). Canadian policy-makers have paid much attention to this issue. It has often come up in parliamentary debates and during election campaigns, and the last two decades have seen several initiatives to assist immigrants in having their qualifications recognized. The Liberal Martin government launched the Foreign Credential Recognition Program, and the subsequent Conservative government established the Foreign Credentials Referral Office within the immigration ministry. In January 2009, federal and provincial governments agreed on a Pan-Canadian Framework for the Assessment and Recognition of Foreign Qualifications. Overall, Canadian politicians have been eager to invest in facilitating the economic integration of immigrants, and they seemed to have become more eager over time.

All in all, then, three main observations characterize the story of recent developments in immigrants' inclusion in the Canadian welfare state. First, while the overall approach is inclusionary – most permanent residents enjoy practically undifferentiated and immediate access to welfare state benefits, as well as a wide range of settlement services – family migrants, temporary migrants, and undocumented migrants experience exclusion from certain programs and services. Second, over the last two decades this approach has not been subject to a backlash but has remained relatively stable. Only when politicians are concerned that program integrity is at stake – as in the case of welfare use by undocumented migrants, "bogus" refugee claimants, and family migrants on a sponsorship agreement – have we seen calls for exclusion. Third and finally, on the few occasions when the costs of immigration have become a widespread concern among politicians, the policy reaction has usually been to amend admission policy, not to restrict the social rights of newcomers who had already been admitted. For the sake of understanding these outcomes, the next section begins by investigating how the position of immigrants in the Canadian welfare state is most commonly discussed and understood.

Faulty Admission and "Bogus" Claimants: Framing Immigrants' Welfare Dependence

The first observation we should make about the political translation of immigrant welfare dependence in Canada is that the issue has not been as salient as in the other two cases examined in this book. Discussions of benefit use by immigrants certainly arise, but not as frequently as elsewhere.[15] More specifically, the issue has not received consistent and sustained attention in Parliament. This is illustrated in Figure 4.1, which shows the number of private motions, questions, and petitions that were tabled on the subject in the House of Commons between 1994 and 2012.[16] For one thing, we can see there has been little parliamentary activity regarding immigrants' access to and use of social benefits. Moreover, we see that the subject has been salient at only three points in time: in the mid-1990s, when Reform politicians frequently criticized the welfare costs of family migrants and undocumented migrants; in 2007, when members of the NDP repeatedly advocated a reduction in the residence requirement for OAS; and in the early 2010s, when opposition parties were criticizing the Conservative government's plans to reduce the health care entitlements of refugees and refugee claimants. Finally, it is worth observing that calls for inclusion have been more frequent than calls for exclusion, especially in recent years.

My interviewees in the civil service indicated that the subject of immigrant benefit use is rarely on the agenda in the Canadian bureaucracy. Perhaps more importantly, they also noted that when levels of welfare dependence are discussed, they appear as an indicator of (unsuccessful) economic integration, not as evidence that immigration poses a "drain." For example, a senior civil servant responsible

Figure 4.1. Questions and motions in Parliament advocating the expansion (black bars) and reduction (white bars) of immigrants' access to welfare state benefits in Canada, 1994–2012

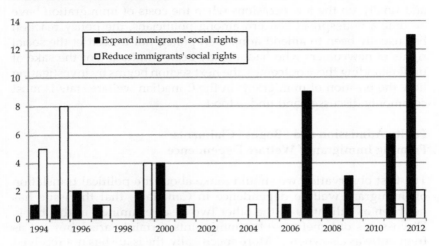

for integration services said that "[welfare use] is one factor that is looked at along with everything else. But it is not the driving force" (interview CAN12). A colleague responsible for admission policies made a similar point: "We don't spend a lot of time looking at the number of people among immigrants who are on welfare" (interview CAN11). And also at the ministry that administers all federally operated social programs in Canada, I was told that immigration is rarely discussed as a threat to the sustainability of the welfare state (interview CAN14). At the provincial level, the story is largely the same. Federal civil servants told me they rarely heard complaints about immigrant use of social assistance when negotiating with the provinces (interviews CAN11, CAN12). My interviewees in Ontario confirmed this. A senior civil servant at the department responsible for Ontario's social assistance program stated:

> Is immigration a cause for concern around the financial sustainability or integrity of the programs? No, we don't particularly feel that that is the case. We are looking at all sorts of things, but we don't have any indication to think so nor is there a political discourse currently that puts a spotlight on that as a reason for concern. (interview CAN21)

Finally, at the provincial ministry of Citizenship and Immigration there did not seem to be any indication of selective solidarity either:

> I don't necessarily worry that immigration is going to make the social assistance system collapse ... So definitely we talk about it, but [not] in terms of "Oh my goodness, the social assistance programs are under such pressure we will have to stop immigration." (interview CAN24)

At least as important as how much attention the subject receives is the way in which it is usually framed. A discourse analysis of parliamentary debates over the last two decades suggests that two frames are particularly common in the occasional criticisms of the social benefit costs incurred by immigrants. The first is to describe (some) refugee claimants and undocumented migrants as people who cheat the system and who thereby offend not only native-born Canadians but also established immigrants who *did* play by the rules as well as current applicants who are following the indicated procedures. This rhetoric was particularly common in the mid-1990s. A good example arose during the parliamentary discussion of immigration targets for 1997, when Val Meredith (RPC) argued that the extant refugee system was unable to properly protect itself against fraud: "Abusers of the systems are causing genuine refugees to be left fearing for their lives while these abusers jump the immigration queue and benefit from Canada's social and health programs" (House of Commons debate/29 October 1996). Equally illustrative is a comment from her party colleague Jay Hill, who mentioned media reports about undocumented migrants receiving welfare payments and commented that "Canadians are compassionate and would like to open their doors to legitimate refugees, but this abuse is an unacceptable drain on our already overburdened social programs" (House of Commons debate/31 January 1994). Provincial politicians made similar comments at that time. For example, in 1993 Cameron Jackson (OPC) complained that "[there are] illegal refugees, approximately 10,000 of them in the city of Toronto, who are on welfare" (Legislative Assembly of Ontario debate/8 July 1993). Similarly, Yvonne O'Neill of the Ontario Liberal Party (OLP) lamented that undocumented migrants could too easily access social assistance because of insufficient information sharing between welfare offices and immigration agencies (Legislative Assembly of Ontario debate/15 November 1994).

This discursive frame has reappeared in recent discussions about refugee claimants' access to health care. Tellingly, the name of the bill in which the proposed IFHP cut first appeared was the Preventing Human Smugglers from Abusing Canada's Immigration System Act. Conservative politicians frequently invoked the language of "queue jumpers" and "bogus refugees" in parliamentary debates. Ed Holder (CPC), for example, lamented that:

> The fact is too many taxpayer dollars are being spent on people who are not fleeing genuine persecution who instead seek to manipulate and take advantage of Canada's generous asylum system to receive lucrative taxpayer-funded health care, welfare and various social benefits. (House of Commons debate/23 April 2012)

Vic Toews (CPC), the public safety minister, defended the IFHP cuts in similar terms:

> The measures which our government is proposing are tough, but they are fair. They are fair to those who legitimately and legally wait, or have waited in line for a better life in Canada ... For those who want to jump the queue or target Canada for criminal gain, these measures are a message, clear and direct. (House of Commons debate/21 June 2011)

Again, it is worth emphasizing that the discursive strategy we see in these examples entails not only framing the targets of policy cuts as cheaters but also suggesting that the policy changes will somehow protect other immigrants in the country.

The second and even more pervasive frame in recent parliamentary discourse is to blame the costs incurred by the welfare system on defects in the immigration system, not on immigrants themselves. As mentioned earlier, concerns about immigrant welfare use have more often led to calls for changes to the admission policy than to immigrants' benefit access. Illustrative here is the following quote from Alice Wong (CPC), then parliamentary secretary for multiculturalism:[17]

> Hon. Members of the House know very well that this government is a strong advocate and supporter of the humanitarian division of our immigration program. [However,] we also face significant challenges ... We have a system where even the most straightforward successful refugee claims are currently taking too long to reach a decision. Unsuccessful refugee claimants regularly take over five years before they finish the various levels of appeals available to them. This is five years of federally funded

health care and provincially funded social programs, on top of court costs and IRB costs. (House of Commons debate/20 April 2009)

In sum, we can conclude that immigrant welfare is not a prominent subject on the agenda and that when it does come up, the costs tend to be blamed either on the admission system or on "queue jumpers" who make the system work worse for everyone. The discourse regarding immigrants already in the country has largely been inclusive and sympathetic.

A look at Canada's welfare system and national identity helps us understand this discourse. At first glance, Canada's liberal welfare regime would seem a fertile context for discussions about whether immigrants truly deserve the benefits they use.[18] In that light, it is unsurprising that it has been with regard to the residual means-tested program of social assistance that the benefit use of undocumented migrants (and more recently, refugee claimants) has come under the most scrutiny. Similarly telling is that in discussions about recent cuts to settlement services, the opposition insisted that integration services should not be viewed as a form of welfare. Gerald Kennedy (LPC), for example, objected to the cuts as follows: "These are not benefits, or money in their pockets. This is language training, assistance to connect and be successful" (House of Commons Debate/1 March 2011).

Recent concerns about refugees' access to health care seem at first glance more difficult to reconcile with our theoretical expectations. After all, while most of Canada's tax-paid social programs are means-tested, the health care system is an exception: according to the Canada Health Act, provincial governments are required to offer *universal* health care to their citizens and permanent residents. For this program, then, we should expect that some of the same theoretical propositions we made about universal welfare states apply: namely, that its structure leaves little room for differentiation, and that the universality principle enjoys much legitimacy among the population.[19] Part of the explanation is that the IFHP is a federal program, separate from the universal programs offered by the provinces. More importantly, the primary discursive strategy of advocates of the cuts has been precisely to argue that the IFHP violates the principle of universalism by offering refugees and refugee claimants more generous health care benefits than they do to native-born Canadians (see, among many examples, parliamentary contributions by Vic Toews on 21 June 2011; Rick Dykstra on 19 September 2011; Roxanne James on 13 June 2012; and Jason Kenney on 27 September 2012). On several occasions, Conservative parliamentarians explicitly framed opponents of the cuts as opponents of universalism. Sadia Groguhé and Paul Dewar (NDP), for example, received the following response from Rick Dykstra when they voiced criticism of the health care cuts:

> We believe they should get and deserve an equal health care system, the same kind of medicare that is offered across this country. If you think they deserve more than every Canadian why do you not stand up in the House and acknowledge that? (House of Commons Debate/11 May 2012)[20]

This strategy seemed to work, at least initially. In the past, advocates of generous entitlements for immigrants frequently invoked the health care system's universality principle. For example, when Art Hanger (RPC) criticized the health care costs incurred by HIV-positive refugee claimants, Mary Clancy (LPC) declared: "This government believes in health care for all Canadians. We believe in health care for people who come to this country" (House of Commons debate/5 May 1995). Some ten years later, Paul Szabo (LPC) made the same point in a general discussion about the Canadian health care system:

> There is universality. This means that health care is going to be available to all in Canada regardless of whether they are citizens or have landed status or, indeed, are refugees. People who are on our shores are going to have accessibility. Health care is going to be universally available to all those who are in Canada. That is our value. (House of Commons debate/14 April 2004)

The proposals for IFHP cuts, however, initially faced much less opposition. The government started to invoke the argument that refugees receive a better deal than native-born Canadians as early as June 2011, but it was not until September that any parliamentarian challenged this argument (see the NDP's Philip Toone's comments on 30 September 2011), and the opposition only started to become vocal in May 2012. Moreover, this opposition has been voiced largely by members of the NDP (and on occasion by BQ MPs), with Liberal MPs mostly remaining silent on the issue.[21] In sum, the Conservatives' appropriation of the universalism frame seems to have muted at least initial opposition to the cuts in refugees' health care services.

Overall, however, the structure of the welfare system helps explain only some aspects of the framing and tone of discussions about immigrants' social rights in Canada.[22] More important is the crucial position immigration occupies in Canada's national identity, which has weakened the purchase of any line of reasoning suggesting that "immigrants" as a group should not be entitled to the programs they use. As a settler society that has relied on immigration for demographic growth throughout its history (Kelley and Trebilcock 1998; Knowles 2007), the country is rightfully described as a "nation of immigrants." According to the 2016 Census, more than 27 per cent of the population over fifteen years old was born outside Canada, and another 15 per cent is made up of immigrants' children. A large portion of the Canadian population therefore identifies itself as immigrant. In the 2015 Canadian Election Studies, less than 17 per cent of respondents self-identified as "Canadian" in answer to the question "To what ethnic or cultural group do you belong?" It is perhaps unsurprising, then, that a welcoming and inclusive approach to newcomers has become a crucial component of "Canadianness."[23]

This understanding of national identity is reflected in Canada's commitment to policies of multiculturalism that recognize and accommodate immigration-induced diversity (Kymlicka 2003; Ryan 2010). As early as 1971, Canada declared itself a multicultural society, and in 1988 Parliament enacted the Multiculturalism Act aimed at protecting the cultural rights of ethnic minorities. Even the Canadian Constitution protects the principle of multiculturalism: Section 27 of the Canadian Charter of Rights and Freedoms (the first part of the Constitution, which outlines fundamental individual human rights) guarantees "the preservation and enhancement of the multicultural heritage of Canadians."

The central importance of diversity to Canada's national identity is apparent in parliamentary discourse as well. Politicians of all stripes often refer to immigration as a defining feature of Canada. In their 2015 campaign manifestos, the Liberals stated that "Canada's story is the story of immigration"; the Conservatives observed that "Canadians take immense pride in the fact that we are a nation of immigrants, and rightly so"; and the NDP referred to Canada's "proud tradition of welcoming newcomers" (Conservative Party of Canada 2015, 32; Liberal Party of Canada 2015, 62; New Democratic Party of Canada 2015, 8).

A telling example is the way then prime minister Jean Chrétien (LPC) finished the very first comment he made in Parliament after the terrorist attacks of 11 September 2001:

> Finally, I want to make another very important point. Canada is a nation of immigrants from all corners of the globe, people of all nationalities, colours and religions. This is who we are. Let there be no doubt. We will allow no

one to force us to sacrifice our values or traditions under the pressure of urgent circumstances. We will continue to welcome people from the whole world. We will continue to offer refuge to the persecuted. I say again, no one will stop this. (House of Commons debate/17 September 2001)

The public seems to have a similar understanding of what it means to be Canadian. Richard Johnston and his colleagues found that national-ist respondents in Canada actually tend to be *more* favourable to immi-gration and immigrants than their less nationalist counterparts (John-ston et al. 2010). More generally, in national surveys many respondents mention their country's stance on immigration and multiculturalism as a source of pride (Adams 2007, 86–7).

One such survey, Environics Focus Canada, asked respondents how important to Canadian identity they believed a variety of symbols to be. The results of the most recent wave of this survey are reported in Figure 4.2. More than 47 per cent of all respondents thought that mul-ticulturalism was "very important" to Canadian identity (with another 39 per cent answering "somewhat important"). As such, multicultur-alism was deemed only marginally less central to Canadian identity than the National Anthem and decidedly more important than hockey, bilingualism, or the Queen.

Figure 4.2. Views on importance of several symbols to Canadian identity, 2012

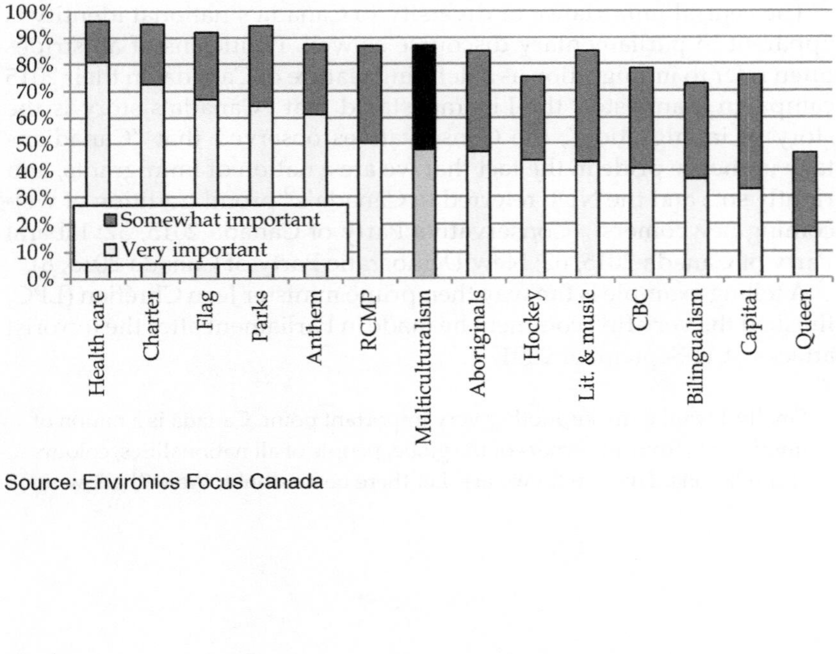

Source: Environics Focus Canada

In the context of these findings, it is instructive to look at a recent Canadian nationalist manifesto (Griffiths 2009). Titled *Who We Are*, the book is clearly presented as the Canadian counterpart to the American *Who Are We?* by Samuel Huntington (2004). But while author Rudyard Griffiths echoes some of Huntington's arguments concerning the importance of teaching national history and infusing public life with more nationalist symbols, his views on immigration are almost the complete opposite. In contrast to Huntington's alarmist discussion about the migration of Latin Americans to the United States, *Who We Are* is unreservedly positive about the role immigration has played in Canada's history (Griffiths 2009, 74–95). Indeed, Griffiths describes immigration as a source of national pride, boasting that "Canada has achieved the status of an immigration powerhouse" (81) and framing his country's stance on immigration as a key component of "Canadian exceptionalism" (Griffiths 2009, 79).

In a country where support for immigration goes hand in hand with nationalism, nationalist appeals for immigrant exclusion are clearly in vain. Indeed, proposals to restrict any aspect of Canadian immigration policy are typically met with references to Canada's history as a country of immigrants. For example, in opposing cuts to the budget for integration services, Justin Trudeau (LPC) began his contribution by stating that "our country was built on immigration" (House of Commons debate/1 March 2011). Parliamentary opposition to the previously mentioned Preventing Human Smugglers from Abusing Canada's Immigration System Act was similarly infused with nationalist rhetoric. We saw one example of this in chapter 2, namely, Saskatchewan premier Ed Wall's description of the bill as "un-Canadian," which was frequently repeated by opposition MPs (see, e.g., contributions by the federal Liberals' Ralph Goodale and the NDP's Jinny Sims on 26 November 2012). Other opponents of the bill used similar language. Liberal Jim Karygiannis argued that "one has to look back in our history and examine the people who have come to our country," and his party colleague Sean Casey described the bill as "purposely mean-spirited, divisive, and anti-Canadian" (House of Commons debate/20 September 2011 and 23 April 2012). The contribution by Raymond Côté (NDP) was perhaps most emphatic:

> Bill C-4 is not only an unacceptable affront to the human dignity of thousands of men, women and children, but it is also a threat to the Canadian values we hold in trust, a heritage reaching back thousands of years that

we cannot betray without serious consequences. (House of Commons debate/3 October 2011)

Politicians invoke nationalism not only in opposition to exclusionary measures but also when arguing for more *inclusion*. For example, Gurbax Malhi (LPC) suggested to ease the sponsorship requirements in family migration on the basis that "Canada is a multicultural country and immigrants are a great contribution to multiculturalism in Canada" (House of Commons debate/13 May 1999). Similarly, his colleague Colleen Beaumier (LPC) finished a plea to reduce the residence requirement for the universal pension program from ten years to three by saying: "I want to remind members of the House that Canada has been, remains, and always will be a country of immigrants" (House of Commons debate/23 October 2007). Olivia Chow (NDP), when proposing to expand the possibilities for family migration, argued that "it is un-Canadian to keep families separate" (House of Commons debate/30 September 2010). And Don Davies defended a similar bill by arguing "we all know that Canada is a nation of immigrants [...] This bill recognizes that history" (House of Commons debate/9 March 2011).

In sum, Canadian nationalism discourages people from viewing immigration as a negative phenomenon and immigrants as dangerous "others." Indeed, Canadians tend to have comparatively positive attitudes about immigration, including its impact on the welfare state (Adams 2007; Banting 2008; Crepaz 2008; Hiebert 2006; Jedwab 2008). It even appears that Canadians who believe that immigrants make heavy use of welfare benefits are more likely to support a redistributive welfare state than others (Banting, Soroka, and Koning 2013). All in all, there is little evidence that sentiments of selective solidarity are widespread among the Canadian electorate.

Moreover, as far as data availability permits us to draw firm conclusions, those sentiments seem to have become scarcer over time. Unfortunately, researchers have only occasionally surveyed Canadian respondents explicitly about immigrants' appropriate position in the welfare system. For example, the 2009 Transatlantic Trends found that 75 per cent of Canadians agreed with the statement that legal immigrants should be given the same access to social benefits as native-born citizens, and the 2010 wave of the same survey found that only 4 per cent supported making health care benefits an exclusive privilege for citizens (with fully 60 per cent indicating that even "illegal immigrants" should have access to health care). However, these questions have not

Figure 4.3. Anti-immigrant attitudes, 1977–2012

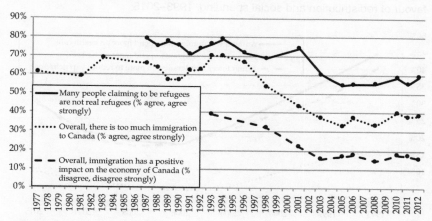

Source: Environics Focus Canada

been asked in different waves of the survey. The Canadian Election Studies asked respondents on five occasions (1997, 2000, 2004, 2008, 2011) whether they agreed with the statement that "we should look after Canadians born in this country first and others second." The percentage of people who answered "agree" or "strongly agree" decreased over time from over 50 in 1997 to less than 38 per cent in 2011,[24] which suggests that selective solidarity is indeed in decline in the country.

For a better sense of how public opinion has evolved over time, we can look at questions measuring more general attitudes towards immigration that have been asked repeatedly over a long period. Figure 4.3 shows the responses to three questions on immigration featured in successive waves of the Environics Focus Canada survey. Since the late 1990s, Canadians seem to have become less likely to think that overall immigration levels are too high, that most refugee claimants are not real refugees, and that immigration has a negative effect on the economy.[25] While this information does not constitute direct evidence on how views on immigrants' social rights have evolved, the striking similarity of the trend across three distinct immigration-related questions makes it plausible that those views have become more positive as well.

More support for that suggestion comes from an analysis that combines different questions from existing surveys. In every wave since 1993, Canadian Election Studies has asked respondents about their

Figure 4.4. Percentage of respondents who are opposed to immigration but in favour of redistribution and social spending, 1993–2015

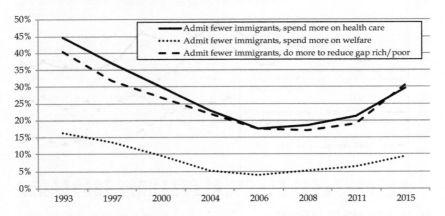

Source: CES, and author's calculations

views on both immigration levels and welfare state institutions. Figure 4.4 shows the percentage of people who argue that fewer immigrants should be admitted to the country but at the same time think that the government should spend more on health care (solid line), that the federal government should spend more on welfare (dotted line), and that more should be done to reduce the gap between the rich and the poor (dashed line). As with the other pieces of (indirect) evidence, this analysis suggests that Canadians display less selective solidarity today than they did twenty years ago, although the graph does seem to suggest an increase over the last ten years.

None of this is to suggest that concerns about immigrant welfare dependence are absent in Canada. A senior civil servant I spoke to rightfully pointed out: "There is lots of public opinion in Ontario that immigrants are a drain on the system. You just have to look at the *Globe*[26] chat rooms to see that" (interview CAN24). Moreover, a number of anti-immigrant interest groups, such as the Centre for Immigration Policy Reform and canadafirst.net, express strong objections to the costs incurred by immigration flows. And one can certainly find criticisms of immigrants' welfare use in public commentaries (Stoffman 2002, 88–93, 108–11), right-wing newspapers (Bissett 2011; Lilley 2011), and televised news (Ibbitson 2012). To be clear, the point is not that there are no immigration sceptics in Canada criticizing the "burden" that immigrants place on the welfare state. Rather, the observation here is that this group is relatively small and seems to be shrinking.

The immigration spokespeople for Canada's three largest federal parties shared this observation when asked about their perceptions of public opinion on this issue. The NDP's Don Davies, for example, told me that most Canadians have a "gut" preference for immigration (interview CAN02). Kevin Lamoureux (LPC) stated that "all in all, I think the vast majority of Canadians are okay with the way that immigration has served our country" (interview CAN03). Rick Dykstra (CPC), finally, was somewhat more cautious, saying that "I think that Canadians do worry about the cost of it ... They want to see that things are managed properly and money isn't wasted." But at the same time he stated that most Canadians would be opposed to a reduction in overall immigration levels: "There is a general consensus from a majority of the people across the country that ... we should leave those numbers where they are" (interview CAN01).

Given these perceptions, it is unsurprising that politicians do their best to position themselves as pro-immigrant in public. In a careful multi-method analysis of the 2004 and 2006 elections, Jerome Black and Bruce Hicks (2008, 254) concluded that "all of the parties worked to convey the impression that they valued immigration and immigrants." Perhaps even more strikingly, they found that when elections become more competitive, political parties try to outbid one another by moving their immigration policies in a more "permissive" direction (255). The dominant view among Canadian policy-makers today seems to be that immigration is a contribution to rather than a drain on the welfare system. All three of the immigration spokespeople I spoke to described immigration as a necessary resource for the future sustainability of the welfare state in light of declining population growth (interviews CAN01, CAN02, CAN03). Such comments can often be heard in Parliament as well.[27]

Concerns remain, of course, especially in two areas. The first of these is more about the immigration system than about immigrants themselves: the fact that refugee claims take a long time to be processed, and that applicants rely on state services in the meantime, still bothers politicians from left to right. And this concern does not only exist among politicians. According to senior staff I spoke to federally at CIC (interviews CAN11, CAN12) and provincially at the departments of social services (interview CAN21, CAN22) and immigration (interview CAN24), discussions about the costs associated with lengthy refugee determination procedures have been frequent within the civil service.

Second, to this day right-wing politicians criticize immigrants' benefit use when the perception arises that newcomers are in some way better treated than the native-born. We already saw one example of this, namely, in the recent attempt to repeal the supplementary health care benefits offered to refugee claimants under the IFHP. A second example can be drawn from the 2011 Ontario provincial elections. When the OLP led by premier Dalton McGuinty proposed offering tax credits to employers who hire recent immigrants, opposition leader Tim Hudak (OCP) denounced the plan as a form of positive discrimination. Within a week, the conservative challenger had drafted a radio ad arguing that the government cares more about newcomers than about native-born Canadians (Radwanski, Howlett, and Paperny 2011).

In order not to exaggerate the importance of these events, two qualifying remarks are in order. First, the political right actively tries to attract the immigrant vote and, despite the occasional flare-up of assimilationist rhetoric, it does so even more today than in the past. This has been noted not only by academics (Marwah, Triadafilopolous, and White 2013) but by politicians as well. In 2005, for example, Liberal MP Wajid Khan remarked sarcastically that "after years of making anti-immigrant statements, the Conservatives are now trying to cast themselves as pro-immigrant" (House of Commons debate/7 April 2005).[28]

Second, when the Conservatives or other right-wing organizations do criticize immigrants' place in the Canadian welfare state, they spur significant opposition. Perhaps the most instructive example in this regard is the reception of a recent study (Grubel and Grady 2011) by the Fraser Institute, a right-wing think tank that has repeatedly criticized Canada's immigration system for being too lax. The report, co-written by former RPC parliamentarian Herbert Grubel, concludes that the average immigrant poses a net fiscal drain of C$6,051 on the Canadian economy and suggests "severely limiting immigrants' access to the benefits of the welfare state" as a possible solution (Grubel and Grady 2011, 23).

These conclusions have not had the impact their authors might have hoped. The *Vancouver Sun* denounced the study as "incomplete" and "disingenuous" (Hume 2011), no politician echoed Grubel's concerns in Parliament, and only two months after the report's publication a network of immigration scholars and policy-makers published a response challenging its main findings (Javdani and Pendakur 2011).[29] Perhaps even more importantly, with the exception of the CPC's Rick Dykstra, all of my interviewees evaluated the report in negative terms. Lamoureux (LPC) simply said he didn't believe the conclusions (interview CAN03), while Davies' (NDP) rejection was more emphatic:

> Mister Grubel is a former member of a far-right party in our Parliament, and the Fraser Institute is an ideologically driven right-wing think tank in this country ... Instead of offering valid comment and research to the debate, they tend to have their conclusion in advance and then try to find the data to support it. (interview CAN02)

The senior civil servants I spoke with described the report as "flawed" (CAN11), "incomplete" (CAN14, CAN15), and "unrealistic" (CAN24), or simply referred to the study by Javdani and Pendakur for their views on the issue (CAN12).

The lack of support among politicians today for reducing immigrants' access to social programs and benefits also becomes apparent when we look at their views on the best way to avoid a large immigrant welfare clientele. Based on party manifestos, legislative behaviour, and personal interviews with each party's spokesperson on immigration, I determined how each of the three largest parties in the Canadian Parliament[30] assesses four possible strategies to achieve that goal: (1) restrict immigrants' access to social benefits, (2) make admission policies more selective, (3) invest more in integration assistance, and (4) implement across-the-board welfare retrenchment. Table 4.2 summarizes the findings.

The most striking observation is just how much politicians of different parties seem to be in agreement. For one thing, Dykstra, Davies, and Lamoureux all expressed support for continued investment in a formidable set of integration and settlement services. And while it is true that the CPC has been less supportive of programs aimed at cultural recognition than the NDP and the LPC (Ryan 2010), the Conservatives have been as eager as their political rivals to invest in programs designed to facilitate economic integration. Indeed, the budget for integration increased considerably when the Conservatives were last in power, with support from both the NDP and the Liberals.[31]

A second and even more relevant subject of consensus is that all three parties reject explicit differentiation in social rights between immigrants and native-born citizens (even though they do support the principle of the sponsorship mechanism for family migration). Certainly, there

Table 4.2. Political parties' views on four possible strategies to avoid/reduce immigrant welfare dependence

Party	Ideology	% seats, (2015 elections)	Restrict access to benefits?	More selective intake?	More integration assistance?	General welfare reform?
LPC	Liberal	54	No	Yes	Yes	Some
CPC	Conservative	26	Some	Yes	Yes	Yes
NDP	Social-dem.	11	No	No	Yes	No

are party differences on this subject. NDP politicians tend to be most adamant in rejecting reductions in immigrants' social rights and in fact frequently advocate *more* inclusion, such as expanding the labour rights of temporary migrants, reducing the residence requirement for the universal pension program, and offering additional benefits to victims of human trafficking (see House of Common debates on 27 November 2007, 30 May 2008, and 25 March 2011, respectively). The CPC, by contrast, has recently made some suggestions for benefit *exclusion*: it has called for reduced IFHP benefits for refugees and for a residence requirement on social assistance for refugee claimants. But overall, even the CPC does not actively advocate IEWRs as the best approach to avoiding a large immigrant welfare clientele. Dykstra (CPC) put it as follows: "Our emphasis isn't on placing restrictions once people are here. Our emphasis is on setting policy in place where those restrictions are unnecessary. [We prefer making] a decision at the front end versus having to regulate at the back end."

This comment echoes Canada's traditional strategy of employing a selective admission policy aimed at immigrants with high human capital who are unlikely to claim welfare services. In the 1990s the Liberal Chrétien governments increased the relative intake of economic migrants from around 40 to well over 60 per cent of the total inflow with the explicit aim of decreasing the pressure on social programs. The immigration minister at the time, Sergio Marchi, justified the increased reliance on economic migration as follows:

Consultations reveal that Canadians are concerned about the sustainability of Canada's social benefit system. The government is addressing that broader challenge by opening a dialogue on improving social security in Canada. For our part we will contribute to the solution by focusing more on those immigrants less likely to require public assistance. Changes to the sponsorship obligations and their more rigorous enforcement will enhance the fairness of access to social benefits. (House of Commons/1 November 1994)

The reliance on economic migration remained around the same level during the incumbency of the Conservative Harper government but has decreased somewhat (to about 52 per cent) since the advent of the Liberal Trudeau government. The NDP is the only Canadian party that seems to take exception to this preference for selective admission policies. The party has frequently objected to the stringent medical requirements applicants need to meet in order to enter the country (see, e.g., House of Common Debates on 20 September 2011 and 4 April 2012), rejected the heavy reliance of the Harper government on temporary migration as a replacement for permanent migrant streams (see below), and advocated a larger intake of refugees and (in particular) family migrants.[32]

Finally, the three parties differ predictably in their views on overall welfare retrenchment as a strategy for facilitating immigrants' integration. The Conservatives and (to a lesser extent) the Liberals generally favour limited state intervention in the market; indeed, both parties have recently cut social programs and reduced redistributive mechanisms while in power (Banting and Myles 2013; P.M. Evans 2002; Kneebone and White 2009). The social democratic NDP, by contrast, advocates a more expansive welfare state; more specifically, it rejects the idea that flexibilization of the labour market or overall retrenchment would facilitate the economic integration of immigrants (interview CAN02).

To wrap up, we have seen that the political translation of levels of immigrant welfare dependence is not as inclusionary as in Sweden, but still avoids the divisive and accusatory tone we will encounter in the Dutch case. The topic of immigrant benefit use does not arise as often as in other immigrant-receiving welfare states, and when it does, discussions tend to focus on faults in the admission system or to target those migrant groups that are easily framed as "queue jumpers" attempting to milk the system. All in all, the belief that immigrants' access to the welfare state should be curtailed certainly exists in Canada, but it is not particularly prominent, and its traction seems to have diminished over time. And while recent years did see some proposals for IEWRs, all political parties today reject differentiating between native-born citizens and immigrants who have already been admitted to the country with regard to access to social programs and benefits. The Canadian model of integration assistance and selective admission policies still seems to enjoy widespread support among today's parliamentarians.

Political Battles at the Margins of the Canadian Model

It is difficult to imagine that the Canadian approach to immigrants' social rights will change dramatically in the near future. This becomes clear when we consider the virtual absence of anti-immigrant politicians, the responses of mainstream politicians to occasional anti-immigrant rhetoric, and the legal hurdles that attempts at IEWRs would face.

To begin, Canada has never had an AIP resembling the ones that have entered the national parliaments of Austria, Denmark, the Netherlands, Norway, Sweden, and Switzerland. That said, some Canadian politicians have tried to attract the anti-immigrant vote. In the 2015 elections the Conservatives described refugee migration as a potential security threat, warned against the "barbaric practices" in some minority communities, and insisted that newcomers should be forbidden to wear a face veil during their citizenship ceremony (Andrew-Gee 2015). One of the most vocal proponents of these proposals, Kellie Leitch, ran for her party's leadership two years later, and distinguished herself most clearly from her opponents by maintaining a hard line on issues of (immigrant-induced) cultural diversity. In both cases, the political strategy did not work: the Conservatives lost the 2015 elections, and Leitch lost the party leadership race.

More successful was the short-lived Reform Party of Canada, which voiced objections to the costs of immigration more than any other party in modern Canadian history. The party sent its first member to the federal Parliament in 1989 in a by-election. In the elections of 1993, it managed to secure 52 of the 295 seats, and in 1997 it became the second-largest party in Parliament, winning 60 of 301 seats. In late 1999, however, the party started to join forces with other right-wing political parties and eventually became part of today's Conservative Party of Canada (Flanagan 2009).

In some respects the RPC was similar to Western European AIPs. For one thing, it was decidedly populist. Its leader, Preston Manning, hailed the "common sense of the common people" as the most useful guideline for political decision-making (Flanagan 2009, 20–36; Manning 2003), and Reform politicians often framed their policy positions accordingly. For example, Ian McClelland finished his plea to cut social assistance to asylum seekers who were appealing a rejection of their refugee claim by saying: "It is not meanspirited; it is merely common sense" (House of Commons debate/March 3, 1997). Just like AIPs in Western Europe, when Reform advocated restrictions in immigration policy it often did so in the name of democracy. Its 1989 election manifesto lamented that "there is perhaps no area of public policy where the views of Canadians have been more systematically ignored through the undemocratic structuring of political debate than the area of immigration" (Reform Party of Canada 1988, 25). In Parliament, RPC members frequently accompanied their pleas for lower immigration levels with public opinion polls that suggested the majority of voters agreed with them.[33] Generous immigration policies, meanwhile, were framed as serving only the "desires of a few special interests" (Art Hanger, House of Commons debate/25 February 1994).

A second way in which Reform resembled other AIPs is that it often raised objections to immigration in largely unrelated discussions. In a debate about emergency assistance to farmers, for example, Preston Manning argued that funds for such assistance would be amply available if the government stopped spending so much money on illegal immigration (House of Commons debate/3 November 1999). Similarly, when the House of Commons debated a proposal to ban the promotion of tobacco products, Ted White (RPC) made a few comments on the actual bill but then quickly changed the subject entirely and started to discuss illegal immigration (House of Commons debate/8 October 1998).

A third reason why Reform might be considered an AIP is that it attracted the support of anti-immigrant organizations and voters. Indeed, some observers have been able to trace connections between the Reform Party and overtly anti-immigrant organizations such as the National Citizens' Coalition and the Northern Foundation (Dobbin 1992, 105–38). Wolfgang Droege, leader and founder of the neo-Nazi movement Heritage Front, publicly commented that he saw the rise of the RPC as a reason for hope, and he was a member of the party until his membership became public knowledge (Dobbin 1992, 131; Flanagan 2009, 92). More generally, RPC voters tended to have more negative attitudes towards immigration and ethnic diversity than those who voted for other parties (Flanagan 2009 41, 148). Data from the Canadian Election Studies of 1993 and 1997, the only two elections in which Reform competed successfully, confirm this conclusion. As Table 4.3 illustrates, in both elections people who reported having voted for the RPC were

Table 4.3. Relationship between self-reported vote for RPC and anti-immigrant attitudes, 1993 and 1997

	1993 vote			1997 vote		
	RPC	Other	τ	RPC	Other	τ
Canada should admit fewer immigrants	74.6%	59.4%	**0.09	56.2%	42.8%	**0.09
Less should be done for racial minorities	48.8%	19.7%	**0.23	34.3%	11.8%	**0.21
We should look after native-born first	52.6%	46.3%	*0.04	62.5%	50.4%	**0.09
Too many immigrants do not want to fit in	76.4%	59.4%	**0.11	86.2%	63.3%	**0.21

Note: Table 4.3 reports summary data. (For the second statement, the percentage includes respondents who indicated that either "much less" or "somewhat less" should be done; for the last two statements, the percentage includes respondents who either "agreed" or "strongly agreed.") The tau-c coefficients, measuring the association between anti-immigrant sentiment and a vote for RPC, have been calculated on the basis of all available ordinal answer categories. Data are drawn from CES 1993 and 1997.

* Significant at level p < 0.05.
** Significant at level p < 0.001.

considerably and significantly more likely than other voters to think that admission levels should be lowered, that less should be done for racial minorities, that the native-born should receive preferential treatment, and that immigrants generally do not want to fit in.[34]

Despite these similarities, it is important to point out a number of crucial differences between the RPC and AIPs such as the Dutch PVV. First, the RPC never really promoted *selective* solidarity: with its squarely right-wing economic agenda (Dobbin 1992; Patten 1999), it did not combine its restrictive stance on immigration policy with support for generous social policies like most modern AIPs do. Second, immigration was never the number one concern on the RPC agenda: tax reduction, democratic reform, and (especially) symmetrical federalism were bigger priorities. Indeed, in RPC election manifestos and other party literature immigration policies tended to occupy a marginal space.[35]

Third, the RPC's electoral strategy in the area of immigration could be described by what Murray Dobbin (1992) calls "calculated ambiguity." While the party did try to cater to the anti-immigrant vote, it was careful not to scare more mainstream voters away in the process. The party elite weeded out overt racists,[36] and it steered clear of plainly discriminatory policy suggestions even when they were voiced by grassroots members.[37] Instead, the party tried to brand itself as a generally pro-diversity party. Between the 1993 and 1997 elections, for example, Reform recruited minority candidates in an attempt to shake off its xenophobic image.[38] Similarly, Reform politicians often prefaced their suggestions for restrictive reforms with a general pro-immigration statement. For example, Art Hanger, who as we have seen was one of the most vocal critics of immigration, repeatedly stated that he was "proud to be a citizen of a country that has gained an international reputation for its fairness, compassion and its acceptance of immigrants of all kinds" (House of Commons debate/2 February 1994).

In sum, the challenge Reform MPs posed to an inclusive approach to immigrants in Canada cannot be equated with the attacks we have seen Sweden Democrats level at the dominant approach in Sweden. Compared to most AIPs, the RPC spent less time priming immigration as an issue of concern, and it tended to frame its criticisms of immigration policies in less extremist and divisive terms. Much the same can be said about Kellie Leitch. On the one hand, she clearly pursued a populist electoral strategy proclaiming to defend "average Canadian workers" against "elites" and "insiders," and she attracted support from anti-immigrant voters and organizations. On the other hand, she paid little attention to the finances of immigration, never portrayed herself as a defender of social programs, and explicitly rejected any comparison to European anti-immigrant politicians (Minsky 2017a).

Not only have explicit anti-immigrant voices been rare in the Canadian House of Commons, the ones that did appear have also been met by a dismissive response. Other politicians have responded to restrictive suggestions by framing them as anti-immigrant and therefore as "un-Canadian" (see above).

Some scholars do argue that the Chrétien governments were affected by a "contagion effect," as evidenced for example by its increased reliance on economic migration, its introduction of a $975 fee for all new immigration applicants, and its reforms of refugee policy (Black and Hicks 2008). Politicians have made this argument as well. Reform's Art Hanger, for example, boasted that his party had "set the agenda in immigration policy" (House of Commons debate/16 November 1996). On the other side of the political spectrum, Osvaldo Nunez (BQ) accused immigration minister Sergio Marchi (LPC) of being "afraid of the Reform Party, and [...] becoming increasingly hard on immigrants and refugees" (House of Commons debate/6 April 1995), and Louise Hardy (NDP) criticized Liberal immigration plans by saying that "this government must advance policies that represent the values of

Canadian citizens rather than reacting to the hysteria of right-wing politicians" (House of Commons debate/27 May 1998).

The comments by Nunez and Hardy, however, are instructive not only in pointing at the limited contagion that did take place, but also in showing the dangers associated with such a strategy: opposition parties are likely to quickly detect a reorientation of immigration policy and frame it as mean-spirited and offensive to a large portion of the Canadian population.

In this light, it is unsurprising that even though the Liberals implemented more restrictive policies at the time of the RPC's ascendance, they certainly did not adopt a more restrictive tone in their discourse. In fact, the Liberals' most common response to Reform's immigration proposals was vehement and at times personal criticism. To give just a few examples, immigration minister Sergio Marchi characterized the RPC as "these customers who continue to spin mythology around immigration" (House of Commons debate/29 September 1994), Brian Tobin lamented that Reform promoted "an irresponsible attitude [...] with respect to Canada's immigrants [and] anybody who does not have a right-wing, narrow-minded, bigoted attitude about people in the country" (House of Commons debate/3 November 1994), and John Richardson accused the party of "fueling fear and hate [by] espousing an extreme Canada that is anti-bilingual, anti-multicultural, anti-rural, anti-immigrant, disunited, weak and Americanized" (House of Commons debate/3 October 1997). Lou Sekora simply called the RPC a "racist" movement (House of Commons debate/3 June 1999), and Sheila Copps went so far as to compare Preston Manning to American Ku Klux Klan leader David Duke (Herrington 1991). Other parties were no less aggressive in their accusations. Even members of the Progressive Conservative Party decried Reform's "racist and discriminatory policy on immigration and refugees" (David Price, House of Commons debate/5 June 2000). More recently, Kellie Leitch faced a similar response. Even prominent Conservatives denounced her platform as "dangerous," "anti-immigrant," and "un-Canadian" (Minsky 2017b; Zimonjic 2017).

In short, party politics are an important factor in explaining the political translation of immigrants' welfare costs in Canada. The only party in recent history that actively opposed immigration and multiculturalism was in Parliament for only a short period of time, rarely framed its critique as an attack on the immigrant population for abusing the welfare system, and received a hostile response from other parties in Parliament. In a country where about 13 per cent of parliamentarians are foreign-born,[39] and about 42 per cent of all residents over 15 are either immigrants or the children of immigrants, the view that the state should privilege native-born citizens enjoys little currency. In other words, we have seen few IEWRs in Canada not only because the political elite considers them undesirable, but also because it has nothing to gain electorally from implementing them.

This is not to say that the politics of left and right are irrelevant to the politics of immigrants' social rights, however. Of the twenty-six motions, petitions, and questions that were tabled in Parliament between 1994 and 2012 criticizing immigrants' use of or access to social programs and benefits, none were brought forward by the left-wing NDP, while the right-wing RPC was responsible for fifteen (see appendix Tables A2.1–A2.3). Conversely, of the forty-eight motions, petitions, and questions that advocated an expansion of immigrants' social rights, thirty were presented by the NDP and another fifteen by the LPC (see appendix Tables A2.4–A2.6).

Today, while all political parties embrace the core features of the Canadian model of immigration and welfare, there are strong disagreements between left and right about the practical interpretation of this model, especially in two areas. First, the right advocates much more rigorous admission policies than the left. According to Rick Dykstra (CPC), on this point there are no large differences between his party and the former RPC:

> [We] place more emphasis on one's ability, or the family's ability, to participate in Canadian society in a much quicker way ... And I'm not so sure it comes from Reform, or Alliance, or what have you. I think it is more a traditional view that is held by, I guess, ... the conservative people in the country, and that is that one's citizenship is to be honoured and one's citizenship is to be earned. (interview CAN01)

As we have seen, this "traditional view" entails support for heavy reliance on economic migration at the expense of family and refugee migration. The Liberal Trudeau government, by contrast, increased not only the overall intake of new migrants but also the relative reliance on family and refugee migration. The contrast between the Conservatives and the NDP on this issue is even starker. For example, NDP members have repeatedly opposed the policy of denying admission to people who are likely to need extensive health care, advocated giving everyone the opportunity to once in their life sponsor the migration of a family member who would not be eligible under the current system, and has been a strong supporter of extensive legal rights for refugee claimants during the application process.[40]

A second area of controversy is temporary migration. The Conservative party is a vocal proponent of the temporary foreign worker program (interview CAN01). The number of individuals on a temporary work permit more than doubled during the incumbency of the successive Harper governments, from roughly 152,000 in 2006 to 384,000 in 2014 (Citizenship and Immigration Canada 2015). Even though the Conservatives implemented some restrictions at the end of their tenure (in particular, enhanced requirements that employers demonstrate that no labour is available domestically before they can hire temporary migrants), they remained warm advocates of the program. By contrast, left-wing politicians in Canada – especially members of the NDP – are virulent critics of current temporary migration policies. Their objections are threefold: first, these migrants should have more options to receive permanent residence status; second, temporary migrants' weak labour rights and limited access to Employment Insurance and health care leave them vulnerable to exploitation; and third, a heavy reliance on temporary migration dampens domestic wages.[41] It is worth quoting Don Davies (NDP) at length:

First of all, it [the reliance on temporary migration] represents a significant departure from Canada's historic approach to immigration, which has been citizenship-track. This can be encapsulated by the slogan: "if you're good enough to work here, you're good enough to be a citizen here." ... There is a place for some intelligent niche Temporary Foreign Worker program. But not the way that this program has developed. This program has developed into, basically, a way to import cheap labour ... If they are exploited, and you know, they in a not insignificant number have been and are, they don't know where to access help or assistance. We deduct Canada Pension Plan premiums from them, Employment Insurance premiums from them, but they'll never get them, so there's a bit of an economic exploitation there ... The Canadian Restaurant Association [and] the agricultural sector in British Columbia ... claim they need to bring in people from Mexico to harvest their vegetables. Well, if you pay twenty dollars an hour, and had a health and welfare plan, and paid pension benefits, maybe you would have domestic Canadians who would come out and do that work. So the fact that they can bring in people from outside I think does have a wage-dampening effect in many industries. I think

that's maybe why the Conservatives like it, and why a number of employers want it. (interview CAN02)

Rick Dykstra's reaction when I presented these kinds of critiques
revealed just how politically sensitive the disagreements on temporary
migration are. He started by dismissing them as "red herring arguments" and "more fallacies than truths," and then proceeded to say:

> I think part of the problem when we talk about this issue, is that people
> forget what the title of the program is. It is a *temporary* foreign worker pro-
> gram. ... In large part it was never meant to be a program of citizenship.
> It was meant to be a temporary program where assistance was provided
> for a period of time to a specific business, to a system through the work
> season. So while I appreciate that there are also those on the sidelines look-
> ing in as to whether a program is successful or not successful, I would
> suggest that if you actually did an in-depth review and understanding of
> what this program has actually provided, you'll see that it is probably one
> of the most successful programs that this country has ever engaged in.
> (interview CAN01)

In sum, while the immigration file is certainly not free of controversy,
one would be hard-pressed to find a Canadian politician in today's
Parliament openly advocating reductions in overall admission levels,
significant cutbacks in integration services, or limits to immigrants'
access to social programs. Moreover, we have seen that when right-
wing politicians do voice suggestions for exclusion, the left does not
feel compelled to give concessions in a restrictive direction out of fear
for electoral repercussions. Since adopting an overtly anti-immigrant
stance can have serious negative electoral consequences (Marwah et al.
2013), we can consider the institutionalized support for immigrant
inclusion a non-trivial obstacle to IEWRs. An interesting consequence
is that politicians intent on implementing restrictive reforms sometimes
resort to the strategy of blame avoidance that has been observed in general social policy reform. For example, the Harper government tried
to obfuscate small cuts in the settlement budget by introducing them
as part of an omnibus budget bill. They used the same strategy for the
proposal to introduce residence requirements on social assistance for
refugee claimants.

The obstacles to IEWRs flowing from the legal system are at least
equally formidable. Canada is not bound by supranational law in the

same way that EU member-states Sweden and the Netherlands are; it is, however, party to the ICESCR, which prohibits discrimination (Article 2) and guarantees all residents the right to "social security, including social assistance" (Article 9). Federal law, in particular the Charter of Rights and Freedoms, is an even more important source of protection against immigrant exclusion. Besides the previously mentioned Section 27 on the protection of multiculturalism, the most relevant Charter rights for our discussion are the principle of non-discrimination (Section 15), the protection against "cruel and unusual treatment" (Section 12), and the "right to life, liberty, and security of the person and the right not to be deprived thereof except in accordance with the principles of fundamental justice" (Section 7). Finally, in Canada human rights are protected at the provincial level as well, which can pose yet another obstacle to differentiations between immigrants and the native-born in the extension of social rights. The Ontario Human Rights Code, for example, guarantees the "right to equal treatment with respect to services, goods and facilities, without discrimination because of race, ancestry, place of origin, colour, ethnic origin, [and] citizenship" (Section 1).

In two respects, the role of the judiciary in the legislative process is much larger in Canada than in the other two cases under study. First, judges in Canada have the power of judicial review and can therefore repeal new or existing laws if they find them to be in violation of the Constitution or provincial human rights legislation. This also means there is considerable space for legal activists to fight exclusionary reforms.[42] For example, the United Food and Commercial Workers International Union has since 2003 been involved in a (so far unsuccessful) attempt to prove that the exclusion of temporary foreign workers from Employment Insurance violates Charter Section 15 (Basok and Carasco 2010, 357–8). As we saw above, activists have been more successful in fighting the cuts to the IFHP program and have convinced the Federal Court that they violate Section 12 of the Charter (*Canadian Doctors for Refugee v. Canada*, 2014). And if the Conservatives had been re-elected in the 2015 elections, their proposals for residence requirements on refugee claimants' access to social assistance would likely have faced similar legal contestation (Vincent and Benzie 2014).

Second, the Canadian legal system is based on the common law tradition in which precedent-setting court decisions constitute a form of legislation. An instructive example for our present discussion is the 1985 Supreme Court of Canada verdict that denying an oral hearing to a refugee claimant constitutes a violation of Section 7 of the Charter (*Singh v. Minister of Employment and Immigration*; see Kelley and Trebilcock 2010, 402–4).[43] On several occasions, politicians have blamed this court decision for the high costs of the refugee system (see, e.g., the contributions by the CA's Randy White, House of Commons debate/27 February 2001; and Ted White, House of Commons debate/31 March 2003). Tony Valeri (LPC) went so far as to suggest repealing Charter rights for refugee claimants altogether (House of Commons debate/22 February 1995).

Furthermore, the federal nature of Canada's welfare system offers a legal safeguard against IEWRs. The Canadian Health and Social Transfer, a federal block transfer that helps fund provincial welfare programs, prohibits any residence requirement for access to social assistance. In 1995, when the province of British Columbia was faced with a sudden influx of interprovincial migration, its provincial government tried to implement a three-month waiting period for newcomers but was forced by the federal government to drop it (National Council of Welfare 1997). For that reason, if the OPC had won the 2011 elections in Ontario, it is unlikely that it would have been able to implement its proposal to "require welfare recipients to be residents of Ontario for one year before collecting benefits" (Ontario Progressive Conservative Party 2011, 30). Besides the unlikelihood that it would survive a human rights challenge, such a proviso would undoubtedly be challenged by the federal government (interview CAN21).

All in all, then, immigrants' access to and reliance on welfare programs have not featured prominently on the Canadian political agenda. While both matters did receive some attention in the mid-1990s – and certainly, some Canadians think that immigrants place a burden on the welfare system – from a comparative perspective political interest in the subject has been small. Equally importantly, whenever the welfare costs of immigration have become a topic of discussion, they have been carefully framed as an indication that admission policies are not working properly, not as evidence that immigrants who have already been admitted to the country are lazy welfare cheats. As we saw in chapter 2, part of this positive reception has something to do with objective economic reality: in comparison to their counterparts in other Western countries, immigrants in Canada tend to be successful in their economic integration and to place little demand on welfare state programs and benefits. But for a more complete explanation we need to look beyond economic facts – after all, even now that immigrants experience more problems on the labour market, the political translation remains largely unchanged. Much of this has to do with the central role that immigration plays in Canada's history and national identity, which makes calls to differentiate between immigrants and the native-born unlikely to surface. Moreover, Canadian politics does not feature a European-style AIP to criticize the overall inclusive approach to immigration and immigrant rights. As a result, there has been a striking degree of policy stability over the last two decades. The Canadian model of taking in a large but carefully selected group of immigrants, offering them extensive integration and settlement services, and providing permanent migrants with the same social protections as native-born citizens, thus seems likely to persist in the future.

The Canadian case highlights the theoretical significance of both political translation and anti-immigrant politics in any explanation of immigrant-excluding welfare reforms. Clearly, concerns about immigrants' use of benefits are not particularly central to Canadian politics, and when they do arise in political discussion, they are more often explained as a consequence of defects in admission policies than blamed on the recipients themselves. Few politicians express interest in disentitling migrants from benefits, not in the least because such attempts carry considerable electoral risks. The result has been a political history of very few efforts to reduce immigrants' entitlements, and even fewer successful ones.

Chapter Five

Netherlands: The Sudden Surge of Selective Solidarity

Students of immigration politics are paying increasing attention to the Netherlands. This is not surprising. After fifty years of experience with large-scale immigration, about 22 per cent of the Dutch population is now either a first- or second-generation immigrant (CBS), and the Netherlands hosts a larger proportion of Muslims than any Western European country except France (Pew Research Center 2012). More important than these raw demographic figures, the nature of Dutch immigration politics has changed drastically over the last twenty years or so. In the mid-1990s the Netherlands had among the most generous immigration policies in the Western world and mostly employed a consensus-oriented and depoliticized approach to immigration policy-making, but in the new millennium immigration has become one of the most prominent and controversial topics on the political agenda. Within just a few years, two prominent immigration critics were assassinated, anti-immigrant parties achieved unprecedented electoral success, and immigration policies became much more restrictive. Compared to twenty years ago, it is now much harder to be admitted to the Netherlands as a family migrant or a refugee, to acquire Dutch citizenship, and to live on Dutch territory without being pressured to conform.

The social rights of immigrants have not survived this restrictive climate unscathed. Starting with a 1998 exclusion of undocumented migrants from social services, the last two decades have seen the adoption of a series of IEWRs. Today, only immigrants with the most robust status are entitled to welfare benefits, and only after they have spent considerable time in the Netherlands and successfully participated in integration and language classes. These policy changes reflect a transformation in the political translation of the subject. In 1996, junior minister Elizabeth Schmitz observed "a foundation of solidarity" towards immigrants among Dutch politicians and citizens (TK13–845, 16 October 1996). Thirteen years later, former immigration minister Rita Verdonk bluntly stated that the Dutch welfare state should only support "citizens" who subscribe to "Dutch norms and values" (TK70–5531, 31 March 2009). In the streets, in the bureaucracy, and in Parliament, one is today bound to encounter the sentiment that the Dutch state owes more to its native-born citizens than to newcomers on its territory.

Unsurprisingly, the Mediterranean refugee crisis brought concerns about the costs of immigration into the political spotlight. At the height of the crisis, conservative prime minister Mark Rutte argued that the only way to manage the intake of refugees would be by reducing new-comers' social rights. And this line of reasoning was not confined to the political right. Labour minister Jeroen Dijsselbloem warned that if the inflow could not be managed at the EU level, "we should be prepared to protect our society and make sure that it will not lead to disruption of our welfare state" (Isitman 2015).

This chapter traces this sudden surge in selective solidarity and the social policy changes it triggered. What we will see is that immigrants' reliance on social benefits has become a high priority on the political agenda and, more importantly, is increasingly framed as the fault of immigrants themselves. At its most benign, immigrant welfare depen-dence has been explained as a sign that immigrants are particularly likely to be caught in a welfare trap and should therefore be "helped" by being pushed off benefits. In other cases, it has been used to fuel the stereotype that immigrants are generally lazy and have an innate tendency to cheat the system. This accusatory and divisive discourse seems difficult to understand at first glance, considering the historical insistence on tolerance, diversity, and solidarity in Dutch social policies. But the sudden success of anti-immigrant politicians thanks to favour-able political and social conditions has challenged this tradition. Not only has the anti-immigrant movement become a powerful player in Dutch politics, but it has also convinced mainstream parties to com-promise and to move in a more restrictive direction out of electoral considerations. In this political context, IEWRs have become a widely accepted policy tool for reducing immigrant welfare use. We will see that exclusionary reforms typically pass with handsome majorities, fac-ing little opposition from progressive parties or societal movements. At the same time, the scope of IEWRs has been constrained by legal roadblocks, in particular by the imperatives of EU law and the ECHR.

This chapter is structured as follows. The next section reviews seven ways in which the Dutch welfare state has become less inclusive of its immigrant population. After that, I describe the change in the political translation of patterns of immigrant welfare use. The final section discusses the key role that anti-immigrant politicians have played in these developments, while simultaneously pointing out that many attempts at IEWRs have been thwarted by legal obstacles.

A Recent History of Immigrant-Excluding Welfare Reforms

In the mid-1990s one could still describe the history of immigrants' formal position in the Dutch welfare state as one of the gradual extension of social rights. In 1993 Menno Vellinga wrote: "Once the immigrants have been legally admitted, they enjoy the same rights and obligations in the economic and social spheres as Dutch nationals" (Vellinga 1993, 156). Three years later Rinus Penninx (1996, 193) reached the same conclusion: "In general, equality for immigrants in this field has been reached" (see also Lucassen and Penninx 1997, 154). Only a decade later, those conclusions had become outdated. Writing in 2004, Godfried Engbersen describes the recent trend as "not in the direction of inclusion, but exactly of exclusion of unwanted migrants" (Engbersen 2004, 33). More recent developments support Engbersen's observation. I will describe seven examples of this restrictive turn.

First, the social rights of undocumented migrants have been stripped away almost entirely. The centre-left Lubbers-III cabinet was the first to state (in 1989) that more needed to be done to prevent undocumented migrants from making use of social benefits and programs (see Table 5.1 below for an overview of Dutch cabinets since 1986). It asked a parliamentary committee (named Zeevalking after its president) to investigate the issue, and it increased identification control in the administration of benefits (Minderhoud 2004). The successor "Purple" cabinet (an alliance of the "red" of the social democratic party PvdA and the "blue" of the conservative party VVD) continued down this road, promising in its 1994 coalition agreement to develop a law to formally disentitle all foreigners without a legal residence permit. In 1995 the government lived up to its promise and proposed a first version of the law, named the Linking Act (*Koppelingswet*) in reference to the link it entailed between social rights and legal residence in the Netherlands. After several parliamentary debates, consultations with advisory organs,[1] and legislative amendments, the law passed in November 1996 and went

Table 5.1. Cabinets of the Netherlands, 1986–2017

Administration	Political complexion	Takes office	Coalition parties	Majority/minority (initial House seats of total 150)
Lubbers II	Center-right	1986/07/14	CDA, VVD	Majority (81)
Lubbers III	Center-left	1989/11/07	CDA, PvdA	Majority (93)
Kok I	Purple*	1994/08/22	PvdA, VVD, D66	Majority (92)
Kok II	Purple*	1998//08/3	PvdA, VVD, D66	Majority (97)
Balkenende I	Right	2002/07/22	CDA, LPF, VVD	Majority (93)
Balkenende II	Center-right	2003/05/27	CDA, VVD, D66	Majority (78)
Balkenende III	Center-right	2006/07/07	CDA, VVD	Minority (71)
Balkenende IV	Center-left	2007/02/22	CDA, PvdA, CU	Majority (80)
Rutte I	Right	2010/10/14	VVD, CDA (PVV#)	Minority (52/76#)
Rutte II	Purple*	2012/11/05	VVD, PvdA	Majority (79)

* In Dutch politics, the label purple is used to refer to coalitions of the social democratic PvdA (which uses red as its party colour) and the conservative VVD (blue). # While the PVV was not a formal coalition partner in the Rutte-I cabinet, it provided "guaranteed support" for the government's agenda in exchange for policy concessions.

into effect on 1 July 1998. Since then, undocumented migrants have been barred from all social benefits and provisions with the exception of education for under-aged children, legal counselling, and emergency medical care.

In recent years there has been much political attention to the rights of denied refugee claimants. Some Dutch municipalities offer these individuals modest accommodation as a way to provide a minimum standard of living and to counter homelessness. In 2015 the political right started to harshly criticize these "bed, bath, and bread" arrangements and advocated cutting the funding of any municipality that offered them. The issue almost led to a government crisis (because coalition partners VVD and PvdA took opposite positions in the debate) and is certain to resurface in future coalitions (Couzy 2016).

Refugees whose claims have not yet been decided have also been targeted. The 1987 Arrangement Accommodation Asylum Seekers (*Regeling Opvang Asielzoekers*) and the subsequent 1994 amendment excluded asylum seekers from all general social services and programs (and from the labour market as well). Instead, all refugee claimants were to be placed in so-called asylum centres with some pocket money and access to health care services for as much time as the authorities needed to determine their status (Minderhoud 1999). The conditions in those centres were deliberately kept as modest as possible.[2] As of 2000, asylum seekers whose claims had failed had to leave the Netherlands within four weeks, after which they lost their benefits and faced arrest (Meyers 2004, 100). And in 2011, the level of pocket money for asylum seekers with large families was reduced by almost 20 per cent (TK19637–1421, 19 May 2011).

Asylum seekers are not the only temporary migrants for whom benefits have become less accessible. The Dutch welfare state distinguishes three types of benefits: (a) employee insurance programs (*werknemersverzekeringen*) such as unemployment benefits and disability benefits, which are accessible to everyone working in the Netherlands and paying premiums; (b) public insurance programs (*volksverzekeringen*) such as child benefits and pension benefits, for which one qualifies either by working in or being a long-term resident of the Netherlands; and (c) social provisions such as social assistance, which are available to long-term residents only. As will be clear, the interpretation of "long-term resident" is relevant here. The meaning of this term has developed over time as the result of jurisprudence, but politicians have been eager to establish formally that public insurance programs and (in particular) social provisions are *not* intended for people with an ephemeral connection to the Netherlands. The 1999 Decision Expansion and Reduction Insurance Sphere Public Insurance Programs (*Besluit Uitbreiding en Beperking kring verzekerden volksverzekeringen*) formalized that people who do not work in the Netherlands must be long-term residents in order to qualify for public insurance programs – international students, for example, are explicitly excluded (Article 20). In 2006 a sweeping social assistance reform explicitly stated that only people with a "durable connection" to the Netherlands are eligible.[3] While these formalizations of existing practices had few practical implications, their political portent was clear.

Third, even the social rights of family migrants and labour migrants have been limited in a number of regards. A prominent example of this is closely related to the above-mentioned considerations regarding temporary migrants. Immigrants to the Netherlands can receive a permanent residence permit only after a prolonged period of time in the Netherlands. For economic migrants, this residence requirement is five years, during which their status is that of a temporary immigrant. People who arrive through the family reunification stream are even more vulnerable in their first years in the Netherlands: their right of residence is dependent on the partner who sponsors them, which means not only that they have no access to any benefits, but also that they must leave the country if the relationship breaks down. This period of "partner-dependent right of residence" was originally three years but was increased to five years in 2012 (32175–21, 17 February 2012).[4]

The residence requirement for a permanent residence permit has consequences for migrants' access to social benefits. As a senior civil servant at the Department of Social Affairs put it, "you can simply make more stringent demands concerning reintegration and access to provisions of people who do not have a permanent residence status" (interview NET13). In other words, the five-year waiting period before migrants can become permanent residents basically implies that social provisions such as social assistance have a five-year residence requirement as well – unless, again, the applicant has a demonstrable "durable link" to the Netherlands. The only immigrants who are exempted from this restriction are recognized refugees: they too have to wait five years before they can acquire a permanent residence permit, but they are eligible for social provisions in the interim.

The residence requirement for social provisions applies to migrants from within the EU as well. In some respects these individuals hold a privileged position in the Dutch welfare state compared to immigrants from outside the EU. To the chagrin of many politicians,[5] they can more easily take Dutch insurance benefits with them when they leave the Netherlands (see below), and they are allowed to count the time they have worked in their country of origin in calculating eligibility for employee insurance programs. But in accessing social provisions, they face the same obstacles as other labour migrants, even though the legal technicalities are slightly different (Kremer 2013, 82–3). In accordance with EU directive 2004/38, no EU citizen has the right to claim benefits in another EU member-state in the first three months of residence. After that period, EU citizens can technically apply for social assistance. However, ever since the 2006 social assistance reform, until they have permanent residence status (which takes at least five years), they can be removed from the Netherlands if they pose an "unreasonable burden" on social assistance. In practice, this means that even for EU migrants there is a five-year residence requirement for complete access to social assistance. After all, as a civil servant explains, "the mere fact that you claim welfare is [usually interpreted as] enough indication that you do not have sufficient means of supporting yourself, and thus that you can be sent back to your country of origin" (interview NET15). In 2012 the government took this restriction one step further and introduced a pilot project in the border municipality of Vaals that involved testing every EU migrant applicant's residence status before any welfare benefit was paid out, thereby depriving applicants of assistance for the duration of the administrative procedure (see 35–12, 13 December 2012).[6] This pilot has since been rolled out in the city of Rotterdam, and the results are likely to inform future legislation.

In contrast to social provisions, public insurance programs are immediately accessible to immigrants. This is *only* the case, however, if they are employed. Family migrants with children, for example, are ineligible for child benefits for the first five years after they arrive, unless they find employment. And even working migrants face some residence requirements. For example, since 1991 a special health care benefit that funds health care costs that are not covered by health insurance (*Algemene Wet Bijzondere Ziektekosten*) has had a residence requirement of one month for each year that the person has not lived in the Netherlands or another EU country, with a maximum of twelve months. Naturally, the stepwise nature of Dutch immigration law is of little relevance for access to employee insurance programs. After all, like native-born Dutch people, migrants build up the right to these programs by working in the Netherlands.[7]

A fourth example of recent attempts in the Netherlands to reduce immigrants' access to social programs regards the universal pension program (*Algemene Ouderdomswet*). To qualify for a full pension, one needs to have lived in the Netherlands uninterruptedly from ages fifteen to sixty-five. Every missing year results in a 2 per cent decrease in the pension benefit. Inevitably, then, many elderly immigrants have a "gap" in their pension benefit. Those immigrants who for that reason fall below a certain income threshold are eligible for a specific type of social assistance called Supplemental Income Provision Elderly (*Aanvullende Inkomensvoorziening Ouderen*, or AIO). In 2006 about 5 per cent of all Dutch residents above the retirement age made use of this supplement, all of whom with an international work history (SVB 2007a). Until recently, many politicians expressed worries about the relatively low level and, in particular, low uptake, of the AIO. In 2004, for example, after a motion by Fatma Koşer Kaya (of liberal party D66), the government transferred the administration of the AIO from the municipal welfare offices to the executive agency administering public insurance programs. The explicit aim of this rearrangement was to increase the take-up of this benefit among elderly migrants who were entitled to it.

In recent years, however, the AIO has often been described as unreasonably generous and expensive, and not only by right-wing parties. In 2007 the centre-left Balkenende-IV cabinet asked a number of governmental and non-governmental research agencies to investigate the feasibility of compelling all incoming migrants to "buy in" their public pension gap on entering the Netherlands. Ultimately, the government decided against such a compulsory buy-in[8], but the opposition to the AIO remained strong.[9] In 2011, Parliament passed a law to reduce the level of this benefit, fully aware that this would affect mainly immigrant elderly.[10]

Fifth, most parliamentary parties have begun formulating objections to the "export" of social insurance programs – that is, to the practice of paying out benefits to people who do not reside in the Netherlands, either because they paid premiums in the past (as in the case of insurance programs) or because they are considered to have a strong connection to the Netherlands (as in the case of child benefits for children who temporarily live abroad while their parents are still in the Netherlands). The first sign of this trend was the Limitation on the Export of Benefits Act (*Wet Beperking Export Uitkeringen*, better known as *Wet Beu*[11]), which went into effect in 2000. The law introduced a "territoriality principle," which implies that insurance benefits can only be exported to EU member-states and countries with which the Netherlands has a bilateral social security agreement (SVB 2007b). Moreover, the law made it far more difficult to export most employee insurance programs (UWV 2007).

The adoption of the *Wet Beu* did not mute politicians' concerns about the export of benefits. A 2011 welfare reform reduced the period during which one can receive social assistance and the AIO benefit abroad to four and eight weeks, respectively. Later that year a large parliamentary majority passed a bill introducing a "country of residence principle" (*woonlandbeginsel*) for the export of child benefits; this adjusted the level of the exported benefit to the standard of living in the country where the recipient resides.[12] During the debate, MPs of coalition parties repeatedly indicated that these restrictions did not yet go quite as far as they would like. Matthijs Huizing (VVD), for example, described the bill as "merely a stopover" en route to more restrictive legislation (22–14, 10 November 2011). And indeed, more restrictions followed. Since 1 January 2014, the country of residence principle has applied to the public pension benefit as well, and child benefits are no longer exported to countries outside the EU with which the Netherlands does not have bilateral social security agreements. Moreover, the successive Rutte governments have attempted to renegotiate the social security agreements with countries that host large numbers of Dutch benefit export recipients with the precise aim of ending the export of benefits to those countries. Negotiations with Morocco proved difficult, and in February 2016 Parliament voted in favour of repealing the bilateral agreement altogether. (Before the implications of this repeal would have come into effect, however, the Netherlands and Morocco were able to renegotiate the agreement.)

Sixth, integration policies in the Netherlands have become decreasingly generous. For the present discussion, two aspects are especially relevant. First, access to a number of benefits has become conditional on successful participation in integration and language classes. Rita Verdonk (at that time VVD immigration and integration minister) was one of the first politicians to suggest (in 2003) cutting the social assistance benefits of immigrants who had not integrated "well enough," but the government did not stay in power long enough for her to execute these plans. Three years later, her suggestion was taken up by PvdA parliamentarians Jeroen Dijsselbloem and Saskia Noorman-Den Uyl, who proposed compelling several groups of immigrants to acquire "sufficient oral and written skills in the Dutch language and knowledge of Dutch society" or risk losing their benefits. The affected groups were social assistance recipients for whom a lack of language skills was proving a barrier to finding employment, social assistance recipients with underage children, and "old-comers" (typically the generation of guest workers who came to the Netherlands in the 1960s and 1970s) in receipt of unemployment or disability benefits (kst-30308–66, 21 June 2006). These suggestions were incorporated into Dutch integration law in December 2006. In 2010, Stef Blok (VVD) introduced a private bill that would have made proficiency in Dutch at the (fairly low) A2 level a condition for access to social assistance benefits, excluding even refugee migrants who would not meet this threshold (kst-32328–2, 4 March 2010). Even though new elections were called before the bill was passed, the subsequent government took up this suggestion and (a slightly amended version of) the law came into effect in January 2016 (Groenendijk and Minderhoud 2016). Finally, in its 2010 coalition agreement the first Rutte cabinet displayed its desire to take the requirement to fit in one step further by stating it would also cut social assistance benefits "in case the behaviour or clothing of someone factually reduces his [*sic*] chances on the labour market" (Government of the Netherlands 2010b).[13]

Besides coupling access to welfare benefits to integration, Dutch policy-makers have also scaled down the number of immigrant-targeted services they are willing to fund. Successive governments have abolished virtually all labour market programs for immigrants, as well as other immigrant-targeted programs such as state-funded interpretation services in health care and affirmative action programs such as preferential hiring of immigrants in the public service. Indeed, the budget for integration has been cut so deeply that a senior civil servant commented somewhat sarcastically: "If you add up everything and end up at 500,000 euro, it would be much" (interview NET11). The government has even become unwilling to pay for the integration classes that immigrants are required to take. The centre-left Balkenende-IV cabinet started asking immigrants to cover part of the expenses, and the Rutte-I cabinet went even further. In a comprehensive integration reform (which also increased fines for not passing integration exams, reduced the period during which immigrants were expected to complete their integration course, and cut societal counselling for refugee migrants), the right-wing government decided to ask all immigrants (including refugees and family migrants) to pay the entire bill for their mandatory integration and language courses. State loans are available to those who do not have sufficient resources.

Finally, in addition to all of these formal measures to restrict immigrants' access to welfare state benefits, the Dutch Parliament has become increasingly attentive to the strict enforcement of those rules. The first signs of this trend became visible after the implementation of the Linking Act. Several politicians complained in Parliament about municipalities that were making exceptions and were extending some benefits to undocumented migrants. For example, when in 2000 the city of Amsterdam offered welfare to migrants who had been in the Netherlands since before 1992 but had lost their residence status as a result of recent legislative changes (often referred to as "white illegals"), Joop Wijn of Christian democratic party CDA suggested reducing intergovernmental transfers to Amsterdam and all other municipalities that similarly violated the Linking Act. Similarly, parliamentarians have repeatedly advocated strict enforcement of the residence requirement of five years on access to social assistance, however "durable" an immigrant's link to the Netherlands might be. In June 2008, Eddy van Hijum (CDA) and Hans Spekman (PvdA) introduced a motion to that effect, which passed with an overwhelming majority (about 93 per cent). A year later, Jan Jacob van Dijk (CDA) again urged the government to enforce the five-year requirement strictly: "We are very worried about this. How will the members of government make sure that someone who has worked here [less than] five years but is not a Dutch citizen will not be claiming welfare? We are worried about the consequences for the Dutch social security system" (kst-1750–368, 26 February 2009).[14] It is unsurprising, then, that governments feel compelled to frequently reassure Parliament that it is not true that "too many foreigners are making use of benefits" (see, e.g., 34–3-12704, 21 January 2009; 35–3-13416, 18 September 2009; or 35–2, 13 December 2012), and even to boast about the number of residence permits it terminated on the basis of excessive welfare use (29407–149, 28 August 2012).

All in all, over the last twenty years the Dutch welfare state has become decidedly less inclusive of the growing immigrant population. A wide range of reforms have restricted access to benefits for all categories of newcomers, limited the possibility of taking benefits across borders, and abolished or downsized social programs that had been designed specifically to assist immigrant integration. While the first of these reforms were implemented in the mid-1990s, the push to differentiate in social rights between immigrants and native-born citizens has become especially pronounced over the last ten years or so. Very quickly, the Netherlands has undergone a far-reaching metamorphosis in its approach to the social rights of newcomers.

From Taboo to Cliché: Increasing Concerns about Immigrants' Welfare Dependence

The transformation in public policy reflects a change over the last two decades in the political translation of the subject of immigrant welfare dependence. First, and most obviously, the issue has attracted more and more attention in recent years. In keeping with the Dutch tradition of depoliticization (Lijphart 1968), immigration was for a long time kept off the political agenda (Lechner 2008, 150; Scheffer 2007, 49–50). Indeed, it had long been considered taboo – even racist – to criticize any aspect of immigration or multiculturalism in political debate (Entzinger 2006, 133; Lechner 2008, 150). Paul Ulenbelt (SP) remembers the reaction when his party first voiced concerns about immigrant integration in 1984:

> At that time, [our party] said: "this is not going well at all" ... We even said back then: "Everything that people have built up in terms of social

premiums, they can take that with them if they return to Morocco, Turkey, or wherever. They can use that money to build up something over there." Well, the SP was then categorized as fascists. That was considered right-wing. (interview NET05)

Similarly, when a new political party that placed immigration critique at the centre of its election manifesto gained electoral representation in 1989 (see below), the mainstream response was to denounce it as the political branch of a dying breed of neo-Nazism.

Slowly, however, immigration critique started to gain traction in political discourse. Government reports explicitly flagged immigration-related problems – including the costs immigrants were placing on the welfare state (Government of the Netherlands 1994) – and similar arguments were disseminated by public commentators (Lakeman 1999). During the 1998 election campaign, complaints about the integration of immigrants (in particular of those of Moroccan and Turkish origin) constituted a non-trivial part of the platform of the VVD (Bale et al. 2010; Erk 2011). In 2000, Labour intellectual Paul Scheffer spoke in a provocative op-ed of a "multicultural drama" that had been ignored for too long, and warned, among other things, of "enormous numbers of stragglers and people without prospect, who will increasingly burden Dutch society" (Scheffer 2000). This led to a nationwide discussion about the merits of immigration, including a highly visible parliamentary debate (70–4700, 18 April 2000). With the entry on the political scene of Pim Fortuyn, who posthumously won a landslide during the 2002 election by running on an anti-immigration platform, the "conspiracy of silence" (Messina 2007) surrounding the subject was definitely over.

In this changed climate, advisory bodies soon started to describe the overrepresentation of immigrants on welfare as "a problem" and "one of the biggest issues of concern" (WRR 2001, 13, 121). A 2003 report by the Netherlands Bureau for Economic Policy Analysis (*Centraal Planbureau*) concluded that "any successful policy will be restrictive as regards access to the country or its welfare arrangements" (Roodenburg, Euwals, and Ter Rele 2003, 9). In a May 2011 report, the Dutch Council for Social Development (*Raad voor Maatschappelijke Ontwikkeling*) made the same recommendation, in surprisingly frank and uncompromising terms:

Who does not contribute (anymore) to welfare and innovation cannot stay and is not allowed to make a claim on the welfare state. Part of the integration problems can be explained because [*sic*] too generous access to benefits undermines the social and financial support for the welfare state ... The maxim is thus: "You are more than welcome, but we are not going to take care of you." (Frissen and Van Diepen 2011)[15]

Unsurprisingly, patterns of immigrant welfare dependence also became a more common subject of parliamentary debate. The topic was covered extensively in the debates that led to the policy reforms reviewed in the previous section, and it even came up frequently in discussions that were not directly related. Moreover, it featured prominently in two parliamentary inquiries (Lower House of Dutch Parliament 2003, 2011) and was the exclusive subject of two emergency debates (5527–70, 31 March 2009; 43–9, 19 January 2012). It would take up too much space to detail all episodes of the increased parliamentary attention to the subject of immigrants' use of welfare state benefits. By means of aggregate illustration, Figure 5.1 reports the number of questions and motions brought forward in Parliament each year from 1995 to 2012 that directly addressed immigrants' access to welfare state benefits.[16]

The figure shows a clear increase in the number of parliamentary motions and questions on this subject. Even more importantly, it reveals

Figure 5.1. Questions and motions in Parliament advocating the expansion (black bars) and reduction (white bars) of immigrants' access to welfare state benefits, 1995–2012

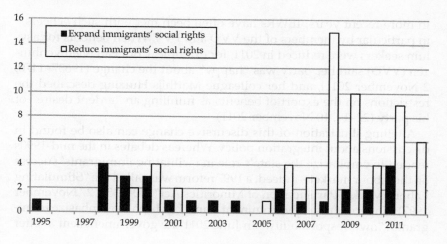

that calls for exclusion have become much more frequent than pleas to expand immigrants' social rights. This brings me to the second main aspect of the change in political translation that is crucial to understanding the adoption of IEWRs in the Netherlands: while debates about immigrants' place in the welfare state were initially similar to the ones we saw in Sweden and Canada, in recent years the dominant frame has become more accusatory and divisive. More specifically, it has become more common to maintain (1) that the state should not take care of immigrants, (2) that it is primarily migrants' fault that they are making disproportionate claims on the welfare state, and (3) that other factors have little to do with it. I will discuss each of these three discursive changes in turn.

First, politicians have started to emphasize that it is not the state's responsibility to take care of immigrants. During discussions of the Linking Act, most politicians (except the CD's Hans Janmaat) labelled the reform controversial and framed their position as reluctantly supporting a policy change that was necessary in order to maintain the system's integrity. Christian Democratic leader Maxime Verhagen, for example, commented:

> I wish to emphasize that of course no one is really cheering at the introduction of the Linking Act. After all, we are talking about people here and it is more satisfactory to give people something than to take something away from them. That applies very markedly to my parliamentary party as well. (16-1112, 23 October 1996)

In more recent years, IEWRs have often been met with such "cheers," in particular by members of the VVD and PVV. When benefits for asylum seekers were reduced in 2011, for example, Cora van Nieuwenhuizen (VVD) said her party was "happy" about the change (19637–1470, 2 November 2011), and her colleague Matthijs Huizing described the restrictions on the export of benefits as fulfilling an "ardent desire" of his party (22–14, 10 November 2011).

A telling illustration of this discursive change can also be found in discussions about integration policy. Whereas debates in the mid-1990s tended to emphasize the state's role in facilitating immigrants' success on the labour market – indeed, a 1997 reform was called the "Stimulating Labour Market Participation of Minorities Act" (30–2357, 27 November 1997) – in recent years the dominant frame has been to emphasize immigrants' "own responsibility." In June 2011 the government sent a letter to Parliament outlining its "new vision on integration, cohesion, and citizenship" (32824–1, 16 June 2011), consisting primarily of the argument that "integration and the acquisition of knowledge and skills that are necessary to maintain oneself independently in Dutch society are the responsibility of everyone who wants to settle here permanently." The following year it passed an integration reform that, tellingly, was titled "An Amendment to the Integration Act and a number of other acts in relation to strengthening the own responsibility of those who have the duty to integrate." The framing of immigrant integration as something the state cannot be asked to contribute to was ubiquitous in the parliamentary debates on the legislative change. Van Nieuwenhuizen (VVD) argued that "the language and the knowledge of Dutch society are things that the state cannot teach people, but people have to do this themselves"; Van Klaveren (PVV) stated that "if people want to take an integration course, they can do that on their own costs"; and Sterk (CDA) posited that integration "is in the first place something of those people themselves, because after all they choose to come to the Netherlands" (74–27 and 75–9, 10 and 11 April 2012). Even opposition parties with objections to the reform adopted this frame. Sadet Karabulut of socialist party SP started her contribution by saying that "it is fine, great even, to appeal to people's own strength"; Cynthia Ortega-Martijn of the leftish Christian party CU stated that "the emphasis with which the newcomer is held personally responsible is, as far as our parliamentary party is concerned, a great thing"; and Tofik Difi of the environmentalist party GL called the emphasis on immigrants' responsibility "a good principle."

A second change has been a growing reluctance to acknowledge that levels of immigrant reliance on state benefits might have something to do with state policies or societal attitudes (Kremer 2013, 70). During the 2000 debate following Paul Scheffer's op-ed on a "multicultural drama," Christian Democratic leader Jaap de Hoop Scheffer reached a balanced conclusion on the subject: "We should also answer the question: whose fault is that [i.e., that the integration of immigrants has not been successful]? Well, that's our fault, of all of us here, of Dutch society and in part of the newcomers themselves" (70–4700, 18 April 2000). In recent years, however, the emphasis has shifted to the last part of this quote. Centre-right politicians have been especially prone to dismiss any suggestions that discrimination might be a relevant factor. For example, when Labour MPs asked questions about a newspaper article that concluded that about 75 per cent of employment agencies discriminated against Turks, Moroccans, and Surinamese migrants, junior minister Paul de Krom (VVD) coolly started talking about the "role for migrants themselves to combat discrimination" (tk-767, 25 November 2011). Something similar happened a few months later, when Fatma Koşer Kaya (D66) specifically asked whether the government believed that discrimination is "part of the problem" related to high unemployment and welfare dependency among non-Western immigrants. De Krom briefly stated that "discrimination could play a role in this" but then quickly started to talk about factors related to the migrants themselves, invoking "differences in qualifications ..., social-normative skills (for example an attitude that is too modest, not being able to present oneself well in work situations and dealing with unwritten rules), and aspects that have to do with the ethnic or religious background of the applicants (lower proficiency in the Dutch language, wearing of a headscarf)" (tk-1712, 2 March 2012).

Jesse Klaver (GL) received a similar response when he tabled the findings of a report by the Netherlands Institute for Social Research concluding that migrants' skills had been improving while their situation on the labour market had not. Minister Kamp (VVD) limited his reaction to stating that discrimination could have something to do with it according to the institute (TK-31066–12, 6 March 2012). During the subsequent committee meeting for which the report was listed as one of the agenda points, no participant actually discussed its main conclusions (TK-29544–409, 6 August 2012).[17]

A debate in 2004 offers a telling illustration of just how common the view had become among Dutch politicians that immigrants should shoulder most of the blame for their disproportionate use of transfer benefits. A parliamentary majority asked Prime Minister Balkenende to inform Parliament about "possibilities to restrict the access of immigrants to social security" (see kst-29861–2, 9 March 2005). Note that the request was not to investigate possibilities for reducing immigrants' *use* of social security. Apparently, the Dutch Parliament saw immigrants' overrepresentation among benefit recipients primarily as a sign that the benefits were too easily accessible for newcomers, not that the Dutch state was doing a poor job at facilitating immigrants' economic integration.

This brings me to the third discursive shift, namely, the increased tendency to suggest that high levels of immigrant welfare dependence reflect a penchant among immigrants to draw benefits. Again, we do not have to go far back in time to find a different discursive climate than today. In November 2000, economic affairs minister Annemarie Jorritsma (VVD) said during a press conference that one reason for high levels of immigrant welfare dependence might be that "in some social groups a culture of drawing benefits might have emerged." Opposition MPs were outraged and called her to Parliament. Jorritsma quickly apologized for her comments, stating that she mostly meant to argue that the state apparatus does not seem as effectively geared towards activation and reintegration as she would like, and that she certainly did not mean to suggest there is a culturally determined penchant for welfare use (TK-28–2369, 28 November 2000). It is difficult to imagine such an episode in contemporary Dutch politics. The argument that there is something about immigrants that makes them more likely than the native-born to make use of benefits has become part and parcel of political debate, and certainly a VVD minister would no longer apologize in Parliament for making that point.

One version of this argument insists that a low standard of living in the country of origin makes welfare benefits particularly attractive to non-Western immigrants. In advocating cutting welfare for migrants who do not speak Dutch, VVD MP Stef Blok argued: "[welfare] benefits are admittedly modest according to Dutch standards, but they do offer a reasonable alternative to low-skill jobs for immigrants from countries where social security is often entirely absent or otherwise very minimal" (kst-32328–3, 4 March 2010). In a similar vein, the PVV's Ino van den Besselaar predicted that Eastern European migrants would soon overflow the Dutch system of benefits, reasoning that:

> not only are wages much lower there, but there is also no social safety net worth mentioning. That has caused the migration streams of labour forces ... Countries with the highest wages, best medical care, and highest benefits, like the Netherlands, make for an attractive target. (50-16, 7 February 2012)

Some politicians take this argument a step further and suggest that the generosity of Dutch social benefits actually attracts immigrants with a dubious work ethic. Eddy van Hijum (CDA), for example, told me that "even someone like *GroenLinks*' Tofik Dibi says that Moroccan youth know perfectly well how high the level of social assistance benefits is in the Netherlands, and consider that a factor to come here" (interview NET04). Similarly, Hans Spekman (PvdA) declared that "[you shouldn't] blindly open provisions to anyone who might show up here on a late afternoon, because otherwise it is of course totally logical that people do show up, because they can then immediately go on welfare or receive child benefits" (interview NET02). And in a committee meeting on the reduction of benefit exports, Karin Straus (VVD) lamented that "the Dutch system of social security seems so attractive to labour migrants that it becomes an independent reason for migration to the Netherlands" (TK-32500-XV-69, 9 March 2011).

Parliamentarians of the PVV have been most explicit in this line of reasoning. For one thing, they have frequently suggested that immigrants are generally lazy. For example, De Jong argued that "it appears too often that non-Western immigrants in particular indicate they do not want to work [...] and prefer to make use of a social benefit" (33000-XV-51, 14 December 2011); Van den Besselaar complained about "the ease with which some cultures abuse our system of social security" (32500-XV-69, 9 March 2011); and Fritsma called an emergency debate to point out that "it is not supposed to be the case that hard-working Dutch people pay taxes for the benefits of healthy [immigrant] youth who simply do not want to work" (43–9, 19 January 2012).[18] In a similar vein, members of the PVV have suggested that some immigrant groups are overrepresented among benefit recipients because they have a natural tendency to cheat the system. The party has asked parliamentary questions about the scope of welfare fraud among immigrants (2012Z10956, 1 June 2012) and has submitted more than one motion to include information on country of origin in government statistics on benefit fraud (33000-XV-53, 14 December 2011; 33207–18, 4 July 2012). Sietse Fritsma contended in Parliament that "for Moroccans and Turks, the Netherlands is apparently one big casino. They enjoy making a fraud gamble with our tax money" (TK70–5527, 31 March 2009). Unsurprisingly, Fritsma also appealed to this line of reasoning when I asked him why his party believed that reductions in immigrants' social rights were the best strategy to decrease immigrant welfare dependence. He replied that "only restrictions in social provisions would give an incentive to this group of people" (interview NET03).

All in all, the political translation of patterns of immigrant welfare dependence has changed markedly over time. The subject has started to occupy a more prominent place in political discourse, and it has become more common to first and foremost blame immigrants themselves for their overrepresentation among benefit recipients. At first glance, this translation might seem difficult to understand, given the relatively egalitarian nature of the Dutch welfare state and the openness to religious and social diversity that has so long been central to public conceptions of Dutch history and identity. In recent years, however, we have witnessed changes in both these respects: the welfare state has undergone restructuring, and public understandings of what it means to be Dutch have become more exclusionary. I will briefly address both these changes in turn.

In comparative studies of social policy, the Netherlands has long stood out as having one of the most encompassing welfare states on the European continent. Data up until the late 1980s consistently placed the country at the top of the list among Western industrialized democracies in levels of social spending, decommodification, equality, transfer payments, and, in particular, spending on the non-aged population (Crepaz and Damron 2009; Huber and Stephens 2001; Pontusson 2005). Besides a health care system and an old age pension benefit that are available to all residents on the same terms, the country also boasts two universal safety nets that are less common in Western welfare states. First, a cornerstone of the Dutch system is the "social minimum," a stipulated level of income that no resident (whatever their assets or savings) is legally allowed to fall under (Cox 1993). This has implications not only for minimum wage settings but also for the level of means-tested benefits such as social assistance. Second, until recently the Netherlands offered a disability benefit that was available to every resident who was unable to work because of long-term sickness or disability, regardless of the length of employment history or contributions to social premiums (Kuipers 2006).

These characteristics have been important in shaping immigrants' social rights. The system's universal character has made it difficult to differentiate between native-born citizens and permanent residents – and as we will see below, this is a continuous source of frustration for current champions of IEWRs. Moreover, universalism has fostered a sense of solidarity and made it less likely that benefit recipients will be singled out as leeches of the system. Indeed, in early discussions about immigrants' access to benefits politicians occasionally framed the subject in terms of the generous nature of the Dutch welfare state and the value of solidarity. Moreover, according to Jan Lucassen and Rinus Penninx the first attempt at developing a coherent integration policy apparatus in the late 1970s was deeply influenced by the extant welfare state system:

> In its ambitiously formulated objectives it is possible to recognize the basic
> principles of the welfare state: a guarantee of minimum standards for all

legal inhabitants (regardless of nationality), equality of rights and opportunities, proportional participation and equal treatment. The [integration] policy can therefore be regarded as a specific form of the policy of such a welfare state ... In the ideology of the welfare state its role with respect to legally admitted aliens should be ...: once legally admitted they should be treated as much as possible as residents. (Lucassen and Penninx 1997, 161, 188)

As noted, however, the characterization of the Dutch welfare state as a source of immigrant inclusion should be qualified in two ways. First, despite its universal features, the Dutch system also has conservative characteristics, in particular the dual preferences to prioritize passive income replacement over labour activation (Binnema 2004; Huo 2009, 59; Visser Hemerijck 1997), and to protect the rights of employees over those of newcomers to the labour market (Rochon 1999, 204; Taylor-Gooby 2004, 23; Van Oorschot 2004).[19] These arrangements have likely contributed to immigrants' overrepresentation in the welfare system. An exacerbating factor is that immediately after the era of guest worker migration the Netherlands went through a severe welfare crisis (Entzinger 1985; Visser and Hemerijck 1997). To make things worse, politicians and civil servants eager to reduce unemployment levels decided to channel large portions of the unemployed population (including many former guest workers) towards the above-mentioned disability benefit (Kuipers 2006, 139–42; Snel, Stavenuiter, and Duyvendak 2002). All in all, it is not surprising that many observers argue that the Dutch welfare state has done more harm than good to its immigrant population (Buruma 2006; Chorny, Euwals, and Folmer 2007, 32; Mollenkopf 2000; Scheffer 2007, 38–40, 113–18, 201).

The second qualification is that the Dutch welfare state was significantly restructured in the 1980s and 1990s. The Lubbers and Kok cabinets introduced a series of reforms that sharpened eligibility requirements and reduced benefit levels (Green-Pedersen 2002; Hemerijck, Unger, and Visser 2000). Sickness (Huber and Stephens 2001), disability (Kuipers 2006), unemployment (Green-Pedersen 2002), and social assistance benefits (Visser and Hemerijck 1997) underwent the most dramatic transformations. The overarching goal of many of these reforms was to reduce the number of benefit recipients by making it harder to qualify for social programs (Green-Pedersen, Van Kersbergen, and Hemerijck 2001; Van Oorschot 2004).

This transformation is of great consequence for our current discussion. First, in an institutional context in which disentitlement is the most common response to rising social expenditure, pushing immigrants off benefits seems a feasible and intuitive strategy for reducing levels of immigrant welfare dependence. Second, given that welfare regimes shape public attitudes about redistribution, we should expect that the cutbacks resulted in heightened attention to recipients' "deservingness." It can be no surprise, then, that immigrants' entitlements have also come under scrutiny, especially since non-Western immigrants are such a visible part of the welfare caseload. Indeed, many of my interviewees – both civil servants and parliamentarians – explicitly linked the general welfare reforms of the 1980s and 1990s to the restrictive changes targeting immigrants. In sum, then, the Dutch welfare system has moved in a less generous direction, with a concomitantly sharper focus on the deservingness of benefit recipients.

Equally important is the development that Dutch nationalism has undergone. The Dutch have long invoked openness towards and tolerance of religious and social diversity as cornerstones of their history and identity (Buruma 2006, 35; Lucassen and Penninx 1997, 3; Scheffer 2007, 149–90). As Lucassen and Penninx (1997) demonstrate, immigration is by no means a new phenomenon in the Netherlands. They conclude that over the centuries the country has welcomed "probably more [immigrants] than any other country in north-western Europe" (19). They estimate that as early as 1620 the immigrant population was around 10 per cent (29) – only a little lower than what it is today. During the "Golden Age" of the Dutch Republic, the Netherlands acquired a reputation as a safe haven for religious minorities (in particular, Protestant groups such as French Huguenots, but Jewish and Catholic migrants as well) and intellectuals (including Descartes, Locke, Hobbes, and Rousseau) escaping oppressive regimes. In the words of one of these intellectuals, Pierre Bayle, the country became known as "la grande arche des fugitifs" (Lucassen and Penninx 1997, qtd at 36).

The depiction of the Netherlands as a tolerant nation, then, refers to more than its contemporary policies on soft drugs, same-sex rights, and euthanasia. It is also rooted in the country's historical treatment of minority groups, in particular religious minorities. The Union of Utrecht (1579), the declaration of independence by the Protestant provinces in the northern Netherlands from the Spanish regime, is often cited as one of the first recognitions of religious freedom in Europe: it included the provision that in two of the provinces citizens could privately profess their religion of choice (even Catholicism). In more recent history, of particular relevance is the so-called Great Pacification of 1917, a compromise that introduced, alongside universal suffrage and proportional representation, the institution of state-financed religious education (De Rooy 2005, 155–7). That agreement ushered in the era of "pillarization": a period lasting until the late 1960s, during which Dutch society was deeply divided into five social groups (Catholics, two Protestant denominations, liberals, and social democrats) but nevertheless managed to coexist relatively peacefully because the pillars' political representatives agreed to cooperate with one another (Lijphart 1968).

Certainly, one could question how tolerant and open the Dutch state has truly been (Scheffer 2007). My main purpose here, however, is to point out that the *perception* that the Netherlands is a minority-friendly country is a powerful one, and that this perception shaped the Dutch approach to migration after the Second World War. Indeed, the first formulations of integration policy in the late 1970s were not only based on welfare state principles (see above), but also couched in terms of tolerance and the value of diversity (Lucassen and Penninx 1997, 150). Moreover, some of the laws to accommodate minorities in the early twentieth century proved to have an important institutional legacy. For example, the protection of state-financed religious education turned into a cornerstone of Dutch integration policy when Islamic minorities started to use this article of the constitution to fund Islamic elementary schools (Koning 2007). Some intellectuals, especially those of a Christian democratic background, even actively defended pillarization as the best approach to integrating Islamic minorities (Scheffer 2007, 170). In sum, while the government's initial response to immigration in the 1970s cannot be described as "multicultural" in the modern sense of the term (Vink 2007), it certainly did entail a relatively generous and inclusive approach that included a comprehensive set of group rights and anti-discrimination measures.

In recent years, however, a broader unease about immigration and multiculturalism has led to a more exclusionary conception of Dutch national identity, one that has created a space for the welfare chauvinist argument that access to social programs should be a *reward* for national belonging rather than a social right in itself. As discussed above, by the new millennium the belief had become widespread that politicians had long been guided by politically correct naivety, that this had led to overly generous immigration policies that made fraud too easy, and that those policies, in turn, were responsible for present-day integration problems. Within a few years, Dutch governments implemented drastic changes not only in admission policies (Lechner 2008; Meyers 2004; Minderhoud 2004) but in naturalization and integration policies as well (De Hart 2007; Joppke 2010). Moreover, the emphasis on cultural assimilation has become more pronounced. In a recent study, Semin Suvarierol characterized the information that aspirant-citizens receive in the Netherlands as follows: "Not only does the citizenship material assume a unitary national identity, but [it also] does not offer any space for divergent practices and at times strongly qualifies these practices as unacceptable" (Suvarierol 2012, 225). The restrictive turn is most obvious in integration policies (Entzinger 2006; Vink 2007). Beginning with the first Purple coalition, governments have steered the group-based integration policy of the 1980s in a more assimilative direction. This has entailed, among other things, abolishing mother-tongue education for immigrants, introducing mandatory integration classes, reducing the funding for accommodative services such as public language assistance, repealing "multicultural" targets in public media, and abolishing quota-based minority employment projects (Entzinger 2006; Geddes 2003).

According to some observers, these policy changes should be understood as a concerted effort to protect the liberal and tolerant characteristics of Dutch national identity from more conservative immigrant cultures (Bosma 2010; Sniderman and Hagendoorn 2007). But if that has been the intention, it seems the baby has been thrown out with the bath water. Instead of reinforcing liberalism and tolerance, the policy changes are encouraging an understanding of Dutch national identity rooted in very different values. They embody a view that government officials have repeatedly voiced (Vink, 2007) and that has become pervasive in media coverage as well (Korteweg 2006; Vliegenthart and Roggeband 2007): the Netherlands should not be open to differences and indeed should *seclude* itself from outside influences.[20] In this view, immigrants have to make a compelling case to explain why they need to be on Dutch territory, and once they are admitted, they must prove themselves before they deserve full inclusion.

Survey data suggest a similar change in the nature of Dutch nationalism. On two occasions the International Social Survey Program has asked respondents in the Netherlands about their views on national identity. And as illustrated in Figure 5.2, the answers were very different before and after the turn of the century. Respondents were significantly more likely in 2003 than in 1995 to think that different ethnic

Figure 5.2. Public opinion on national identity, 1995 and 2003

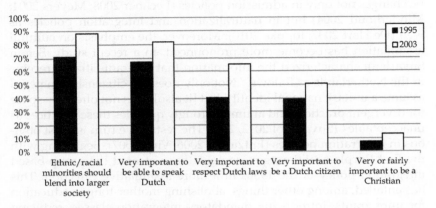

Source: International Social Survey Program

groups should blend into the larger society and that in order to be truly Dutch it is important to speak Dutch, to respect Dutch laws, to be a Dutch citizen, and to be a Christian.[21]

The relevance of this changed understanding of national identity is that it can be used to justify differentiation in social policies between newcomers and the native-born. We have already seen a good example of this practice, namely, Verdonk's claim that social policies should only be used to protect people who were raised according to Dutch norms and values. Other instances of this discourse abound. For example, Stef Blok (VVD) objected to the income supplement for elderly immigrants (AIO) by stating: "I wouldn't know how you could justify it to Dutch tax-payers who are not on welfare [...] That people come here from countries without old age security is not our fault" (kst-29389–17, 25 May 2009). In our personal interview, Cora van Nieuwenhuizen explained the VVD's position as follows: "Where other parties often start with "people should be able to share in our welfare and to vote in our elections," we do not start with sharing, voting, or talking, but with participating ... Dutch citizenship needs to be earned, we always say. It's worth the investment" (interview NET01). This frame is especially common in discussions about the export of benefits. Social affairs minister Henk Kamp (VVD), for example, objected to the principle that emigrants can enjoy contributory benefits they paid premiums for on the basis that "the benefit is intended for people in the Netherlands"

(32500-XV-69, 9 March 2011; see also comments in the same debate by conservative MP Strauss).

The role of this view as a driver of IEWRs can be inferred in a different way as well. Even when I specifically asked about social policies or immigrants' welfare dependence, some of the politicians I interviewed changed the subject to more general concerns regarding immigration's threat to Dutch identity. Fritsma (PVV), for example, repeatedly emphasized that the main goal of his party's immigration proposals is to "stop the Islamization of the Netherlands" (interview NET03). Paul Ulenbelt (SP) elaborated on cultural differences that cause neighbourhood disturbances. Van Nieuwenhuizen (VVD) talked about crime, alcoholism, and homophobia among immigrants, as well as the "uncomfortable feeling" she has when sitting in a train where people are speaking in a different language (interview NET01). That politicians explicitly invoke cultural concerns when asked to comment on immigrants' position in the welfare state illustrates the importance of the more general backlash against immigration and multiculturalism for the increase in selective solidarity.

All in all, the structure of the Dutch welfare state and the traditional conception of Dutch identity long placed the Netherlands on an inclusive path with regard to immigrants' social rights. But in recent years we have seen changes in both these respects. In this light, it is not surprising that we see increasing support for immigrant welfare exclusion among both the public and the political elite.

Unfortunately, Dutch respondents have only occasionally been surveyed on the subject of immigrants' social rights. Nevertheless, two pieces of indirect evidence do suggest that Dutch citizens have become less willing to share their welfare state with newcomers. First, while public opinion seems to be relatively stable or to have become more positive over time on a number of questions that have repeatedly been asked about ethnic diversity and immigration (Government of the Netherlands 2007), the results are different when people are probed specifically about immigrants' access to state-funded services. Figure 5.3 shows results from three questions from the Cultural Changes in the Netherlands Survey that have been asked annually from 1978 to 2010. While on two questions there is no evidence of an increase in anti-immigrant attitudes over time, the number of people who agree with the only question that directly asks whether native-born Dutch should have more entitlements to a social service than immigrants increased steadily after the late 1980s and has remained more or less stable since the late 1990s.

Figure 5.3. Anti-immigrant attitudes, 1978–2010

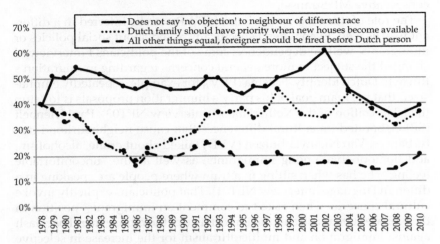

Source: Cultural Changes in the Netherlands Survey

Second, in the absence of questions that directly measure selective solidarity, we can approximate the concept by combining existing survey questions. In each wave of the Dutch Parliamentary Election Studies (DPES) since 1998, all respondents have been asked to place themselves on a scale from 1 to 7 concerning both income redistribution (where 1 means "income differences should be larger" and 7 means "income differences should be smaller") and asylum seekers (where 1 means "the Netherlands should admit more" and 7 means "asylum seekers should be sent back to their country of origin"). Figure 5.4 shows the percentage of respondents, in each wave of the DPES since 1998, who give at least a score of 5 on both questions, indicating that they are at the same time in favour of income redistribution and opposed to asylum seekers. The proportion of voters who demonstrate this type of selective solidarity is decidedly larger after 2006 than in earlier election years.

The widespread support for restricting immigrants' social rights may not be surprising, considering that it is no longer taboo to note that immigrants are laying larger than average claims on the welfare system. Still, it is important to reiterate that acknowledging immigrants' overrepresentation does not logically necessitate support for IEWRs, and one can think of at least three alternative strategies for reducing

Figure 5.4. Percentage of respondents in favour of income redistribution and opposed to asylum seekers, 1998–2012 (with 95% CIs)

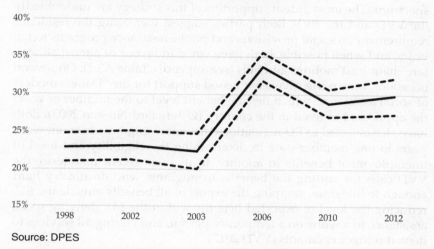

Source: DPES

Table 5.2. Political parties' views on four possible strategies to avoid/reduce immigrant welfare dependence

Party	Ideology	% seats, 2017 elections	Restrict access to benefits?	More selective intake?	More integration assistance?	General welfare reform?
VVD	Conservative	22	Yes	Yes	No	Yes
PVV	Anti-immigrant	13	Yes	Yes	No	No
CDA	Christian dem.	13	Yes	Yes	No	Some
D66	Liberal	13	Some	No	Yes	Yes
SP	Socialist	9	Some	Yes	Yes	No
GL	Green	9	No	No	Yes	No
PvdA	Labour	6	Some	Some	Some	No

immigrants' reliance on welfare benefits (selective admission policies, more aggressive integration policies, and across-the-board welfare cuts). Table 5.2 summarizes the position of the seven largest parties in Parliament on each of these four strategies, based on legislative behaviour, party platforms, and interviews with the relevant spokesperson of each party.[22]

The first observation we should make is that the option of restricting immigrants' access to social benefits is popular across the ideological spectrum. The most ardent supporters of this strategy are undoubtedly the VVD and the PVV. Both parties suggest increasing the residence requirement on social provisions and public insurance programs to ten years, and when possible, both have voted in favour of almost all welfare chauvinist motions and bills (see appendix Table A3.2). On several occasions, both parties have expressed support for the "Danish model" of social assistance, which ties the benefit level to the number of years the applicant has lived in the country (Østergaard-Nielsen 2003). Both have also objected to EU regulations that allow migrants to count work years in one member-state in determining the eligibility and level of unemployment benefits in another. In its most recent manifesto, the VVD calls for cutting the benefits to migrants who do not try hard enough to integrate, stopping the export of all benefits outside the EU, reducing the level of exported benefits within the EU, denying social assistance to anyone on a temporary permit, and cutting all services to denied refugee claimants (VVD 2017).

The CDA, too, has advocated scaling back immigrants' access to benefits, but it has not embraced all the proposals that the VVD and PVV champion. Eddy van Hijum describes his party's position as follows:

I think that the welfare state has gone too far in the last decades, both in the direction of immigrants and in the direction of benefit recipients in the Netherlands ... But at the same time we have said: "there are also boundaries that we do not want to touch." The five-year period for welfare, for example, that the VVD and PVV want to extend to ten years or longer, we said about that: "we are not going to touch that." [Similarly,] we try to draw a very sharp distinction between [social provisions] and insured rights that you build up here – if you work here you are insured for unemployment, disability, and old age – you should be able to take those rights with you. That applies to immigrants, that applies to everyone; we are not going to touch that. (interview NET04)

The other parties are more reluctant to advocate differential treatment between newcomers and native-born citizens. Indeed, they have criticized some restrictive policy changes and have occasionally advocated an expansion of immigrants' social rights. All four parties, for example, recently defended municipalities that offer "bed, bath, and bread" to denied refugee claimants. When asked, Hans Spekman

(PvdA), Paul Ulenbelt (SP), and Fatma Koşer Kaya (D66) all rejected the thesis that immigration threatens the future of the Dutch welfare state. Moreover, as soon as restrictions on immigrants' access to benefits came up, both Koşer Kaya and Ulenbelt hurried to emphasize their commitment to the principle of non-discrimination. For example, Ulenbelt declared: "When people are ultimately here, you need to treat them like any other. Even the Polish labourer who is here for three years and becomes occupationally incapacitated in a greenhouse should get a disability benefit. It is simple: sauce for the goose is sauce for the gander" (interview NET05).

Nevertheless, all of these parties do advocate some restrictions, except perhaps for GL. The current residence requirements for access to social assistance are supported by all four parties, even though D66 and GL voted against a 2008 motion (by Van Hijum and Spekman) to enforce those requirements without exceptions. The PvdA and D66 were in favour of a 2008 suggestion to investigate a stricter "grow-in" model of social security, and all parties except GL have supported the restrictions on the export of benefits. The proposal to tie immigrants' eligibility for social assistance benefits to participation in integration and language classes was brought forward by the PvdA and was supported by all parties in Parliament.

The second option – employing a more selective admission policy – enjoys a similar level of support in the Dutch Parliament. Indeed, the reduction of migration flows is often mentioned as a policy goal in parliamentary debates, without garnering much opposition (see, e.g., 33000-VII-53, 14 November 2011). The PVV advocates the most restrictive policy. In the 2012 elections it proposed halting all non-refugee migration from "Muslim countries," reducing the number of refugees, increasing the requirements for family migration, and exclusively admitting temporary labour migration. Its 2017 manifesto is less detailed but equally clear: it simply states "close the borders" (PVV 2017). The VVD's position is only marginally less drastic: the overarching message of its stance on immigration is to stop admitting migrants who are "without prospect" (*kansloos*). To that end, it advocates tighter requirements for family migration, the exclusive admission of high-skilled labour migrants, resistance to any EU efforts to facilitate labour migration from outside the union, and a complete halt to all (!) asylum claims from people outside Europe. The CDA advocates a similar but much more modest package of restrictions (selective labour migration, stricter requirements on family migration, reduction in asylum migration).

At the other end of the political spectrum, the SP also proposes a sharp reduction in the intake of migrants, but its opposition is mostly rooted in the belief that open borders not only exploit immigrants who are willing to work for low pay but also reduce wages for the native-born population. For that reason, it advocates more restrictions on labour migration than on family or asylum migration. The PvdA proposes fewer restrictions than these four parties but nevertheless believes that the overall intake should decrease, advocating reductions in labour migration (for similar reasons as the SP) an income threshold for family migrants, and increased efforts to accommodate refugees close to the region they are fleeing from rather than resettling them in the Netherlands. Among the major Dutch parties, then, only D66 and GL do not propose restrictions in admission policy. While D66's 2017 manifesto does state that labour migration should be guided primarily by the demands of the Dutch economy, most of the party's proposals seem interested in *increasing* the number of newcomers; it advocates active recruitment of educated labour migrants and rejects some of the recent restrictions on family and asylum migration. The GL's position is largely similar.

In sharp contrast to these two restrictive policy options, fewer parties endorse efforts to stimulate economic integration through targeted labour market programs. Fritsma (PVV) dismissed immigrant-targeted policies on the basis that "there have always been programs to encourage labour market participation, but the problem has never been solved" (interview NET03). Cora van Nieuwenhuizen explains the position of the VVD in similar terms:

> All those organizations with an addiction for subsidies, we should stop with that. That goes for targeted policies as well. It is some sort of hugging culture and a pampering that all these organizations cling to, because "it is all so necessary." Then I think that if that policy would be the solution, we wouldn't have these problems anymore, because we've been doing it like that forever. (interview NET01)

Similarly, while the CDA does support some investment in language courses on public media, the party is overall "critical" of this strategy (interview NET04).

Left-of-centre parties are more supportive of this approach. The SP and GL advocate immigrant-targeted labour market programs, anti-discrimination initiatives, and diversity quotas in the public sector, as well as a reversal of the decision to have immigrants pay for their own integration courses. Although it often criticizes targeted policies for "treating people in groups" (interview NET06), D66 supports the same set of policy initiatives, except for diversity quotas in the public sector. The PvdA, finally, is largely supportive of public funding to ameliorate immigrants' standing in the labour market but has no objection to the policy of requiring immigrants to pay for their own integration classes.

Finally, the general positions of these parties on the appropriate size of the welfare state are predictable. The VVD and, to a lesser extent, the CDA champion less intervention in the market (indeed, the Rutte-I cabinet, a coalition of these two parties, scaled down both youth disability benefits and means-tested social services). Meanwhile, the SP, GL, and PvdA advocate preserving or enhancing available services and programs. The positions of D66 and the PVV deserve some more attention. D66 is the only party that advocates welfare reform for the explicit reason that a rigid labour market and passive welfare benefits constrain the opportunities of newcomers in the labour market. Koşer Kaya:

> Do you know why there are so many entrepreneurs among Turkish Dutch people? Because they do not get the opportunities, so they think: I will do it myself. That's great, very innovative, and very positive, but it is a consequence of [the structure of the labour market]. So you have to dare looking at that system, but also at the system of social security ... You have to make sure that you on the one hand change something about the duration of a benefit, but on the other hand that people can more easily go from one job to another ... Whether we're talking about immigrant or native-born, if we want a future-proof system, then we need to dare changing it now. (interview NET06)

What is noteworthy about the PVV is that it actively resists most proposals for welfare retrenchment. It was perhaps the most vocal critic of the 2010 increase in the retirement age,[23] and it withdrew its support from the Rutte-I cabinet in April 2012 precisely because it refused to support plans for further retrenchment. MP Léon de Jong explicitly stated that "the PVV is not an anti-welfare party" (30545–110, 4 January 2012). Party ideologue Martin Bosma (Bosma 2010, 36) has described the PVV creed as follows:

> The state has the responsibility to protect the weak. Thus we will strive for excellent health care, benefits for people who want to work but are

unable to, and a decent [public pension.] But besides the new party will distinguish itself by a hard line on the issue of mass immigration and islamisation.

This pro-welfare position is relevant not only because it shows that among all parties in Parliament the PVV most clearly champions *selective* solidarity but also because it distinguishes the PVV from earlier Dutch AIPs. Both the CD and Pim Fortuyn's LPF often described immigration as a threat to the welfare state, but neither party ever expressed warm support for generous social policies in the first place. Indeed, Fortuyn's argument that "the very carefully crafted arrangements of the welfare state are under pressure because of [immigration]" (Fortuyn 2001, 121) seems curious coming from a person who advocated the most residual of welfare states, consisting of a single means-tested benefit to replace all current arrangements (Fortuyn 2001, 84–5).[24]

All in all, over the past twenty years, immigrants' position in the Dutch welfare state has gone from being a taboo issue to a prominent topic of discussion. The public and, more clearly, the political elite have become increasingly attentive to immigrants' reliance on social programs and benefits. More importantly, the dominant frame for discussing the subject is one that justifies IEWRs by blaming immigrants themselves for their overrepresentation in the welfare system, trivializing other factors and emphasizing that it is first and foremost immigrants' own responsibility to make sure they are doing well economically. It is therefore unsurprising that the majority of Dutch parliamentarians now agree that the most appropriate strategy for addressing levels of immigrant welfare dependence is to make restrictive changes not just to admission policies but to immigrants' access to benefits as well.

Reaching the Boundaries of Exclusion

As we saw in chapter 2, it is difficult to find an economic explanation for the sudden concerns in the Netherlands about immigrants' reliance on social benefits. In fact, the economic integration of the migrant population has improved considerably over the same time period that suggestions for IEWRs have become more frequent. The explanation should therefore be sought in political factors, in particular the increased prominence of anti-immigrant politicians and their ability to sway the mainstream in a more restrictive direction. I will discuss both these factors in

Figure 5.5. Share of seats in Lower House of Parliament occupied by anti-immigrant parties, 1991–2017

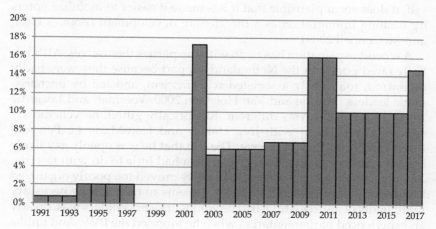

turn, after which I will turn to the legal and institutional obstacles that attempts at IEWRs have faced.

The Netherlands' extremely proportional electoral system (the electoral threshold is only 0.67 per cent) facilitates the emergence of new parties, but as Figure 5.5 shows,[25] AIPs did not achieve significant electoral success until the twenty-first century. But since the 2002 elections, which saw the meteoric rise and assassination of Pim Fortuyn, this type of party has occupied a central place in the Dutch party system.

While this is largely beyond the scope of this chapter, we might reflect briefly on the reasons why AIPs have recently become so much more successful. Two types of explanations seem particularly helpful. The first focuses on the political and social conditions that facilitated their rise. The year 2002 was a particularly opportune time to voice the populist message that there was no real choice in Dutch politics. At that time the country had been governed for eight years by a coalition of the PvdA and the VVD, the two parties that traditionally shaped the main fault line in party politics. In the absence of clear cleavages between existing political parties, it was easy for Fortuyn to frame the 2002 election as a battle between him and the established elite. Moreover, a common line of reasoning among anti-immigrant politicians is that multiculturalism is an elitist project that silences any opposition. That argument became gruesomely plausible after the assassination of Fortuyn and, two years later, of movie director, columnist, and Islam critic Theo van Gogh. And while this obviously cannot explain the initial success of Fortuyn himself, it does seem plausible that it has made it easier to mobilize voters by framing immigration as a threatening development (Boin, 't Hart, and McConnell 2009).

A second explanation has to do with the parties themselves. AIPs initially fared poorly in the Netherlands in part because they were badly organized, too closely associated with fascism, and led by uncharismatic leaders (Mudde and Van Holsteyn 2000; Voerman and Lucardie 1992). Pim Fortuyn was different. Rhetorically gifted, he vehemently rejected comparisons with Jörg Haider and Jean-Marie Le Pen and insisted he was a true democrat. The fact that he was openly gay likely helped convince people that his platform had little to do with fascism. After his assassination, however, his party proved too poorly organized to have any lasting success. The PVV seems to have all the necessary ingredients of a successful AIP. The eloquent Geert Wilders was already an experienced parliamentarian when he founded the PVV. And unlike AIPs of the past, the Freedom Party boasts a relatively solid organization. It quickly managed to develop a wide network of sponsors, and while in recent years there certainly has been internal dissent, the leadership structure of the party has so far remained soundly intact. Perhaps most importantly for our current discussion, the PVV has established a niche in the Dutch party system as the only outspoken pro-welfare but anti-immigrant party. (For a more detailed discussion of the fortunes of AIPs in the Netherlands, see Koning 2017a.)

The sustained presence of a large AIP over the last decade has had two important effects. First, the LPF and especially the PVV have actively primed the costs of immigration and the overreliance of immigrants on the welfare system. During its first five years in Parliament the party initiated two emergency debates on the subject (5527–70, 31 March 2009; 43–9, 19 January 2012) and tabled more than twenty parliamentary questions and motions criticizing immigrants' social rights.

Perhaps the best example in this regard has already been mentioned: the series of questions Sietse Fritsma (PVV) asked in July 2009 about spending on non-Western immigrants, and the incomplete response he received from Labour minister Eberhard van der Laan. Predictably, the government's reluctance to fully answer Fritsma's questions merely added fuel to the fire. Once again the PVV could make a plausible case that the Dutch immigration system was being run by elitists who valued political correctness over democratic transparency (and this is

exactly what Fritsma argued when I asked him about the episode; interview NET03). The clash between Van der Laan and Fritsma received
much attention, both within and outside Parliament. Some journalists
even made attempts to do the calculations for Fritsma (Wynia 2009).
The PVV itself launched a website titled "What does the mass immigration cost?," inviting citizens to share any worries they might have about
the costs of immigration.[26] Moreover, it paid an independent research
agency to make the calculations instead (Van der Geest and Dietvorst
2010) and with much fanfare presented the finding that a typical non-
Western immigrant costs the Dutch welfare state 50,000 euros per year.[27]

Besides placing the costs of immigration on the political agenda
explicitly, the PVV also increased parliamentary attention to this subject
by raising it in unrelated discussions. For example, in his contribution
to a discussion about the increase in the retirement age and the reform
of the universal public pension, Tony van Dijck quickly changed the
subject from pension reform to the costs of immigration:

> This debate is not about the affordability of the [pension program] or
> about ageing. It is about cold retrenchment. It is about a black hole in
> the public treasury [...] This government [...] is deaf and blind [...] to the
> financial dike breach that is occurring behind its back: the costs of mass
> migration [...] The PVV chooses the conservation of our social security
> or of what is left of it. The PVV chooses the conservation of the [pension
> program]. And it is possible. Stop the immigration from Muslim coun-
> tries now and we can all have our pension when we reach 65. That is the
> essence of this debate: do we choose the Netherlands or do we choose
> even more immigration? (TK24-2071, 12 November 2009)

To give a few more examples, members of the PVV tabled the complaint that foreigners do not pay motor vehicle tax during a general
discussion on government finance (TK-33403–6, 11 October 2012),
commented that "our painstakingly built welfare state [has] become a
magnet for non-Western immigrants" in a debate on a welfare reform
affecting youth under twenty-seven (8–8, 5 October 2011), and asked in
a discussion about violence against social services personnel whether
there is "any connection between the level of violence and the fact that
more than half of those who are eligible for welfare are migrants" (7–3,
4 October 2011).

It is also worth reiterating that anti-immigrant politicians tend to
frame the subject in divisive terms. More specifically, they not only tend

to describe immigration as irreconcilable with generous social benefits but also state frequently that a choice must be made between caring for "us" or "them." Just how central this frame is to the PVV's rhetoric quickly becomes clear when one looks at its latest party manifesto, which is titled "The Netherlands Ours Again" and summarizes its agenda as follows: "Here is our plan: instead of financing ... people we don't want here, we spend the money on the normal Dutchman" (PVV 2017).

Even more consequential than the behaviour of the LPF and the PVV themselves has been the response to their electoral success from the mainstream parties. The LPF came out of nowhere to win twenty-six seats (out of 150) and become the second-largest party in 2002. The PVV came close to repeating that feat in 2010 when it won twenty-four seats, and in 2017 it became the second-largest party as well. The consequence has been a comparatively accommodating reaction from mainstream parties. Indeed, there is ample evidence of both compromise and contagion, even though all mainstream parties currently exclude the possibility of ever entering a coalition with the PVV (again).

Before the breakthrough elections of 2002, most politicians paid little attention to occasional anti-immigrant contributions in parliamentary debate. For example, in the long series of debates on the Linking Act, no one responded to any of the contributions by the CD's leader Hans Janmaat.[28] The only exception was when the Speaker of the House forced Janmaat to retract the comment that civil servants of immigrant background would likely attempt to sabotage the coupling of databases on welfare and residence status (8–439, 3 October 1996). When the parliamentary presence of the anti-immigrant voice suddenly grew much larger, this strategy no longer seemed feasible. Certainly, there are recent examples of the kind of name-calling to which MPs of Reform and the Sweden Democrats have been subjected. Martijn van Dam (PvdA), for example, dismissed Joram van Klaveren's (PVV) contribution as just another one of the "sad little speeches he always holds" (94–9, 16 June 2011), and Sadet Karabulut (SP) classified comments by Léon de Jong (PVV) as "disgusting" (104–15, 4 July 2012). And as evidenced by the scarcity of motions that have been jointly introduced by the LPF or PVV and one of the mainstream parties, politicians have remained careful not to associate themselves too closely with the AIPs. At the same time, however, the balance they have to strike is a precarious one, because rejecting these successful parties in too strong terms carries the risk of coming across as elitist and not taking the views of a large portion of the electorate seriously.

Often, therefore, MPs premise their disagreement with anti-immigrant politicians by conceding some points. For example, in the parliamentary debate on the 2012 integration policy reform, many started their contributions by implicitly thanking the LPF and PVV for drawing attention to problems with immigrant integration (74–27, 10 April 10, 2012). Mirjam Sterk (CDA) stated:

> [in the past] the pedagogical effect of forcing people to learn the Dutch language was doubted; even my parliamentary party had that view I believe. When I look around here, I think that fortunately by now much has changed in the thinking about integration.

In similar terms, Karabulut (SP) argued that "the importance of speaking the language has long been underestimated by politicians," and Dibi (GL) began by saying: "I think it is appropriate to express my appreciation for [former minister and later independent anti-immigrant politician] ms. Verdonk, because the importance of integration cannot be underestimated. For a long time it has been by the government."

In other instances, parliamentarians have chosen to let opportunities for name-calling slide that Swedish or Canadian MPs would undoubtedly have capitalized upon. When the PVV launched a website in February 2012 inviting people to share their objections to the presence of migrants from Central and Eastern Europe, the outrage in the subsequent parliamentary debate (53–3, 14 February 2012) was surprisingly mild. Some politicians who criticized the website employed the strategy mentioned above and began by conceding points to the PVV. Frans Timmermans (PvdA):

> I don't think that any parliamentary party in this Chamber still closes its eyes for the problems that relate to labour migration. I admit that this has happened in the past. Mister Bontes [PVV] rightly points at the problems that exist in the big cities.

Perhaps even more telling was that the cabinet refused to publicly criticize the website altogether. Prime Minister Rutte's (VVD) cool reaction nicely illustrates the calculated approach of distancing oneself from the PVV without denouncing it: "It is an initiative of the PVV … I am not going to comment on the actions of political parties."

The most important reason for the government's disinterested reaction was undoubtedly that it relied on the AIP for majority support in

Parliament. After the 2010 elections the PVV struck a deal with coalition partners CDA and VVD: it agreed to support the minority government in Parliament in exchange for restrictive reforms in integration and immigration policies. These reforms included four IEWRs: the increase in the residence requirement for family migrants' access to social benefits and popular insurance programs; the reduction of benefit export outside of the EU; the requirement that migrants pay for their own mandatory integration programs; and the welfare cuts for burqa-clad women (Government of the Netherlands 2010a).[29]

This was not the first example of compromise with anti-immigrant politicians. The same two parties that negotiated Wilders's "guaranteed support" in 2010 had forged a coalition with the LPF after the 2002 election. The AIP managed to negotiate the creation of a new ministry titled "Foreigners Affairs and Integration," with an LPF minister at the helm (Hilbrand Nawijn), and was able to see some of its party's suggestions for IEWRs folded into the government agreement – in particular, cuts to legal aid for asylum seekers, a reduction of welfare benefits for immigrants who had not completed their integration classes, and a requirement that immigrants pay for their own mandatory integration courses (Chorus and De Galan 2002; Government of the Netherlands 2002). The government fell within three months of its appointment and was thus unable to bring about any of these reforms. However, these ideas have since been picked up by politicians from other parties. The requirement that migrants pay for their own integration classes was included in the sweeping integration reform of 2012, and it was a motion by two Labour Party MPs that first made benefit access conditional on successfully completing integration programs.

For the moment, it seems doubtful that an anti-immigrant party will join a coalition government again in the near future. After the first Rutte government fell in 2012, the CDA declared that it would never rely on the PVV again, and in the 2017 election campaign, prime minister and VVD leader Rutte similarly excluded any future cooperation with the anti-immigrant party. According to Rutte, he reached this decision because Wilders was "more left-wing than [socialist leader] Roemer" and was making proposals that were "in violation of Dutch freedoms" (Rusman 2017). It seems likely he had at least one other reason for this decision – he probably expected it would attract PVV voters. In the very same statement, Rutte explicitly addressed PVV voters, saying he did not mean to alienate them and that he took their concerns very seriously. Moreover, he ran on a platform featuring a wide range of restrictive immigration reforms and adopted clear anti-immigrant rhetoric during the campaign, suggesting that people "who don't like how we treat each other in this country" should leave, and stating that people of Turkish background who do not feel a connection to the Netherlands should "piss off" (Moerman 2017).

This brings me to the mechanism of contagion: the success of first the LPF and then the PVV has incentivized mainstream parties to move in a more restrictive direction on issues of immigration (Bale et al. 2010; Koning 2017a). While my interviewees rejected the suggestion that their parties had adopted a more restrictive line on immigration for electoral reasons, some of their comments in fact lend credence to this argument.

For example, when asked whether the VVD's proposals had been inspired by growing public dissatisfaction over immigration, Cora van Nieuwenhuizen wholeheartedly agreed. The SP's Paul Ulenbelt was even clearer on this point: "The parliament represents the people. That thus means that you have to voice public opinion in politics. If you don't do that, you will not be elected and someone else will. It's as simple as that" (interview NET05). Christian Democrat Eddy van Hijum specifically referred to the PVV when describing how he saw his role as a representative of the people:

> Of course it is the case that political parties' viewpoints are reactions to the discontent that is felt in society. The problem is sometimes rather that we identify and translate it too late, and that therefore let us say populist parties get the chance to cater to this in an in my view rather unhealthy way, than that we have been too early with it. I think it is a function of the political system to exactly detect that kind of discontent, not to repeat it like some sort of megaphone, but to address the underlying problem. (interview NET04)

The result of the dual mechanisms of compromise and contagion has been that many suggestions for IEWRs have passed through Parliament with a handsome majority. A closer look at the parliamentary votes on the bills and private motions that reduced immigrants' access to the Dutch welfare state illustrates this point forcefully (Table 5.3). While a few bills on this file could count on only a small majority, by and large the picture is clear: calls for IEWRs have tended to generate widespread support from Dutch politicians.

At times, even politicians who expressed reservations about a bill indicated that they supported the principle behind it. For example, the

Table 5.3. Passed welfare chauvinist bills and motions, 1995–2012

Government Bill (year)	Short description	% supp.
Wajong Reform (1996)	Requires 6 years residence for youth disability benefit	64.7
Linking Act (1998)	Disentitles undocumented migrants	95.3
BUP (1999)	Formalizes exclusion of temporary migrants	[a]
Beu Act (2000)	Limits export of benefits	100.0
Alien Act Reform (2000)	Disentitles asylum seekers	[b]70.0
WWB Reform (2006)	Formalizes residence requirements for welfare	100.0
Cut in asylum seekers benefits (2011)	Reduces pocket money for asylum seekers with large families	[a]
Country of Residence Principle Act (2011)	Introduces "country of residence principle" in the export of child benefits	85.3
Reduction of AIO (2011)	Reduces additional income supplement for elderly citizens with a pension gap	52.0
Integration Policy Reform (2012)	Repeals state funding of integration services, increases sanctions for unsuccessful integration	52.0
Child Benefit Reform (2012)	Stops export of child benefits outside EU (pending renegotiation of social security agreements)	55.3
Family Migration Reform (2012)	Extends residence requirement for benefit access for family migrants from 3 to 5 years	[a]

Private motion (date)[c]	Short description	% supp.
Kamp c.s. (2000/6/8)	Cuts legal aid of asylum seekers who appeal a decision without presenting new information	89.3
Dijsselbloem, Noorman-Den Uyl (2006/6/12)	Makes access to welfare conditional on learning Dutch for immigrants outside labour market	100.0
Visser (2006/10/26)	Installs committee to investigate legal leeway for disentitlement of immigrants	100.0
Van Hijum (2008/1/17)	Calls for EU negotiation that social rights do not automatically translate to the Netherlands	92.0
Van Hijum, Spekman (2008/6/25)	Calls for reduced welfare dependence of CEE immigrants or repeal of their residence permit	79.3
Van Hijum, Blok (2008/11/27)	Asks government to investigate possibilities to reduce immigrants' utilization of social system	95.3
Kamp, Van de Camp (2008/12/10)	Asks government to develop plans for a stricter grow-in model of social security	73.3
Van de Camp (2008/12/10)	Asks government to ensure that no parent family migrant can access welfare	68.0
Van Toorenburg (2009/3/31)	Strictly enforces benefit cuts for migrants who do not complete their language course	100.0
Van Hijum, Spekman (2009/12/10)	Presses government to consider ending the export of child benefits	95.3

[a] This bill has not been voted on but has been passed as a "Royal Decision."
[b] The CDA (19% of MPs) voted against this bill, feeling that it did not go *far enough* in excluding asylum migrants.
[c] This overview omits 19 motions that did not pass. Eighteen of these motions were submitted by the PVV or VVD or by independent MPs who previously belonged to one of these parties, and 14 of them were exclusively supported by these three groups of MPs.

environmentalist party GL and the SP both voted against the Linking Act and suggested amendments to reduce its severity. However, they both subscribed to the overall goal the bill was trying to achieve. GL, for example, stated: "The members of the parliamentary party of GL [...] can appreciate the principle that people who are here unlawfully in principle cannot access any of the collective services. [But] that principle can already be realized by applying existing policies" (kst-24233–76c, 23 May 1997). Similarly, Socialist senator Jan de Wit said that his party agreed on the basic principle behind the law, but felt it was "redundant" and that its implementation was little more than "symbolic politics" (ek25–1255, 24 March 1998).

Something similar happened with the *Beu* Act. The SP and GL raised objections to the law, but mostly because they feared it would be implemented before pending negotiations over social security agreements were finalized, not because they fundamentally opposed it. In the end, the law passed through Parliament without a vote. We can see the same dynamic in the 2011 reform that adjusted the level of child benefits to the standard of living in the child's country of residence. The SP ended up voting against the legislation, but the amendments it suggested were mostly technical in nature (its most radical suggestion was to grandfather existing cases) and party members repeatedly stated in Parliament that they had no principled objections to the reform (see Ulenbelt, 22–14, 10 November 2011).

There are many more examples of IEWRs that faced little opposition. For example, the lengthening of the residence requirement for family migrants' access to social provisions and popular insurance programs was challenged by no other party than the SP (TK-32175–36, 26 July 2012), and the only challenge to the reduction in pocket money for asylum seekers was a sarcastic remark by Tofik Dibi (GL) (TK-19637–1470, 2 November 2011). Even the opposition to two of the reforms in Table 5.3 that passed through Parliament with a slim majority was relatively marginal. The objections to the 2012 cuts in child benefit export were mostly about the legal feasibility of the reform (and indeed, a 2009 motion suggesting to end the export of child benefits was supported by more than 95 per cent of Parliament), and some of the parties voting against the comprehensive integration reform of 2012 objected to only some of the cuts (the Labour Party, for example, agreed with most of the cutbacks but wanted to preserve a societal guidance program for refugees).

The Parliament-wide support for these proposals, however, should not be taken to mean that political stripe is irrelevant. One way we can see this is by looking again at the questions and motions that have been introduced in Parliament regarding immigrants' access to the welfare state (see appendix Tables A3.1–A3.4). Roughly three in four of those that criticized immigrants' use of social programs and/or proposed IEWRs came from the VVD and the PVV. Conversely, more than half of the twenty-seven questions and motions advocating inclusion came from left-wing parties SP and PvdA. Moreover, it is telling that the only government in the last twenty years that did not introduce restrictions on immigrants' access to welfare benefits was the centre-left Balkenende-IV cabinet – the only coalition in which the VVD did not take part. However, in the absence of a government pushing for exclusion, opposition parties enthusiastically took over that role. Indeed, no government faced more questions and motions criticizing immigrants' use of the welfare system than the fourth Balkenende government.

The conclusion to draw from all this seems to be that in the Netherlands conservative governments and political parties have more often proposed IEWRs than their more progressive counterparts, but that once such proposals are on the table other parties feel compelled to vote in favour of them. Because parties do not depend on the people affected by the reforms for their re-election but potentially have much to lose by opposing reforms that are framed as "commonsense" reforms of a dysfunctional system, the objections to IEWRs tend to be limited in number and muted in tone.[30]

While the scarcity of parliamentary opposition facilitated the adoption of restrictive policy changes, national and especially international legal prohibitions on differential treatment have impeded efforts to disentitle immigrants. These roadblocks have proven so formidable that the exclusion of immigrants would have been more dramatic in their absence, and that it seems unlikely the Netherlands will go much further in disentitling immigrants than it already has.

Probably most importantly, it is impossible in the Netherlands to implement any policy that directly discriminates between native-born citizens and legal immigrant residents. The principle of non-discrimination is codified in Article 1 of the Dutch Constitution and is also guaranteed in several treaties to which the Netherlands is party – in particular, the ECHR, the UDHR, and the ICESCR. Similarly, whatever reforms Dutch politicians might design, under no circumstances can they violate the nationally and internationally codified obligation to offer every legal resident a minimum standard of living and the right to a private life. Finally, suggestions for IEWRs are constrained by the

social security agreements the Netherlands has struck with other countries, either bilaterally or as part of their membership in the EU. As we
will see, the principle that EU migrants can count their work experience
in other member-states in the calculation of eligibility for employee
insurance programs has proven a particular source of irritation for proponents of IEWRs.

Besides posing legal obstacles, these commitments are a source of
normative pressure. Indeed, many of my interviewees felt compelled
to point out that the differentiations they endorse are not forms of discrimination. A senior civil servant at the Department of Social Affairs
said it seemed highly unlikely that overtly discriminatory changes in
social policy would ever be implemented:

> Some members of parliament think that you should further distinguish
> even after you have been admitted. But we have always said about that:
> the Netherlands is committed to all kinds of things within the EU, all kinds
> of things within the ILO, all kinds of things within the UN, otherwise with
> the Council of Europe; we are simply built in entirely. The principle of
> equal treatment is simply sacred. Period. (interview NET13)

When devising ways to limit immigrants' access to the Dutch welfare state, politicians thus need to inform themselves about the legal
feasibility of their plans. In 2006, Arno Visser (VVD) proposed that a
committee be struck to investigate "which international treaties are
relevant in regards to the file 'migration and social security,' and the
ways in which it is possible within international law to withdraw from,
or amend these treaties" (TK18–1259, 26 October 2006). Moreover, the
author of almost every welfare chauvinist proposal needs to explain
at length why it does not violate the non-discrimination principle. For
example, when suggesting tying immigrants' eligibility for social assistance to language proficiency in Dutch, Stef Blok (VVD) spent much
time arguing that it fell within the ECHR provisos outlining under
which conditions differential treatment is justified. During our interview, Cora van Nieuwenhuizen (VVD) shared her frustration over the
obligation to justify differential treatment, arguing that it should be easier to extend more rights to those who have lived in the Netherlands for
a longer time: "See, that is the difficulty we have with the Convention
of Human Rights and the principle of non-discrimination ... If people
have worked longer, they [should] receive a benefit longer. That's certainly a problem we have in Europe" (interview NET01).

We can distinguish four different strategies that Dutch politicians have followed in trying to deal with these legal commitments. First, they have worked around them. Perhaps the most straightforward evidence of this strategy is the simple observation that the most dramatic IEWRs have targeted those immigrants who enjoy the least legal protection: temporary and, in particular, undocumented migrants. We can also point to the above-mentioned Visser motion (which was supported by all MPs). Its explicit purpose was to map the legal obstacles to restrictions in migrants' social rights so that future proposals would focus on restrictions that were legally feasible. Similarly, the first Rutte cabinet quickly learned that its proposal for a "country of residence principle" in the export of benefits (adjusting benefit levels to the country in which the recipient resides) would be impossible to implement within the framework of EU legislation, and therefore decided to redraft the bill and make it apply to benefit recipients outside of the EU only (TK-32878-B, 9 December 2011). The bill that cut the social assistance of migrants with low levels of language proficiency has undergone a similar transformation. The Council of State – the most important legal-constitutional advisory organ – commented on an early version of the bill that it would violate the equality principle because it would subject immigrants to requirements that native-born citizens did not have to satisfy. In response, Van Nieuwenhuizen (VVD) changed the bill and made Dutch-language proficiency a requirement for all welfare recipients, regardless of country of birth (see TK-32328-5, 21 February 2011; TK-32328-9, 15 May 2012).

A second and related strategy has been to "patch up" unchangeable institutions by adding or amending other policies that make the original institution perform in the desired fashion. For example, the legal obligation (per Article 20 of the Constitution, Article 22 of the UDHR, and Article 9 of the ICESCR) to offer everyone in the Netherlands a minimally decent standard of living has made it impossible to strip social assistance from legal residents. That is why residence requirements for welfare are accompanied by the provision that newcomers lose their legal residence status as soon as they apply for social assistance. Similarly, confronted with the impossibility of disentitling permanent migrants from social provisions, champions of IEWRs have shifted their attention to lengthening the residence requirement to acquire a permanent residence permit. This applies not only to the proposals by the VVD and PVV to place a ten-year residence requirement on access to permanent residence status, but also to the 2012 reform of family migration law that has extended the period during which family migrants are on a "partner-dependent residence permit" from three years to five. Immigration minister Gerd Leers (CDA) explicitly stated that the primary goal of the change was "to prevent a reliance on social assistance for two more years" (TK-32175–21, 17 February 2012). Other examples of this sort of "policy layering" are the decision to ban the practice of hiring labour migrants on part-time contracts under the minimum wage because otherwise these migrant workers would become eligible for social assistance (TK-32144–5, 11 April 2011) and the decision to allow refugee claimants to work for only twenty-four weeks a year because they would otherwise start building up eligibility for employment insurance (TK-32144–9, 23 June 2011).

A final albeit less common strategy has been to amend or abolish the legal obstacles. The *Beu* Act, which limits the export of benefits, had a transition period of three years, meaning that after its ratification in 2000 people could still receive benefits abroad until 2003. On 14 March of that year, however, the Central Appeals Tribunal (*Centrale Raad van Beroep*, the highest court for administrative law) ruled that the act violated ILO Convention 118, which includes, among other things, an unconditional requirement to export long-term disability benefits. In response, the Netherlands withdrew from the convention and then introduced the bill again. The first Rutte cabinet (2010–2012) pursued a similar strategy to push through some of its proposals. Eddy van Hijum (CDA) mentioned that within the coalition there have been frequent discussions about "efforts in the European context to amend some rules" (interview NET04). In similar terms, cabinet ministers have repeatedly declared their "explicit ambition to change legislation in the European context in order to be able to set more onerous demands on family migration for the purpose of a more auspicious integration" (TK-32175–15, 14 January 2011). The cabinet has also aimed its arrows at bilateral social security agreements. In 2010, then social affairs minister Henk Kamp (VVD) started renegotiating forty such agreements in order to implement the "country of residence principle," and the succeeding government continued this work. As we saw above, these renegotiations almost led to the abolition of the bilateral agreement with Morocco.

Many of the legal commitments that hinder IEWRs, however, have proven difficult to abandon. Indeed, when junior minister Henk van Hoof (VVD) commented on the possibility of withdrawing from international legal obligations in response to the previously mentioned Visser motion, he made it clear that most restrictions on differential treatment were directly linked to the Netherlands' membership in the EU and the Council of Europe and that withdrawal from those treaties would have consequences that a majority in Parliament would not want to accept. Similarly, after the first Rutte cabinet presented its government agreement, the so-called Meijers Committee (an independent organization that gives legal advice to the EU and its member-states on immigration, refugee, and criminal law) was quick to point out that many of the proposals for IEWRs would violate both EU law and the ECHR (Commissie Meijers 2010). In many cases, then, Dutch politicians simply have had to accept that their legislative powers are not infinite. We saw this earlier in case of the five-year residence requirement on access to social provisions: even though the government of the Netherlands established in 2005 that any non-permanent immigrant claiming social assistance should be deported, in practice deportation is rare because in many cases it would violate the right of immigrants to a private and family life as enshrined in Article 8 of the ECHR (Zorlu, Hartog, and Beentjes 2010, 11). Another example comes from 2012, when a migrant receiving social assistance argued that the administrative charge that had been levied on his application for family reunification violated Article 8 of the ECHR. The ECHR ruled in his favour (*G.R. v. The Netherlands*, 2012), and the government was compelled to reduce the landing fee for people in his situation (TK-32175–28, 13 April 2012). In these examples, the immutability of the legal framework means that attempts to reduce immigrants' access to welfare state benefits do not work as effectively as their instigators would want.

In other examples, attempts at welfare exclusion have failed altogether. For example, the CDA proposed to include a provision in the Linking Act that would have made it impossible for anyone to appeal a rejection of benefits based on residence status. But because this provision would have violated Article 6 of the ECHR, it never made it into the bill. Something similar happened with the VVD's proposal for the "Danish model" in social assistance law, which ties the level of a benefit to the number of years the recipient has lived in the country. Unlike its Danish counterpart, the Dutch judiciary can directly test whether legislation is in line with European law. Since the model violates Article 14 of the ECHR, the VVD has, at least for the time being, abandoned this proposal (interview NET01). Finally, after repeated failed attempts to repeal the EU principle that migrants can count their work experience in other member-states in calculating benefit eligibility, it seems this IEWR has been abandoned as well. This is well illustrated by subsequent comments by former social affairs minister Kamp (VVD). In April 2011 he declared enthusiastically that he was planning to raise the issue at EU Council meetings (TK-29407–118, 18 April 2011), but by October he was less optimistic, stating that "we are doing our best [...], but we have not really garnered much support" (TK-21501–31, 27 October 2011. A few months later he stated flat out that he estimated the chances of amending this rule to be "nil" (50–16, 7 February 2012).

All in all, it seems therefore that the Netherlands has almost reached the limit of how far it can realistically go in excluding immigrants from the welfare state. This has been communicated to Parliament on several occasions. In 2007, for example, the Socio-Economic Council advised that "the possibility for further measures [to exclude migrants] is very limited, especially because of international legal obligations" (SER 2007, 124). Similarly, in 2009 social affairs minister Jan Piet Hein Donner (CDA) concluded the following regarding recent adjustments to the Dutch welfare state:

In demarcating our social security system a balance has been sought between the desire to offer social protection to labour migrants who contribute to the economy on the one hand and preventing that by offering this protection the Dutch social security would become a pull factor in itself to reside here on the other. The government concludes that this balance has been reached. Further measures to restrict access to our system, for example a grow-in model through the formulation of residence requirements, would not only distort this balance, but also result in unequal treatment in equal cases. (35-3-13416, 18 September 2009)

In this context, it is instructive to look at a letter then junior minister Van Hoof (VVD) sent four years earlier, outlining possibilities for restrictions on immigrants' access (kst-29861–2). This welfare chauvinist wish list contained six[31] proposals: (1) cut welfare for temporary migrants who do not have a durable connection to the Netherlands; (2) increase information-sharing between municipal welfare offices and immigration services; (3) extend the residence requirement for family migrants from three to five years; (4) cut the welfare of refugee claimants in an appeal procedure; (5) force all incoming migrants to buy in their pension gap or renounce the right to the AIO supplement; and (6) introduce a Danish model of social assistance. As we have seen, the first three proposals have already been implemented, and the last three are legally and/or practically unachievable. This of course will not prevent politicians from continuing to propose restrictions that are unlikely to pass constitutional muster or to make a substantial difference,[32] but it does imply that additional far-reaching IEWRs seem unlikely in the immediate future.

Another reason is that further restrictions, such as cutting the welfare of refugees who do not speak Dutch, extending the residence requirement on social assistance to ten years, implementing residence requirements on employer insurance programs, or restricting the export of unemployment and contributory pension benefits, do not enjoy support from any party other than the VVD, the PVV, and possibly the new populist party FVD.[33] The CDA, which has been instrumental in many of the reforms discussed in this chapter, is a pivotal player in this regard. As we saw in the quote by Donner, and earlier in Van Hijum's remark that there are certain "boundaries he does not want to touch," there seems to be little enthusiasm among the Christian Democrats for more drastic measures. At the end of our interview, Van Hijum came back to this point:

> In my opinion [we should be in favour of] a grow-in model, in which you need to emphasize the autonomy of people much more, especially when they come here, but you will have to do that within the framework of international rules of the game and also the fact that you have to recognize that our society is simply becoming more open and international. And that thus also means that you must be able to build up social security rights, also as a labour migrant. And that if it is about [public pensions] or disability, you shouldn't fuss about the export of it. That I really consider very clear boundary conditions that we have set, just like social assistance for refugees ... After several reforms and restrictions, we are by now at a level where you also have to ask yourself what you want to preserve. (interview NET04)

So it seems that more drastic IEWRs, even if they could survive legal scrutiny, would only be possible if the VVD, the PVV, and/or potentially a different AIP somehow managed to form a majority government. This seems unlikely. For one thing, as mentioned, the VVD currently excludes the possibility of again entering a government with the PVV. More importantly, over the last three parliamentary elections, the VVD, PVV, and FVD have won a combined total of 55, 56, and 55 seats, respectively. It seems difficult to believe that a coalition of these parties will ever be able to acquire the additional twenty seats that would be

Figure 5.6. "Virtual" parliamentary presence of VVD and anti-immigrant parties, 2000–June 2017

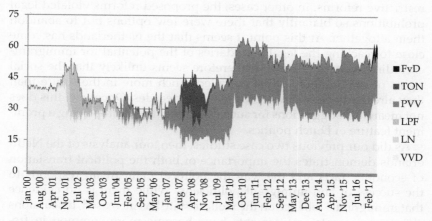

Source: Synovate

necessary for a parliamentary majority. At any rate, opinion polls suggest that outcome is unlikely. Figure 5.6 shows, since the beginning of this century, how many seats the VVD, the PVV, and other AIPs would have in the Lower House of Parliament according to a weekly opinion poll (Synovate). Since 2010, this number has hovered continuously around 55, and none of the peaks has exceeded 65.

In conclusion, over the last two decades the Netherlands has restricted immigrants' access about as much as possible. Recent Dutch history has featured a long series of IEWRs, including exclusions of undocumented migrants, the lengthening of residence requirements, limitations on benefit export, the abolition of programs that assist migrants, and the implementation of requirements that tie immigrants' access to successful participation in (unfunded) integration programs. This development has followed a change in the political climate. In a context of welfare cuts and increased unease over multiculturalism and immigrant diversity, anti-immigrant politicians have successfully challenged the dominant approach to immigrants' social rights. Not only did they manage to change the nature of political discourse on the subject, they also convinced more mainstream politicians to adopt a more restrictive line on immigration and to cooperate in reducing immigrants' benefit access. National and international legal commitments, however, have frustrated some of these efforts. In some cases, policy-makers have worked around or amended legal roadblocks in order to implement restrictive reforms. In other cases, the proposed reforms violated legal prohibitions so blatantly that there were few options but to abandon them altogether. At this point it seems that the Netherlands has come close to reaching the legal boundaries of the potential for immigrant-excluding welfare reforms. It therefore seems unlikely that the social rights of immigrants will be curtailed much more in the future than they already have been over the last two decades. Of course, this does not mean that suggestions for such curtailments will stop being a prominent feature of Dutch politics.

As did our previous two case studies, then, our analysis of the Netherlands demonstrates the importance of both the political translation of economic facts and the way the political mainstream responds to the success of anti-immigrant politicians. While there is no evidence that immigrants' reliance on the welfare state has increased, discussions about immigrants' entitlements have become more common in frequency and more accusatory in tone. In particular, politicians are now more likely to blame immigrants for their difficulties on the labour market and to reject the notion that the state has any responsibility to help them. Moreover, we have seen that the success of anti-immigrant politicians has been particularly consequential because, in sharp contrast to what we saw in the Swedish case, mainstream parties have responded to AIPs by co-legislating with them and adopting a more restrictive line on immigration themselves. Finally, the Dutch case illustrates a theoretical point that was less obvious in our investigation of Sweden and Canada: the institutional dynamics of implementing IEWRs are very different from what we know about more general social policy reform. A key insight in the scholarship on welfare retrenchment is that attempts at across-the-board cutbacks will likely face popular opposition and are therefore electorally risky. We have seen almost the exact opposite in the adoption of IEWRs in the Netherlands. Once proposals for disentitling immigrants were on the table, politicians seemed to consider it far less electorally risky to support them than to oppose them. The most significant hurdles to the implementation of IEWRs in the Netherlands, then, have come not from society or Parliament but from the national and international legal system.

Chapter Six

Conclusions

Immigration has become one of the most salient subjects on the political agenda of Western democracies. Humanitarian crises, global inequality, and enhanced opportunities for international travel have placed pressure on European and North American governments to take in more newcomers. But the subject generates controversy, which in many countries plays out in a context of lingering and sometimes escalating tensions between native-born and migrant groups. Politicians and citizens are sharply divided not only on whether immigrants should be admitted in the first place, but also on the rights and responsibilities they should have if they *are* eventually admitted. A particularly thorny issue is immigrants' access to social benefits and services. Some reason that exclusion from welfare arrangements places migrants, especially those with precarious status, in a vulnerable and marginalized socio-economic position; others argue that granting immediate access can threaten the future of welfare state arrangements, not only because of the financial costs of such access but also because of the resentment it might trigger among the native-born about the welfare state in general and the benefits immigrants can make use of in particular.

Academic literature has by no means ignored these developments. So far, however, it has paid little systematic attention to the efforts of some politicians to disentitle immigrants from benefits and services – policy adjustments I have referred to here as immigrant-excluding welfare reforms (IEWRs). The few recent studies on this subject are primarily interested in either offering an empirical overview of immigrants' social rights in one or more countries (Boucher and Carney 2009; Koning and Banting 2013; Sainsbury 2012) or in investigating the consequences of reforms that have reduced immigrants' benefit access (Fix 2009;

Sabates-Wheeler and Feldman 2011). Most other research on the relationship between immigration and welfare has investigated aggregate effects, examining whether cross-border mobility has a negative impact on national economies in general and welfare state systems in particular. We now know that this is not the case. Politicians who are worried about immigration's impact on the welfare budget have more options at their disposal than pushing for a general retrenchment of the welfare state. Especially in the context of widespread anti-immigrant sentiment, the alternative option of reducing immigrants' access to benefits is likely to be much more popular. In contrast to a central assumption in the available literature, this research finds that xenophobia *reduces* the likelihood of across-the-board welfare retrenchment. In the case of the Netherlands, we saw that policy-makers tend to respond to economic pressure by reducing immigrants' welfare access, not by making the system as a whole less generous. Ironically, the Swedish case suggests that social policy ctbacks of a general nature are a more likely response in communities that are firmly committed to equality.

An additional reason to pay more attention to IEWRs is that the theoretical tools political scientists have developed to understand other social policy changes do not seem applicable to this type of reform. A large literature on the "new politics of the welfare state" has explored how policy-makers can tackle the challenges of today (such as aging, economic globalization, and the emergence of the hourglass economy) in face of widespread public support for most welfare state institutions. While scholars have occasionally noted that changes in eligibility requirements are among the most feasible reforms in the era of the institutionalized welfare state (Pierson 1996, 174; Visser and Hemerijck 1997, 77), the theoretical relevance of policy changes that disentitle newcomers to the political community seems to have been underappreciated. After all, by targeting unprotected groups with little organization behind them, IEWRs avoid the mass objections other policy changes are likely to solicit. At the same time, they face very different institutional obstacles in the form of legal prohibitions on differential treatment. In sum, in contrast to what seems to be the tacit assumption in existing studies of immigrants' social rights, this research shows that the implementation of this specific subtype of social policy change proceeds very differently from the kinds of changes on which the literature has based its theoretical propositions.

The scarcity of theoretical accounts of IEWRs has not prevented politicians, public commentators, and academics from speculating freely about the origins of these policy changes. Political proponents tend to justify these exclusions as a response to "incontrovertible facts" about immigrants' use of social benefits. Immigrants make so much use of social programs, so the explanation goes, that unlimited access will surely make a redistributive welfare state an unsustainable project. As Martin Bosma, commonly viewed as the brain behind the Dutch anti-immigrant party PVV, puts it, "the facts are the facts, and that's what we should base our actions on" (Bosma 2010, 206). Similarly, many observers have pointed to the tension between open borders and generous welfare policies to argue that differentiation in social rights or even the downright exclusion of (some groups of) migrants from certain benefits is no more than a necessary response to the economic pressure generated by immigration (Engelen 2003; Goodhart 2004).

A key conclusion of this research is that this "intuitive" explanation is wrong. To be sure, some types of differentiation between immigrants and the native-born can be justified by considerations of both practicality and fairness. For example, a public pension benefit without a residence requirement would seem difficult, if not impossible, to finance. Besides, in case of immigrants who move from one well-developed welfare state to another, it is not clear why old age security should be paid for exclusively by the country where they happen to be residing on the day they pass retirement age. For similar reasons, one can reasonably defend the tendency that immigrants have less access to contributory programs such as sickness insurance and unemployment insurance than the native-born, because the mechanism of insurance premiums implies that applicants can only access this type of program after they have helped finance it. Another type of differentiation where arguments about necessity make sense is offering fewer services and programs to undocumented migrants than to documented migrants. Especially in countries that border on emigration countries, the welfare system risks making admission policies obsolete if it treats migrants with a valid permit in the same way as undocumented migrants, in particular illegal entrants.

In this sense, I do not disagree with authors who advocate "differentiated citizenship" (Engelen 2003). However, if these are the kinds of differentiation advocates have in mind, the societal relevance of their pleas is unclear. After all, every Western welfare state places a residence requirement on their public pension benefit, and none of them give immigrants easier access to insurance programs than native-born citizens, or offer undocumented migrants the exact same set of benefits as documented migrants. In other words, the kinds of differentiation in social rights that are most justifiable are present in every immigrant-receiving welfare state. As we saw in the previous three chapters, however, the suggestions for welfare exclusion that immigration critics have put forward over the last two decades tend to go much further. They include proposals to deny emergency health care and the most residual cash benefit to undocumented migrants even if they cannot feasibly be deported, to give legal immigrants less or no access to programs of last resort, to restrict the possibility of bringing built-up entitlements to contributory programs across borders, to deny immigrants access to benefits they pay into, and to impose eligibility requirements on immigrants that native-born citizens do not have to satisfy.

When it comes to these kinds of differentiation, arguments about economic necessity are unconvincing. As we have seen, the common argument that these kinds of restrictions are necessary to fend off those who merely move to a country to avail themselves of the benefits of the welfare state has found very little empirical support in economic studies (Barrett and McCarthy 2008; Kvist 2004; Voss, Hammer, and Meier 2001; WRR 2001; Yang and Wallace 2007). Similarly, the suggestion that access should be curtailed because immigrants have a larger propensity than native-born citizens to draw benefits goes against all the available evidence that immigrants are actually *less* likely than the native-born to claim the benefits they are entitled to (Boeri 2009, 20; Capps, Hagan, and Rodriguez 2004; Castronova et al. 2001; Dörr and Faist 1997; Kretsedemas 2004; Ma and Chi 2005; Moon, Lubben, and Villa 1998; Reitz 1995; Sainsbury 2012, 126; Tienda and Jensen 1986).

Third, there is little reason to suggest that IEWRs would address the problems they are supposed to tackle better than alternative solutions such as employing more selective admission policies, investing in integration policies, or implementing across-the-board welfare reforms. As said, proposals for disentitlement tend to rely on faulty assumptions regarding the nature of immigrant welfare dependence, and we have seen that some of these reforms have led to very few practical cost savings. Moreover, welfare exclusion is likely to have a number of counterproductive consequences. For one thing, some studies have concluded that exclusion from one type of benefit is likely to increase the caseload of other, potentially more costly, programs and services (Doctors Without Borders 2005; Kahanec, Kim, and Zimmerman 2013). Moreover, IEWRs are likely to reinforce tensions between immigrants and native-born citizens – not only because they are likely to widen the economic gap between immigrants and native-born and thus contribute to intergroup tension (Horowitz 2000; R. Wilkinson and Pickett 2010), but also because they make the distinction between native-born insider and immigrant outsider an institutionalized feature of the social policy apparatus. Especially when these exclusionary reforms come about after politicized and divisive debates, they are likely to contribute to the very integration difficulties their champions predict them to address.[1]

Fourth, and finally, this research has offered ample evidence that economic reality has little to do with proposals for IEWRs. There is some indication that concerns about immigrants' welfare use become more pronounced in economically difficult times. For example, it was in the context of the declining growth rates and budget deficits of the early 1990s that concerns about the welfare use of "bogus" refugees were most pronounced in Canada. Similarly, parties advocating immigrant exclusion were most successful in Sweden during the two most significant recessions the country has faced over the last two decades, the periods between 1990 and 1994 and after 2008. There is no evidence, however, that calls for the exclusion of immigrants from social programs have been loudest where and when immigrants are most reliant on the welfare system. In other words, the welfare costs of immigrants cannot explain cross-national or cross-temporal differences in the politics of immigrants' social rights. Several pieces of evidence support this conclusion.

First, a quantitative comparison of a dozen Western welfare states found no positive relationship between levels of immigrant welfare use and public sentiments of selective solidarity. In some countries, such as Austria and Ireland, concerns about immigrant welfare use are widespread despite the fact that the actual welfare costs of immigration are low by comparative standards. Conversely, in other countries, such as Sweden and Norway, respondents display few signs of selective solidarity even though immigrants are making heavy use of transfer benefits. This finding is not just based on a simple aggregate comparison. When we control for individual characteristics (such as religion, age, and employment status) and for country characteristics (such as welfare regime type and nation-building policies), the conclusion stands: respondents in countries where immigrants make much use of transfer benefits are *not* more likely to evince selective solidarity than their counterparts in communities where immigrant welfare dependence is low. Moreover, we find the same result if we base our calculations on different types of transfer benefits, different indicators of immigrant welfare dependence, different indicators of selective solidarity, different time periods, and different country samples.

Second, the more qualitative investigation of our three case studies, which allows us to look beyond public opinion and scrutinize political discourse and policy developments, further supports this conclusion. Most obviously, the Dutch and Swedish approaches to immigrants' welfare rights are wildly different, even though levels of immigrant welfare dependence are not higher in the Netherlands than in Sweden. Moreover, economic facts regarding the welfare costs of immigration cannot explain diachronic differences within each country. In the Netherlands, selective solidarity seems to have spread over the last fifteen years while immigrants' employment outcomes have improved. In Canada, conversely, over the last twenty years newcomers have started to turn to the state for support in larger numbers, but this has not led to a concomitant rise in selective solidarity. An analysis of political discourse further suggests that politicians' position on the social rights of immigrants is primarily motivated by other than economic reasons. Some of my interviewees freely admitted that their plans to reduce immigrants' benefit access were not based on a careful cost–benefit analysis. And even in those instances that politicians do invoke economic arguments for placing limits on immigrants' access to social programs, they often depend on a rather opportunistic use of facts. Champions of IEWRs have often aimed their arrows at targets that involve few costs, relied on exaggerations when describing economic reality, or even changed the facts according to political expediency.

All in all, then, the politics of immigrant social rights seem mostly detached from economic reality. In many cases, the economic justification for immigrant welfare exclusion seems to be little more than a façade for hiding ideological objections to immigration and ethnic diversity. (And conversely, the occasional economic arguments for immigrant inclusion in Swedish debate seem but a reflection of their authors' more principled stance on migrant rights.)

To many political scientists, this finding might seem unsurprising. A large literature shows that the same social facts can receive a very different treatment in different political communities. In the comparative literature on social policy change, for example, many have noted that the ways political elites talk about pressures on the welfare system, and the frequency with which they do so, have a large influence on whether retrenchment ultimately takes place. The importance of such processes of political translation of economic facts is particularly large, however, when it comes to the welfare costs of immigration. Immigration is a topic that is particularly sensitive to framing effects. Changes to immigrants' welfare access are motivated not only by considerations of the economic sustainability of the welfare state, but also by beliefs regarding the entitlements of newcomers. Therefore, instead of focusing primarily on the actual costs of immigrants' welfare dependence, we need to look at how these costs are translated into political discourse. In some contexts, immigrant welfare costs are carefully kept off the table. In others, they are at the centre of political attention. In some settings, the costs are explained as the outgrowth of immigrants' difficulties on the labour market and therefore serve as an argument for expanding state efforts to assist integration. In others, they are framed as evidence that immigrants are lazy and have a tendency to take advantage of the system.

The qualitative case studies reveal large differences in the nature of political discourse between Sweden, Canada, and the Netherlands. The differences are particularly stark between the Netherlands on the one hand and Sweden and Canada on the other. For example, not a single Dutch party contests the current arrangement under which permanent migrants are barred from social provisions in the first years after their arrival in the Netherlands. In Canada and Sweden, the political views on such a requirement could not be more different. When during a 1994 convention of the Reform Party – certainly the most immigration-critical party in recent Canadian history – some party members made this very suggestion, party leader Preston Manning dismissed the proposal as too extreme (Flanagan 2009, 197). And when I asked the immigration spokesperson of the explicitly anti-immigrant party Sweden Democrats how he felt about such a residence requirement, he responded that "of course" his party rejected such differentiations between immigrants and the native-born (interview SWE05).

More generally, we can state that country-level differences in the dominant discourse on immigrants' social rights turn out to be much more important than party-level differences in ideological orientation. In other words, two ideologically different parties in one country are more likely to see eye to eye on this subject than two ideologically similar parties in different countries. This does not mean that party differences are non-existent or irrelevant. In all three countries, parties of the left are more likely to advocate inclusion than parties of the right. But the more striking observation is that in each of these three countries, political parties are by and large in agreement about the desirability of

IEWRs. With hardly any opposition from inside or outside Parliament, Dutch governments have scaled down the entitlements of migrants in a large number of ways: they have stripped undocumented migrants of almost all benefits, mandated that only individuals with a "durable connection" can make use of social assistance and other social provisions, increased residence requirements for family migrants, reduced the benefit available to elderly people with a pension gap, made it harder to export benefits abroad, and scrapped almost the entire budget for integration services. In Sweden, meanwhile, reforms aimed at *more* welfare inclusion, such as the expansion of social rights for undocumented migrants, an increase in services available to refugee claimants, the implementation of a variety of immigrant-targeted labour market programs, and the introduction of a specifically immigrant-tailored pension benefit, have gone through Parliament with a similar level of consensus. In Canada, there certainly are important disagreements between the right and the left (concerning, in particular, the appropriate emphasis on economic migrants, or the entitlements of temporary migrants), but few parliamentarians challenge the model of carefully selecting newcomers, offering them a wide range of settlement services, and extending the same benefits to permanent residents as to native-born citizens.

Other examples further illustrate that similar developments have found a very different translation in the three countries under study. The Mediterranean refugee crisis is but the most recent example. Far away from the streams of asylum seekers, the issue became a central topic in the 2015 Canadian elections. The incumbent Conservatives, who invoked arguments about national security and the protection of "Canadian values" to advocate caution in resettlement efforts, lost that election dramatically. More significantly, it lost to a party that insisted that openness to refugees was exactly what Canadian values are about, that objected to the cuts in refugee health care the Conservatives had implemented, and that vowed to settle a large number of refugees as soon as it took office. In Sweden, the initial response was to declare that all asylum seekers with a Syrian passport were welcome. And even though the government introduced border controls and extended temporary permits when the intake exceeded expectations, none of the mainstream parties advocated curtailing the civil and social rights of asylum claimants. In the Netherlands, the refugee crisis reignited concerns about immigration and the costs of immigrant integration. The conservative VVD of prime minister Mark Rutte went so far as to advocate a complete halt on accepting asylum claims from outside the European Union and the denial of even the most basic services for unsuccessful claimants in the Netherlands.

Equally telling is the variation in responses to the economic crisis in the mid-1990s, which in all three countries led to an increase in immigrant unemployment. In the Netherlands, politicians undertook more efforts to make sure undocumented migrants could not make use of social assistance or other transfer benefits. This culminated in the Linking Act, which formally excluded everyone without a legal residence permit from all benefits and programs except emergency care and education for children. In Canada, by contrast, the Liberal government decided to adjust its admission policy so as to ensure that a larger share of the annual intake of newcomers would consist of people who had been specifically selected on the basis of economic criteria. In Sweden, finally, the reaction was yet different. It introduced changes to social policy of a general nature and required *all* welfare recipients to demonstrate they were actively seeking work or improving their qualifications.

The response to family migration in these three countries offers another instructive example. Again, it is the Netherlands that has moved most clearly in an exclusionary direction: by lengthening the waiting period before migrants can claim independent permanent residence status, it has made sure that family migrants are unable to access any residence-based social benefits in their first years in the country. In Canada, those types of arrangements were already in place, but policymakers did not choose to lengthen the duration of sponsorship agreements; instead they increased governmental oversight on whether these agreements were being upheld in practice. Sweden, finally, did not introduce any mechanism of this sort until 2007, and in sharp contrast to the other two cases, this policy change has met fierce criticism from opposition parties. Moreover, the arrangement is decidedly less restrictive than what the Netherlands and Canada have implemented. The so-called Support Requirement affects only a small portion of all incoming family migrants[2] and entails a one-time test whether the "sponsor" has sufficient housing space and makes at least the minimum wage. Most importantly, it does not include any restrictions on benefit access for the migrants themselves.

More generally, there are large differences between these countries in the popularity of the various strategies policy-makers can make use of to avoid or reduce high levels of immigrant welfare dependence. Figure 6.1 shows the percentage of political parties that are in favour

Figure 6.1. Political party support for different responses to Progressive's Dilemma, Sweden, Canada, and the Netherlands

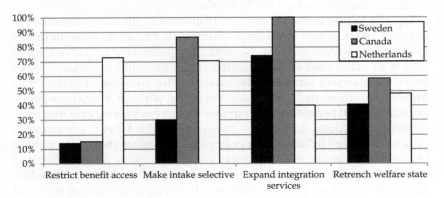

of addressing this issue by restricting benefit access, adopting selective admission policies, investing in integration services, and implementing across-the-board cutbacks, weighted by the percentage of seats they occupy in Parliament.[3]

The picture that emerges is striking. In the Netherlands, more than 70 per cent of Parliament favours restrictions on immigrants' access to social programs and benefits and a similar percentage supports employing a more selective admission policy. The two other options enjoy much less support. Perhaps most strikingly, only about two in five Dutch parliamentarians advocate improving immigrants' social position through immigrant-targeted integration services. In contrast, in Canada the dominant view is that immigrant welfare dependence can best be avoided by combining expanded integration services with selective admission policies. The idea of disentitling immigrants from social programs and benefits receives little support from the major federal political parties. It is in Sweden, finally, that politicians favour the most inclusionary approach. Very few advocate either welfare exclusion or restrictive admission policies, and except for the anti-immigrant party Sweden Democrats, all parties favour at least some integration programs and services. In addition, all right-of-centre parties believe that a flexibilization of the labour market and an overall cut in welfare generosity could improve the economic integration of the immigrant population.

Table 6.1. Relevant comparisons in the politics of immigrants' social rights in the Netherlands, Canada, and Sweden

	Sweden	Canada	Netherlands
Immigrant welfare dependence	Very high	Low	High
Institutional context			
Welfare regime	Universal	Liberal	Hybrid
National identity	Inclusive egalitarian	Inclusive multiculturalist	Decreasingly inclusive
Anti-immigrant politics			
Success of AIPs	Increasing	Very small	Large
Contagion	Some	Some	Much
Compromise	None	None	Much
Political translation			
Salience	High	Low	High
Dominant frame	Integration policy failed	Admission policy failed	Migrants have welfare penchant
Policy outcome			
Preferred strategy to handle Progressive's Dilemma	Investment and general reform	Selective intake and investment	Selective intake and disentitlement
Overall policy direction	Inclusion	Stability	Exclusion

To understand the sharp differences between these three countries, it is helpful to look at both historical factors that have shaped the boundaries of policy-making and political factors that are more recent. Table 6.1 summarizes this theoretical framework, as applied to the three cases under study.[4]

Two institutional characteristics are of particular relevance in shaping the context of immigrants' social rights: the structure of the welfare state, and the nature of national identity. To begin with the first of these factors, IEWRs seem least likely to be considered in a welfare system that is based on universalist principles. We have seen that Swedish respondents express the lowest level of selective solidarity among all the countries investigated in chapter 2 and that Swedish policy-makers have responded to high levels of immigrant welfare dependence with some of the same tools that have been used in the past to encourage the labour market participation of marginalized groups. While not to

the same extent as its Swedish counterpart, the comparatively generous Dutch welfare state initially fostered a similarly inclusive approach
to immigrants: the policy apparatus that was built in the 1970s was
couched explicitly in the inclusive terms of the Dutch *verzorgingsstaat*,
and the social rights this entailed were not seriously contested until the
mid-1990s. At the same time, the more conservative nature of the Dutch
welfare state structure and its traditional reliance on passive benefits
rather than active programs did leave benefit reduction as a more likely
answer to increases in the size of the welfare clientele. (And indeed, in
recent Dutch policy documents and parliamentary debates, the phrases
"reducing immigrants' reliance on programs" and "reducing immigrants' access to programs" are used almost interchangeably.) Finally,
one might expect disentitlement to be a more common response in Canada as well, considering the relatively ungenerous nature of its welfare
system and the large number of means-tested programs. In line with
such an expectation, immigrants to Canada (especially family migrants
and temporary migrants) have indeed been faced with more restrictions on benefit access than their Swedish counterparts. Moreover, in
the few examples from recent Canadian history that politicians contested immigrants' use of social programs (in particular the objections
to the welfare use of "bogus" refugee claimants and the concerns that
recognized refugees receive better health care than native-born Canadians), we observe exactly the invocations of "deservingness" that institutional theories of social policy predict in a residual welfare state. The
bigger story, however, is that the number of such examples is small and
that the multitude of integration services aimed at ameliorating immigrants' economic performance that have been offered since at least the
1980s have gone largely unchallenged and indeed have been expanded.

The second institutional characteristic explains this outcome. A key
component of Canada's national identity is its history of immigration
and its comparatively inclusive approach to (immigration-induced)
diversity. As a consequence, suggestions to restrict immigrants' rights
are easily depicted as "un-Canadian." We can say something similar
about Swedish national identity. Following the tradition of egalitarianism, Swedish politicians tend to understand the equal treatment of
diverse groups as a fundamental characteristic of "Swedishness," and
this has made suggestions for immigrant exclusion difficult to defend.
The values of openness and tolerance have long been seen as central
to the character of the Netherlands as well, but in recent years the
understanding of what it means to be Dutch seems to have undergone

a significant transformation. The argument that the state owes more to "true" Dutch people than to immigrants has become more common, and at times politicians have explicitly framed cultural belonging as a condition for enjoying equal social rights.

In sum, immigrants' use of welfare benefits is unlikely to become a combustible issue in political communities that encourage cohesion. At the same time, however, the Dutch case illustrates that such institutions are neither immutable nor capable of protecting immigrants' social rights from all political challenges. This is where the second step of our theoretical framework comes into play: when the political climate makes it electorally advantageous to present oneself as "tough" on immigration, IEWRs become more likely policy outcomes. As we have seen, the sustained presence of a large anti-immigrant party (AIP) in the Netherlands over the last ten years or so has made the social rights of immigrants a more common subject of political contestation. This is not simply because more anti-immigrant politicians are participating in political debate. It is also because these incoming politicians have been able to influence government policy and the policy positions of mainstream parties. Even though it is true that Dutch AIPs have been met with accusations of xenophobia, their electoral success has led mainstream politicians to cooperate with them and to embrace a more restrictive position on immigration themselves. All the spokespeople of mainstream parties I interviewed asserted that the ascendance of AIPs demonstrates that the political elite has unjustly ignored concerns about immigration and that such concerns must be taken more seriously in the future.

In Canada and Sweden, conversely, such a political climate does not exist, at least not at the moment. True enough, the Liberal Party of Canada adopted a more restrictive position on admission policy right at the time that a populist party seemed to be reaping electoral benefits from its immigration critiques, and the Swedish Social Democrats explicitly justified restrictions on refugee policy as a way to defuse the looming success of the AIP Sweden Democrats. Overall, however, the response from mainstream parties to anti-immigrant voices has tended to be dismissive and hostile. Another relevant difference is that Dutch AIPs have been propagating selective solidarity much more explicitly than either the Canadian Reform Party or the Sweden Democrats. While it is true that all of these parties have repeatedly drawn attention to the welfare costs that immigrants incur, Dutch AIPs (especially the PVV) have framed their critiques in more explicitly divisive terms. Most importantly, while the PVV has proposed a wide range of IEWRs, immigration critics in the Canadian and Swedish parliaments have made very few such suggestions. Indeed, the Reform Party of Canada hardly ever targeted immigrants who already had been admitted and tended to advocate restrictions in admission policy rather than in immigrants' access to programs and benefits. The Sweden Democrats have certainly made some suggestions for welfare exclusion but have been cautious in doing so when communicating with the public at large. When I asked about these plans, the SD immigration spokesperson simply denied they existed.

It would be wrong to suggest, however, that we only need to investigate the success of anti-immigrant politicians when explaining the adoption of IEWRs. As the Dutch case makes clear, national and international legal structures can pose a significant obstacle to attempts at disentitling immigrants. It seems safe to say that policy-makers would have gone further in excluding migrants from the welfare state if the Netherlands were not bound by national and international legal prohibitions on differential treatment. In 2006 the Dutch Parliament unanimously adopted a motion asking the government to investigate the legal possibilities of implementing a range of disentitling reforms, but those changes proved legally impossible and have therefore been abandoned. Similarly, EU legislation has repeatedly frustrated attempts to reduce EU migrants' access to employee insurance programs. In other cases, welfare exclusion could only come about after governments withdrew from international conventions or carefully navigated the legal obstacles.

Again, it is worth emphasizing that it is in these institutional dynamics of policy implementation that we notice a clear difference between IEWRs and more general social policy changes. Much literature has noted that across-the-board cutbacks in social programs tend to solicit large-scale opposition from the electorate. IEWRs are likely to meet less public resistance. Few voters will themselves be affected by policy changes aimed at disentitling future newcomers to the country. In other words, IEWRs tend to target people who have little voice in decision-making, most obviously when the reforms grandfather existing cases and target future newcomers. Instead of democratic opposition, a more significant obstacle to exclusionary welfare reforms is posed by prohibitions on differential treatment flowing from domestic and international legal structures. To push through their proposals, politicians seeking to disentitle immigrants are therefore forced to employ different strategies than their counterparts who are intent on scaling back social programs in a more general fashion. In particular, the implementation of IEWRs necessitates dealing with legal roadblocks in one way or another, either by working around them, layering additional policies on top of them, or amending them.

The central findings of this project have at least three important implications. First, they demonstrate the need for more attention to the politics of immigrants' social rights. Reforms that disentitle a growing subset of immigrant-receiving welfare states raise serious concerns about the future of social protection, yet we know strikingly little about the conditions under which they come about. This is all the more pressing considering that there are good reasons to believe that the implementation of IEWRs operates very differently from what we know about more general welfare retrenchment. This research has aimed to contribute to our understanding by comparing three very different political settings and investigating how the politics of social rights have played out in each of them. This comparison suggests that any explanation for the emergence of IEWRs should pay serious attention to political translation, to the political mainstream's response to anti-immigrant politicians, and to the extent to which immigrants' social rights are protected in existing legal frameworks. But more research on the subject is clearly warranted, not least because we cannot be certain about the external validity of these conclusions based on the intensive investigation of only three cases.

Second, the findings of this research suggest that when immigration becomes a salient political cleavage, it can transcend the boundaries of immigration politics and affect policy-making in at best indirectly related areas. Indeed, many of the suggestions for IEWRs have more to do with concerns about immigration in general than about social policy in particular. The implications for the study of public policy are clear: any explanation for policy change is potentially incomplete if it only considers policy areas that are directly related or focuses primarily on the likely consequences of the reform under investigation. In other words, if politicians believe that proposing or supporting a policy change helps make them appear sensitive to issues of concern to voters, analysing the details of a bill in the relevant policy context will offer little insight into the reasons for its adoption.

Finally, this observation has important political implications as well: when it comes to the politics of immigrants' social rights, we should be sceptical about explanations that politicians offer for their positions, especially when they are couched in economic reasoning. As attested by the many proposals we have seen that are vague, legally unfeasible, unsupported by evidence, inconsequential, and/or counterproductive, the politics of immigrant welfare exclusion often seem more about politicizing the issue than about making genuine suggestions for reform.

Appendix Tables

Appendix 1. Questions and motions on immigrants' welfare use in Sweden

Table A1.1. Interpellations criticizing immigrants' use of / access to welfare benefits

Date (code)	Party	Content
1993/3/30 (86: 27–32)	ND	Cut services for refugees who leave region where they were settled
1994/3/21 (76: 12–19)	ND	Give coupons to refugee claimants instead of pocket money to avoid fraud
1994/5/27 (112: §9)	ND	Benefit fraud by immigrants
1995/4/3 (84: 36–42)	M	Level of welfare benefit for refugees is too high
1996/2/8 (52: 17–23)	M	Welfare fraud by foreigners
1998/3/25 (86: 55–67)	M	Map costs of refugee policy for Swedish welfare state
2000/4/25 (99: 24–30	M	Map costs of refugee policy for Swedish welfare state
2011/3/10 (70: 39–42)	SD	Abolish *nystartzoner*
2011/3/17 (74: 60–63)	SD	Reduce undocumented migrants' access to benefits
2011/11/24 (36: 90–93)	SD	Costs of immigration
2012/3/20 (85: 57–60)	SD	Costs of immigration
2012/10/4 (8: 18–21)	SD	Costs of immigration
2012/11/16 (26: 22–28)	SD	Abuse of SFI system as welfare guarantee by illiterate immigrants
2012/12/6 (38: 39–42)	SD	Reduce exceptions to support requirement in family migration

Table A1.2. Motions proposing to curtail immigrants' access to welfare state benefits

Date (code)	Party	Content
1992/5/11 (Fi42)	ND	Stop funding of education in native tongue
1992/11/1 (Fi36)	ND	Stop funding education in native tongue, reduce financial assistance to refugees
1993/1/26 (Sf628)	ND	Reduce immigrant services, refugee accommodation, and cash assistance
1993/1/26 (Fi211)	ND	Reduce financial assistance for refugees, decrease funding of Swedish language classes, stop funding education in native tongue
1993/2/3 (Sf22)	ND	Cut benefits of refugees who do not work in allocated employment or learn Swedish, decrease assistance for legal aid, stop export of all benefits, cut social assistance for immigrant women who do not speak Swedish, make asylum seekers pay for medical services, stop funding of native tongue education
1993/5/6 (Fi93)	ND	Cut benefits of refugees who do not work in allocated employment or learn Swedish, reduce settlement services by 20%, stop export of benefits, make asylum seekers pay for medical services, reduce social assistance in first two years by 20%; stop funding of native tongue education; cut immigrant-targeted ALMPs
1994/1/13 (Sf607)	S	Make immigrant associations and advocacy groups largely in charge of asylum centres, to reduce costs
1994/1/20 (Sf621)	ND	Reduce refugee settlement and integration services
1994/1/25 (A262)	ND	Repeal immigrant job training programs, cut benefits to those who do not participate in language classes
1994/5/10 (Fi31)	ND	Reduce refugee settlement services, abolish native tongue education
1995/1/16 (Sf608)	M	Devolve immigrant settlement to advocacy groups, replace settlement benefit with loan
1996/10/7 (So665)	M	Prevent immigrants from using social assistance for trips to country of origin
1996/10/7 (Sf630)	M	Reduce benefits for immigrants who do not participate in integration programs
1997/10/3 (Sf04)	M	Decrease funding for native tongue education, introduce loan system for new immigrants
1999/9/24 (Sf603)	M	Map costs of asylum and refugee policy since 1985
2000/4/28 (Fi49)	M	Stop subsidies for immigrant-dense neighbourhoods
2000/9/21 (Sf603)	M	Map costs and benefits of immigration policy since 1985
2000/9/28 (Sf610)	M	Force newly arrived migrants to take care of themselves "for a certain time"
2001/9/21 (Sf208)	M	Map costs of immigration and refugee policy since 1985

Date (code)	Party	Content
2002/10/16 (Sf216)	L	Introduce three-year support requirement for all family migrants except refugees
2003/10/6 (Sf396)	C	Cut social assistance of immigrants who do not make use of internship offers
2003/10/7 (Sf388)	L	Introduce three-year support requirement for all family migrants except refugees
2004/2/6 (Sf32)	M	Cut allowance of asylum seekers who refuse to reveal identity, conditionalize introduction benefit
2004/3/29 (Sf44)	KD	Conduct annual study on effects of immigration from new EU countries on Swedish social security system, review 10-hours rule
2004/3/25 (Sf39)	L	Repeal 10-hours rule, deny part-time labourers in Sweden without residence permit all social benefits, repeal export possibilities of range of social programs
2004/9/30 (Sf248)	L	Implement three-year waiting period before labour migrants can access social security, implement five-year support requirement for family migration
2005/9/30 (Sf255)	M	Strictly enforce cutting introduction benefit to those who do not follow language classes or are otherwise engaged in their introduction plan
2006/2/24 (Sf19)	L	Investigate possible changes to EU labour law so a support requirement can be installed for labour migrants
2010/10/26 (Fi231)	SD	Introduce five-year support requirement for family migration, no sponsoring for people who have received welfare in last year
2011/5/3 (Fi11)	SD	Repeal *instegsjobb* and EBO law, introduce five-year support requirement for family migration, no sponsoring for people who have received welfare in last year
2011/9/27 (Sk230)	M	Share population register data with other Nordic states to avoid voting fraud and benefit fraud among migrants
2011/9/29 (Fi242)	SD	Repeal *instegsjobb* and EBO law, introduce five-year support requirement for family migration, no sponsoring for people who have received welfare in last year
2011/9/29 (Fi307)	SD	Cut subsidies to ethnic organizations
2011/10/4 (Sf348)	SD	Collect information on place of birth in statistics of all welfare sectors
2011/10/4 (Sf352)	SD	Introduce five-year support requirement for family migration, no sponsoring for people who have received welfare in last year
2011/10/5 (Sf347)	SD	Restrict immigrants' access to parental benefits
2012/4/23 (Fi15)	SD	Repeal *instegsjobb*, introduce support requirements in family migration
2012/9/26 (Sf217)	SD	Restrict immigrants' access to parental benefits

(Continued)

216   Appendix Tables

Table A1.2. (Continued)

Date (code)	Party	Content
2012/10/2 (A331)	SD	Abolish *instegsjobb*, reduce immigration and use extra funds for welfare provisions for native-born Swedes
2012/10/2 (Fi219)	SD	Abolish *instegsjobb* and all mother-tongue education
2012/10/3 (Fi256)	SD	Collect more fine-grained data on immigrant welfare use
2012/10/3 (Sf316)	SD	Introduce five-year sponsorship requirement
2012/10/3 (Ub323)	SD	Fight use of SFI as welfare guarantee; increase financial incentives to complete

Table A1.3. Interpellations defending immigrants' use of/access to welfare benefits

Date (code)	Party	Content
1994/5/27 (112: 1–10)	V	Increase services to immigrant communities and refugee families
1997/1/29 (56: 22–25)	MP	Offer pension benefit for immigrants with pension gap
1997/2/13 (65: 1–6)	MP	Extra support services for elderly immigrants, including a pension benefit
1999/3/4 (63: 54–57)	S	Pension access for elderly migrants
1999/3/4 (63: 78–81)	L	Access to health and sick care for undocumented immigrants' children
1999/5/18 (98: 32–35)	MP	Extra psychotherapeutic help for refugee children
2000/1/18 (51: 68–74)	C	More financial security for newcomers, in particular elderly migrants
2000/4/4 (91: 23–30)	S	Extra funding for settlement services
2002/11/28 (25: 93–99)	MP	Social rights of refugee children, in particular access to health care
2004/6/14 (127: 72–78)	L	More opportunities for adult immigrant schooling
2004/12/14 (50: 46–52)	L	More funding for reschooling opportunities
2007/6/4 (119: 1–7)	MP	Increase pension uptake by refugees
2008/12/9 (45: 88–95)	MP	Extend medical care to undocumented immigrants
2011/3/8 (*s.f.* 362)	S	Subsidize Uppsala program offering postgraduate education to foreign civil engineers
2011/4/20 (*s.f.* 458)	S	Offer language training for longer than two years
2011/6/17 (118: 103–9)	V	Offer more assistance to immigrant women in finding a job
2011/11/18 (33: 73–81)	S	Offer more assistance to immigrant women in finding a job
2012/3/15 (83: 72–75)	M	Waive sponsorship requirements when sponsor dies
2012/11/22 (29: 77–80)	MP	Investigate possibilities of offering more care to traumatized refugees

Table A1.4. Motions proposing to expand immigrants' access to welfare state benefits

Date (code)	Party	Content
1991/1/22 (Sf260)	MP	Give immigrants access to public pension
1991/1/25 (Sf357)	L	Review access to public pension for immigrants
1992/1/16 (Sf601)	S	Introduce introduction benefit
1992/10/20 (Sf1)	V	Give access to public pension for all categories of refugees
1992/10/22 (Sf2)	S	Count years in country of origin in calculation of public pension for convention refugees, war resisters, and *de facto* refugees
1993/1/25 (A477)	S	Expand immigrant-targeted active labour market programs in Stockholm
1993/12/6 (Sf12)	V	Repeal reduction in daily benefit for asylum seekers who avoid authorities; introduce program for torture victim refugees; reduce medical fees for asylum seekers
1994/4/26 (So61)	V	Open mental health institute for refugees who have been victims of torture
1995/1/18 (A276)	S	Implement more immigrant-targeted labour market programs
1995/1/23 (Sf615)	L	Develop plans for "carrot" benefit to entice refugees to stay where they were placed
1995/1/25 (A287)	V	Spend additional 125 million SEK (about C$18 million) on immigrant ALMPs
1995/5/4 (A56)	MP	Offer state loans to immigrants starting an own business, offer individual-tailored education for immigrants, decrease premiums for employers who hire immigrants
1996/2/6 (Ub9)	L	Expand education program for immigrants
1996/10/3 (Sf212)	S	Give tax reduction for people who receive a partial pension benefit from another EU country so as to cancel the costs associated with international money transfers
1996/10/6 (Sf624)	V	Develop pension plan for elderly immigrants
1996/10/7 (Sf633)	MP	Introduce introduction benefit higher than SA, expand education in native tongue, facilitate immigrant entrepreneurialism, expand immigrant-targeted ALMPs
1997/9/29 (U203)	S	Develop benefit to assist migrants who return to country of origin in first three years
1997/10/1 (Sf208)	S	Develop a state-funded pension for immigrants
1997/10/3 (Sf11)	KD	Increase funding of immigrant organizations, facilitate immigrant entrepreneurship (e.g., by offering loans)
1997/10/3 (Sf10)	MP	Introduce introduction benefit higher than SA, expand immigrant-targeted ALMPs (e.g., decrease employer premiums for those hiring immigrants)

(Continued)

Table A1.4. (Continued)

Date (code)	Party	Content
1997/10/6 (Sf622)	MP	Offer newly arrived immigrants a benefit higher than SA, offer language training to all incoming migrants (not just asylum seekers), expand immigrant-targeted ALMPs
1997/10/6 (So432)	V	Invest in language services in elder care, offer public pension to elderly immigrants
1997/10/6 (N307)	L	Develop a start-up capital benefit for immigrant entrepreneurs
1998/4/29 (So62)	MP	Offer benefit for elderly immigrants without income from social insurance/pensions
1998/4/29 (Sf40)	V	Offer public pension to all categories of refugees (not just UN refugees), make sure that any new income provision for elderly immigrants works retroactively
1998/4/29 (Fi65)	V	Offer education to children of asylum seekers
1998/10/12 (A1)	V	Expand immigrant-targeted ALMPs, offer public pension to elderly immigrants
1998/10/22 (Ub709)	KD	Compensate immigrants for taking SFI during studies
1998/10/22 (Sf608)	C	Increase subsidies for immigrant organizations, offer relocation support for immigrant families with children in racist environments
1998/10/23 (So311)	V	Offer public pension to elderly immigrants
1998/10/23 (Sf222)	S	Give tax reduction for people who receive a partial pension benefit from another EU country so as to cancel the costs associated with international money transfers
1998/10/25 (Sf612)	V	Offer education to children of asylum seekers, offer public pension to elderly migrants
1998/10/27 (Sf634)	L	Make start-up benefit available to immigrants on social assistance
1998/10/28 (Sf635)	MP	Open SFI to all immigrants (not just refugees), guarantee education in native tongue
1998/10/28 (Sf263)	S	Explore reducing (now 3-year) waiting period for early retirement benefit for refugees
1999/9/27 (Sf3)	V	Ensure that common EU policy does not infringe upon immigrants' social rights, equate humanitarian migrants with convention refugees for social protection
1999/10/3 (A230)	L	Launch work/education programs for migrant women, start-up benefit for immigrants
1999/10/4 (Sf259)	KD	Increase benefits for adoption parents
1999/10/5 (Sf640)	MP	Introduce introduction benefit higher than SA, open SFI to all immigrants (not just refugees), guarantee state-funded education in native tongue

Date (code)	Party	Content
2000/2/9 (Sf3)	V	Reject government's proposal to only register refugees who come to Sweden as the result of mass refugee situation after three years and keep it at one
2000/4/27 (Fi46)	S	Invest more in development projects in immigrant-dense neighbourhoods
2000/9/25 (Ub228)	KD	Stop denying primary education to adult immigrants on welfare
2000/9/28 (Sf611)	C	Develop national pension plan for elderly migrants
2000/10/4 (Sf634)	V	Make naturalization procedure free for applicants
2000/10/4 (Sf625)	S	Make sure that immigrants on welfare do not pay interest on "home equipment loan"
2000/10/4 (Sf303)	S	Develop a pension plan for elderly immigrants
2000/10/5 (A812)	L	Offer child care during Swedish language instruction
2000/10/3 (Sf274)	MP	Make sure that non-registered children have access to education and social services
2001/09/20 (Sf1)	M	Extend export time of ÄFS from three to six months
2001/9/30 (N263)	C	Develop loan programs, work resource centre, and consultant services for immigrants
2001/10/1 (Sf341)	V	Investigate possibility for export of public pension to non-EU countries
2001/10/1 (Sf300)	S	Offer welfare recipients extra incidental social assistance to pay for naturalization
2001/10/3 (A319)	M	Investigate how immigrants are treated by employment services and improve
2001/10/4 (Sf363)	S	Relax repay requirements for immigrant home equipment loans
2001/10/5 (Sf400)	MP	Develop a pension plan for elderly immigrant women
2001/10/5 (Sf348)	V	Conduct a systematic investigation of all the ways that the social security system discriminates against immigrants indirectly, as in the case of the public pension
2002/4/4 (Sf31)	MP	Invest in translation services, prohibit cutting welfare for poor performance in language classes, encourage education uptake among undocumented children
2002/10/15 (A320)	KD	Start a "job guides" program to help immigrants to a job
2002/10/22 (N306)	C	Develop loan programs, work resource centre, and consultant services for immigrants
2002/10/23 (Ub484)	S	Fund elementary education classes of adult students without gainful employment
2003/2/4 (Sf7)	M	Guarantee full access to education and care for refugee claimant children
2003/3/24 (A5)	KD	Start a "job guides" program to help immigrants to a job

(Continued)

Table A1.4. (Continued)

Date (code)	Party	Content
2003/9/29 (So406)	V	Fund research on negative health outcomes among immigrants and solutions
2003/10/1 (So417)	V	Expand social services for asylum seekers' children
2003/10/2 (So343)	C	Expand preventive health care for children of immigrants
2003/10/5 (N329)	C	Develop immigrant entrepreneur program
2003/10/7 (Sf403)	KD	Offer authorized translation services to refugee claimants during the application
2003/10/7 (Sf402)	KD	Give every immigrant the right to mother tongue education, start "job guides" program
2004/9/7 (Ju293)	L	Start information outreach for shelter services for violence-exposed migrant women
2004/11/12 (Sf9)	KD	Reject government's proposal to cut housing allowance for asylum seekers
2005/9/30 (So556)	L	Give refugee children full access to health care
2005/9/30 (Ju380)	L	Start information outreach for shelter services for violence-exposed migrant women
2005/10/1 (Sf333)	C	Offer new start jobs to immigrants
2005/10/4 (A363)	C	Offer new start jobs to immigrants
2005/10/4 (So551)	C	Investigate ways to improve social services' treatment of elderly migrants
2005/10/4 (Sf336)	V	Expand study allowances, improve pension outcomes for immigrants
2005/10/5 (Sf430)	M	Offer new start jobs, introduce employment support program for immigrants
2005/10/5 (A420)	KD	Offer new start jobs to immigrants
2006/3/29 (K22)	MP	Develop additional protocol to the ESCR Convention, ratify UN agreement on social rights of labour migrants, give two individual cases (torture victims) access to benefits
2006/4/6 (So41)	C	Analyse sources of low uptake of social services by elderly immigrants
2006/10/24 (C276)	V	Improve conditions in asylum seeker housing, reintroduce housing allowance
2006/10/25 (Sf268)	S	Make public pension exportable
2006/10/27 (N295)	KD	Develop a language course for immigrant women who are starting a company
2006/10/27 (Sf219)	MP	Offer public pension to all quota refugees, war resisters, and de facto refugees

Date (code)	Party	Content
2006/10/30 (A270)	V	Develop labour market program for migrant women, investigate indirect discrimination of immigrants in unemployment benefits, expand benefits for migrant students
2006/10/31 (Sf296)	MP	Extend health care to all "hidden" refugees
2007/10/4 (C300)	V	Guarantee higher minimum quality of asylum seeker housing
2008/10/1 (N387)	KD	Develop a language course for immigrant women who are starting a company
2008/10/3 (So392)	L	Cut immigrant on welfare less in their welfare if they start working more
2008/10/7 (A377)	MP	Increase micro-credits available for immigrant entrepreneurs
2009/9/24 (Sf206)	MP	Give all declined refugee claimants their built-up pension rights with them
2009/10/5 (Sf372)	MP	Give adult and "hidden" refugees right to health care, increased housing allowance
2011/10/4 (Fi243)	V	Offer immigrants elderly care in mother tongue, extend introduction time
2011/10/4 (So521)	S	Offer immigrants elderly care in mother tongue
2011/10/5 (Fi241)	MP	Invest more in mother-tongue instruction
2011/10/5 (So590)	V	Offer immigrants elderly care in mother tongue
2012/4/28 (…)	V	Offer immigrants elderly care in mother tongue
2012/9/10 (Sf207)	V	Sign migrant worker convention, enhance social rights of migrant workers
2012/9/25 (So506)	S	Offer more targeted elderly migrant care, including service in mother tongue
2012/9/28 (So536)	S	Offer more targeted elderly migrant care, including service in mother tongue
2012/10/1 (So557)	S	Offer more targeted elderly migrant care, including service in mother tongue
2012/10/2 (So540)	MP	Invest more in post-traumatic stress treatment of refugees, in particular specialized treatment for traumatized children
2012/10/3 (So487)	V	Improve possibilities for immigrant-targeted elderly care
2012/10/5 (A360)	S	Investigate options for extending introduction benefit support after 2 years (for municipalities, not for migrants)
2012/10/5 (A393)	MP	Abolish support requirement, expand mother-tongue education, ratify migrant worker convention, increase level of financial assistance to asylum seekers
2012/10/5 (Fi303)	MP	Expand mother tongue education, expand undocumented migrants' social rights
2012/10/5 (Sf389)	MP	Facilitate public pension export to Chile

Appendix 2. Questions, motions, and petitions on immigrants' welfare use in Canada

Table A2.1. Questions criticizing immigrants' use of/access to welfare benefits

Date (y/m/d)	Interpellant (party)	Subject of criticism/inquiry
1994/2/22	Grubel (RPC)	Costs of medical services for family migrants
1994/4/15	Hanger (RPC)	Costs in health services for HIV positive immigrants
1994/4/21	Lee (LPC)	Costs of failed refugee claimants
1994/10/24	Hanger (RPC)	Sponsorship breakdowns
1994/10/24	Hanger (RPC)	People on benefits while sponsoring relatives
1995/3/22	T. White (RPC)	Immigrants who claim child benefits but do not report full world income
1995/4/24	Harper (RPC)	Lawsuit levelled by sponsored immigrants on welfare in Ontario
1995/5/5	Hanger (RPC)	Health care access of refugee claimants
1995/10/6	Hanger (RPC)	Health care costs of refugee claimants
1995/11/6	Meredith (RPC)	Costs of sponsorship breakdown
1995/12/4	Hanger (RPC)	Sponsored migrants on welfare
1995/12/14	Meredith (RPC)	Absence of bonds to ensure compliance with sponsorship agreements
1999/10/13	Benoit (RPC)	Costs of immigrants in Toronto
1999/12/6	McKay (LPC)	Costs of refugee claimants' use of health and housing services
2001/9/21	R. White (CA)	Costs of family reunification for health care and social programs
2004/11/2	R. White (CPC)	Criminal refugees' access to medical benefits and cash assistance
2005/4/22	D'Amours (LPC)	Costs for health care of parents' and grandparents' family migration
2005/5/18	Folco (LPC)	Costs of parents' and grandparents' family migration
2011/2/16	Menegakis (CPC)	Welfare and health care use of "bogus refugee claimants"
2012/4/26	Bateman (CPC)	Health care benefits for asylum seekers
2012/6/18	James (CPC)	Health care benefits for asylum seekers

Table A2.2. Motions and private bills proposing to curtail immigrants' access to welfare state benefits

Date y/m/d	Mover (party)	Content
1997/3/3	Hanger (RPC)	Reduce social assistance for failed refugee claimants
1999/10/14	Benoit (RPC)	Hold emergency debate about costs of immigration

Table A2.3. Petitions proposing to curtail immigrants' access to welfare state benefits

Date (y/m/d)	Petitioner (party)	Content
1995/2/22	Valeri (LPC)	Exclude undocumented migrants and refugee claimants from Charter of Rights and Freedoms
1999/2/19	Cummins (RPC)	Deport criminal illegal immigrants who abuse the system
2009/11/2	Wrzesnewskyi (LPC)	Deny veteran benefits to those who fought on side of Red Army

Table A2.4. Questions defending immigrants' use of/access to welfare state benefits

Date (y/m/d)	Interpellant (party)	Subject of criticism/inquiry
1994/11/29	Ianno (LPC)	Misconception that immigrants are a drain on social security
1999/10/28	McKay (LPC)	Ontario premier's exaggeration of sponsorship breakdowns
1999/12/6	McKay (LPC)	Limited health and housing services for refugee claimants
2000/2/28	Bulte (LPC)	Immigrant children in Ontario who are denied education
2000/4/7	Szabo (LPC)	Immigrant children in Ontario who are denied education
2007/2/16	Chow (NDP)	Rationale for the "cruel" 10-year residence requirement on OAS
2009/10/8	Chow (NDP)	Temporary workers' limited EI and health care eligibility
2011/1/31	Minna (LPC)	Cuts in immigrant settlement services
2011/2/7	Oliphant (LPC)	Cuts in immigrant settlement services
2011/6/23	Harris (NDP)	Cuts in immigrant settlement services
2011/11/29	Sitsabaiesan (NDP)	Cuts in immigrant settlement services

(*Continued*)

Table A2.4. (Continued)

Date (y/m/d)	Interpellant (party)	Subject of criticism/inquiry
2012/3/14	Sitsabaiesan (NDP)	Cuts in immigrant settlement services
2012/5/9	Sims (NDP)	Cuts in Interim Federal Health Program
2012/5/11	Groguhé&Dewar (NDP)	Cuts in Interim Federal Health Program
2012/6/11	Sims&Groguhé (NDP)	Cuts in Interim Federal Health Program
2012/6/18	Bennett (LPC), Groguhé&Sims (NDP)	Cuts in Interim Federal Health Program
2012/6/20	Sims&Groguhé (NDP)	Cuts in Interim Federal Health Program
2012/10/5	Sims&Groguhé (NDP)	Cuts in Interim Federal Health Program
2012/10/26	Groguhé (NDP)	Cuts in Interim Federal Health Program
2012/11/22	Goodale (LPC)	Case of asylum seeker without health care
2012/11/23	Sims&Hughes (NDP)	Cuts in Interim Federal Health Program
2012/11/26	Goodale (LPC), Sims&Groguhé (NDP)	Cuts in Interim Federal Health Program
2012/11/27	Lamoureux (LPC), Sims&Groguhé (NDP)	Cuts in Interim Federal Health Program
2012/11/30	Sitsabaiesan (NDP)	Cuts in Interim Federal Health Program

Table A2.5. Motions and private bills proposing to expand immigrants' access to welfare state benefits

Date (y/m/d)	Mover (party)	Content
1995/6/5	Fillion (BQ)	Restore veteran benefits to immigrants who fought on allied side
1997/3/4	Taylor (NDP)	Negotiate with British government that pensions to British immigrants in Canada are indexed
2000/6/8	Graham (LPC)	Give access to student assistance to persons determined convention refugees but not yet landed (Bill C-487)
2006/10/25	Beaumier (LPC)	Reduce OAS requirement to 3 years (Bill C-362)
2009/6/18	Dhalla (LPC)	Reduce OAS requirement to 3 years (Bill C-428)
2011/3/1	Chow (NDP)	Reverse $53 million cuts in settlement services
2011/3/25	Leslie (NDP)	Expand health care benefits for human trafficking victims

Table A2.6. Petitions proposing to expand immigrants' access to welfare state benefits

Date (y/m/d)	Petitioner (party)	Content
1996/3/12	Riis (NDP)	Restore HRDC-funded services for immigrants
1996/6/14	Riis (NDP)	Restore HRDC-funded services for immigrants
2000/3/23	Grewal (RPC)	Offer same OAS to all citizens
2001/3/14	Patry (LPC)	Abolish 10-year residency requirement on OAS
2007/4/17	Masse (NDP)	Abolish 10-year residency requirement on OAS, GIS
2007/4/19	Chow (NDP)	Abolish 10-year residency requirement on OAS and GIS, waive sponsorship agreement in case of breakdown involving a senior
2007/5/1	Mathyssen (NDP)	Abolish 10-year residency requirement on OAS and GIS, waive sponsorship agreement in case of breakdown involving a senior
2007/5/2	Wasylycia-Leis (NDP)	Abolish 10-year residency requirement on OAS and GIS, waive sponsorship agreement in case of breakdown involving a senior
2007/5/9	Chow (NDP)	Eliminate 10-year residency requirement
2007/5/16	Carlton (NDP)	Eliminate 10-year residence requirement
2007/5/29	Chow (NDP)	Eliminate residence requirement on OAS and GIS
2007/6/1	Siksay (NDP)	Eliminate residence requirement on OAS and GIS
2008/4/10	Black (NDP)	Eliminate 10-year residence requirement on OAS, and waive sponsorship breakdowns involving seniors
2009/3/2	Sweet (CPC)	Provide victims of human trafficking with residence status, housing, legal counselling, health care, and other social services

Appendix 3. Questions, motions, and private bills on immigrant welfare use in the Netherlands

Table A3.1. Questions in Dutch parliament criticizing immigrants' use of/access to welfare benefits

Date (y/m/d)	Interpellant(s) (party)	Subject of criticism/inquiry
1995/6/20	Hoogervorst, Van Hoof (VVD)	Ease of claiming Dutch disability benefits in Morocco
1998/7/13	Verhagen (CDA)	Slow implementation of Linking Act
1998/9/29	Kamp (VVD)	Leiden University's refusal to follow Linking Act
1998/10/28	Kamp (VVD)	Some municipalities' refusal to follow Linking Act
1999/1/14	Kamp (VVD)	Two cities' refusal to follow Linking Act
1999/6/8	Kamp (VVD)	Use of welfare to fund family reunification
2000/3/23	Wilders (VVD)	Burden of asylum seekers on disability benefits
2000/5/30	Wijn (CDA)	"White illegals'" receipt of benefits in Amsterdam
2001/7/25	Kamp (VVD)	Social insurance number fraud by undocumented migrants with the aim of claiming social benefits
2001/12/12	Kamp (VVD)	Refugees on welfare receiving additional benefits to fund family reunification
2005/5/12	Weekers, Van Baalen (VVD); Van As, Varela (LPF)	Immigrants forging marriage and birth certificates in order to apply for social benefits
2006/1/30	Visser (VVD)	Adoptive parents of children without legal status receiving benefits
2006/2/15	Huizinga-Heringa (CU), Visser (VVD)	Trafficking of Somali children with the aim of child benefit fraud
2007/5/2	Fritsma, Van Dijck (PVV)	Polish migrants' "massive" use of unemployment benefits
2007/5/25	Nicolaï (VVD)	Welfare fraud among Somali refugee claimants
2008/2/27	Spekman (PvdA)	The welfare costs associated with the recent amnesty policy for long-term asylum seekers
2008/4/7	Ulenbelt (SP)	The costs of (CEE) immigration
2008/5/13	Fritsma (PVV)	Welfare dependence of CEE immigrants
2009/7/17	Fritsma (PVV)	A series of 4 questions regarding costs incurred by non-Western immigrants
2009/8/13; 2009/8/14	Van Hijum (CDA)	Uncritical extension of unemployment benefits to immigrants in town of Winterswijk
2010/2/8	De Krom, Blok, Meeuwis (VVD)	Study benefits for refugees

Date (y/m/d)	Interpellant(s) (party)	Subject of criticism/inquiry
2010/2/9	De Krom (VVD)	Increase in illegal migration to Spain, and the danger that many will end up on Dutch welfare
2010/9/8	Van Hijum (CDA)	SVB campaign to raise awareness about AIO benefit for elderly immigrants with pension gap
2011/1/10	Van Klaveren (PVV)	Benefit export to Bosnian remigrants
2011/1/10	Spekman, Eijsink (PvdA)	Benefit export to Bosnian remigrants
2011/2/11	Van Klaveren, Fritsma, De Jong (PVV)	Unemployment, benefit dependence, and different "work mentality" among non-Western immigrants
2011/5/4	Azmani (VVD)	Scope of welfare fraud among East Europeans
2011/8/5	Azmani (VVD)	"Welfare tourism" in border municipality Vaals
2011/8/22	Van Hijum, Knops (CDA)	Court decision to extend child benefits to asylum seekers awaiting decision on claim
2011/11/17	De Jong, Van Klaveren (PVV)	Penchant for welfare fraud and laziness among immigrants
2012/4/19	Fritsma (PVV)	Welfare costs of amnesty regulation
2012/6/1	Van Klaveren, De Jong (PVV)	Welfare fraud among non-Western immigrants
2012/7/17	Van Klaveren, De Jong, Wilders (PVV)	High rates of unemployment and welfare dependency among immigrant youth

Table A3.2. Motions and private bills proposing to curtail immigrants' access to welfare state benefits

Date (y/m/d)	Mover(s)	Content	Parties in support (rejected/passed)
2000/6/8	Kamp (VVD), Dittrich (D66), Albayrak, Middel (PvdA)	Cut legal aid for asylum seekers who appeal a denied claim without bringing forth new information	PvdA, D66, VVD, CDA, GPV, SGP, RPF (passed)
2000/6/8	Wijn (CDA)	Differentiate in benefit access between different asylum seekers	CDA (rejected)
2006/6/12	Dijsselbloem, Noorman-Den Uyl (PvdA)	Make access to welfare conditional on learning Dutch for immigrants outside labour market	No vote; became law on 2006/12/5

(Continued)

Table A3.2. (Continued)

Date (y/m/d)	Mover(s)	Content	Parties in support (rejected/passed)
2006/10/26	Visser (VVD)	Install an independent committee to research how much leeway for immigrant disentitlement there is in international and European law	CDA, PvdA, VVD, GL, D66, SP, SGP, LPF, CU, Wilders (passed)
2007/12/12	Fritsma (PVV)	Install 10-year residence requirement for all social services and programs	PVV, Verdonk (rejected)
2008/1/17	Fritsma (PVV)	Deport EU citizens who are in the country for longer than three months and are on welfare	PVV, VVD, Verdonk (rejected)
2008/1/17	Van Hijum (CDA)	In EU negotiations, ensure that social rights of migrants in one member state do not automatically translate to the Netherlands	SP, PvdA, GL, PvdD, VVD, CU, SGP, CDA, Verdonk (passed)
2008/1/17	Fritsma (PVV)	Enforce the restriction on EU citizens' access to welfare in the first three months more strictly	VVD, PVV, Verdonk (rejected)
2008/3/27	Kamp (VVD), Dibi (GL)	Force parents of Antillian descent to apply for jobs or lose welfare	GL, D66, VVD, PVV (rejected)
2008/6/25	Van Hijum (CDA), Spekman (PvdA)	Reduce unemployment and welfare dependence of immigrants from CEE countries or repeal their residence permit	SP, PvdA, PvdD, CU, SGP, CDA, PVV, Verdonk (passed)
2008/7/3	Teeven, Kamp (VVD)	Repeal residence permit of any EU migrant who claims welfare within first 10 years in the country	VVD, PVV, Verdonk (rejected)
2008/7/3	Teeven, Kamp (VVD)	Adjust contributory programs paid out to EU citizens to premiums paid in the country of origin	VVD, PVV, Verdonk (rejected)
2008/7/3	Teeven, Kamp (VVD)	Cut welfare of CEE labour migrants who are able to work and for whom work is available	VVD, PVV, Verdonk (rejected)
2008/9/24	Fritsma (PVV)	Include all welfare-receiving refugees in the calculation of the costs of the general amnesty	VVD, PVV, Verdonk (rejected)

Date (y/m/d)	Mover(s)	Content	Parties in support (rejected/passed)
2008/11/27	Van Hijum (CDA), Blok (VVD)	Investigate access to and utilization of the social system by immigrants and the possibilities to reduce their utilization; also, cooperate with export countries to combat fraud and abuse	CDA, PvdA, VVD, D66, SP, SGP, CU, PVV, PvdD, Verdonk (passed)
2008/12/10	Kamp (VVD), Van de Camp (CDA)	Develop plans for a stricter grow-in model of social security	PvdA, D66, VVD, SGP, CDA, PVV, Verdonk (passed)
2008/12/10	Van de Camp (CDA)	Make sure that no parent family migrant can access welfare	SP, D66, VVD, SGP, CDA, PVV, Verdonk (passed)
2009/3/31	Fritsma (PVV), Verdonk (indep.)	Stop all child benefits to children resident in Morocco or Turkey	VVD, PVV, Verdonk (rejected)
2009/3/31	De Krom (VVD), Van Toorenburg (CDA)	Force municipalities to consistently charge contributions for mandatory integration courses from all participants	VVD, SGP, CDA, PVV, Verdonk (rejected)
2009/3/31	Van Toorenburg (CDA)	Make sure benefit cuts for migrants who do not complete their language course are more strictly enforced	Passed without vote
2009/6/25	Fritsma (PVV)	Make immigrants pay the entire bill for mandatory integration courses	SGP, PVV, Verdonk (rejected)
2009/11/5	De Krom (VVD)	Deport labour migrants on welfare; stop export of social services and popular insurance programs; increase residence requirement for family migrants from 3 to 5 years; and only give benefits to refugees who participate in integration classes	VVD, PVV, SGP (rejected)
2009/12/10	Blok (VVD)	Stop export of child benefits to all non-EU countries	VVD, SGP, PVV, Verdonk (rejected)
2009/12/10	Van Hijum (CDA), Spekman (PvdA)	In reconsidering the export of unemployment benefits, the government should also consider ending the export of child benefits and other benefits as well	SP, PvdA, D66, PvdD, VVD, CU, SGP, CDA, PVV, Verdonk (passed)

(Continued)

Table A3.2. (Continued)

Date (y/m/d)	Mover(s)	Content	Parties in support (rejected/passed)
2010/2/25	Blok; since 2011/2/21 Van Nieuwenhuizen (VVD)	Make access to social assistance conditional on language proficiency	Personal vote, passed 105–42
2011/5/19	Wilders (PVV)	Introduce a system that only extends rights to immigrants gradually	VVD, PVV (rejected)
2011/12/14	De Jong (PVV)	Introduce "coffee house inspection" to curtail welfare use among non-Western immigrants	PVV (rejected)
2012/2/29	Van den Besselaar (PVV)	Ensure that work years in other EU states cannot be counted in determining unemployment benefit	PVV (rejected)
2012/7/4	De Jong, van den Besselaar (PVV)	Require 10-year uninterrupted residence and work history without any criminal offence for welfare	VVD, PVV, 3 independents (rejected)
2012/7/4	De Jong, van den Besselaar (PVV)	Start investigation of welfare fraud among non-Western immigrants	PVV, 2 independents (rejected)

Table A3.3. Questions in Dutch parliament defending immigrants' use of/access to welfare benefits

Date (y/m/d)	Interpellant(s) (party)	Subject of criticism/inquiry
1995/11/9	Noorman-Den Uyl (PvdA)	Lack of special benefits for asylum seekers
1998/1/8	Van Dijke (RPF)	Reduction in allowance for asylum seekers
1998/2/3	Sipkes (GL)	Lack of access to welfare for citizens from Dutch Antilles when looking for a job in the Netherlands
1998/6/19	Van Zijl (PvdA)	Case of legal resident not receiving child benefits
1998/8/11	Halsema, Van Gent, Rosenmöller (GL)	Lack of access to social services for foreigners involved in lengthy appeal procedures
1999/4/16	Albayrak (PvdA)	Lack of medical care for migrants awaiting permit
1999/10/20	Verburg (CDA)	Lack of health insurance for seniors abroad

Date (y/m/d)	Interpellant(s) (party)	Subject of criticism/inquiry
1999/12/21	Stroeken, Verburg (CDA)	Legality of decision to cut temporary migrants' access to benefits
2000/1/18	Stroeken, Bijleveld-Schouten (CDA)	Exempt emigrants from paying benefit premiums
2000/8/9	De Wit (SP)	Unfair grounds for guest workers' lower disability benefits
2000/9/5	Santi (PvdA)	Restrictions on benefit export to Suriname
2002/3/22	Marijnissen (SP)	Lower tax breaks for people with a pension gap
2003/11/13	Kant (SP)	Six-year residence requirement on Wajong
2006/5/19	Verbeet, Meijer, De Vries (PvdA)	Pension rights of refugees in relation to Article 24 of Geneva Convention
2007/2/28	Spekman (PvdA)	Administrative negligence leading to failure to pay out benefits to immigrant children
2008/9/16	Karabulut (SP)	Ineligibility for secondary education of refugees on welfare
2009/9/8	Spekman (PvdA)	Immigrant parents in EU losing custody over children for being dependent on state
2009/9/29	Karabulut (SP)	Financial problems among young human trafficking victims
2010/11/22	Spekman, Dijsselbloem (PvdA)	Health care insurance for undocumented children

Table A3.4. Motions and private bills proposing to expand immigrants' access to welfare state benefits

Date (y/m/d)	Mover(s)	Content	Parties in support (rejected/passed)
2001/11/20	De Wit (SP)	Stop rent subsidy reductions for roommates of undocumented migrants	SP, GL (rejected)
2004/11/24	Koşer Kaya (D66)	Transfer administration of AIO from municipal welfare office to SVB in order to increase uptake	CDA, PvdA, SP, GL, LPF, D66, CU, SGP (passed)
2006/02/07	De Wit (SP), Van der Staaij (SGP), De Vries (PvdA), Vos (GL)	Make sure all asylum seekers who are lawfully in the Netherlands have right to shelter	SP, GL, PvdA, D66, CU, SGP (rejected)

(*Continued*)

Table A3.4. (Continued)

Date (y/m/d)	Mover(s)	Content	Parties in support (rejected/passed)
2010/11/2	Spekman (PvdA), Sterk (CDA), Anker (CU)	Make family members of refugees on a temporary residence permit eligible for social benefits and health care insurance	Dropped before put to vote
2011/10/5	Ortega-Martijn (CU), Sterk (CDA)	Exempt refugee youth from 4-week wait time for welfare	SP, PvdD, PvdA, GL, D66, SGP, CU, CDA (passed)
2011/10/5	Sterk (CDA)	Extend period of possible welfare receipt abroad for people over 65 to 13 weeks	SP, PvdD, PvdA, GL, D66, CU, CDA (passed)
2011/11/17	Gesthuizen (SP)	Reverse changes to medical care provisions for asylum seekers	SP, PvdD (rejected)
2011/11/17	Van Dam (PvdA)	Exempt refugees from duty to pay for own integration classes	SP, PvdD, PvdA, GL, D66, CU (rejected)

List of Interviews

CAN01: Interview with Rick Dykstra (Conservative Party of Canada, at the time Parliamentary Secretary to the Minister of Citizenship and Immigration), Ottawa, 6 December 2011.

CAN02: Interview with Don Davies (New Democratic Party of Canada, at the time immigration critic), Ottawa, 1 March 2012.

CAN03: Interview with Kevin Lamoureux (Liberal Party of Canada, at the time immigration critic), Ottawa, 29 September 2011.

CAN11: Interview with senior civil servant in the ministry of Citizenship and Immigration Canada, Ottawa, June 2011.

CAN12: Interview with senior civil servant in the ministry of Citizenship and Immigration Canada, Ottawa, August 2011.

CAN13: Interview with senior civil servant in the ministry of Citizenship and Immigration Canada, Ottawa, August 2011.

CAN14: Interview with senior civil servant in the ministry of Human Resources and Skills Development Canada, Gatineau, September 2011.

CAN15: Interview with senior civil servant in the ministry of Human Resources and Skills Development Canada, Gatineau, September 2011.

CAN16: Interview with senior civil servant in the ministry of Veteran Affairs Canada, phone interview, October 2011.

CAN21: Interview with senior civil servant in the Ontario Ministry of Community and Social Services, Toronto, August 2011.

CAN22: Interview with senior civil servant in the Ontario Ministry of Community and Social Services, Toronto, August 2011.

CAN23: Interview with senior civil servant in the Ontario Ministry of Community and Social Services, Toronto, August 2011.

CAN24: Interview with senior civil servant in the Ontario Ministry of Citizenship and Immigration, videocall interview, September 2011.

NET01: Interview with Cora van Nieuwenhuizen (VVD, then spokesperson on immigration), The Hague, 10 February 2011.

NET02: Interview with Hans Spekman (PvdA, then spokesperson on immigration), The Hague, 2 February 2011.

NET03: Interview with Sietse Fritsma (PVV, then spokesperson on immigration), The Hague, 14 January 2011.

NET04: Interview with Eddy van Hijum (CDA, then spokesperson on social policy), The Hague, 26 January 2011.

NET05: Interview with Paul Ulenbelt (SP, then spokesperson on immigration), The Hague, 19 January 2011.

NET06: Interview with Fatma Koşer Kaya (D66, then spokesperson on social affairs), The Hague, 21 January 2011.

NET11: Interview with senior civil servant in Ministry of Immigration, The Hague, February 2011.

NET12: Interview with senior civil servant in Ministry of Immigration, phone interview, February 2011.

NET13: Interview with senior civil servant in Ministry of Social Affairs, The Hague, January 2011.

NET14: Interview with senior civil servant in Ministry of Social Affairs, The Hague, January 2011.

NET15: Interview with senior civil servant in Ministry of Social Affairs, The Hague, January 2011.

NET16: Interview with senior civil servant in Ministry of Health Care, email interview, February 2011.

SWE01: Interview with Magdalena Streijffert (S, former spokesperson on social policy), Stockholm, 7 April 2011.

SWE02: Interview with Mikael Cederbratt (M, at the time spokesperson on immigration), Stockholm, 5 April 2011.

SWE03: Interview with Ulf Nilsson (L, at the time spokesperson on immigration), Stockholm, 7 March 2011.

SWE04: Interview with Fredrick Federley (C, at the time spokesperson on immigration), Stockholm, 7 April 2011.

SWE05: Interview with Erik Almqvist (SD, at the time spokesperson on immigration), Stockholm, 21 March 2011.

SWE06: Interview with Christina Höj Larsen (V, at the time spokesperson on social policy), Stockholm, 7 April 2011.

SWE07:   Interview with Emma Henriksson (KD, at the time spokes-person on social policy), Stockholm, 10 March 2011.

SWE11:   Interview with senior civil servant in Ministry of Employ-ment, Stockholm, March 2011.

SWE12:   Interview with senior civil servant in Ministry of Health and Social Welfare, Stockholm, March 2011.

SWE13:   Interview with senior civil servant at National Board of Health and Welfare, Stockholm, March 2011.

SWE14:   Interview with senior civil servant in Ministry of Health and Social Welfare, email interview, April 2011.

SWE15:   Interview with senior civil servant in Ministry of Immigra-tion, email interview, May 2011.

Notes

Introduction

1   Even though Canada has historically had a larger annual intake than the Netherlands and Sweden, this difference has become much smaller since the 1990s. Today, each of these countries admits seven or eight foreign-born individuals per 1,000 citizens per year (OECD). The three countries have also gone through similar economic cycles. Even though there are differences in timing and severity, they all went through recessions in the early 1990s, early 2000s, and late 2000s and faced similar economic pressures at roughly the same points in time. The methodological advantage of these similarities is that we cannot attribute any differences we might observe between these countries in their exclusion of immigrants from benefits to differences in the size of the recent immigrant population or to differences in budgetary pressures.

2   I analysed all documents in their original language. In my analysis of parliamentary debates and policy documents in the Netherlands, I relied on the official database of parliamentary documents (zoek. officielebekendmakingen.nl) and searched the entire timeline under investigation for any document in the policy areas of finance, economics, social security, and labour that included immigration-related terms (more specifically, I used search term migr* OF immigr* OF allochto* OF vluchtelin* OF asielzoek* OF buitenlande* OF vreemdelin* OF integratie) and any document in the policy area of immigration and integration that included social policy–related terms (more specifically, I used search term bijstand OF WW OF AOW OF arbeidsongeschi* OF verzorgingsstaat OF pensioe* OF uitkerin*). Similarly, in my analysis of relevant debates and documents in Sweden, I relied on the official database of parliamentary

attitudes towards immigration) were overrepresented compared to previous iterations of the survey (Ahmadi, Palm, and Ahmadi 2016, 64). Second, the response rate in 2016 was lower than in earlier waves (30 per cent, compared to about 45 per cent in 2010), which likely increased the relative size of the most opinionated. (Many thanks to Irving Palm for sharing data on response rates with me.)

19 Respondents were asked to say whether they thought "Taking in fewer refugees," "Reducing social benefits," and "Reducing income differences in society" were "very good," "fairly good," "neither good nor bad," "fairly bad," or "very bad" ideas. Figure 3.2 shows the percentage of people who thought that reducing the intake of refugees was either a "very good" or a "fairly good" idea and who also believed it would be a "very good" or "fairly good" idea to reduce income differences (dotted line); and the percentage who favoured reducing the refugee intake and who at the same time thought it was a "very bad" or "fairly bad" idea to reduce social benefits (dashed line). Non-responses and "don't knows" have been excluded from the analysis. Many thanks to Dennis Anderson and Henrik Oscarsson for making the relevant data from the 2014 survey available to me before they were released officially.

20 Particularly controversial has been a 1997 party document in which the Moderates describe what the "ordinary Swede" tends to think of immigrants: "He can't avoid seeing what immigrants receive. They receive social assistance, they have their rent paid for, they have free public transit passes, child care that's practically free. With three children, they receive a standard of living that would correspond to a before-tax income of multiple hundreds of thousands [of Swedish crowns]. He can't help but think about that. Every time he sees a black-skinned family he thinks about that" (Moderaterna 1997).

21 In response, Andersson quit the party and completed his mandate as an independent. In 2002, he became a member of the Sweden Democrats.

22 The figure excludes motions and interpellations that, while related to the social rights of immigrants, were primarily about something else (such as increasing the compensation municipalities receive for refugee accommodation, changing social programs for all recipients, or amending admission policy).

23 Unfortunately, the MP refused to participate in this research.

24 Even regarding the expansion of health care access for undocumented migrants that the Reinfeldt government introduced, the support of the Moderates can at best be described as lukewarm. Reinfeldt himself justified this policy change as follows: "This has been important for the

documents (riksdagen.se/sv.dokument-lagar) and searched the timeline under investigation for any document that simultaneously included immigration-related and social policy-related terms (more specifically, I used search term (invandr* ELLER "utrikes föd" ELLER utrikesföd* ELLER flyktin*) OCH (försörjningsstöd ELLER socialförsäkring ELLER a-kassa ELLER välfärdsstat ELLER socialbidrag ELLER pension ELLER äldreförsörjningsstöd)). Unfortunately, the search engine on the website of the Canadian parliament does not feature advanced search options like its Dutch and Swedish counterparts. Instead, I searched for relevant policy documents on the individual websites of the departments of immigration and social affairs. I also used private website openparliament.ca to search in each available parliamentary debate in the time period under investigation for immigration-related terms (more specifically, I used search terms "immigr," "migr," "refuge," "asyl," "foreigne," and "newcome," going through each debate with the browser search function), judging in each instance whether the discussion had any bearing on discussions about social policy. I conducted my interviews in the Netherlands in Dutch, while my interviews in Sweden and Canada took place in English. I will refer to the interviews by a simple code consisting of the first three letters of the country and a two-digit number (for example, I will refer to the fourth interview I conducted in Sweden as "SWE04"). For reasons of confidentiality, I will be intentionally vague about the identity of the civil servants I interviewed. See also the list of interviews included at the end of the book.

1. Theorizing Immigrant-Excluding Welfare Reforms

1 As we will see, even some politicians cite Putnam in arguing that immigration threatens the welfare state.
2 Putnam's theory seems to offer more grounds to expect an overall decrease in solidarity, but as we have seen, he mostly theorizes about diversity's effects on social trust and social capital, and those effects do not necessarily translate into a decrease in support for social programs. Moreover, Putnam's findings have not been replicated in studies outside the United States (Banting 2008; Gesthuizen, Van der Meer, and Scheepers 2009).
3 In Sainsbury's account, the welfare regime, the incorporation regime, admission policy, the framing of immigration, the policy venues where immigrants' social rights are established, party politics, the territorial arrangement of a country, and the efforts of immigrant organizations all

matter for the politics of immigrants' social rights. Her book does not address, however, *how* exactly these factors matter. There is no discussion of the relative leverage of each of the variables, their interactions, or the stage in the causal sequence during which they are most important. As such, it is difficult to derive generalizations or observable implications from her explanation. An additional problem is that her model makes no analytic distinction between IEWRs and general cutbacks in social policies, assuming the two types of policy change are driven by the same logic (see, in particular, 40–1, 281). As we will see, however, we can expect that when it comes to IEWRs, the importance of political translation is larger, and the institutional obstacles are different. See also (Koning 2013).

4 One ground that is omitted from this discussion, and that matters for social rights in some idiosyncratic cases, is ethnicity. Ethnic German immigrants (so-called *Aussiedler*), for example, used to have more access to the German welfare state than guest workers with the same status and length of residence (Bommes 2000, 101; Kaiser and Paul 2011). Zeev Rosenhek (2000) observes similar privileges for ethnic Jews in Israel.

5 Unless stated otherwise, all translations are mine.

6 This study only considers domestic responses to the tension between immigration and welfare systems. Some scholars have argued that immigrants' welfare could be effectively enhanced by more international cooperation, in particular regarding the portability of social security rights (Kremer 2013; Sabates-Wheeler and Feldman 2011). A discussion of such international solutions is beyond the scope of this analysis.

7 It seems plausible that the nature of admission policy might also indirectly affect the currency of selective solidarity. After all, we know that the public tends to view highly skilled labour migrants more favourably than family migrants or asylum seekers (Hanson, Scheve, and Slaughter 2005; Menz 2006), and we might therefore expect calls for immigrant exclusion to be louder in countries that admit larger proportions of "unpopular" migrants. As we will see, however, such an explanation does not take us very far in understanding the differences between our three case studies. The reliance on asylum and family migration is much greater in Sweden than in the Netherlands, yet selective solidarity pervades Dutch politics much more than Swedish politics.

8 Of course, immigration critics would argue that the restrictive policy changes they propose are necessary responses to the economic pressure that immigration places on the welfare system, and that political correctness and pro-immigration lobbying have prevented previous policy-makers from coming to this realization. Such an account does not

challenge my main point here, which is that objective indicators of the size of immigration-related problems are of little use in predicting the political salience or dominant framing of those problems.

9 None of this should be taken to mean that objections to immigration have nothing to do with economic concerns. There is much scholarly evidence supporting the "realistic conflict theory," which suggests that working-class citizens tend to have more negative attitudes towards immigrants in part because they compete for low-skilled jobs (Sniderman, Peri, De Figueiredo, and Piazza 2000). My point here is merely that objections to immigrants' use of welfare benefits are not likely to originate in a careful analysis of actual levels of immigrant welfare dependence.

10 In 1990 the UN General Assembly also adopted a convention on the protection of the rights of migrant workers, which explicitly guarantees the right of all immigrants to enjoy the same working conditions (Article 25) and access to social benefits (Article 27) as native-born citizens. So far, however, the convention has only been signed by emigration countries.

11 Not to be confused with the European Council (which is one of the two executive branches of the EU), the Council of Europe is a human rights organization with forty-seven member states. This includes every recognized country in Europe in its broadest definition, with the exception of Belarus.

12 For this reason, the labels "extreme right," "far right," and "radical right" that some scholars employ to denote these parties are becoming increasingly misleading.

13 Indeed, a cynic might reason that since these politicians' electoral fortunes depend on the continued existence of these problems, they have little to gain from addressing them directly.

2. The Limits of Economic Explanations

1 There have been many waves of the LIS. Table 2.1 shows data from the 2000 wave because it maximizes the number of countries for which data are available. Some of the regression analyses in this chapter do make use of other data points.

2 There is no variable for immigrant status in the United Kingdom, but there is a question on ethnicity. I have therefore calculated the overrepresentation of non-white respondents instead. Despite the strong overlap in the United Kingdom between ethnicity and immigrant status, this approach obviously raises concerns about the comparability of the data. In the subsequent statistical investigations, I have therefore

conducted all analyses without the UK as well. The conclusions are very similar.

3 Some might argue that a more appropriate indicator would be an estimate of the total objective "costs" of immigration. (Such an estimate would also account, among other things, for the costs incurred by immigration in other areas of the budget, as well as for the benefits immigrants bring to the host country's economy.) However, not only would it be difficult to develop such an indicator that is comparable from one country to another, but this approach would also be less useful for theoretical reasons. After all, what interests me is the desire to exclude immigrants from social programs and transfers, not unease about immigration in general. Others might agree with the focus on transfer benefits but still suggest other indicators, such as (1) a comparison of the *percentages* of immigrants and native-born that receive benefits, or (2) a measure exclusively based on how much immigrants are receiving in benefits *without comparing this to how much native-born citizens are receiving*. Both these measures have disadvantages. The former measure does not capture that the level of a benefit can differ substantially between one recipient and another, and therefore is an imprecise indicator of welfare dependence (Mood 2011). The latter measure is troubled by cross-national differences in benefit generosity and eligibility requirements, and is a poorer indicator from a conceptual point of view (after all, by their very nature, feelings of selective solidarity entail comparing the deservingness of immigrants with that of the native-born). Despite these conceptual problems, however, I have rerun all analyses with these alternative operationalizations for the purpose of cross-validation, and the conclusions are very similar (the results are available upon request). Finally, some might question the rationale of focusing on these specific three sets of transfer benefits. The reasons are threefold. First, public support tends to be lower for means-tested programs such as social assistance than for more universal programs such as public pension programs. The estimates of overrepresentation, therefore, can be placed on a scale of "deservingness": if immigrants' overrepresentation in welfare programs indeed spurs selective solidarity, we should expect the effect to be larger for social assistance than for all transfer benefits. Second, these sets allow us to acknowledge the interplay of the various transfer programs in a system of welfare provision. In many countries, an important reason for immigrants' overrepresentation among recipients of social assistance is their failure to qualify for programs with higher benefit levels. For that reason, it makes more sense to calculate overrepresentation for different *sets* of transfers

than for each benefit in isolation. (Moreover, such a strategy also makes little sense from a conceptual point of view. It seems implausible, both intuitively and theoretically, that selective solidarity could be driven by an overrepresentation of immigrants among recipients of, for example, child benefits in particular.) Finally, when accounting for cross-national differences in welfare systems it makes sense to focus on "core" transfers only (social assistance, unemployment, family, and pension benefits). The set of benefits a state offers varies considerably from one country to another, and this is reflected in the LIS data as well. Data for social assistance, unemployment, family, and pension benefits, however, are available in the data set for every welfare state under study.

4 From the ISSP, I measure the proportion of respondents in these countries who believe that (1) the government spends too much money assisting immigrants; (2) legal immigrants should not have the same rights as citizens; (3) immigrants are not good for the economy; and (4) immigrants take jobs away from native-born citizens. From the WVS, I calculate how many respondents (1) express more concern about immigrants than about the elderly, sick, and unemployed; (2) indicate less willingness to help immigrants than the elderly and sick; (3) believe that employers should prioritize the native-born when jobs are scarce; and (4) are in favour of redistribution but opposed to immigration.

5 Since data on these eight variables were not available for all twelve countries, I decided to estimate the overall level of selective solidarity by a country's average distance from the mean rather than by a summary index. Overall, it seems reasonable to suggest that the eight indicators tap the same underlying sentiment. The average correlation of the country-level percentages is 0.57, and combining all percentages in one scale yields a very high Cronbach's alpha (0.91).

6 In the ISSP data of 2003, the dependent variable is composed of respondents' positions on four statements: immigration is good for the economy; immigrants take jobs away from the native-born; the government spends too much money on immigration; and legal non-citizen immigrants should have the same rights as citizens. In the 1995 wave of the ISSP, only the first two items are available. In the analysis of the 1999–2000 wave of the WVS, I rely on four items: (1) respondents' position on whether employers should prioritize the native-born when jobs are scarce, (2) the extent to which respondents simultaneously express support for redistribution but opposition to immigration, (3) the extent to which respondents express a lower degree of concern for immigrants than for elderly, unemployed, and sick and disabled people in their

country, and (4) the extent to which respondents express less willingness to help improve the conditions of immigrants than of elderly and sick and disabled people in their country. In the analysis of the most recent available WVS data, the dependent variable is a composite index of only the first two of these items.

7 As Table 2.1 makes apparent, the distribution of these estimates is far from normal (most obviously, the scores on overrepresentation in social assistance are much higher in the Scandinavian countries than elsewhere). To avoid modelling such a skewed distribution linearly, I transformed the values for each analysis in such a way that they can be used in linear regression analysis. Using Tukey's ladder of powers (Scott n.d.), I have transformed the variables in such a way as to best approximate a straight line when ordering the cases from low to high (and indeed, after the transformations, the rank order on each overrepresentation variable can be captured by a straight line with a minimum explained variance of 0.9). All in all, I made the following transformations: for ISSP 2003 log(social assistance), (two benefits)$^{0.5}$, (four benefits + 80)^2; for ISSP 1995 (social assistance)$^{0.2}$, (four benefits + 20)$^{0.35}$; for wave 4 and 5 of the WVS (social assistance + 1)$^{0.25}$, (two benefits + 1)$^{0.5}$; and for wave 4 of the WVS log(social assistance). Unfortunately, the different timing of the various waves of the LIS, ISSP, and WVS made it impossible to always match data from the same years, or to consistently employ the same lag between data on immigrant benefit use and public opinion data. In order to maximize the number of cases, I use a three-year lag for the analysis of ISSP data from 2003, a five-year lag for the analysis based on the most recent WVS data, and no lag in the other two analyses.

8 While imperfect, nation-building policies are commonly used indicators for measuring national identity. In this case, the main alternative measure, namely survey data, would introduce several methodological problems. In particular, an indicator based on survey data would result in a particularly undemanding test of the hypothesis that national identity matters for selective solidarity: it would measure whether a group of respondents that indicates it is comfortable with granting immigrants easy access to citizenship would also be likely to formulate few restrictions on immigrants' access to social benefits.

9 One might level two types of objections at the findings of the regression analyses. First, one might rightly point out that the low number of country cases casts doubt on the validity of the regression results. For reasons of both data availability and comparability of cases, I am not able to address this by expanding the sample of countries. Instead, I

have cross-validated the findings by rerunning the statistical models in various ways (using multiple data sets, rerunning all analysis without the UK, and using different indicators of immigrant welfare dependence; see also notes 2 and 3). As an additional robustness test, I have employed a technique called qualitative comparative analysis, a method of data analysis that has been specifically designed to deal with a medium-sized sample (Nelson 2005; Ragin 1994). This involves dichotomizing the variables of interest and then using the Boolean method to ascertain whether they are systematically related. The main conclusions are largely in line with the regression results. The analysis suggests that countries lacking both a universal welfare system and an inclusive national identity will experience high levels of selective solidarity, even if immigrants' objective burden on the welfare state is relatively low. Moreover, even if they promote an inclusive national identity, non-universal welfare states still appear susceptible to selective solidarity when immigrants are strongly overrepresented in the welfare system. (The outcome of the analysis, in Boolean terminology, is as follows: UWR + over*uwr*INI → wc; and OVER*uwr + uwr*ini → SS; with "+" referring to "or," "*" to "and," upper case letters indicating the presence of a variable, lower case letters the absence of a variable, UWR standing for a universal welfare regime, OVER for a high immigrant overrepresentation, INI for inclusive national identity, and SS for high levels of selective solidarity.) A second objection one might rightly raise is that in static comparisons it is difficult to capture countervailing effects. More specifically, in the absence of longitudinal analysis a negative covariance can be interpreted in a very different manner: the more immigrants become overrepresented among welfare recipients, the more pervasive selective solidarity becomes; the more pervasive selective solidarity, the higher the likelihood of exclusionary reforms; and finally, if these reforms are implemented, we would expect them to decrease immigrants' reliance on transfer programs. In this interpretation, then, in the short run high overrepresentation leads to higher levels of selective solidarity, but in the longer run such sentiments lead to lower levels of overrepresentation. To a certain extent, this observation highlights the limitations of the methodology I have employed. The kinds of fine-grained comparative and longitudinal indicators of the main dependent and independent variables that would allow me to control for endogeneity are simply not available. However, as far as we are able to assess, there is not much evidence that the possibility of this feedback loop has significantly distorted our conclusions. First, if short-term effects and long-term effects run counter to each other, we would expect there to be more evidence of a negative effect when the lag between income and survey data is larger. However, the analysis of the ISSP data from 2003 (which uses a three-year lag) does not show stronger evidence of a negative relationship than the ISSP data from 1995 (no lag), and neither is there more evidence of a negative relationship in the most recent WVS data (five-year lag) than in the data from 2000 (no lag). Second, if selective solidarity is a response to patterns of immigrant welfare use, we should at least observe a positive relationship in *changes* in these two variables; in other words, we should expect it to increase in countries where immigrants' reliance on transfer programs is becoming larger, and vice versa. This does not seem to be the case either: changes between the first and last available estimates of immigrant overrepresentation are unrelated to changes over the same years in agreement with the statement that employers should prioritize native-born citizens when jobs are scarce (the only item that has been asked over a long period of time). The correlation is low (0.15) and statistically insignificant (p = 0.7, two-tailed test).

10 There is some evidence, however, that objections to immigrants' access to welfare state benefits tend to be loudest in economically difficult times. In Sweden, both public and political unease about the costs of immigration were at their highest during the economic crisis of the early 1990s. When the Swedish economy shrank three years in a row (from 1991 to 1993), a new AIP called New Democracy played a vocal role in public debate, mainstream parties defended their most restrictive immigration agendas in two decades, and public opinion polls pointed to widespread unease about immigrants' place in the welfare system. Meanwhile, a similar storm was raging in Canada. In a context of large budget deficits and high unemployment rates the right-wing Reform Party attempted (albeit with limited success) to mobilize public discomfort about immigration and multiculturalism and occasionally suggested IEWRs. The crisis in the early 1990s did not hit the Netherlands as hard, but during a later recession, in the early 2000s, the first successful Dutch anti-immigrant politician, Pim Fortuyn, rose to prominence and led his party to a landslide victory (a victory he himself could not witness – he was assassinated nine days before the election took place).

11 The Netherlands only started to collect data on social benefit use by country of origin after it was explicitly instructed to do so by a 1999 motion introduced by conservative MP Henk Kamp. Over the time span for which these data are available, the level of welfare dependence among immigrants seems to have remained largely stable: from 2001 to 2015, the

share of immigrants on social assistance has consistently hovered around 12.5 per cent (CBS).

12 For other examples, see comments by Kalle Larsson (*Pr.* 2007/08:43, *anf.* 2, 13 December 2007); Tobias Billström (*Pr.* 2011/12:85, *anf.* 57, 20 March 2012); Leif Blomberg (*Pr.* 1994/1995:84, *anf.* 36, 3 April 1995); or Emma Henriksson (*Pr.* 2011/12:94, *anf. 49*, 11 April 2012).

13 The analysis includes statements from the period 1991–2012 for Sweden, 1994–2012 for Canada, and 1995–2012 for the Netherlands. Since critiques of immigrants' access to welfare are much more prevalent in the Netherlands than in the other two cases, for the Dutch case I only coded statements that criticized immigrants' access to social assistance benefits in particular. In total, I coded 63 statements from Swedish debates, 170 statements from Canadian debates, and 93 statements from Dutch debates. Full results are available upon request.

14 Of course, one might suspect that such motivations also underlie some of the economic comments or principled comments about system integrity or integration reviewed above, but such suspicions are difficult to substantiate.

15 See, for example, House of Commons debates from 2 February, 22 February, 7 March, 15 April, and 23 September 1994, as well as from 13 October 13 and 9 November 1999, for the suggestion that immigrants' access to benefits should be reduced because of their poor economic integration; and from 13 February 1994 and 30 March and 6 April 1995 for the argument that employment equity policies are unnecessary because of immigrants' successful economic integration.

16 See comments by Sergio Marchi, House of Commons debate, 2 February 1994.

17 For example, the United States and Germany admitted more immigrants than Canada in absolute terms, while Sweden and Switzerland took in larger numbers relative to population size.

18 This argument is also used by proponents of migration in the other two cases. See, for example, the contribution of Jenny Sims in Canada (House of Commons debate, 26 April 2012), and comments by Tofik Dibi in the Netherlands (TK-20–23, 8 November 2011).

19 The document quotes a Eurobarometer survey, which found that 59 per cent of the unemployed who migrated found a job within a year, as opposed to 33 per cent of those who stayed in their home country (Moderaterna 2010, 124). At most, however, these data tell us that immigration reduces unemployment in Europe. Besides, on the basis of this information we cannot tell whether these people found a job because they migrated or migrated because they found a job abroad.

3. Sweden: Universalism, Even for Newcomers?

1 In fact, with the exception of asylum seekers, every migrant from outside the EU and EEA is expected to acquire a residence permit even before travelling to Sweden.

2 Undocumented migrants, according to 2008 data, comprised only 0.11 per cent of the population, the fourth-lowest among the then twenty-seven EU member states (Papadopoulos 2012).

3 Eighteen per cent of municipalities indicated that they had granted a social assistance benefit to an undocumented migrant, while 14 per cent reported having denied a social assistance benefit to this category of migrant. Taking the possibility of overlap into account, this means that between 68 and 82 per cent of all municipalities had never seen undocumented migrants at their welfare office.

4 In addition, a number of voluntary organizations have opened clinics that offer undocumented migrants the services they are ineligible for, free of charge (*SOU* 2011, 48).

5 Until 2015, the party was called *Folkpartiet Liberalerna*. I will consistently use its current name.

6 Since 2001, Swedish social insurance law has distinguished between benefits for which one qualifies by residing in Sweden (such as child benefits and housing allowance) and those that require employment history (such as sickness insurance and income-related parental benefits) (Försäkringskassan, 2010). I will discuss the latter category of insurance programs later in this section.

7 EBO is short for *eget boende*, or "own housing."

8 The large number of people who applied for temporary protection in Sweden during and in the aftermath of the wars in former Yugoslavia would, according to the law at the time, be registered in the national register because they were expected to stay in Sweden for at least a year and, therefore, enjoy the exact same health care access as any native-born Swede. The Persson governments (with support from the Moderates) saw this as an undesirable outcome and decided that any refugee claimant applying for temporary protection or arriving as the result of a mass refugee situation could not be registered until he or she had lived in the country for three years. This led to vehement criticism from all other parties in Parliament (*Pr.* 2002/03:33, *anf.* 33–68, 10 December 2002; see also Försäkringskassan 2010). Interestingly, the Löfven government responded differently to the more recent refugee crisis. Like its counterpart some fifteen years earlier, the government decided to extend only

temporary permits to new refugees, but it set those permits at thirteen months so that all newcomers would qualify for residence-based social programs.

9 See, for example, the speech by Lars Biörck (M) (*Pr.* 1992/93:55, *anf.* 55, 21 January 1993).

10 As further evidence that this has little to do with an unwillingness to extend benefits to newcomers, it is worth noting that the Sweden Democrats do not oppose the *vårdnadsbidrag* (see *Pr.* 2011/12:46, *anf.* 169, 12 December 2011).

11 Overall, we can say that the contributory employment-based pension programs Sweden has had since 1959 have hardly entailed any direct exclusion of newcomers, but for the reasons mentioned above they have been scarcely available to, in particular, recent immigrants (Johansson 2010).

12 This has occasionally been criticized in Parliament. In 2006, Yilmaz Kerimo (S) tabled a (unsuccessful) motion suggesting to enable the export of the public pension to all countries (*Mo.*2006/07:*Sf*268, 25 October 2006).

13 Some observers have described the overhaul of the integration system as a "restrictive" reform (Schierup & Ålund 2011, 58). From a comparative perspective, such a classification is difficult to understand. After all, immigrants who decide not to participate in the integration trajectory do not face any economic sanctions, or consequences for their residence status.

14 Interestingly, most right-wing politicians reject the label "immigrant-targeted programs" in order to distinguish these policies from the targeted programs that existed under the social democratic integration regime.

15 As a result of the 2010 reform, this benefit has been replaced by the "Establishment Benefit" (*etableringsersättning*), which is available to every refugee migrant who follows the integration trajectory.

16 Interestingly, ND's Lars Moquist suggested the mechanism that, as we will see in chapter 5, has been adopted in the Netherlands: "Just set requirements for documented skills in Swedish – couple it to economic sanctions in the form of heavily reduced social assistance" (*Pr.* 1992/1993:60, *anf.* 233, 11 February 1993).

17 All of the politicians I interviewed agreed that immigrants are overrepresented among welfare recipients, and many of them mentioned data from recent studies to specify the size of this overrepresentation.

18 There are two additional reasons why it seems premature to make too much of the single data point from 2016. First, in this wave of the survey the elderly and less educated (two groups that tend to have less positive

Environment Party and for my Alliance friends, and I have listened" (*Pr.* 2010/11:74, *anf.* 61, 17 March 2011).

25 The Moderates still emphasize that other EU countries should take in more refugee migrants. However, according to Mikael Cederbratt that is not to reduce the inflow to Sweden. He described his position as asking other EU states: "We are the best in the class, why don't you do like we do?" (interview SWE02).

26 See, for example, the contribution by Göte Wahlström (*Pr.* 2007/08:83, *anf.* 1, 26 March 2008).

27 See, for example, comments by Christian Democrat Alf Svensson (*Pr.* 1995/96:3, *anf.* 46, 4 October 1995) and Centre Party MP Birgitta Carlsson (*Pr.* 1999/2000:, *anf.* 139–44, 3 February 2000).

28 Comments like this come up in almost every debate on immigration. For particularly pertinent examples, see Moderate motions *Mo.* 2001/02:Sf400, 5 October 2001 and *Mo.* 2002/03:A229, 23 October 2002; and comments in Parliament by Lennart Rodin (L) (*Pr.* 1996/97:106, *anf.* 7, 21 May 1997); Stefan Attefall (KD) (*Pr.* 1998/99:23, *anf.* 158, 26 November 1998); Karin Pilsäter (L); (*Pr.* 1998/99:42, *anf.* 58, 20 January 1999); and Göran Lindblad (M) (*Pr.* 1999/2000:91, *anf.* 25, 4 April 2000).

29 Again, this line of reasoning is almost ubiquitous. See comments by Ana Maria Narti (L) (*Pr.* 1999/2000:96, *anf.* 110, 12 April 2000), Tobias Billström (M) (*Pr.* 2004/05:66, *anf.* 9, 28 January 2005), and Maria Lundqvist Brömster (L) (*Pr.* 2010/11:61, *anf.* 92, 17 February 2011).

30 Frederick Federley (C), for example, described the anti-immigrant party as follows: "They are like a classical social democratic party, with racism. So the addition is the racist part and the islamophobic part" (interview SWE04).

31 This is all the more impressive considering that polls tend to underestimate support for anti-immigrant parties. For example, the last poll before the 2010 election estimated SD's support at 3.8 per cent while the party in fact garnered 5.7 per cent of the vote, and these numbers were 10.3 and 12.9, respectively, in the 2014 election.

32 The other two cases are William Petzäll, who was asked in September 2011 to give up his seat because of alcoholism problems, and Anders Forsberg, who left the party in May 2017 when it became clear he had embezzled more than a million crowns (about C$150,000) from the party treasury.

33 While beyond the scope of the current discussion, it seems worth repeating that not all political scientists agree that a dismissive strategy is most effective in muting the electoral success of AIPs (Bale et al. 2010; Loxbo 2010). Here, however, my main interest is in illustrating that the

Sweden Democrats have had little success at changing mainstream policy positions, not in providing an explanation for the SD's electoral fortunes.

34 Some have been especially prone to hurl insults at any suggestion for restrictive measures. A case in point is Kalle Larsson (V), who accused the Liberals of being racist for suggesting the inclusion of a language test in the naturalization procedure (*Pr.* 2005/06:41, *anf.* 76, 30 November 2005), and who called the Support Requirement in family migration a form of discrimination (*Pr.* 2009/10:85, *anf.* 9, 10 March 2010).

35 Politicians have not been alone in attempting to silence anti-immigrant movements in this way. Swedish media deliberately ignored the SD entirely until the International Free Press Society criticized this boycott in 2006 (Cohen 2009). Still today, the SD faces uncooperative media. In the run-up to the 2010 elections, no television station was willing to air the party's campaign video (interview SWE05) and the largest daily newspaper *Aftonbladet* refused to run any SD campaign ads (Helin and Mellin 2009).

4. Canada: Stability in a Country of Immigrants

1 This chapter will by and large ignore developments in Quebec. The centrality of sub-state nationalism in Quebec politics lends a distinct character to that province's political discourse on immigration and integration (Jenson 1997; Rocher et al. 1999) that is beyond the scope of this book to explore.

2 The 1990s were turbulent times for the political right in Canada. Reform succeeded in replacing the existing Progressive Conservative Party (PCP) as the largest party on the right but quickly realized it would need to build coalitions if it ever hoped to win an election. In 2000 it joined forces with a number of former members of the PCP and other (provincial) conservative parties to form the Canadian Alliance (CA). In 2003 the Alliance and the PCP merged to create the Conservative Party of Canada (CPC), which is the still the largest right-of-centre party today.

3 See, for example, comments by Derek Lee (House of Commons debate, 21 April 1994) and Martin Cauchon (House of Commons debate, 19 September 1994) of the LPC, and by Réal Ménard of the BQ (House of Commons debate, 5 March 1999).

4 Examples of this critique abound. In Ontario, see comments by Elaine Ziemba (NDP) on 18 April 1994; Cameron Jackson (OPC) on 16 November 1994; and Carl DeFaria (OPC) on 28 June 2001 and 16 June 2003. On the federal level, see comments by Derek Lee (LPC) on 21 April 1994; Art

Hanger (RPC) on 9 February, 1 March, and 14 December 1995 and 13 May 1996; Oscar Nunez (BQ) on 11 February, 3 March, and 9 April 1997; Leon Benoit (RPC) on 13 October and 14 October 1999; Bernard Bigras (BQ) on 1 May 2000; Madeleine Dalphon-Duiral (BQ) on 4 June 2001; Gurmant Grewal (CA) on 4 June 2001; Randy White (CPC) on 2 November 2004; Ed Komarnicki (CPC) on 29 January 2007); Nina Grewal (CPC) on 2 March 2007; and Alice Wong (CPC) on 20 April 2009.

5   See, for example, in Ontario, comments by Cameron Jackson (OPC) on 2 May 1991; or, on the federal level, comments by Art Hanger (RPC), 3 March 1997, Grant McNally (RPC), 5 February 1999; and Randy White, 27 February 2001 (CA).

6   About 50 per cent of temporary workers and almost all international students have a closed permit, which means they are not allowed to work for more than one employer. They therefore cannot meet the "available for work" test for unemployment benefits.

7   A telling example of permanent residents' equal treatment is that they can even access veterans' benefits provided that they fought on the same side as Canada in the Second World War or the Korean War. This arrangement was repealed in 1995 but reintroduced in 2009. Parenthetically, the reintroduction led to strong objections from Boris Wrzesnewskyj (LPC), who was concerned that the policy change would enable some Red Army veterans to access these benefits as well (House of Commons Debate, 2 November 2009).

8   The only exceptions I am aware of are the suggestion by some members of the Bloc Québécois to waive the sponsorship agreement once an immigrant acquires Canadian citizenship (see, for example, the plea by Raymond Gravel, House of Common Debates, 23 October 2007), and the suggestion by some Liberal MPs to relax sponsors' income requirements (see Gurbax Malhi, House of Common Debates, 13 May 1999).

9   Because the 2001 elections took place before the bill could pass, it was retabled in the new parliament as Bill C-11.

10 New labour market entrants need to have a minimum work history of 910 hours – the rough equivalent of half a year of full-time work – before they are eligible for EI. Also relevant is that the EI program provides more generous terms regarding both eligibility and benefits in areas of high unemployment. Immigrants tend to live in areas where unemployment is low and where the EI system is correspondingly less generous.

11 According to a senior civil servant at the responsible department, deterring EI use among immigrants in particular has not been the policy intention of any of these program features (CAN14).

12 When the program was first created in 1952, this requirement was twenty years. To encourage immigration, however, it was lowered to ten years only five years later.

13 This means that these applicants now only receive the partial OAS (which theoretically can be as low as 1/40th of the full OAS). Only the very small group of elderly immigrants who have been in the country for less than ten years, were born in a country with which Canada has a bilateral agreement, and are not under a sponsorship agreement can still receive a partial OAS with a GIS top-up.

14 This position has been defended on one or more occasions by the NDP's Dawn Black, Chris Carlton, Olivia Chow, Libby Davies, Brian Masse, Irene Mathyssen, Penny Priddy, and Bill Siksay; the LPC's Colleen Beaumier, Sukh Dhaliwal, Ruby Dhalla, Maria Minna, Bernard Patry, and Bob Rae; the BQ's Nicole Demers and Raymond Gravel; and the CA's Gurmant Grewal.

15 For example, between 1994 and 2012 there were 168 oral questions and motions on the subject in Sweden but only 64 in Canada.

16 The figure only includes motions, questions, and petitions that were clearly accompanied by a normative evaluation (and thus excludes, for example, questions that seemed genuinely aimed at acquiring information). The graph also excludes comments that, while related to immigrants' social rights, were mostly about something else (such as admission policy or more general social policy changes).

17 This rhetoric is so pervasive that it would be impossible to list all examples. To give just a few, see contributions by Art Hanger (RPC, 3 February 1994), Osvaldo Nunez (BQ, 3 March 1997), David Price (PC, 23 March 1999), and Boris Wrzesnewskyi (LPC, 2 December 2009).

18 In this context, the way Osvaldo Nunez (BQ) responded to a Reform Party motion that social assistance be cut for refugee claimants is as confusing as it is ironic: "The very spirit of this motion is disturbing. [It] goes against the universality principle, which is fundamental to our social security system" (House of Commons debate, 3 March 1997).

19 The results of a recent analysis of Canadian public opinion are interesting in this context. Respondents who believed that immigrants were making heavy use of welfare were found to be less supportive of social assistance benefits, but *more* supportive of universal health care, than those who thought few immigrants were on welfare (Banting, Soroka, and Koning 2013). Also worth noting are the results of an Environics Focus Canada survey, which found that Canadians considered their health care system the single most important aspect of Canadian identity (see Figure 4.2).

20 For a similar example, see the interaction between Libby Davies (NDP) and Jason Kenney and Diane Finlay (CPC) on 1 June 2012.

21 The Liberals have criticized the cuts only indirectly, for example, by asking what kind of evidence the cuts have been based on (House of Commons debate, 6 November 2012), by referring to the critiques of others (House of Commons debate, 26 November 2012), or by making sarcastic remarks about the immigration minister's use of limousine services at a time when refugees' health care was being cut (House of Commons debate, 5 October 2012).

22 One feature of the Canadian welfare state that helps explain why we have seen few suggestions overall for limiting immigrants' access to welfare programs in federal politics is that most social programs are administered at the provincial level. This is, for example, how Keith Banting explains why during the mid-1990s Canada decided to take in fewer refugee and family migrants (Banting 2010, 807), and some of my interviewees made similar comments (interviews CAN11, CAN14). The importance of this factor should not be exaggerated, however. While the federal nature of the Canadian welfare state might explain why objections to immigrants' access to welfare benefits have been rare in federal politics, they do not explain why we have not heard more of them at the provincial level, in particular in the most immigrant-dense province of Canada, Ontario.

23 Again, it is worth noting that the generalizations I am making apply primarily to Canada outside Quebec. The distinct nature of Québécois identity has made the discourse on cultural diversity there quite different than in the rest of Canada.

24 More specifically, in 1997, 50.7 per cent of respondents gave one of these two answers; the percentages were 40.7 per cent in 2000, 39.2 per cent in 2004, 30.4 per cent in 2008, and 37.7 per cent in 2011.

25 The longitudinal comparison is somewhat troubled by the fact that the surveys did not offer "neither" as a possible answer to these questions before 2003 but did do so afterwards. However this might have affected the response patterns, it clearly cannot account for the overall decrease in anti-immigrant attitudes (especially since it mostly occurred before 2003).

26 The *Globe and Mail* is a national newspaper headquartered in Toronto.

27 See, for example, John Cannis (LPC): "Our birth rate in Canada is not that high [...] If we are going to grow and sustain the social safety net that Canada is so recognized for, then we need immigration. We need input" (House of Commons debate, 22 September 2010).

28 Ironically, Khan defected to the CPC only two years later.

29 Mohsen Javdani and Krishna Pendakur argue that the report is swamped with methodological flaws and that an accurate calculation arrives at a

net fiscal transfer of 450 dollars per immigrant (or 7 per cent of Grubel and Grady's estimate). Moreover, they challenge the report's political interpretation: "The main result ... is driven by the fact that immigrants have lower incomes than do Canadian-born workers. [However,] lower average wage of immigrants provides a cheap labour input for firms ... Immigrants increase the production and variety of goods and services in the economy [and] also provide a boost to international trade" (Javdani and Pendakur 2011, 13).

30 This overview omits the sub-state nationalist Bloc Québécois and the environmentalist Green Party of Canada, which currently hold ten and 1 seat(s) in Parliament, respectively.

31 In 2011 the Conservatives made a slight cut to the integration budget, and the political reactions were illustrative. The LPC and NDP vehemently criticized the cuts (using them as an important point of criticism of the government during the 2011 election and raising the subject repeatedly between December 2010 and May 2012), while the CPC insisted that the funding change did not really constitute a cut but rather reflected changed settlement patterns among immigrants.

32 Unsurprisingly, Davies expressed his dislike of the other two parties' emphasis on economic migration: "I quite frequently think of what's written on the Statue of Liberty in the United States: 'give me your tired, give me your poor, give me your huddled masses yearning to breathe free.' That was an immigration policy that didn't say: 'give me your wealthy, give me your rich, give me your highly skilled, highly trained to build my economy.' And I would argue that the United States' economic growth from say, the middle of the 19th century ... to now has been pretty good!" (Interview CAN02.)

33 See, for example, contributions by Art Hanger (House of Commons debate, 15 March and 28 September 1994), Sharon Hayes (House of Commons debate, 9 June 1994); Philip Mayfield (House of Commons debate, 19 September 1994), and Ted White (House of Commons debate, 14 February 1994).

34 In reviewing studies conducted with these same data, Jerome Black and Bruce Hicks (2008, 246) concluded that "Reform voters were not particularly more inclined to admit fewer immigrants." This conclusion, however, was based on analyses that included anti-immigrant attitudes along with many other independent variables such as age, gender, and religiosity. While including such controls makes sense for certain purposes, it does not for ours. For example, the findings that men were more likely to express anti-immigrant attitudes than women, and that men were more

likely to vote RPC than women, by no means shows that anti-immigrant attitudes played no role in an RPC vote. A more plausible interpretation is that part of the reason why men were more likely to vote RPC is that they were more likely to hold anti-immigrant attitudes.

35 Reform's 1989 election manifesto dedicated barely one page of a total of 29 to immigration (Reform Party of Canada 1988). Its 1996 and 1999 "Blue Books" (statements of principles and policies) similarly devoted only about 2 per cent of their pages to immigration (Reform Party of Canada 1996, 1999). It is also worth noting that Preston Manning does not discuss immigration *at all* in his political autobiography (Manning 2003) – the only thing he mentions is that he has been called "anti-immigrant" by his opponents.

36 For example, when Doug Collins, a man who had made racist comments in his past, was supported by acclamation as the candidate for Capilano–Howe Sound in the 1989 election, Preston Manning asked him to provide a written condemnation of racism. Collins refused and was consequently not nominated (Dobbin 1992, 145; Manning 2003, 33).

37 During a 1994 party convention in Ottawa, Manning rejected almost all grassroots resolutions on immigration for being too extreme, including one suggesting to bar all immigrants from social benefits during their first five years in Canada (Flanagan 2009, 197). (Parenthetically, we will see that this position has been adopted by most mainstream parties in the Netherlands.)

38 None of the fifty-two members of the 1993 RPC House caucus were non-white or born outside the Western world, but by 1997 the caucus included four non-Western immigrants: Gurmant Grewal (born in India), Rahim Jaffer (born in Uganda), Inky Mark (born in China), and Deepak Obhrai (born in Tanzania). As such, the RPC caucus that year was much more diverse than the factions of the Bloc, NDP, and PCP, which included no non-Western immigrant members at all, and only slightly less diverse than the Liberal parliamentary party (13 of the 158, or 8.2 per cent, of Liberal parliamentarians were non-Western immigrants, whereas the proportion was 4 out of 60, or 6.7 per cent, for Reform).

39 In 2017, 43 of the 338 Members of the House of Commons were born outside Canada, 32 of them in a non-Western country.

40 See, for example, parliamentary contributions by Bill Siksay on 9 May 2006; by Judy Wasylycia-Leis on 12 December 2007, 11 March 2008, 27 January 2009, and 19 June 2010; by Olivia Chow on 17 June 2010; or by Don Davies on 20 September 2011 and 4 April 2012.

41 Examples of these critiques abound. To give just a few: on the first point, see Olivia Chow (House of Commons debates, 8 October 2009 and 21 November, 2009); on the second point, see comments by Dick Proctor (25 September 2003), Pat Martin (30 March 2008), and Olivia Chow (17 April 2008); on the last point, see contributions by Bill Siksay (2 June 2006) and Olivia Chow (26 February 2009). One could argue that in criticizing temporary migration, the NDP's rhetoric sometimes came close to the kind of anti-immigrant rhetoric we can observe in other countries. For example, in criticizing the temporary foreign worker program, Yvon Godin (NDP) complained that immigrants were taking the jobs of native-born citizens (8 June 2011), and Thomas Mulcair argued that the program was contributing to native-born unemployment (19 September 2012). Usually, however, NDP MPs are careful not to couch their criticisms in such divisive terms, and as said, such criticisms are often accompanied by concerns about the social rights of temporary workers. A good example is the following contribution: "That is the trick that the government has devised. Foreign workers will come and work in the plants because Atlantic Canadians will have headed west. Then foreign workers will go home and will not get employment insurance. They will not receive benefits" (Yvon Godin, 30 October 2012).

42 Of course, legal activists can also attempt to contest legislation on the basis of international law. For example, after the Supreme Court ruled that the exclusion of undocumented migrants from health care services did not violate Sections 7 or 15 (*Toussaint v. Canada, 2009*), activists challenged the exclusion as a violation of the International Covenant on Civil and Political Rights. The case is currently before the UN Human Rights Committee.

43 Because Section 7 guarantees legal rights to "everyone," the Supreme Court of Canada reasoned that even though refugee claimants do not have landed immigrant status, they still have the right to a fair trial that, in case their claim is denied, explains the reasons for the denial and offers the opportunity to respond.

5. Netherlands: The Sudden Surge of Selective Solidarity

1 This is not to say that the government followed all the advice it solicited. The Council of State (the most important legal-constitutional advisory organ) recommended on several occasions to include a stipulation allowing for the provision of welfare in exceptional situations, but the government decided against including such a proviso.

2 In 1996, these conditions were made somewhat *more* generous. A proposal to increase the municipal benefits available to asylum seekers was passed

by an overwhelming majority (only the fringe anti-immigrant party CD voted against the bill).

3 While the exact content of this term is unclear and in fact judges enjoy quite some interpretative leeway in practical cases, this connection is measured along three dimensions: a legal dimension (measured by applicants' residence status), a social dimension (measured by the scope of their network of Dutch family members and friends), and a financial dimension (measured by employment history in the Netherlands).

4 Interestingly, Rita Verdonk, certainly one of the most welfare chauvinist cabinet members the Netherlands has seen, decided against extending this period to five years during her incumbency as Minister of Immigration and Integration (2002–2003), out of worry this would leave female migrants in too vulnerable a position.

5 See for example PVV motion 32680–25, 29 February 2012; written questions and answers on 2 October 2012 (21501–31–293); or parliamentary debates on 8 November 2011 (20–23) and 7 February 2012 (50–16).

6 Before that, the applicant's residence status was established only after the welfare benefit was paid out.

7 There is one employee insurance program that has a residence requirement, the costly *Wet Werk en Arbeidsondersteuning Jonggehandicapten*, a disability benefit for people who became disabled before adulthood or during their studies. A comprehensive 1996 reform introduced, among other things, a residence requirement of six years (article 10.2). This policy, however, has been all but phased out. A 2015 reform restricted the eligibility requirements so sharply that only about 10 per cent of all recipients were able to retain the benefit.

8 The main reason was that the costs would be unreasonably high for immigrants with a large gap. Immigrants arriving in the Netherlands at age forty, for example, could be looking at costs as high as 80,000 euros, or about C$120,000 (SVB 2007a, 18).

9 Other suggestions for reducing elderly immigrants' dependence on AIO, such as cutting the residence requirement of the universal pension program from fifty to forty years, have occasionally been made but have never been taken seriously. When the largest Dutch trade union suggested such a cut, PvdA junior minister Ahmed Aboutaleb immediately dismissed it, contending that such a measure "would affect a much larger group and have ... large budgetary effects" (kst-29549–13, 19 November 2007).

10 Before the bill was passed, the social affairs committee was informed that only 10 per cent of AIO recipients were native-born citizens (32777–6, 27 June 2011).

11 While it is unclear whether much should be read into this, it seems worth noting that the law's acronym – "beu" – is also the Dutch word for being sick of or fed up with something.

12 This adjustment is made only when the standard of living is lower than in the Netherlands. The benefit does not become more generous for emigrants residing in a country with a higher standard of living.

13 As early as 2006, then Amsterdam alderman Ahmed Aboutaleb (PvdA) argued that burqa-wearing women should not be entitled to social assistance. His comment was widely covered in the national press, and pollster Maurice de Hond even surveyed the public on the issue. According to this survey, only 20 per cent of respondents disagreed with Aboutaleb.

14 It would take up too much space to mention all relevant examples here. For a few more examples, see comments by Malik Azmani (VVD, 2011Z15945, 5 August 2011), Raymond Knops (CDA, 14–16, 25 October 2011), and Cora Van Nieuwenhuizen (VVD, 30545–114, 4 July 2012).

15 The government at the time responded enthusiastically to the RMO's report. The only critique it levelled was that the report did not go far enough and that it should have advocated *more* restrictions on the right of migrants to take built-up benefits with them when they leave the country (tk-30573–76).

16 Figure 5.1 excludes motions and questions that were unaccompanied by a clear evaluation on behalf of their author (e.g., questions that seemed to be asked primarily to acquire information), as well as motions and questions that, while related to the position of immigrants in the welfare state, were mostly about something else (such as motions proposing to attract more high-skilled migrants, or to make a benefit more generous for all recipients).

17 This discourse changed somewhat after a new government took office in November 2012. When Steven van Weyenberg (D66) asked questions in Parliament about yet another report detailing discriminatory practices in employment agencies, the new responsible junior minister Jetta Klijnsma (from the social democratic party PvdA) responded more sympathetically: "I wholeheartedly agree with Mr. Van Weyenberg that this persistent phenomenon of discrimination in the labour market is unacceptable" (TK-36–7, 18 December 2012). At the same time, however, she did add immediately that this was not a subject of discussion in negotiations with social partners and that she was unwilling to consider any of the anti-discrimination measures D66 and the SP were proposing.

18 For other examples, see questions by Van Klaveren, Fritsma, and De Jong (2011Z02826, 11 February 2011); De Jong and Van Klaveren (2011Z23335,

17 November 2011); and Van Klaveren, De Jong, and Wilders (2012Z14575, 17 July 2012).

19 These preferences have produced such a rigid and inaccessible system, that until 1980 the Netherlands had the lowest female labour force participation of all OECD countries. It still scores comparatively low in this regard (Huber and Stephens 2001, 166; Seeleib-Kaiser, Van Dyke, and Roggenkamp 2008, 25; Van Kersbergen 1995).

20 This view is not shared, however, by all advisory bodies. The Scientific Council for Government Policy argued in a 2007 report that rather than asserting one unchangeable national identity, the Netherlands should promote various modes of identification with the Netherlands and leave room for simultaneous ties to other national or sub-national communities (WRR 2007).

21 All differences are statistically significant at level $p < 0.001$. Respondents were also asked how important they considered being born in the Netherlands and having lived in the Netherlands for most of one's life to be. The differences in responses to these questions were smaller and not statistically significant.

22 My interviews were with Cora van Nieuwenhuizen (VVD), Hans Spekman (PvdA), Sietse Fritsma (PVV), Eddy van Hijum (CDA), Paul Ulenbelt (SP), and Fatma Koşer Kaya (D66). Unfortunately, the environmentalist party GL refused to be interviewed for this study. Table 5.2 omits six small parties (each with five seats or fewer in parliament): leftish Christian party CU, animal rights party PvdD, seniors' rights party 50+, orthodox Christian party SGP, minority rights party DENK, and Eurosceptic party FVD.

23 PVV's opposition to the pension reform brought then VVD leader (and later prime minister) Mark Rutte to state: "Our colleague Pechtold [D66] has been worrying recently about the alleged extreme right-wing tendencies of his colleague Wilders [PVV], but as far as I'm concerned the fact that colleague Wilders on the point of the [pension reform] is cosily taking sides with the SP and leans up against [union leader] Jongerius indicates the ultimate unmasking of the PVV. As far as I'm concerned the PVV is not extreme right-wing but extreme left-wing" (TK24–2066, 12 November 2009). Other right-wing critics of the PVV have made similar comments. Former PVV MP Marcial Hernandez, for example, mentions "the increasingly left-wing course of the Freedom Party on, among other things, the health care file" and his belief that the party "was increasingly turning out to be an extreme left party in many areas" among his reasons for stepping out of the party (Hernandez 2014, 106, 111).

24 This difference between the PVV and earlier anti-immigrant parties also becomes apparent when we look at the attitudes of voters. Data from the Dutch DPES suggest that those who voted for the CD and the LPF were significantly less likely to favour income redistribution than other voters. PVV voters, by contrast, turned out to be either equally or *more* likely to advocate a reduction in income differences. These conclusions are based on a comparison of CD and non-CD voters in the DPES of 1994 and 1998, LPF and non-LPF voters in the DPES of 2002, 2003, and 2006, and PVV and non-PVV voters in the DPES of 2010 and 2012 (the PVV also competed in the election of 2006, but it was impossible to make the comparison for this election because the variable on vote choice did not include the PVV as a separate answer option). The calculations are not shown but can be made available upon request.

25 The graph maps the percentage of seats taken by the CD, the LPF, the PVV, and the newly minted FVD, as well as by independents Geert Wilders and Rita Verdonk (who both started an anti-immigrant movement after their break with the VVD – the PVV and Proud of the Netherlands, respectively).

26 Interestingly, the website www.watkostdemassaimmigratie.nl never offered an answer to its name-giving question. It merely offers a platform for people to post complaints about the costs of immigration.

27 It is worth noting that the report does not attempt to calculate the overall net effect of immigration on the Dutch economy. It explicitly states at the outset that it is a "partial" study that does not account for, among other things, the effects of immigration on the labour market or on economic growth in general (Van der Geest and Dietvorst 2010, 7).

28 For another example, see the 1998 debate on remigration policy in which no politician responds to the contributions by CD's Wim Elsthout (71–5322, 8 April 1998).

29 While one could speculate that the VVD (and perhaps even the CDA) might have proposed the first two of these changes in the absence of the PVV as well, the latter two can directly be traced to the PVV – in fact, when in 2009 the party suggested to make immigrants pay the full costs of integration courses, both the VVD and CDA voted against the motion (see appendix table A3.2.).

30 There are certainly exceptions to this pattern, but they tend to be levelled precisely against reforms that affect existing immigrant groups that have a role to play in the election process (as opposed to future migrants who by definition are excluded from the vote). A good example is the opposition to changes in the AIO – the top-up benefit intended for those elderly who because of an international life history are only eligible for an incomplete

pension benefit. The 2011 reduction in the benefit level was one of only two IEWRs from 1995 to 2012 that were opposed by all opposition parties. Moreover, when it comes to the AIO we encounter occasional strong language. When the first Rutte cabinet reduced the number of weeks during which one can enjoy AIO abroad, for example, Hans Spekman (PvdA) cried out: "this is nothing but bullying immigrant elderly of Surinamese, Turkish and Moroccan background who have worked here for very long, but have not built up a complete pension. There is no other way I can see this" (8–8, 5 October 2011).

31 The letter contained eight suggestions in all, but two of those were amendments to admission policies and will therefore not be considered here.

32 The PVV, for example, continues to advocate many of the IEWRs that have proven impossible to implement, including the Danish model of social assistance and the lowering of unemployment benefits for EU migrants.

33 The party *Forum voor Democratie* first participated in national elections in 2017, when it won two seats. While it has not taken an explicit stance on any of these specific proposals, it seems likely that it would support them warmly. In its election manifesto it advocates a wide range of far-reaching restrictions in immigration and integration policies, including the abolition of extending permanent residence permits to refugees and the deportation of immigrants who do not "assimilate" or have "extreme political views."

6. Conclusions

1 The other three policy responses seem more effective. First, by mere mathematical necessity across-the-board cuts reduce social spending to a larger extent than cutbacks aimed at only a portion of recipients. Second, as the Canadian case shows, a selective admission policy can effectively avoid a large immigrant welfare clientele. And third, since lower levels of human capital are a crucial explanation for immigrants' overrepresentation among welfare dependents, the rationale for programs aimed at increasing immigrants' human capital seems obvious. (At the same time, however, we should not attribute panacean qualities to this policy response. As the Swedish case shows, even in the presence of generous integration services, the combination of an almost exclusive intake of refugee and family migration on the one hand and protective labour market institutions on the other is still likely to result in overall troubled economic integration.)

2 Initially the government expected the support requirement to apply to about one in four incoming family migrants, but in practice this share is even smaller. In 2011, the first year that the requirement went into force,

only 350 of a total of 23,000 incoming family migrants (barely 1.5 per cent) were affected by the requirement.

3 In cases where a party exhibits only partial support for a strategy, I coded the party as being half in favour. The results for Canada omit the Bloc Québécois and Green Party, which together occupy 11 of the 338 seats in Parliament; the results for the Netherlands do not include the six smallest parties, which collectively account for less than 15 per cent of the seats in Parliament. See the country chapters for a more elaborate discussion of the position of each political party.

4 To be clear, my main goal is explain why different countries have responded very differently to the tension between immigration and welfare, and in particular, why support for excluding migrants from benefits is more pronounced in some contexts than in others. A systematic explanation for cross-national differences in the politics of immigration in general is beyond the scope of this research.

References

Aalandslid, Vebjørn. 2009. *A Comparison of the Labour Market Integration of Immigrants and Refugees in Canada and Norway.* Oslo: Statistics Norway.

Adams, Michael. 2007. *Unlikely Utopia: The Surprising Triumph of Canadian Multiculturalism.* Toronto: Penguin.

Ader, Christine R. 1995. "A Longitudinal Study of Agenda Setting for the Issue of Environmental Pollution." *Journalism Mass Communication Quarterly* 72(2): 300–11.

Adsera, Alicia, and Barry R. Chiswick. 2006. "Divergent Patterns in Immigrant Earnings across European Destinations." In *Immigration and the Transformation of Europe*, ed. C.A. Parsons and T.M. Smeeding, 85–111. Cambridge: Cambridge University Press.

Ahmadi, Fereshteh, Irving Palm, and Nader Ahmadi. 2016. *Mångfaldsbarometern 2016* [Diversity Barometer 2016]. Gävle: Högskolan i Gävle.

Akbari, Ather H. 1989. "The Benefits of Immigrants to Canada: Evidence on Tax and Public Services." *Canadian Public Policy* 15(4): 424–35.

Åkesson, Jimmy. 2008. Främst var det EU-frågan som drog mig till politiken (It was the question of the EU that first drew me to politics). In *20 röster om 20 år. Sverigedemokraterna 1988–2008* [20 voices over 20 years. The Sweden Democrats, 1988–2008], ed. J. Leandersson Stockholm: Blåsippans Förlag.

Alesina, Alberto, and Eliana La Ferrara. 2002. "Who Trusts Others?" *Journal of Public Economics* 85(2): 207–34.

Alesina, Alberto, and Edward L. Glaeser. 2004. *Fighting Poverty in the US and Europe. A World of Difference.* Oxford: Oxford University Press.

Alexander, Shannon. 2010. "Humanitarian Bottom League? Sweden and the Right to Health for Undocumented Migrants." *European Journal of Migration and Law* 12(2): 215–40.

Alliansen. 2014. Vi bygger Sverige: Alliansens Valmanifest 2014–2018 [We build Sweden: Alliance's election manifesto 2014–2018].

Andersen, John, Jørgen Elm Larsen, and Iver Hornemann Møller. 2009. "The Exclusion and Marginalisation of Immigrants in the Danish Welfare Society: Dilemmas and Challenges." *International Journal of Sociology and Social Policy* 29(5–6): 274–86.

Andersen, Jørgen Goul, and Tor Bjørklund. 2000. "Radical Right-Wing Populism in Scandinavia: From Tax Revolt to Neo-Liberalism and Xenophobia." In *The Politics of the Extreme Right: From the Margin to the Mainstream*, ed. P. Hainsworth, 193–223. London: Pinter.

Andrew-Gee, Eric. 2015. "Conservatives vow to establish 'barbaric cultural practices' tip line." *Globe and Mail*, 2 October.

Appelbaum, Lauren D. 2001. "The Influence of Perceived Deservingness on Policy Decisions regarding Aid to the Poor." *Political Psychology* 22(3): 419–42.

Ariely, Gal. 2011. "Globalization, Immigration and National Identity: How the Level of Globalization Affects the Relations between Nationalism, Constructive Patriotism, and Attitudes toward Immigrants." *Group Processes & Intergroup Relations* 15(4): 539–57.

Aylott, Nicholas. 2015. "The Sweden Democrats: Ostracised and Energised?" *Policy Network*, 22 January. http://www.policy-network.net/pno_detail .aspx?ID=4823&title=The-Sweden-Democrats-Ostracised-and-energised.

Baker, Michael, and Dwayne Benjamin. 1995. "The Receipt of Transfer Payments by Immigrants to Canada." *Journal of Human Resources* 30(4): 650–76.

Baker, Michael, Dwayne Benjamin, and Elliott Fan. 2009. *Public Policy and the Economic Wellbeing of Elderly Immigrants*. Vancouver: Canadian Labour Market and Skills Researcher Network.

Bale, Tim, Christoffer Green-Pedersen, André Krouwel, Kurt Richard Luther, and Nick Sitter. 2010. "If You Can't Beat Them, Join Them? Explaining Social Democratic Responses to the Challenge from the Populist Radical Right in Western Europe." *Political Studies* 58(3): 410–26.

Banting, Keith G. 2000. "Looking in Three Directions: Migration and the European Welfare State in Comparative Perspective." In *Immigration and Welfare: Challenging the Borders of the Welfare State*, ed. M. Bommes and A. Geddes, 13–33. London: Routledge.

– . 2008. "Canada as Counternarrative: Multiculturalism, Recognition, and Redistribution." In *The Comparative Turn in Canadian Political Science*, ed. L.A. White, R. Simeon, R. Vipond, and J. Wallner, 59–76. Vancouver: UBC Press.

– . 2010. "Is There a Progressive's Dilemma in Canada? Immigration, Multiculturalism, and the Welfare State." *Canadian Journal of Political Science* 43(4): 797–820.

Banting, Keith G., and Will Kymlicka. 2011. Multiculturalism Policy Index.

Banting, Keith G., and John Myles. 2013. *Inequality and the Fading of Redistributive Politics*. Vancouver: UBC Press.

Banting, Keith G., Stuart N. Soroka, and Edward A. Koning. 2013. "Multicultural Diversity and Redistribution." In *Inequality and the Fading of Redistributive Politics*, ed. K.G. Banting and J. Myles, 165–86. Vancouver: UBC Press.

Barkman, Tobias. 2017. "'Moderaterna kontrar efter S krav på färre flyktingar till Malmö: 'Inte några alls'" [Moderates counter Social Democrats' demand for fewer refugees to Malmö: "none at all"]. *Sydsvenskan*, 23 April.

Barrett, Alan, and Bertrand Maître. 2013. "Immigrant Welfare Receipt across Europe." *International Journal of Manpower* 34(1–2): 8–23.

Barrett, Alan, and Yvonne McCarthy. 2008. "Immigrants and Welfare Programmes: Exploring the Interactions between Immigrant Characteristics, Immigrant Welfare Dependence, and Welfare Policy." *Oxford Review of Economic Policy* 24(3): 542–59.

Basok, Tanya. 2003. *Human Rights and Citizenship: The Case of Mexican Immigrants in Canada*. San Diego: Center for Comparative Immigration Studies.

Basok, Tanya, and Emily Carasco. 2010. "Advancing the Rights of Non-Citizens in Canada: A Human Rights Approach to Migrant Rights." *Human Rights Quarterly* 32(2): 342–66.

Bay, Ann-Helén, and Axel West Pedersen. 2006. "The Limits of Social Solidarity. Basic Income, Immigration, and the Legitimacy of the Universal Welfare State." *Acta Sociologica* 49(4): 419–36.

Bergmark, Åke, and Joakim Palme. 2003. "Welfare and the Unemployment Crisis: Sweden in the 1990s." *International Journal of Social Welfare* 12(2): 108–22.

Betz, Hans-Georg. 2001. "Exclusionary Populism in Austria, Italy, and Switzerland." *International Journal* 56(3): 393–420.

Betz, Hans-Georg, and Carol Johnson. 2004. "Against the Current – Stemming the Tide: The Nostalgic Ideology of the Contemporary Radical Populist Right." *Journal of Political Ideologies* 9(3): 311–27.

Bijl, Rob, Jeroen Boelhouwer, Mariëlle Cloïn, and Evert Pommer. 2011. *De sociale staat van Nederland 2011* [The social state of the Netherlands 2011]. The Hague: Sociaal en Cultureel Planbureau.

Biles, John. 2008. "Integration Policies in English-Speaking Canada." In *Immigration and Integration in Canada in the Twenty-First Century*, ed. J. Biles, J. Frideres, and M. Burstein, 139–86. Montreal and Kingston: McGill–Queen's University Press.

Binnema, Harmen. 2004. "The Netherlands: How OECD Ideas Are Slowly Creeping In." In *The OECD and European Welfare States*, ed. K. Armingeon and M. Beyeler, 113–25. Cheltenham: Edward Elgar.

Birkland, Thomas A. 1997. *After Disaster: Agenda-Setting, Public Policy, and Focusing Events*. Washington, DC: Georgetown University Press.

Bissett, James. 2011. "Immigration isn't as beneficial as politicians claim." *Calgary Herald*, 20 May.

Black, Jerome H., and Bruce M. Hicks. 2008. "Electoral Politics and Immigration in Canada: How Does Immigration Matter?" *International Migration & Integration* 9(3): 241–67.

Blackwell, Tom. 1999. "Ontario continues to get tough: Throne Speech promises Common Sense Revolution." *Gazette*, 22 October, A10.

Bloch, Alice, and Lisa Schuster. 2002. "Asylum and Welfare: Contemporary Debates." *Critical Social Policy* 22(3): 393–414.

Boeri, Tito. 2009. *Immigration to the Land of Redistribution*. London: London School of Economic and Political Science.

Boeri, Tito, Gordon H. Hanson, and Barry McCormick. 2009. *Immigration Policy and the Welfare System*. Oxford: Oxford University Press.

Boin, Arjen, Paul 't Hart, and Allan McConnell. 2009. "Crisis Exploitation: Political and Policy Impacts of Framing Contests." *Journal of European Public Policy* 16(1): 81–106.

Bommes, Michael. 2000. "National Welfare State, Biography, and Migration: Labour Migrants, Ethnic Germans, and the Re-Ascription of Welfare State Membership." In *Immigration and Welfare: Challenging the Borders of the Welfare State*, ed. M. Bommes and A. Geddes, 90–108. London: Routledge.

Bommes, Michael, and Andrew Geddes. 2000. "Immigration and the Welfare State." In *Immigration and Welfare: Challenging the Borders of the Welfare State*, ed. M. Bommes and A. Geddes, 1–12. London: Routledge.

Borevi, Karen. 2012. "Sweden: The Flagship of Multiculturalism." In *Immigration Policy and the Scandinavian Welfare State 1945–2010*, ed. G. Brochmann and A. Hagelund, 25–96. Basingstoke: Palgrave.

Borjas, George J. 1999. *Heaven's Door: Immigration Policy and the American Economy*. Princeton: Princeton University Press.

Bosma, Martin. 2010. *De Schijnélite van de Valse Munters. Drees, Extreem Rechts, de Sixties, Nuttige Idioten, Groep Wilders en Ik* [The Fake Elite of the Forgers. Drees, Extreme Right, the Sixties, Useful Idiots, Group Wilders and Me]. Amsterdam: Bert Bakker.

Boucher, Anna, and Terry Carney. 2009. "Social Security and Immigration: An Agenda for Future Research." *Journal of Foreign and International Labour and Social Security Law* 23(1): 36–57.

Breunig, Christian, and Adam Luedtke. 2008. "What Motivates the Gatekeepers? Explaining Governing Party Preferences on Immigration." *Governance: An International Journal of Policy, Administration, and Institutions* 21(1): 123–46.

Brochmann, Grete. 1996. *European Integration and Immigration from Third Countries*. Oslo: Scandinavian University Press.

Brooks, Clem, and Jeff Manza. 2007. *Why Welfare States Persist. The Importance of Public Opinion in Democracies*. Chicago: University of Chicago Press.

Bullock, Heather E. 1999. "Attributions for Poverty: A Comparison of Middle-Class and Welfare Recipient Attitudes." *Journal of Applied Social Psychology* 29(10): 2059–82.

Burgoon, Brian. 2011. *Immigration, Integration, and Support for Redistribution in Europe*. Madrid: Center for Advanced Study in the Social Sciences.

Burns, Peter, and James G. Gimpel. 2000. "Economic Insecurity, Prejudicial Stereotypes, and Public Opinion on Immigration Policy." *Political Science Quarterly* 115(2): 201–25.

Buruma, Ian. 2006. *Murder in Amsterdam*. New York: Penguin.

Caldwell, Christopher. 2009. *Reflections on the Revolution in Europe. Immigration, Islam and the West*. New York: Anchor Books.

Canadian Press. 2012. "Wall slams refugee health cuts." *Calgary Herald*, 23 November.

Capps, Randy, Jacqueline Hagan, and Nestor Rodriguez. 2004. "Border Residents Manage the U.S. Immigration and Welfare Reforms." In *Immigrants, Welfare Reform, and the Poverty of Policy*, ed. P. Kretsedemas and A. Aparicio, 229–50. Westport: Praeger.

Carens, Joseph H. 1988. "Immigration and the Welfare State." In *Democracy and the Welfare State*, ed. A. Guttman, 207–30. Princeton: Princeton University Press.

Carter, Elisabeth L. 2002. "Proportional Representation and the Fortunes of Right-Wing Extremist Parties." *West European Politics* 25(3): 125–46.

– . 2005. *The Extreme Right in Western Europe: Success or Failure?* Manchester: Manchester University Press.

Castles, Stephen, and Godula Kosack. 1985. *Immigrant Workers and Class Structure in Western Europe*, 2nd ed. Oxford: Oxford University Press.

Castronova, Edward J., Hilke Kayser, Joachim R. Frick, and Gert G. Wagner. 2001. "Immigrants, Natives, and Social Assistance: Comparable Take-Up under Comparable Circumstances." *International Migration Review* 35(3): 726–48.

Chiswick, Barry R., and Michael E. Hurst. 1998. "The Labor Market Status of U.S. Immigrants: A Synthesis." In *Immigration, Citizenship, and the Welfare State in Germany and the United States: Immigrant Incorporation*, ed. H. Kurthen, J. Fijalkowski, and G.G. Wagner, 73–94. Stamford: Jai Press.

Chong, Dennis, and James N. Druckman. 2007. "Framing Theory." *Annual Review of Political Science* 10: 103–26.

Chorny, Victoria, Rob Euwals, and Kees Folmer. 2007. *Immigration Policy and Welfare State Design. A Qualitative Approach to Explore the Interaction.* The Hague: CPB Netherlands Bureau for Economic Policy Analysis.

Chorus, Jutta, and Menno De Galan. 2002. *In de ban van Fortuyn. Reconstructie van een politieke aardschok* [Under the Spell of Fortuyn. Reconstruction of a Political Earthquake]. Amsterdam: Olympus.

Citizenship and Immigration Canada. 2015. *Facts and Figures.* Ottawa.

Clark, William A.V., and Freya Schultz. 1998. "Mass Migration, Dependency, and Poverty in the United States." In *Immigration, Citizenship, and the Welfare State in Germany and the United States: Immigrant Incorporation,* ed. H. Kurthen, J. Fijalkowski, and G.G. Wagner, 15–33. Stamford: Jai Press.

Cohen, James. 2009. "Locking Out the Swedish Democrats." *International Free Press Society,* 18 September.

Collett, Elizabeth. 2011. *Immigrant Integration in Europe in a Time of Austerity.* Washington, DC: Migration Policy Institute.

Commissie Meijers. 2010. "Notitie immigratie en asiel in het Regeerakkoord VVD-CDA 30 september 2010" [Memorandum immigration and asylum in government agreement VVD-CDA, 30 September 2010]. Utrecht.

Conservative Party of Canada. 2015. *Protect our Economy. Our Conservative Plan to Protect the Economy.* Ottawa.

Couzy, Michiel. 2016. "Onderhandeling over bed-bad-brood strandt" [Negotation about bed-bath-bread fails], *Het Parool,* 21 November.

Cox, Robert Henry. 1993. *The Development of the Dutch Welfare State.* Pittsburgh: University of Pittsburgh Press.

– . 2001. "The Social Construction of an Imperative. Why Welfare Reform Happened in Denmark and the Netherlands but not in Germany." *World Politics* 53(3): 463–98.

Crepaz, Markus M. 2006. "'If you are my brother, I may give you a dime!' Public Opinion on Multiculturalism, Trust, and the Welfare State." In *Multiculturalism and the Welfare State. Recognition and Redistribution in Contemporary Democracies,* ed. K.G. Banting and W. Kymlicka, 92–117. Oxford: Oxford University Press.

– . 2008. *Trust beyond Borders: Immigration, the Welfare State, and Identity in Modern Societies.* Ann Arbor: University of Michigan Press.

Crepaz, Markus M., and Regan Damron. 2009. "Constructing Tolerance: How the Welfare State Shapes Attitudes about Immigrants." *Comparative Political Studies* 42(3): 437–63.

d'Appollonia, Ariane Chebel, and Simon Reich. 2008. *Immigration, Integration, and Security. America and Europe in Comparative Perspective.* Pittsburgh: University of Pittsburgh Press.

Dagens Industri. 2016. "Anna Hagwall tvingus ut ur SD" [Anna Hagwall forced out the SD], 28 October.

Dagens Nyheter. 2012. "Isovaara lämnar riksdagen efter ny SD-skandal" [Isovaara leaves parliament after new SD scandal]. *Dagens Nyheter*, 29 November.

– . 2016. "DN Debatt: 'Föreslagna flyktinglagarna försämrar integrationen'" [DN debate: "Proposed refugee laws deteriorate integration"].

Dagevos, Jaco, Mérove Gijsberts, and Carlo Van Praag. 2003. *Rapportage Minderheden 2003: Onderwijs, arbeid en sociaal-culturele integratie* [Report Minorities 2003: Education, labour, and socio-economic integration]. The Hague: Sociaal en Cultureel Planbureau.

Dahlberg, Mats, Karin Edmark, and Heléne Lundqvist. 2012. "Ethnic Diversity and Preferences for Redistribution." *Journal of Political Economy* 120(1): 41–76.

Dahlström, Carl, and Peter Esaiasson. 2013. "The Immigration Issue and Anti-Immigrant Party Success in Sweden 1970–2006: A Deviant Case Analysis." *Party Politics* 19(2): 343–64.

Damen, Sofie. 2001. "Strategieën tegen extreem-rechts. Het cordon sanitaire onder de loep" [Strategies against Extreme Right. The Cordon Sanitaire under Investigation]. *Tijdschrift voor Sociologie* 22(1): 89–110.

De Hart, Betty. 2007. "The End of Multiculturalism: The End of Dual Citizenship? Political and Public Debates on Dual Citizenship in The Netherlands 91980–2004." In *Dual Citizenship in Europe: From Nationhood to Societal Integration*, ed. T. Faist, 77–102. Aldershot: Ashgate.

De Koster, Willem, Peter Achterberg, and Jeroen Van der Waal. 2012. "The New Right and the Welfare State: The Electoral Relevance of Welfare Chauvinism and Welfare Populism in the Netherlands." *International Political Science Review* 34(1): 3–20.

De Lange, Sarah L. 2007. "A New Winning Formula? The Programmatic Appeal of the Radical Right." *Party Politics* 13(4): 411–35.

De Leeuw, Jan, Erik Meijer, and Harvey Goldstein. 2008. *Handbook of Multilevel Analysis.* New York: Springer.

De Rooy, Piet. 2005. *Republiek van rivaliteiten. Nederland since 1813* [Republic of Rivalries. The Netherlands since 1813]. Amsterdam: Mets & Schilt.

De Wijk, Rob. 2008. "Boerka is niet het probleem, maar flauwekuldebatten" [The burqa is not the problem, silly debates are]. *Trouw*, 2 May.

Demleitner, Nora. 1998. "Power, Perceptions, and the Politics of Immigration and Welfare." In *Immigration, Citizenship, and the Welfare State in Germany and the United States: Welfare Policies and Immigrants' Citizenship*, ed. H. Kurthen, J. Fijalkowski, and G.G. Wagner, 9–28. Stamford: Jai Press.

Derks, Anton. 2008. "Populist Challenges to the Welfare State in Belgium: On the Susceptibility of the Underprivileged for Anti-Welfare State Discourse and Politics." In *Social Justice, Legitimacy, and the Welfare State*, ed. S. Mau and B. Veghte, 169–92. Aldershot: Ashgate.

DeVoretz, Don J. 1995. "New Issues, New Evidence, and New Immigration Policies for the Twenty-First Century." In *Diminishing Returns: The Economics of Canada's Recent Immigration Policy*, ed. D.J. Devoretz, 1–30. Toronto and Vancouver: C.D. Howe Institute and the Laurier Institution.

DeVoretz, Don J., and Sergiy Pivnenko. 2004. "Immigrant Public Finance Transfers: A Comparative Analysis by City." *Canadian Journal of Urban Research* 13(1): 155–69.

Dobbin, Murray. 1992. *Preston Manning and the Reform Party*. Halifax: Formac.

Doctors Without Borders. 2005. Gömda i Sverige. Utestängda från Hälso- och Sjukvård [Forgotten in Sweden. Excluded from Health and Sick Care]. Stockholm.

Dörr, Silvia, and Thomas Faist. 1997. "Institutional Conditions for the Integration of Immigrants in Welfare States: A Comparison of the Literature on Germany, France, Great Britain, and the Netherlands." *European Journal of Political Research* 31(4): 401–26.

Doyle, Nicola, Gerard Hughes, and Eskil Wadensjö. 2006. *Freedom of Movement for Workers from Central and Eastern Europe*. Stockholm: Swedish Institute for European Policy Studies.

Dwyer, Peter. 2006. "Governance, Forced Migration, and Welfare." In *Migration, Immigration, and Social Policy*, ed. C.J. Finer, 63–80. Malden: Blackwell.

Eastmond, Marita. 2011. "Egalitarian Ambitions, Constructions of Difference: The Paradoxes of Refugee Integration in Sweden." *Journal of Ethnic and Migration Studies* 37(2): 277–95.

Eger, Maureen E. 2010. "Even in Sweden: The Effect of Immigration on Support for Welfare State Spending." *European Sociological Review* 26(2): 203–17.

Ekberg, Jan. 1983. *Inkomsteffekter av invandring* [Income Effects of Immigration]. Växjö: Växjö University College.

– . 1999. "Immigration and the Public Sector: Income Effects for the Native Population in Sweden." *Journal of Population Economics* 12: 278–97.

– . 2009. *Invandringen och de offentlige finanserna* [Immigration and the Public Finances]. Stockholm: Ministry of Finance.

Ekelund, Martin. 2013. Sd-ledamot stöttar Svenskarnas parti [SD MP supports Party of the Swedes]. *Aftonbladet*, 13 December.

Engbersen, Godfried. 2004. "De muur rond de verzorgingsstaat" [The Wall around the Welfare State]. *Amsterdams Sociologisch Tijdschrift* 31(1): 20–37.

Engelen, Ewald. 2003. "How to Combine Openness and Protection? Citizenship, Migration, and Welfare Regimes." *Politics & Society* 31(4): 503–36.

Entzinger, Han. 1985. "The Netherlands." In *European Immigration Policy: A Comparative Study*, ed. T. Hammar, 50–88. Cambridge: Cambridge University Press.

– . 2006. "The Parallel Decline of Multiculturalism and the Welfare State in the Netherlands." In *Multiculturalism and the Welfare State: Recognition and Redistribution in Contemporary Democracies*, ed. K.G. Banting and W. Kymlicka, 177–201. Oxford: Oxford University Press.

Entzinger, Han, and Jelle Van der Meer. 2004. *Grenzeloze Solidariteit. Naar een Migratiebestendige Verzorgingsstaat* [Solidarity without Borders. Towards a Migration-Proof Welfare State]. Amsterdam: De Balie.

Eriksson, Jonas. 2006. "The Pre-Enlargement Debate in Sweden." In *Freedom of Movement for Workers from Central and Eastern Europe*, ed. N. Doyle, G. Hughes, and E. Wadensjö, 77–90. Stockholm: Swedish Institute for Policy Studies.

Erk, Jan G. 2005. "From Vlaams Blok to Vlaams Belang: The Belgian Far-Right Renames Itself." *West European Politics* 28(3): 493–502.

– . 2011. "The Famous Dutch (In)Tolerance." *Current History* 110(734): 110–16.

Escandell, Xavier, and Alin M. Ceobanu. 2010. "Nationalism and Anti-Immigrant Sentiment in Spain." *South European Society & Politics* 15(2): 157–79.

Esping-Andersen, Gøsta. 1990. *The Three Worlds of Welfare Capitalism*. Princeton: Princeton University Press.

– . 1992. "The Making of a Social Democratic Welfare State." In *Creating Social Democracy: A Century of the Social Democratic Labor Party in Sweden*, ed. K. Misgeld, K. Molin, and K. Åmark, 35–66. University Park: Penn State University Press.

– . 1996a. "Positive-Sum Solutions in a World of Trade-Offs." In *Welfare States in Transition. National Adaptations in Global Economies*, ed. Esping-Andersen, 256–67. London: Sage.

– . 1996b. "Welfare States without Work: The Impasse of Labour Shedding and Familialism in Continental European Social Policy." In *Welfare States in Transition. National Adaptations in Global Economies*, ed. Esping-Andersen, 66–87. London: Sage.

Esses, Victoria M., Ulrich Wagner, Carina Wolf, Matthias Preiser, and Christopher J. Wilbur. 2006. "Perceptions of National Identity and Attitudes toward Immigrants and Immigration in Canada and Germany." *International Journal of Intercultural Relations* 30(6): 653–69.

Evans, Geoffrey. 1996. "Cross-National Differences in Support for Welfare and Redistribution: An Evaluation of Competing Theories." In *Understanding Change in Social Attitudes*, ed. B. Taylor and K. Thomson, 185–208. Aldershot: Dartmouth.

Evans, Patricia M. 2002. "Downloading the Welfare State, Canadian Style." In *Diminishing Welfare: A Cross-National Study of Social Provision*, ed. G.S. Goldberg and M.G. Rosenthal, 75–102. Westport: Auburn House.

Expressen. 2013. "Förundersökning mot Thoralf Alfsson inleds" [Preliminary investigation started against Thoralf Alfsson]. *Expressen*, 18 November.

Faist, Thomas. 1995. "Boundaries of Welfare States: Immigrants and Social Rights on the National and Supranation Level." In *Migration and European Integration: The Dynamics of Inclusion and Exclusion*, ed. R. Miles and D. Tränhardt, 177–95. London: Pinter.

– . 1996. "Immigration, Integration, and the Welfare State: Germany and the USA in a Comparative Perspective." In *The Challenge of Diversity. Integration and Pluralism in Societies of Immigration*, ed. R. Bauböck, A. Heller, and A.R. Zolberg, 227–58. Aldershot: Avebury.

Ferrer, Ana, and W. Craig Riddell. 2008. "Education, Credentials, and Immigrant Earnings." *Canadian Journal of Economics / Revue Canadienne d'Economique* 41(4): 186–216.

Finseraas, Henning. 2012. "Anti-Immigration Attitudes, Support for Redistribution, and Party Choice in Europe." In *Changing Social Equality. The Nordic Welfare Model in the 21st Century*, ed. J. Kvist, J. Fritzell, B. Hvinden, and O. Kangas, 23–44. Bristol: The Policy Press.

Fix, Michael E. 2009. *Immigrants and Welfare. The Impact of Welfare Reform on America's Newcomers*. New York: Russel Sage Foundation.

Flanagan, Thomas. 2009. *Waiting for the Wave: The Reform Party and the Conservative Movement*. Montreal and Kingston: McGill–Queen's University Press.

Fleury, Dominique. 2007. *A Study of Poverty and Working Poverty among Recent Immigrants to Canada*. Ottawa: Human Resources and Skills Development Canada.

Flood, Lennart, and Andreea Mitrut. 2010. *Ålderspension för invandrare från länder utanför OECD-området* [Old age pension for immigrants from countries outside the OECD area]. Stockholm: SOU.

Fong, Cara M. 2007. "Evidence from an Experiment on Charity to Welfare Recipients: Reciprocity, Altruism, and the Emphatic Responsiveness Hypothesis." *Economic Journal* 117(522): 1008–24.

Ford, Robert. 2015. "Who Should We Help? An Experimental Test of Discrimination in the British Welfare State." *Political Studies* 64(3): 630–50.

Försäkringskassan. 2010. Förändringar inom socialförsäkrings- och bidragsområderna 1968–01–01–2010–07–01 [Changes in social insurance and benefits areas January 1968–July 2010]. Stockholm.

Fortuyn, Pim. 2001. *Droomkabinet. Hoe Nederland geregeerd moet worden* [Dream Cabinet. How the Netherlands Should Be Governed]. Amsterdam: Van Gennep.

Fragomen, Austin T. 1997. "The Illegal Immigration Reform and Immigrant Responsibility Act of 1996: An Overview." *International Migration Review* 31(2): 438–60.

Franzén, Eva. 2004. "Invandrare och socialbidragsmottagare" [Immigrants and welfare recipients]. In *Egenförsörjning eller bidragsförsörjning? Invandrarna, arbetsmarknaden och välfärdsstaten* [Autonomy or Welfare Dependence? The Immigrants, the Labour Market, and the Welfare State], 103–32. Stockholm: SOU.

Freeman, Gary P. 1986. "Migration and the Political Economy of the Welfare State." *Annals of the American Academy of Political and Social Science* 485: 51–63.

– . 2009. "Immigration, Diversity, and Welfare Chauvinism." *Forum* 7(3): 1–16.

Frissen, Paul, and Albertine Van Diepen. 2011. "Migranten zijn van harte welkom maar we gaan niet voor ze zorgen" [Migrants are more than welcome but we will not take care of them]. *Volkskrant*, 26 May.

Geddes, Andrew. 2003. "Migration and the Welfare State in Europe." In *The Politics of Migration: Managing Opportunity, Conflict and Change*, ed. S. Spencer, 150–62. Malden: Blackwell.

Genschel, Philipp. 1997. "The Dynamics of Inertia: Institutional Persistence and Institutional Change in Telecommunications and Health Care." *Governance: An International Journal of Policy, Administration and Institutions* 10(1): 43–66.

Gerdes, Christer. 2011. "The Impact of Immigration on the Size of Government: Empirical Evidence from Danish Municipalities." *Scandinavian Journal of Economics* 113(1): 74–92.

Gerdes, Christer, and Eskil Wadensjö. 2008. *Immigrants from the New EU Member States and the Swedish Welfare State*. Stockholm: Swedish Institute for European Policy Studies.

– . 2012. "Is Immigration Challenging the Economic Sustainability of the Nordic Welfare Model?" In *Changing Social Equality. The Nordic Welfare Model in the 21st Century*, ed. J. Kvist, J. Fritzell, and B. Hvinden, 187–99. Bristol: The Policy Press.

Gesthuizen, Maurice, Tom Van der Meer, and Peer Scheepers. 2009. "Ethnic Diversity and Social Capital in Europe: Tests of Putnam's Thesis in European Countries." *Scandinavian Political Studies* 32(2): 121–42.

Ghorashi, Halleh. 2005. "Agents of Change or Passive Victims: The Impact of Welfare States (the Case of the Netherlands)." *Journal of Refugee Studies* 18(2): 181–98.

Gibson, Rachel K. 2002. *The Growth of Anti-Immigrant Parties in Western Europe.* Lewiston: Edwin Mellen Press.

Gilens, Martin. 1999. *Why Americans Hate Welfare.* Chicago: University of Chicago Press.

Ginsburg, Helen Lach, and Marguerite G. Rosenthal. 2002. "Sweden: Temporary Detour or New Directions?" In *Diminishing Welfare: A Cross-National Study of Social Provision,* ed. G.S. Goldberg and Rosenthal, 103–148. Westport, CT: Auburn House.

Girard, Erik R., and Harald Bauder. 2007. "Assimilation and Exclusion of Foreign Trained Engineers in Canada: Inside a Professional Regulatory Organization." *Antipode* 39(1): 35–53.

Giulietti, Corrado, Martin Guzi, Martin Kahanec, and Klaus F. Zimmerman. 2013. "Unemployment Benefits and Immigration: Evidence from the EU." *International Journal of Manpower* 34(1–2): 24–38.

Goodhart, David. 2004. "Too Diverse?" *Prospect* (February), 30–7.

Gorodzeisky, Anastasia, and Moshe Semyonov. 2009. "Terms of Exclusion: Public Views towards Admission and Allocation of Rights to Immigrants in European Countries." *Ethnic and Racial Studies* 32(3): 401–23.

Gortázar Rotaeche, Cristina J. 1998. "Racial Discrimination and the European Convention on Human Rights." *Journal of Ethnic and Migration Studies* 24(1): 177–88.

Gould, Arthur. 2001. *Developments in Swedish Social Policy: Resisting Dionysus.* Basingstoke: Palgrave Macmillan.

Government of the Netherlands. 1994. *Contourennota Integratiebeleid* [Report Framework Integration Policy]. The Hague.

– . 2002. *Werken aan vertrouwen, een kwestie van aanpakken. Strategisch akkoord voor kabinet CDA, LPF, VVD* [Working on Trust, a Matter of Tackling Things. Strategic Agreement for Cabinet CDA, LPF, VVD]. The Hague: SDU.

– . 2007. *Integratienota 2007–2011: Zorg dat je erbij hoort!* [Integration Report 2007–2011: Make Sure to Belong!]. The Hague: VROM/WWI.

– . 2010a. *Gedoogakkoord VVD-PVV-CDA* ["Guaranteed support" agreement VVD-PVV-CDA]. The Hague: SDU.

– . 2010b. *Vrijheid en Verantwoordelijkheid: Regeerakkoord VVD en CDA* [Freedom and Responsibility: Governing Agreement VVD and CDA]. The Hague: SDU Publishers.

Government Offices of Sweden. 2009. "Swedish Integration Policy. Fact Sheet." Stockholm.

Graefe, Deborah Roempke, Gordon F. De Jong, Matthew Hall, Samuel Sturgeon, and Julie Van Eerden. 2008. "Immigrants' TANF Eligibility,

1996–2003: What Explains the New Across-State Inequalities." *International Migration Review* 42(1): 89–133.

Green, David A., and Christopher Worswick. 2010. "Entry Earnings of Immigrant Men in Canada: The Roles of Labour Market Entry Effects and Returns to Foreign Experience." In *Canadian Immigration: Economic Evidence for a Dynamic Policy Environment*, ed. T. McDonald, E. Ruddick, A. Sweetman, and C. Worswick, 77–110. Montreal and Kingston: McGill–Queen's University Press.

Green, Eva G.T., Oriane Sarrasin, Nicole Fasel, and Christian Staerklé. 2011. "Nationalism and Patriotism as Predictors of Immigration Attitudes in Switzerland: A Municipality-Level Analysis." *Schweizerische Zeitschrift für Politikwissenschaft* 17(4): 369–93.

Greenfeld, Liah. 1992. *Nationalism: Five Roads to Modernity*. Cambridge, MA: Harvard University Press.

Green-Pedersen, Christoffer. 2002. *The Politics of Justification. Party Competition and Welfare-State Retrenchment in Denmark and the Netherlands from 1982 to 1998*. Amsterdam: Amsterdam University Press.

Green-Pedersen, Christoffer, Kees Van Kersbergen, and Anton Hemerijck. 2001. "Neo-Liberalism, the 'Third Way' or What? Recent Social Democratic Welfare Policies in Denmark and the Netherlands." *Journal of European Public Policy* 8(2): 307–25.

Griffiths, Rudyard. 2009. *Who We Are. A Citizen's Manifesto*. Vancouver: Douglas and McIntyre.

Groenendijk, Kees. 2006. "Family Reunification as a Right under Community Law." *European Journal of Migration and Law* 8(2): 215–30.

Groenendijk, Kees, and Paul Minderhoud. 2016. "Taaleis in de bijstand: Discriminerend, disproportioneel en onnodig" [Language requirement in social assistance: Discriminating, disproportionate, and unnecessary]. *Nederlands Juristenblad* 22(1): 183–8.

Grönqvist, Hans, Per Johansson, and Susan Niknami. 2012. "Income Inequality and Health: Lessons from a Refugee Residential Assignment Program." *Journal of Health Economics* 31(4): 617–29.

Grubel, Herbert, and Patrick Grady. 2011. *Immigration and the Canadian Welfare State 2011*. Vancouver: Fraser Institute.

Guibernau, Montserrat. 2010. "Migration and the Rise of the Radical Right: Social Malaise and the Failure of Mainstream Politics." *Policy Network* (March), 1–19.

Guiraudon, Virginie. 2000. "The Marshallian Triptych Reordered. The Role of Courts and Bureaucracies in Furthering Migrants' Social Rights." In *Immigration and Welfare: Challenging the Borders of the Welfare State*, ed. M. Bommes and A. Geddes, 72–89. London: Routledge.

– . 2002. "Including Foreigners in National Welfare States: Institutional Venues and Rules of the Game." In *Restructuring the Welfare State: Political Institutions and Policy Change*, ed. B. Rothstein and S. Steinmo, 129–56. New York: Palgrave Macmillan.

Gustafsson, Björn, and Torun Österberg. 2001. "Immigrants and the Public Sector Budget – Accounting Exercises for Sweden." *Journal of Population Economics* 14: 689–708.

Hainmueller, Jens, and Michael J. Hiscox. 2010. "Attitudes toward Highly Skilled and Low-Skilled Immigration: Evidence from a Survey Experiment." *American Political Science Review* 104(1): 61–84.

Hainsworth, Paul. 2000. "Introduction: The Extreme Right." In *The Politics of the Extreme Right: From the Margins to the Mainstream*, ed. P. Hainsworth, 1–18. London: Pinter.

Halvorsen, Knut. 2007. "Legitimacy of Welfare States in Transitions from Homogeneity to Multiculturality: A Matter of Trust." In *Social Justice, Legitimacy and the Welfare State*, 239–60. Aldershot: Ashgate.

Hammar, Tomas. 1985. "Sweden." In *European Immigration Policy: A Comparative Analysis*, ed. T. Hammar, 17–49. Cambridge: Cambridge University Press.

– . 1990. *Democracy and the Nation State: Aliens, Denizens, and Citizens in a World of International Migration*. Aldershot: Avebury.

Hammarstedt, Mats. 2009. "Assimilation and Participation in Social Assistance among Immigrants." *International Journal of Social Welfare* 18(1): 85–94.

Handler, Joel F. 2009. "Welfare, Workfare, and Citizenship in the Developed World." *Annual Review of Law and Social Science* 5: 71–90.

Hanson, Gordon H., Kenneth F. Scheve, and Matthew J. Slaughter. 2005. "Individual Preference over High-Skilled Immigration in the United States." In *Skilled Immigration Today: Prospects, Problems, and Policies*, ed. J. Bhagwati and G.H. Hanson, 458–87. Oxford: Oxford University Press.

Hartog, Joop. 1999. "Wither Dutch Corporatism? Two Decades of Employment Policies and Welfare Reforms." *Scottish Journal of Political Economy* 46(4): 458–87.

Heclo, Hugh. 1974. *Modern Social Policies in Britain and Sweden*. New Haven: Yale University Press.

Heclo, Hugh, and Henrik Madsen. 1987. *Policy and Politics in Sweden: Principled Pragmatism*. Philadelphia: Temple University Press.

Heitmueller, Axel. 2005. "Unemployment Benefits, Risk Aversion, and Migration Incentives." *Journal of Population Economics* 18(1): 93–112.

Helin, Jan, and Lena Mellin. 2009. "Därför stoppar vi SD:s valannonser" [This is why we refuse SD's campaign ads]. *Aftonbladet*, 17 September.

Hello, Evelyn, Peer Scheepers, and Peter Sleegers. 2006. "Why the More Educated Are Less Inclined to Keep Ethnic Distance: An Empirical Test of Four Explanations." *Ethnic and Racial Studies* 29(5): 959–85.

Hemerijck, Anton, Brigitte Unger, and Jelle Visser. 2000. How Small Countries Negotiate Change: Twenty-Five Years of Policy Adjustment in Austria, the Netherlands, and Belgium. In *Welfare and Work in the Open Economy*, vol. 2: *Diverse Responses to Common Challenges*, ed. F.W. Scharpf and V.A. Schmidt, 175–263. Oxford: Oxford University Press.

Hennebry, Jenna L., and Kerry Preibisch. 2012. "A Model for Managed Migration? Re-examining Best Practices in Canada's Seasonal Agricultural Worker Program." *International Migration* 50(1): e19–40.

Hernandez, Marcial. 2014. *Geert Wilders ontmaskerd. Van messias tot politieke klaploper* [Geert Wilders Unmasked. From Messiah to Political Freeloader]. Soesterberg: Aspekt.

Hero, Rodney E., and Robert R. Preuhs. 2007. "Immigration and the Evolving American Welfare State: Examining Policies in the US States." *American Journal of Political Science* 51(3): 498–517.

Herrington, Doug. 1991. "Copps likens Preston Manning to David Duke." *Ottawa Citizen*, 19 November, A4.

Hiebert, Daniel. 2006. "Winning, Losing, and Still Playing the Game: The Political Economy of Immigration in Canada." *Tijdschrift voor Economische en Sociale Geografie* 97(1): 38–48.

Hilson, Mary. 2008. *The Nordic Model: Scandinavia Since 1945*. London: Reaktion Books.

Hojem, Petter, and Martin Ådahl. 2011. *Kanadamodellen: Hur Invandring Leder Till Job* [The Canadian Model: How Immigration Leads to Jobs]. Stockholm: Fores.

Hooghe, Marc, Ann Trappers, Bart Meuleman, and Tim Reeskens. 2008. "Migration to European Countries: A Structural Explanation of Patterns, 1980–2004." *International Migration Review* 42(2): 476–504.

Horowitz, Donald L. 2000. *Ethnic Groups in Conflict*. Berkeley: University of California Press.

House of Lords. 2008. *The Economic Impact of Immigration*. London: HMSO.

Howard, Marc M. 2006. "Comparative Citizenship: An Agenda for Cross-National Research." *Perspectives on Politics* 4(3): 443–55.

Huber, Evelyne, and John D. Stephens. 2001. *Development and Crisis of the Welfare State. Parties and Policies in Global Markets*. Chicago: University of Chicago Press.

Huisman, Charlotte. 2009. "Geen inburgering, minder uitkering" [No integration, lower welfare benefit]. *Volkskrant*, 23 September.

Hume, Stephen. 2011. "The big picture shows immigrants a good bet: Fraser Institute's disingenuous study of newcomer costs looks at one small part of a complex phenomenon." *Vancouver Sun*, 30 May.

Humphreys, Adrian. 2011. "Illegal immigrants have no right to free health care." *Vancouver Sun*, 8 July.

Huntford, Roland. 1971. *The New Totalitarians*. London: Penguin Books.

Huntington, Samuel P. 2004. *Who Are We? The Challenges to America's National Identity*. New York: Simon and Schuster.

Huo, Jingjing. 2009. *Third Way Reforms: Social Democracy after the Golden Age*. Cambridge: Cambridge University Press.

Ibbitson, John. 2012. CTV News, 16 February.

Ignazi, Piero. 2003. *Extreme Right Parties in Western Europe*. Oxford: Oxford University Press.

Ireland, Patrick. 2004. *Becoming Europe: Immigration, Integration, and the Welfare State*. Pittsburgh: University of Pittsburgh Press.

Isitman, Elif. 2015. "Rutte: 'Je kunt niet doorgaan met deze instroom'" [Rutte: "This inflow cannot continue"]. *Elsevier*, 27 November.

Ivarsflaten, Elisabeth. 2005. "The Vulnerable Populist Right Parties: No Economic Realignment Fuelling Their Electoral Success." *European Journal of Political Research* 44(3): 465–92.

Iyengar, Shanto, and Donald Kinder. 1987. *News That Matters: Television and American Opinion*. Chicago: University of Chicago Press.

Jaeger, Mads Meier. 2007. "Are the 'Deserving Needy' Really Deserving Everywhere? Cross-Cultural Heterogeneity and Popular Support for the Old and the Sick in Eight Western Countries." In *Social Justice, Legitimacy and the Welfare State*, ed. S. Mau and B. Veghte, 73–94. Aldershot: Ashgate.

– . 2012. "Do We All (Dis)like the Same Welfare State? Configurations of Public Support for the Welfare State in Comparative Perspective." In *Changing Social Equality. The Nordic Welfare Model in the 21st Century*, ed. J. Kvist, J. Fritzell, B. Hvinden, and O. Kangas, 45–68. Bristol: The Policy Press.

Javdani, Mohsen, and Krishna Murthy Pendakur. 2011. "Fiscal Transfers to Immigrants in Canada." Metropolis British Columbia, Centre of Excellence for Research on Immigration and Diversity.

Jedwab, Jack. 2008. "Receiving and Giving: How Does the Canadian Public Feel about Immigration and Integration?" In *Immigration and Integration in Canada in the Twenty-First Century*, ed. J. Biles, M. Burstein, and J. Frideres, 211–30. Montreal and Kingston: McGill–Queen's University Press.

Jenson, Jane. 1997. "Fated to Live in Interesting Times: Canada's Changing Citizenship Regimes." *Canadian Journal of Political Science* 30(4): 627–44.

– . 2012. "Changing Perspectives on Social Policy: A Cross-Time Comparison." In *Social Policy and Citizenship. The Changing Landscape*, ed. A. Evers and A.-M. Guillemard, 57–79. Oxford: Oxford University Press.

Jenson, Jane, and Denis Saint-Martin. 2003. "New Routes to Social Cohesion? Citizenship and the Social Investment State." *Canadian Journal of Sociology* 28(1): 77–99.

Johansson, Peter. 2010. *Sociala rättigheter och migration. Det svenska pensionssystemet i internationella situationer 1946–1993* [Social Rights and Migration: The Swedish Pension System in an International Context]. Stockholm: Institutet för Framtidsstudier.

Johansson-Murie, Amanda. 2012. "Peter Mangs kommer att dömas för mord" [Peter Mangs has been convicted of murder]. *Dagens Nyheter*, 24 July.

Johnston, Richard, Keith Banting, Will Kymlicka, and Stuart Soroka. 2010. "National Identity and Support for the Welfare State." *Canadian Journal of Political Science* 43(2): 349–78.

Joppke, Christian. 2001. "The Legal-Domestic Sources of Immigrant Rights: The United States, Germany, and the European Union." *Comparative Political Studies* 34(4): 339–66.

– . 2010. *Citizenship and Immigration*. Cambridge: Polity Press.

Jurado, Elena, and Grete Brochmann. 2013. *Europe's Immigration Challenge: Reconciling Work, Welfare and Mobility*. London: L.B. Tauris.

Kaestner, Robert, and Neeraj Kaushal. 2005. "Immigrant and Native Responses to Welfare Reform." *Journal of Population Economics* 18(1): 69–92.

Kahanec, Martin, Anna Myung-Hee Kim, and Klaus F. Zimmerman. 2013. "Pitfalls of Immigrant Inclusion into the European Welfare State." *International Journal of Manpower* 34(1): 39–55.

Kaiser, Lutz C., and Regine Paul. 2011. "Differential Inclusion in Germany's Conservative Welfare State: Policy Legacies and Structural Constraints." In *Migration and Welfare in the New Europe: Social Protection and the Challenges of Integration*, ed. E. Carmel, A. Cerami, and T. Papadopoulos, 121–43. Bristol: The Policy Press.

Kaushal, Neeraj. 2005. "New Immigrants' Location Choices: Magnets without Welfare." *Journal of Labor Economics* 23(1): 59–80.

Kelleher, Christine A., and Jennifer Wolak. 2006. "Priming Presidential Approval: The Conditionality of Issue Effects." *Political Behavior* 28: 193–210.

Kelley, Ninette, and Michael J. Trebilcock. 1998. *The Making of the Mosaic: A History of Canadian Immigration Policy*. Toronto: University of Toronto Press.

Kingdon, John W., and James A. Thurber. 1984. *Agendas, Alternatives, and Public Policies*. Boston, MA: Little, Brown.

Kitschelt, Herbert. 2001. "Partisan Competition and Welfare State
Retrenchment: When Do Politicians Choose Unpopular Policies?" In *The
New Politics of the Welfare State*, ed. P. Pierson, 265–302. Oxford: Oxford
University Press.

Kitschelt, Herbert, and Anthony J. McGann. 1995. *The Radical Right in Western
Europe. A Comparative Analysis*. Ann Arbor: University of Michigan Press.

Kleinman, Mark. 2003. "The Economic Impact of Labour Migration." In
The Politics of Migration: Managing Opportunity, Conflict and Change, ed.
S. Spencer, 59–74. Malden: Blackwell.

Kloosterman, Robert. 2000. "Waltzing Elephants? Mollenkopf's View on
Assimilating Immigrants in Old and New Amsterdam." *Netherlands Journal
of Social Sciences* 36(2): 35–9.

Kneebone, Ronald D., and Katherine G. White. 2009. "Fiscal Retrenchment
and Social Assistance in Canada." *Canadian Public Policy* 35(1): 21–40.

Knowles, Valerie. 2007. *Strangers at Our Gates: Canadian Immigration and
Immigration Policy, 1540–2006*. Toronto: Dundum Press.

Kogan, Ireen. 2004. "Last Hired, First Fired? The Unemployment Dynamics
of Male Immigrants in Germany." *European Sociological Review* 20(5):
445–61.

Koning, Edward A. 2007. "Erfenis van de verzuiling. Politieke partijen over
islamitische basisscholen" [A Legacy of Pillarization. Political Parties on
Islamic Elementary Schools]. *Liberaal Reveil* 48(3): 156–61.

– . 2011. "Ethnic and Civic Dealings with Newcomers: Naturalization Policies
and Practices in Twenty-Six Immigration Countries." *Ethnic and Racial
Studies* 34(11): 1974–94.

– . 2013. "Book Review of *Welfare States and Immigrant Rights* by Diane
Sainsbury." *Journal of European Social Policy* 23(4): 451–2.

– . 2017a. "Making Xenophobia Matter: The Consequences of the 2002
Elections for Dutch Immigration Politics." In *The Strains of Commitment:
The Sources of Solidarity in Diverse Societies*, ed. K. Banting and W. Kymlicka,
268–99. Oxford: Oxford University Press.

– . 2017b. "Selecting, Disentitling, or Investing? Exploring Party and Voter
Responses to Immigrant Welfare Dependence in Fifteen West European
Welfare States." *Comparative European Politics* 15(4): 628–60.

Koning, Edward A., and Keith G. Banting. 2013. "Inequality Below the
Surface: Reviewing Immigrants' Access to and Utilization of Five Canadian
Welfare Programs." *Canadian Public Policy* 39(4): 581–601.

Koopmans, Ruud. 2010. "Trade-Offs between Equality and Difference:
Immigrant Integration, Multiculturalism, and the Welfare State in Cross-
National Perspective." *Journal of Ethnic and Migration Studies* 36(1): 1–26.

Korpi, Walter. 1978. *The Working Class in Welfare Capitalism: Work, Unions, and Politics in Sweden*. Abigdon: Taylor and Francis.

– . 1980. "Social Policy and Distributional Conflict in the Capitalist Democracies: A Preliminary Comparative Framework." *West European Politics* 3(3): 296–316.

Korteweg, Anna C. 2006. "The Murder of Theo van Gogh: Gender, Religion, and the Struggle over Immigrant Integration in the Netherlands." In *Migration, Citizenship, Ethnos*, ed. M. Bodemann and G. Yurdakul, 147–66. New York: Palgrave Macmillan.

Kremer, Monique. 2013. *Vreemden in de Verzorgingsstaat* [Aliens in the Welfare State]. Den Haag: Boom Lemma.

Kretsedemas, Philip. 2004. "Avoiding the State: Haitian Immigrants and Welfare Services in Miami–Dade County." In *Immigrants, Welfare Reform, and the Poverty of Policy*, ed. P. Kretsedemas and A. Aparicio, 107–33. Westport: Praeger.

Kretsedemas, Philip, and Ana Aparicio. 2004. *Immigrants, Welfare Reform, and the Poverty of Policy*. Westport: Praeger.

Kuipers, Sanneke. 2006. *The Crisis Imperative: Crisis Rhetoric and Welfare State Reform in Belgium and the Netherlands in the Early 1990s*. Amsterdam: Amsterdam University Press.

Kunovich, Robert M. 2009. "The Sources and Consequences of National Identification." *American Sociological Review* 74(4): 573–93.

Kurthen, Hermann. 1998. "Fiscal Impacts of Immigration on the American and German Welfare States." In *Immigration, Citizenship, and the Welfare State in Germany and the United States: Immigrant Incorporation*, ed. H. Kurthen, J. Fijalkowski, and G.G. Wagner, 175–211. Stamford: Jai Press.

Kvist, Jon. 2004. "Does EU Enlargement Start a Race to the Bottom? Strategic Interaction among EU Member States in Social Policy." *Journal of European Social Policy* 14(3): 301–18.

Kvist, Jon, Johan Fritzell, Bjørn Hvinden, and Olli Kangas. 2012. *Changing Social Equality: The Nordic Welfare Model in the 21st Century*. Bristol: The Policy Press.

Kvistad, Gregg O. 1998. "Membership without Politics? The Social and Political Rights of Foreigners in Germany." In *Immigration, Citizenship, and the Welfare State in Germany and the United States: Welfare Policies and Immigrants' Citizenship*, ed. H. Kurthen, J. Fijalkowski, and G.G. Wagner, 141–57. Stamford: Jai Press.

Kymlicka, Will. 2003. "Canadian Multiculturalism in Historical and Comparative Perspective: Is Canada Unique?" *Constitutional Forum* 13(1): 1–8.

Lakeman, Pieter. 1999. *Binnen zonder kloppen: Nederlandse immigratiepolitiek en de economische gevolgen* [Enter without Knocking: Dutch Immigration Policy and the Economic Consequences]. Amsterdam: Meulenhoff.

Lancee, Bram, and Jaap Dronkers. 2011. "Ethnic, Religious, and Economic Diversity in Dutch Neighbourhoods: Explaining Quality of Contact with Neighbours, Trust in the Neighbourhood, and Inter-Ethnic Trust." *Journal of Ethnic and Migration Studies* 37(4): 597–618.

Larsen, Christian Albrekt. 2008. "The Institutional Logic of Welfare Attitudes: How Welfare Regimes Influence Public Support." *Comparative Political Studies* 41(2): 145–68.

Lechner, Frank J. 2008. *The Netherlands: Globalization and National Identity*. London: Routledge.

Leigh, Andrew. 2006. "Trust, Inequality, and Ethnic Heterogeneity." *Economic Record* 82(258): 268–80.

Leiken, Robert S. 2005. "Europe's Angry Muslims." *Foreign Affairs* 84(4): 120–35.

Letki, Natalia. 2008. "Does Diversity Erode Social Cohesion? Social Capital and Race in British Neighbourhoods." *Political Studies* 56(1): 99–126.

Liberal Party of Canada. 2015. *Real Change. A New Plan for a Strong Middle Class*. Ottawa.

Lijphart, Arend. 1968. *The Politics of Accommodation: Pluralism and Democracy in the Netherlands*. Berkeley: University of California Press.

Lilley, Brian. 2011. "Immigrants' Use of Welfare a Mixed Bag, Documents Show." *Toronto Sun*, 11 January.

Lindquist, Gabriella Sjögren. 2007. "Unemployment Insurance, Social Assistance, and Activation Policy in Sweden." Peer Review Programme of the European Employment Strategy, *Implementierung the New Basic Allowance for Job Seekers*, Berlin, 17–18 April.

Lower House of Dutch Parliament. 2003. *Onderzoek Integratiebeleid* [Inquiry Integration Policy]. The Hague: SDU.

– . 2011. *Parlementair onderzoek Lessen uit recente arbeidsmigratie* [Parliamentary Inquiry: Lessons from Recent Labour Migration]. The Hague: SDU.

Loxbo, Karl. 2010. "The Impact of the Radical Right: Lessons from the Local Level in Sweden, 2002–2006." *Scandinavian Political Studies* 33(3): 295–315.

Lucassen, Jan, and Rinus Penninx. 1997. *Newcomers. Immigrants and Their Descendants in the Netherlands 1550–1995*. Amsterdam: Het Spinhuis.

Lundberg, Urban. 2005. "Social Democracy Lost: The Social Democratic Party in Sweden and the Politics of Pension Reform, 1978–1998." In *Welfare Policies Cross-Examined: Eclecticist Analytical Perspectives on Sweden and the Developed World, from the 1880s to the 2000s*, ed. E. Carroll and L. Eriksson, 117–45. Amsterdam: Aksant.

Lundgren, Sofia. 2009. "Anders Lago positiv till ändringar i ebo-lagen" [Anders Lago positive about changes to law on own housing]. *Dagens Nyheter*, 30 October.

Luttmer, Erzo F. 2001. "Group Loyalty and the Taste for Redistribution." *Journal of Political Economy* 109(3): 500–28.

Ma, Ambrose, and Iris Chi. 2005. "Utilization and Accessibility of Social Services for Chinese Canadians." *International Social Work* 48(2): 148–60.

Magnusson, Erik. 2017. "Anna Kinberg Batra: Så ska dialogen mellan M och SD gå till [Anna Kinberg Batra: This is how the dialogue between the Moderates and the Sweden Democrats will take place]. *Sydsvenskan*, 30 January.

Magnussen, Örjan, and Thomas Larsson. 2011. "Regeringen och MP överens om migrationspolitiken [Government and Environment Party in accord about migration policy]. *Sverige Nyheter*, 3 March.

Mahoney, James. 2000. "Path Dependence in Historical Sociology." *Theory and Society* 29(4): 507–48.

Mahoney, Jill. 2010. "Kenney urges provinces to review 'generous' welfare for refugees." *Globe and Mail*, 31 March.

Manning, Preston. 2003. *Think Big: My Adventures in Life and Democracy*. Toronto: McClelland and Stewart.

Marshall, T.H. 1950. *Citizenship and Social Class*. London: Pluto Press.

Marwah, Inder, Triadafilos Triadafilopolous, and Stephen White. 2013. "Immigration, Citizenship, and Canada's New Conservative Party." In *Conservatism in Canada*, ed. J. Farney and D. Rayside, 95–119. Toronto: University of Toronto Press.

Masso, Anu. 2009. "A Readiness to Accept Immigrants in Europe? Individual and Country-Level Characteristics." *Journal of Ethnic and Migration Studies* 35(2): 251–70.

Matthews, J. Scott, and Lynda Erickson. 2008. "Welfare State Structures and the Structure of Welfare State Support: Attitudes towards Social Spending in Canada, 1993–2000." *European Journal of Political Research* 47(4): 411–35.

Mau, Steffen, and Christoph Burkhardt. 2009. "Migration and Welfare State Solidarity in Western Europe." *Journal of European Social Policy* 19(3): 213–29.

Meinecke, Friedrich. [1907]1970. *Cosmopolitanism and the National State*. Princeton: Princeton University Press.

Menz, Georg. 2006. "'Useful' Gastarbeiter, Burdensome Asylum Seekers, and the Second Wave of Welfare Retrenchment: Exploring the Nexus between Migration and the Welfare State." In *Immigration and the Transformation of Europe*, ed. C.A. Parsons and T.M. Smeeding, 393–418. Cambridge: Cambridge University Press.

– . 2013. "European Employers and the Rediscovery of Labour Migration." In *Europe's Immigration Challenge: Reconciling Work, Welfare and Mobility*, ed. E. Jurado and G. Brochmann, 105–24. London: L.B. Tauris.

Messina, Anthony M. 2007. *The Logics of Politics of Post-WWII Migration to Western Europe*. Cambridge: Cambridge University Press.

Mewes, Jan, and Steffen Mau. 2013. "Globalization, Socio-Economic Status and Welfare Chauvinism: European Perspectives on Attitudes toward the Exclusion of Immigrants." *International Journal of Comparative Sociology* 54(3): 228–45.

Meyers, Eytan. 2004. *International Immigration Policy: A Theoretical and Comparative Analysis*. New York: Palgrave Macmillan.

Migrationsverket. 2010. *Rapport Migration 2000–2010* [Migration Report 2000–2010]. Stockholm.

Miller, Paul W., and Leanne M. Neo. 2003. "Labour Market Flexibility and Immigrant Adjustment." *Economic Record* 79(246): 336–56.

Minderhoud, Paul E. 1999. "Asylum Seekers and Access to Social Security: Recent Developments in the Netherlands, United Kingdom, Germany, and Belgium." In *Refugees, Citizenship, and Social Policy in Europe*, ed. A. Bloch and C. Levy, 132–48. Houndmills: Macmillan.

– . 2004. "Het Immigratiebeleid" [The Immigration Policy]. In *Grenzeloze Solidariteit. Naar een Migratiebestendige Verzorgingsstaat* [Solidarity without Borders. Towards a Migration-Proof Welfare State], ed. H. Entzinger and J. van der Meer, 11–25. Amsterdam: De Balie.

Minsky, Amy. 2017a. "'Canada's Donald Trump': Kellie Leitch blasts 'elites' and 'insiders' during Fox interview." *Global News*, 4 January.

– . 2017b. "Kellie Leitch firm on screening immigrants for 'Canadian values' in wake of Quebec shooting." *Global News*, 1 February.

Moderaterna. 1997. "Land för hoppfulla. Manifest för ett nytt sekel" [Country for the Hopeful. Manifesto for a New Century]. Stockholm.

– . 2010. "Med blicken mot framtiden" [With the Eye to the Future]. Stockholm.

Moerman, Thomas. 2017. "Nu Mark Rutte samenwerking met Geert Wilders uitsluit, doet hij hard z'n best om Henk en Ingrid te charmeren" [Now Mark Rutte excludes cooperation with Geert Wilders, he is doing his best to woo PVV voters]. *Business Insider*, 23 January.

Mollenkopf, John. 2000. "Assimilating Immigrants in Amsterdam: A Perspective from New York." *Netherlands Journal of Social Sciences* 36: 126–45.

Mols, Frank. 2012. "What Makes a Frame Persuasive? Lessons from Social Identity Theory." *Evidence & Policy* 8(3): 329–45.

Mood, Carina. 2011. "Lagging Behind in Good Times: Immigrants and the Increased Dependence on Social Assistance in Sweden." *International Journal of Social Welfare* 20(1): 55–65.

Moon, Ailee, James E. Lubben, and Valentine Villa. 1998. "Awareness and Utilization of Community Long-Term Care Services by Elderly Korean and non-Hispanic White Americans." *Gerontologist* 38(3): 309–16.

Morency, Jean-Dominique, Éric Caron Malenfant, and Samuel MacIsaac. 2017. *Immigration and Diversity: Population Projections for Canada and Its Regions, 2011 to 20136*. Ottawa: Statistics Canada.

Mudde, Cas. 2000. *The Ideology of the Extreme Right*. Manchester: Manchester University Press.

– . 2010. "The Populist Radical Right: A Pathological Normalcy." *West European Politics* 33(6): 1167–86.

Mudde, Cas, and Joop J. Van Holsteyn. 2000. "The Netherlands: Explaining the Limited Success of the Extreme Right." In *The Politics of the Extreme Right: From the Margins to the Mainstream*, ed. P. Hainsworth, 144–71. London: Pinter.

Myles, John. 2002. "A New Social Contract for the Elderly?" In *Why We Need a New Welfare State*, ed. G. Esping-Andersen, 130–72. Oxford: Oxford University Press.

Mynott, Ed, Elizabeth Humphries, and Steve Cohen. 2002. "Introduction: Locating the Debate." In *From Immigration Controls to Welfare Controls*, ed. S. Cohen, E. Humphries, and E. Mynott, 1–8. London: Routledge.

Nadeau, Richard, Richard Niemi, and Jeffrey Levine. 1993. "Innumeracy about Minority Populations." *Public Opinion Quarterly* 57(3): 332–47.

Nakache, Delphine, and Paula J. Kinoshita. 2010. *The Canadian Temporary Foreign Worker Program: Do Short-Term Economic Needs Prevail over Human Rights Concerns?* Montreal: Institute for Research on Public Policy.

National Council of Welfare. 1997. *Another Look at Welfare Reform*. Ottawa.

Nelson, Kenneth. 2005. "The Last Resort: Determinants of the Generosity of Means-Tested Income Protection in Welfare Democracies." In *Welfare Politics Cross-Examined: Eclecticist Perspectives on Sweden and the Developed World, from the 1880s to the 2000s*, ed. E. Carroll and L. Eriksson, 85–116. Amsterdam: Aksant.

Nergelius, Joakim. 2011. *Constitutional Law in Sweden*. Alphen aan den Rijn: Kluwer Law International.

Neubeck, Kenneth J., and Noel A. Cazenave. 2001. *Welfare Racism: Playing the Race Card against America's Poor*. New York: Routledge.

New Democratic Party of Canada. 2015. *Building the Country of Our Dreams. Tom Mulcair's Plan to Bring Change to Ottawa*. Ottawa.

Nickel, Stephen. 1997. "Unemployment and Labor Market Rigidities: Europe versus North America." *Journal of Economic Perspectives* 11(3): 55–74.

Nordlund, Madelene, Tom Stehlik, and Mattias Strandh. 2013. "Investment in Second-Chance Education for Adults and Income Development in Sweden." *Journal of Education and Work* 26(5): 514–38.

Norris, Pippa. 2005. *Radical Right: Voters and Parties in the Electoral Market*. Cambridge: Cambridge University Press.

O'Connell, Michael. 2005. "Economic Forces and Anti-Immigrant Attitudes in Western Europe: A Paradox in Search of an Explanation." *Patterns of Prejudice* 39(1): 60–74.

O'Connor, Julia. 1993. "Gender, Class, and Citizenship in the Comparative Analysis of Welfare State Regimes." *British Journal of Sociology* 44(3): 501–18.

O'Malley, Eoin. 2008. "Why Is There No Radical Right Party in Ireland?" *West European Politics* 31(5): 960–77.

Oesch, Daniel. 2008. "Explaining Workers' Support for Right-Wing Populist Parties in Western Europe: Evidence from Austria, Belgium, France, Norway, and Switzerland." *International Political Science Review* 29(3): 349–73.

Olwig, Karen Fog. 2011. "Integration: Migrants and Refugees between Scandinavian Welfare Societies and Family Relations." *Journal of Ethnic and Migration Studies* 37(2): 179–96.

Ontario Progressive Conservative Party. 2011. *Changebook. OPC Platform for 2011 Elections*. Toronto.

Orloff, Ann Shola. 1993. "Gender and the Social Rights of Citizenship." *American Sociological Review* 58(3): 303–28.

Ornbrant, Birgitta, and Markku Peura. 1993. "The Nordic Pact: An Experiment in Controlled Stability." In *The Politics of Migration Policies: The First World into the 1990s*, ed. D. Kubat, 202–30. New York: Center for Migration Studies.

Østergaard-Nielsen, Eva. 2003. "Counting the Costs: Denmark's Changing Migration Policies." *International Journal of Urban and Regional Research* 27(2): 448–54.

Pal, Michael, Sujit Choudry, and Matthew Mendelsohn. 2011. *The Impact of Regionally Differentiated Entitlement to EI on Charter-Protected Canadians*. Toronto: Mowat Centre for Policy Innovation.

Papadopoulos, Theodoros. 2012. "Immigration and the Variety of Migrant Integration Regimes in the European Union." In *Migration and Welfare in the New Europe: Social Protection and the Challenges of Integration*, ed. E. Carmel, A. Cerami, and T. Papadopoulos, 23–48. Bristol: The Policy Press.

Patten, Steve. 1999. "The Reform Party's Re-Imagining of the Canadian Nation." *Journal of Canadian Studies / Revue d'Etudes Canadiennes* 34(1): 27–51.

Pehrson, Samuel, Vivian L. Vignoles, and Rupert Brown. 2009. "National Identification and Anti-Immigrant Prejudice: Individual and Contextual Effects of National Definitions." *Social Psychology Quarterly* 72(1): 24–38.

Penninx, Rinus. 1996. "Immigration, Minorities Policy, and Multiculturalism in Dutch Society Since 1960." In *The Challenge of Diversity: Integration and*

Pluralism in Societies of Immigration, ed. R. Bauböck, A. Heller, and A.R. Zolberg, 187–206. Aldershot: Avebury.

Pettigrew, Thomas, and Roel Meertens. 1995. "Subtle and Blatant Prejudice in Western Europe." *European Journal of Social Psychology* 25(1): 57–75.

Pew Research Center. 2012. *The Global Religious Landscape. A Report on the Size and Distribution of the World's Major Religious Groups as of 2010*. Washington, DC: Pew Research Center's Forum on Religion & Public Life.

Pierson, Paul. 1994. *Dismantling the Welfare State?* Cambridge: Cambridge University Press.

– . 1996. "The New Politics of the Welfare State." *World Politics* 48(2): 143–79.

– . 2001. "Post-Industrial Pressures on the Mature Welfare State." In *The New Politics of the Welfare State*, ed. P. Pierson, 80–104. Oxford: Oxford University Press.

– . 2004. *Politics in Time: History, Institutions, and Social Analysis*. Princeton: Princeton University Press.

Pinsonneault, Gérard, Aline Lechaume, Chakib Benzakour, and Pierre Lanctôt. 2010. *Recours au programme d'aide sociale par les immigrants de la catégorie des travailleurs qualifiés: échec ou transition dans le processus d'intégration?* Quebec: Ministère de l'Emploi et de la Solidarité sociale.

Pontusson, Jonas. 2005. *Inequality and Prosperity: Social Europe vs. Liberal America*. Ithaca: Cornell University Press.

Pralle, Sarah B. 2009. "Agenda-Setting and Climate Change." *Environmental Politics* 18(5): 781–99.

Putnam, Robert D. 2007. "E Pluribus Unum: Diversity and Community in the Twenty-First Century: The 2006 Johan Skytte Prize Lecture." *Scandinavian Political Studies* 30(2): 137–74.

PVV. 2017. "Nederland weer van ons! PVV verkiezingsprogramma 2017–2021" [The Netherlands Ours Again! PVV Election Manifesto 2017–2021]. The Hague.

Radwanski, Adam, Karen Howlett, and Anna Mehler Paperny. 2011. "Ontario campaigns bog down over tax-credit obsession." *Globe and Mail*, 13 September.

Ragin, Charles C. 1994. "Introduction to Qualitative Comparative Analysis." In *The Comparative Political Economy of the Welfare State*, ed. T. Janoski and A.M. Hicks, 298–317. Cambridge: Cambridge University Press.

Reeskens, Tim, and Wim Van Oorschot. 2012. "Disentangling the 'New Liberal Dilemma': On the Relation between General Welfare Redistribution Preferences and Welfare Chauvinism." *International Journal of Comparative Sociology* 53(2): 120–39.

Reform Party of Canada. 1988. *The West Wants In! 1988 Election Platform of the Reform Party of Canada*. Edmonton.

–. 1996. *A Fresh Start for Canadians. Blue Book 1996–1997. Principles and Policies of the Reform Party of Canada*. Edmonton.

–. 1999. *The Blue Book. Principles and Policies of the Reform Party of Canada*. Edmonton.

Rehm, Philip. 2001. "Who Supports the Welfare State? Determinants of Preferences Concerning Redistribution." In *Social Justice, Legitimacy, and the Welfare State*, ed. S. Mau and B. Veghte, 47–72. Aldershot: Ashgate.

Reitz, Jeffrey G.1995. *A Review of the Literature on Aspects of Ethno-Racial Access, Utilization and Delivery of Social Services*. Ontario: Multicultural Coalition for Access to Family Services.

–. 2001. "Immigrant Skill Utilization and the Canadian Labour Market: Implications of Human Capital Research." *Journal of International Migration and Integration* 2(3): 347–78.

Rocher, François, Micheline Labelle, Anne-Marie Field, and Jean-Claude Icart. 1999. *Le concept d'interculturalisme en contexte Québécois: Généalogie d'un néologisme*. Montreal: Centre de recherche en immigration, ethnicité et citoyenneté.

Rochon, Thomas R. 1999. *The Netherlands: Negotiating Sovereignty in an Interdependent World*. Boulder: Westview Press.

Roodenburg, Hans, Rob Euwals, and Harry Ter Rele. 2003. *Immigration and the Dutch Economy*. The Hague: CPB Netherlands Bureau for Economic Policy Analysis.

Rosenhek, Zeev. 2000. "Migration Regimes, Intra-State Conflicts, and the Politics of Exclusion and Inclusion: Migrant Workers in the Israeli Welfare State." *Social Problems* 47(1): 49–67.

Rothstein, Bo. 1998. *Just Institutions Matter. The Moral and Political Logic of the Universal Welfare State*. Cambridge: Cambridge University Press.

Ruist, Joakim. 2014. "Free Immigration and Welfare Access: The Swedish Experience." *Fiscal Studies* 35(1): 19–39.

Rusman, Floor. 2017. "Rutte: kans op samenwerking met PVV is 'nul'" [Rutte: chance of cooperation with PVV is "zero"]. *NRC Handelsblad*, 15 January.

Ryan, Paul. 2010. *Multicultiphobia*. Toronto: University of Toronto Press.

Rydgren, Jens. 2003. "Meso-Level Reasons for Racism and Xenophobia. Some Converging and Diverging Effects of Radical Right Populism in France and Sweden." *European Journal of Social Theory* 6(1): 45–68.

–. 2006. *From Tax Populism to Ethnic Nationalism. Radical Right-Wing Populism in Sweden*. New York: Berghahn Books.

Ryner, Magnus. 2000. "European Welfare State Transformation and Migration." In *Immigration and Welfare: Challenging the Borders of the Welfare State*, ed. M. Bommes and A. Geddes, 51–89. London: Routledge.

Sabates-Wheeler, Rachel, and Rayah Feldman. 2011. *Migration and Social Protection. Claiming Social Rights beyond Borders*. Houndmills: Palgrave.

Sachweh, Patrick, Carsten G. Ullrich, and Bernhard Christoph. 2007. "The Moral Economy of Poverty: On the Conditionality of Public Support for Social Assistance Schemes." In *Social Justice, Legitimacy and the Welfare State*, ed. S. Mau and B. Veghte, 123–44. Aldershot: Ashgate.

Sainsbury, Diane. 2006. "Immigrants' Social Rights in Comparative Perspective: Welfare Regimes, Forms of Immigration Policy, and Immigration Policy Regimes." *Journal of European Social Policy* 16(3): 229–44.

– . 2012. *Welfare States and Immigrant Rights. The Politics of Inclusion and Exclusion*. Oxford: Oxford University Press.

Sales, Rosemary. 2002. "The Deserving and the Undeserving? Refugees, Asylum Seekers and Welfare in Britain." *Critical Social Policy* 22(3): 456–78.

Sassen, Saskia. 1996. *Losing Control? Sovereignty in an Age of Globalization*. New York: Columbia University Press.

Scharpf, Fritz W., and Vivien A. Schmidt. 2000. *From Vulnerability to Competitiveness*, vol. 1: *Welfare and Work in the Open Economy*. Oxford: Oxford University Press.

Scheffer, Paul. 2000. "Het multiculturele drama" [The multicultural drama]. *NRC Handelsblad*, 29 January.

– . 2004. "De fictie van grenzeloze solidariteit" [The fiction of boundless solidarity]. *NRC Handelsblad*, 10 January.

– . 2007. *Het land van aankomst* [The Country of Arrival]. Amsterdam: De Bezige Bij.

Scheve, Kenneth F., and Matthew J. Slaughter. 2001. "Labor Market Competition and Individual Preferences over Immigration Policy." *Review of Economics and Statistics* 83(1): 133–45.

Schierup, Carl-Ulrik, and Aleksandra Ålund. 2011. "The End of Swedish Exceptionalism? Citizenship, Neoliberalism, and the Politics of Exclusion." *Race & Class* 53(1): 45–64.

Schierup, Carl-Ulrik, Peo Hansen, and Stephen Castles. 2006. *Migration, Citizenship, and the European Welfare State*. Oxford: Oxford University Press.

Schmidt, Alexander W., and Dennis C. Spies. 2014. "Do Parties 'Playing the Race Card' Undermine Natives' Support for Redistribution? Evidence From Europe." *Comparative Political Studies* 47(4): 519–49.

Schmidt, Vivien A. 2000. "Values and Discourse in the Politics of Adjustment." In *Welfare and Work in the Open Economy*, vol. 1: *From Vulnerablity to Competitiveness*, ed. F.W. Scharpf and V.A. Schmidt, 229–309. Oxford: Oxford University Press.

Schuster, Liza. 2000. "A Comparative Analysis of the Asylum Policy of Seven European Governments." *Journal of Refugee Studies* 13(1): 118–32.

Sciortino, Giuseppe. 2013. "Immigration in Italy: Subverting the Logic of Welfare Reform?" In *Europe's Immigration Challenge: Reconciling Work, Welfare, and Mobility*, ed. E. Jurado and G. Brochmann, 77–94. London: L.B. Tauris.

Scott, David. n.d. "Tukey's Ladder of Powers." In *Online Statistics Education: A Multimedia Course of Study*, ed. D.M. Lane.

Seeleib-Kaiser, Martin, Silke Van Dyke, and Martin Roggenkamp. 2008. *Party Politics and Social Welfare. Comparing Christian and Social Democracy in Austria, Germany, and the Netherlands.* Cheltenham: Edward Elgar.

SER. 2007. *Arbeidsmigratie en sociale zekerheid* [Labour Migration and Social Security]. The Hague: SER.

Shayo, Moses. 2009. "A Model of Social Identity with an Application to Political Economy: Nation, Class, and Redistribution." *American Political Science Review* 103(2): 147–74.

Sheridan, Paul, and Ketan Shankardass. 2016. "The 2012 Cuts to Refugee Health Coverage in Canada: The Anatomy of a Social Policy Failure." *Canadian Journal of Political Science* 48(4): 905–31.

Sides, John, and Jack Citrin. 2007. "European Opinion about Immigration: The Role of Identities, Interests, and Information." *British Journal of Political Science* 37(3): 477–504.

Simich, Laura, Morton Beiser, Miriam Stewart, and Edward Mwakarimba. 2005. "Providing Social Support for Immigrants and Refugees in Canada: Challenges and Directions." *Journal of Immigrant Health* 7(4): 259–68.

Simpson, Jeffrey. 2013. "Has Kenney Found the Right Balance?" *Globe and Mail*, 23 January.

Sjöberg, Ola. 2005. "How to Maintain a Big Tax Welfare State?" In *Social Policy and Economic Development in the Nordic Countries*, ed. O. Kangas and J. Palme, 241–64. Basingstoke: Palgrave.

Skenderovic, Damir. 2007. "Immigration and the Radical Right in Switzerland: Ideology, Discourse, and Opportunities." *Patterns of Prejudice* 41(2): 155–76.

Snel, Erik, Monique Stavenuiter, and Jan Willem Duyvendak. 2002. *In de Fuik. Turken en Marokkanen in de WAO* [Trapped: Turks and Moroccans in the WAO]. Utrecht: Verwey Jonker Instituut.

Sniderman, Paul, and Louk Hagendoorn. 2007. *When Ways of Life Collide: Multiculturalism and Its Discontents in the Netherlands.* Princeton: Princeton University Press.

Sniderman, Paul, Pierangelo Peri, Rui J.P. de Figueiredo Jr., and Thomas Piazza. 2000. *The Outsider*. Princeton: Princeton University Press.

Socialförsäkring. 2005. *Vad Är Arbetslinjen?* [What Is the Work Principle?]. Stockholm.

Socialstyrelsen. 2005. "Hur tillämpas bestämmelsen i 4 kap. 4§ socialtjänstlagen?" [How is chapter 4, article 4, of the Social Services Act applied?]. Stockholm.
– . 2010. *Social Rapport 2010* [Social Report 2010]. Västerås: Edita Västra Aros.
Soroka, Stuart N. 2002. *Agenda-Setting Dynamics in Canada.* Vancouver: UBC Press.
Soroka, Stuart N., Richard Johnston, and Keith G. Banting. 2004. "Ethnicity, Trust, and the Welfare State." In *Cultural Diversity versus Economic Solidarity,* ed. P. Van Parijs, 279–303. Brussels: Deboeck Université Press.
Soroka, Stuart N., Richard Johnston, Keith G. Banting, Anthony Kevins, and Will Kymlicka. 2013. "Migration and Welfare State Spending." Paper presented at the annual meeting of the Canadian Political Science Association, Victoria.
Soysal, Yasemin N. 1994. *Limits of Citizenship: Migrants and Postnational Membership in Europe.* Chicago: University of Chicago Press.
– . 2012. "Citizenship, Immigration, and the European Social Project: Rights and Obligations of Individuality." *British Journal of Sociology* 63(1): 1–18.
Spies, Dennis. 2013. "Explaining Working-Class Support for Extreme Right Parties: A Party Competition Approach." *Acta Politica* 48(3): 296–325.
Stjernquist, Nils. 1990. "Judicial Review and the Rule of Law: Comparing the United States and Sweden." *Policy Studies Journal: The Journal of the Policy Studies Organization* 19(1): 106–15.
Stoffman, Daniel. 2002. *Who Gets In: What's Wrong with Canada's Program – and How to Fix It.* Toronto: MacFarlane, Walter & Ross.
Stokke, Øyvind. 2007. "Membership and Migration: Market Citizenship or European Citizenship." In *Citizenship in Nordic Welfare States,* ed. B. Hvinden and H. Johansson, 155–69. Abingdon: Routledge.
Storesletten, Kjetil. 2000. "Sustaining Fiscal Policy through Immigration." *Journal of Political Economy* 108(2): 300–23.
– . 2003. "Fiscal Implications of Immigration – a Net Present Value Calculation." *Scandinavian Journal of Economics* 105(3): 487–506.
Streeck, Wolfgang, and Kathleen Thelen. 2005. "Introduction: Institutional Change in Advanced Political Economies." In *Beyond Continuity: Institutional Change in Advanced Political Economies,* ed. Streeck and Thelen, 1–39. New York: Oxford University Press.
Sundberg, Marit. 2017. "Därför har Moderaterna ändrat sig om SD" [Why the Moderates have changed their position on the SD]. *SVT Nyheter,* 24 January.
Suvarierol, Semin. 2012. "Nation-freezing: Images of the Nation and the Migrant in Citizenship Packages." *Nations and Nationalism* 18(2): 210–29.
Svallfors, Stefan. 2006. *The Moral Economy of Class: Class and Attitudes in Comparative Perspective.* Stanford: Stanford University Press.
SVB. 2007a. *AOW inkopen of niet* [Buying in AOW or not?]. The Hague.

– . 2007b. *Cijfers bij Migratie en Sociale Zekerheid*. [Data on Migration and Social Security]. The Hague.

SvD Nyheter. 2012. "Almqvist från riksdag till mediejobb" [Almqvist from parliament to media job]. *SvD Nyheter*, 30 December.

Svensson, Niklas. 2015. "Löfven: Invandringen en stor ansträngning" [Löfven: Immigration a large strain]. *Expressen*, 25 June.

Sverigedemokraterna. 2007. *Invandringspolitiskt program* [Immigration policy program]. Stockholm: Sverigedemokraterna.

Sverigedemokraterna. 2014. "Vi väljer välfärd! Sverigedemokratiskt valmanifest – valet 2014" [We choose welfare! Sweden Democratic Party manifesto – 2014 elections].

Swedish Ministry of Finance. 2007. "Arbetsutbud och sysselsättning bland personer med utländsk bakgrund. En kunskapöversikt" [Labour and employment among individuals with a foreign background. An overview]. Stockholm.

Swedish Ministry of Health and Social Affairs. 2003. *The Swedish National Pension System*. Stockholm.

Sweetman, Arthur. 2001. "Immigrants and Employment Insurance." In *Essays on the Repeat Use of Unemployment Insurance*, ed. S. Schwartz and A. Aydemir, 123–54. Ottawa: SRDC.

Tajfel, Henri. 1982. *Social Identity and Intergroup Relations*. Cambridge: Cambridge University Press.

Taylor-Gooby, Peter. 2002. "The Silver Age of the Welfare State: Perspectives on Resilience." *Journal of Social Policy* 31(4): 597–621.

– . 2004. *New Risks, New Welfare: The Transformation of the European Welfare State*. Oxford: Oxford University Press.

The Local. 2015. "Løkke and Cameron find common ground on refugees and welfare." 22 September.

Tienda, Marta, and Leif Jensen. 1986. "Immigration and Public Assistance Participation: Dispelling the Myth of Dependency." *Social Science Research* 15(4): 372–400.

Transatlantic Trends. 2010. "Immigration: Key Findings 2010." The German Marshall Fund of the United States.

Triadafilopolous, Triadafilos. 2012. *Becoming Multicultural. Immigration and the Politics of Membership in Canada and Germany*. Vancouver: UBC Press.

UN. 2016. "International Migration Report 2015: Highlights." New York.

UN Human Rights Council. 2007. "Report of the Special Rapporteur on the Right of Everyone to the Enjoyment of the Highest Attainable Standard of Physical and Mental Health Paul Hunt, on his Mission to Sweden."

UWV. 2007. "Export Uitkeringen 2006" [Benefit Export 2006]. Amsterdam.

Valenty, Linda O., and Ronald D. Sylvia. 2004. "Thresholds for Tolerance: The Impact of Racial and Ethnic Population Composition on the Vote for California Propositions 187 and 209." *Social Science Journal* 41(3): 433–46.

Van der Geest, L., and A.J.F. Dietvorst. 2010. *Budgettaire Effecten van Immigratie van Niet-Westerse Allochtonen* [Budgetary Effects of Immigration of Non-Western Migrants]. Utrecht: Nyfer.

Van der Veen, Romke, and Willem Trommel. 1998. *The Dutch Miracle: Managed Liberalisation of the Dutch Welfare State*. London: IPPR.

Van der Waal, Jeroen, Peter Achterberg, Dick Houtman, Willem De Koster, and Katerina Manevska. 2010. "'Some are more equal than others': Economic Egalitarianism and Welfare Chauvinism in the Netherlands." *Journal of European Social Policy* 20(4): 350–63.

Van der Waal, Jeroen, Willem De Koster, and Wim Van Oorschot. 2013. "Three Worlds of Welfare Chauvinism? How Welfare Regimes Affect Support for Distributing Welfare to Immigrants in Europe." *Journal of Comparative Policy Analysis* 15(2): 164–81.

Van Kersbergen, Kees. 1995. *Social Capitalism: A Study of Christian Democracy and the Welfare State*. New York: Routledge.

Van Oorschot, Wim. 2004. "Flexible Work and Flexicurity Policies in the Netherlands: Trends and Experiences." *European Review of Labour and Research* 10(2): 208–25.

Van Oorschot, Wim, and Wilfred Uunk. 2007. "Multi-Level Determinants of the Public's Informal Solidarity towards Immigrants in European Welfare States." In *Social Justice, Legitimacy and the Welfare State*, ed. S. Mau and B. Veghte, 217–38. Aldershot: Ashgate.

Van Spanje, Joost. 2010. "Contagious Parties: Anti-Immigration Parties and Their Impact on Other Parties' Immigration Stances in Contemporary Western Europe." *Party Politics* 16(5): 563–86.

Vänsterpartiet. 2014. *Vänsterpartiets valttform för riksdagvalet 2014*. Stockholm.

Van Tubergen, Frank. 2006. "Occupational Status of Immigrants in Cross-National Perspective: A Multilevel Analysis of Seventeen Western Societies." In *Immigration and the Transformation of Europe*, ed. C.A. Parsons and T.M. Smeeding, 147–71. Cambridge: Cambridge University Press.

Vellinga, Menno. 1993. "The Benelux Countries: Divergent Paths toward Restrictive Immigration." In *The Politics of Migration Policies*, ed. D. Kubat, 141–63. New York: Center for Migration Studies.

Venturini, Alessandra. 2004. *Postwar Migration in Southern Europe, 1950–2000*. Cambridge: Cambridge University Press.

Vermeulen, B.P., J.P. Loof, B. Wegelin, N. Doorn-Harder, T. Loenen, F. Leemhuis, and A. Van Bommel. 2006. *Overwegingen bij een boerka verbod. Zienswijze van de deskundigen inzake een verbod op gezichtsbedekkende kleding* [Considerations on a Burqa Ban: Viewpoint of the Experts regarding a Prohibition of Face-covering Clothing]. The Hague: SDU.

Vincent, Donovan, and Robert Benzie. 2014. "Refugee advocates battle federal government over welfare." *Toronto Star*, 18 November.

Vink, Maarten P. 2007. "Dutch 'Multiculturalism' beyond the Pillarisation Myth." *Political Studies Review* 5(3): 337–50.

Visser, Jelle, and Anton Hemerijck. 1997. *A Dutch Miracle. Job Growth, Welfare Reform, and Corporatism in the Netherlands*. Amsterdam: Amsterdam University Press.

Vliegenthart, Rens, and Conny Roggeband. 2007. "Framing Immigration and Integration: Relationships between Press and Parliament in the Netherlands." *International Communication Gazette* 69(3): 295–319.

Voerman, Gerrit, and Paul Lucardie. 1992. "The Extreme Right in the Netherlands: The Centrists and Their Radical Rivals." *European Journal of Political Research* 22(1): 35–54.

Voges, Wolfgang, Joachim R. Frick, and Felix Büchel. 1998. "The Integration of Immigrants into West German Society: The Impact of Social Assistance." In *Immigration, Citizenship, and the Welfare State in Germany and the United States: Immigrant Incorporation*, ed. H. Kurthen, J. Fijalkowski, and G.G. Wagner, 159–74. Stamford: Jai Press.

Voss, Paul R., Roger B. Hammer, and Ann M. Meier. 2001. "Migration Analysis: A Case Study for Local Public Policy." *Population Research and Policy Review* 20(6): 587–603.

VVD. 2017. *Zeker Nederland. VVD Verkiezingsprogramma 2017–2021* [Secure Netherlands: VVD Election Manifesto 2017–2021].

Wadensjö, Eskil. 1973. *Immigration och samhällsekonomin* [Immigration and the Swedish Economy]. Lund: Studentlitteratur.

Waslander, Bert. 2003. "The Falling Earnings of New Immigrant Men in Canada's Large Cities." In *Canadian Immigration Policy for the 21st Century*, ed. C.A. Beach, A.G. Green, and J.G. Reitz, 335–72. Kingston: JD Institute for the Study of Economic Policy.

Weaver, R. Kent. 2010. "Paths and Forks or Chutes and Ladders? Negative Feedbacks and Policy Regime Change." *Journal of Public Policy* 30(2): 137–62.

Westin, Charles. 1996. "Equality, Freedom of Choice and Partnership: Multicultural Policy in Sweden." In *The Challenge of Diversity: Integration and Pluralism in Societies of Immigration*, 207–26. Aldershot: Avebury.

Wilkinson, Mick, and Gary Craig. 2012. "Wilful Negligence: Migration Policy, Migrants' Work, and the Absence of Social Protection in the UK." In *Migration and Welfare in the New Europe: Social Protection and the Challenges of*

Integration, ed. E. Carmel, A. Cerami, and T. Papadopoulos, 177–98. Bristol: The Policy Press.

Wilkinson, Richard, and Kate Pickett. 2010. *The Spirit Level: Why Equality Is Better for Everyone*. London: Penguin.

Wind, Marlene. 2010. "The Nordics, the EU, and the Reluctance towards Supranational Judicial Review." *Journal of Common Market Studies* 48(4): 1039–63.

Wong, Cara J. 2007. "'Little' and 'Big' Pictures in Our Heads: Race, Local Context, and Innumeracy about Racial Groups in the United States." *Public Opinion Quarterly* 71(3): 392–412.

Wong, Winnie. 2008. *From Immigration to Participation: A Report on Promising Practices in Integration*. Ottawa: Public Policy Forum.

Wright, Gerald C., Jr. 1977. "Racism and Welfare Policy in America." *Social Science Quarterly* 57(4): 718–30.

Wright, Matthew, and Tim Reeskens. 2013. "Of What Cloth Are the Ties That Bind? National Identity and Support for the Welfare State across 29 European Countries." *Journal of European Public Policy* 20(10): 1443–63.

WRR. 2001. *Nederland als Immigratiesamenleving* [The Netherlands as a Country of Immigration]. The Hague: SDU.

– . 2007. *Identificatie met Nederland* [Identification with the Netherlands]. Amsterdam: Amsterdam University Press.

Wynia, Syp. 2009. "Immigratie kostte tweehonderd miljard euro" [Immigration Cost Two Hundred Billion Euros]. *Elsevier*.

Yang, Joshua S., and Steven P. Wallace. 2007. *Expansion of Health Insurance in California Unlikely to Act as Magnet for Undocumented Migration*. Los Angeles: UCLA Center for Health Policy Research.

Zimonjic, Peter. 2017. "Tory leadership candidate Kellie Leitch wants immigrants to be asked: 'Are men and women equal?'" *CBC*, 7 March.

Zorlu, Aslan, Joop Hartog, and Marieke Beentjes. 2010. *Uitkeringsgebruik van Migranten* [Migrants' Welfare Use]. Amsterdam: Amsterdam Institute for Advanced Labour Studies.

Index

STUDIES IN COMPARATIVE POLITICAL ECONOMY AND
PUBLIC POLICY

Printed and bound by CPI Group (UK) Ltd, Croydon, CR0 4YY

16/04/2025

14658338-0002